The North Atlantic World

in the Seventeenth Century

Europe and the World in the Age of Expansion

edited by Boyd C. Shafer

The North Atlantic World in the Seventeenth Century

by
K. G. DAVIES

UNIVERSITY OF MINNESOTA PRESS □ MINNEAPOLIS

Library of Congress Catalog Card Number: 74-78994

ISBN 0-8166-0713-3

Europe and the World
in the Age of Expansion

SPONSORS

Department of History of the
University of Minnesota

James Ford Bell Library of the
University of Minnesota Library

SUPPORTING FOUNDATIONS

Louis W. and Maud Hill Family
Foundation, St. Paul

James Ford Bell Foundation,
Minneapolis

ADVISORY COUNCIL

Robert I. Crane
*Lawrence H. Gipson
Lewis Hanke

J. H. Parry
Francis M. Rogers
A. P. Thornton

EDITORS

Boyd C. Shafer
*Herbert Heaton, founding editor
Burton Stein, founding associate editor

deceased

Editor's Foreword

The expansion of Europe since the thirteenth century has had profound influences on peoples throughout the world. Encircling the globe, the expansion changed men's lives and goals and became one of the decisive movements in the history of mankind.

This series of ten volumes explores the nature and impact of the expansion. It attempts not so much to go over once more the familiar themes of "Gold, Glory, and the Gospel," as to describe, on the basis of new questions and interpretations, what appears to have happened insofar as modern historical scholarship can determine.

No work or works on so large a topic can include everything that happened or be definitive. This series, as it proceeds, emphasizes the discoveries, the explorations, and the territorial expansion of Europeans, the relationships between the colonized and the colonizers, the effects of the expansion on Asians, Africans, Americans, Indians, and the various "islanders," the emergence into nationhood and world history of many peoples that Europeans had known little or nothing about, and, to a lesser extent, the effects of the expansion on Europe.

The use of the word *discoveries*, of course, reveals European (and American) provincialism. The "new" lands were undiscovered only in the sense that they were unknown to Europeans. Peoples with developed cultures and civilizations already had long inhabited most of the huge areas to which Europeans sailed and over which they came to exercise their power and influence. Nevertheless, the political, economic, and social expansion that came with and after the discoveries affected the daily lives, the modes of producing and sharing, the ways of governing, the customs, and the values of peoples everywhere. Whatever their state of development, the expansion also brought, as is well known, tensions, conflicts, and much injustice. Perhaps most important in our own times, it led throughout the developing world to the rise of nationalism, to reform and revolt, and to demands (now largely realized) for national self-determination.

The early volumes in the series, naturally, stress the discoveries and explorations. The later emphasize the growing commercial and political involvements, the founding of new or different societies in the "new" worlds, the emergence of different varieties of nations and states in the often old and established societies of Asia, Africa, and the Americas, and the changes in the governmental structures and responsibilities of the European imperial nations.

The practices, ideas, and values the Europeans introduced continue, in differing ways and differing environments, not only to exist but to have consequences. But in the territorial sense the age of European expansion is over. Therefore the sponsors of this undertaking believe this is a propitious time to prepare and publish this multivolumed study. The era now appears in new perspective and new and more objective statements can be made about it. At the same time, its realities are still with us and we may now be able to understand intangibles that in the future could be overlooked.

The works in process, even though they number ten, cover only what the authors (and editors) consider to be important aspects of the expansion. Each of the authors had to confront vast masses of material and make choices in what he should include. Inevitably, subjects and details are omitted that some readers will think should have been covered. Inevitably, too, readers will note some duplication. This arises in large part because each author has been free, within the general themes of the series, to write his own book on the geographical area and chronological period allotted to him. Each author, as might be expected, has believed it necessary to give attention to the background of his topic and has also looked a bit ahead; hence he has touched upon the time periods of the immediately preceding and following volumes. This means that each of the studies can be read independently, without constant reference to the others. The books are being published as they are completed and will not appear in their originally planned order.

The authors have generally followed a pattern for spelling, capitalization, and other details of style set by the University of Minnesota Press in the interests of consistency and clarity. In accordance with the wishes of the Press and current usage, and after prolonged discussion, we have used the word *black* instead of *Negro* (except in quotations). For the most part American usages in spelling have been observed. The last is sometimes difficult for historians who must be concerned with the different spellings, especially of place names and proper nouns, at different times and in different languages. To help readers the authors have, in consequence, at times added the original (or the present) spelling of a name when identification might otherwise be difficult.

The discussions that led to this series began in 1964 during meetings of the Advisory Committee of the James Ford Bell Library at the University of Minnesota, a library particularly interested in exploration and discovery. Members of the university's Department of History and the University of Minnesota Press, and others, including the present editor, joined in the discussions. Then, after the promise of generous subsidies from the Bell Foundation of Minneapolis and the Hill Family Foundation of St. Paul, the project began to take form under the editorship of the distinguished historian Herbert Heaton. An Advisory Council of six scholars was appointed as the work began. Professor Heaton, who had agreed to serve as editor for three years, did most of the early planning and selected three authors. Professor Boyd C. Shafer of Macalester College (now at the University of Arizona) succeeded him in 1967. He selected eight authors and did further planning. He has been in constant touch with all the authors, doing preliminary editing in consultation with them, reading their drafts, and making suggestions. The Press editors, as is usual at the University of Minnesota Press, have made valuable contributions at all stages. Between Professor Shafer and the authors — from England, Canada, New Zealand, and the United States — there have been voluminous and amicable as well as critical exchanges. But it must be repeated, each author has been free to write his own work within the general scope of the series.

Kenneth Gordon Davies, the author of this book, volume IV in the series, has had varied experience in study, travel, research, and editing.

He learned about British colonial archives as assistant keeper in the Public Record Office where, as he writes, he "fell over" the records of the Royal African Company and became interested in the slave trade. While he taught at the London School of Economics, at Oxford (New College), and at the University of Bristol, he found time to become acquainted with economic, with European, and with North American history. He has written *The Royal African Company*, edited Hudson Bay Records, contributed papers on the fur trade, and is now responsible for the *Calendar of State Papers*, America and the West Indies, as well as editing (single-handed) a twenty-volume series of British documents of the American Revolution. For the most part Professor Davies has worked in seventeenth-century history, the century of his volume in this series.

Boyd C. Shafer

University of Arizona

Preface

Richard Pares wrote in 1937 that "the most important thing in the history of an empire is the history of its mother-country."[1] That view seems a little old-fashioned today. Four centuries of Europe's primacy over the rest of the world have not only ended but been seen to have ended. The interest of historians, in West Africa for example or in the Indians of North America, has shifted from what the Europeans brought to what was there before the Europeans came and what survived their coming. The "most important thing" in imperial history, or one of the most important, has become resistance to Europe.

The Europeans were opposed in the seventeenth century and I have tried to do justice to this opposition in the following pages. But in the Caribbean and North America resistance was ineffectual; and in West Africa, where the Europeans had limited objectives, it was not of the strongest. Nothing stopped the establishment of white communities on the western shores of the Atlantic and nothing stopped the growth of a slave trade out of Africa. The tide of European manufactures washed away most of the opposition. European daring and European acquisitiveness did the rest. Like it or not, the Atlantic Ocean, north of the equator, was transformed in the course of the seventeenth century into a European lake.

This is a book about Europeans: the people of the seaports in the

[1] Richard Pares, "The Economic Factors in the History of the Empire," reprinted in *The Historian's Business* (Oxford: Clarendon Press, 1961), p. 50.

maritime crescent from the Zuider Zee to the Bay of Biscay; fishermen and fur traders; emigrants who made new homes across the Atlantic; Dutch, French, and English capitalists who risked their own money and other people's lives; and European rulers who tried to control and exploit the founding of colonies. Africans and Indians enter the story as the human material on which the Europeans worked, usually clumsily, often disgracefully, but seldom without effect. Europe's style was both courageous and ignoble, Europe's achievement both magnificent and appalling. There is less need, now that Europe's hegemony is over, for pride or shame to color historical judgments.

I wish to record my thanks to the general editor of the series in which this book appears for much-needed encouragement and much-valued criticism, and especially for his disarming confidence in his authors which in the end planted a small portion of the dedication he himself brought to the task. Mrs. Geraldine M. Bell typed and retyped several of the chapters with patience and expedition. The copy editors of the University of Minnesota Press translated my prose, so far as was within anyone's power, into the American language, saved me from many inaccuracies and infelicities, and are not to blame for those that remain. Much of the reading for this book was completed during a year I spent as Visiting Fellow at All Souls College, Oxford. I am grateful to the Warden and Fellows for their favor.

K. G. Davies

Bristol, England
October 16, 1973

Contents

List of Maps

The North Atlantic World

in the Seventeenth Century

CHAPTER 1

PROBES

Spain and Her Enemies

The exploration of the Atlantic Ocean in the fifteenth and early sixteenth centuries was the work of southern Europeans: of Portuguese captains like Gil Eanes, Bartholomeu Dias, and Pedro Cabral, and of professional Italian pilots like Cadamosto, Columbus, Cabot, Vespucci, and Verrazano. Every major discovery in Africa and America, except John Cabot's voyage to Newfoundland, was financed and directed by Spain or Portugal, and it was to these countries that the returning benefits of the New World first accrued. It was the Portuguese who devised, in West Africa and later in the Far East, methods of trading in regions they were not able to conquer or occupy. And it was the Spaniards who took the first steps in colonization and thus set in motion a train of events leading toward, though it never reached, the subjection of the rest of the world by Europe.

Northwestern Europe, despite an advantageous geographical position and despite vigorous maritime traditions, came late to the feast and in a more tentative spirit. Spanish and Portuguese achievements at first excited envy more than emulation. For a long time the rulers of France and England merely flirted with empire, avoiding the commitment and lacking the purpose of the Iberians. For a long time the merchants and sea captains of the ports of Normandy and Brittany, south and southwestern England, Holland and Zeeland aspired to be no more than parasites feeding on the Atlantic empires of southern Europe or at most summer visitors to the remoter parts of the Spanish and Portuguese estates. Both activities proved practicable and, often enough, profitable. From about the middle of the sixteenth century, encouraged by Spain's involvement in war, the northwestern Europeans mounted, not a concerted campaign, but a succession of hit-and-run raids on the Iberian preserves. In the course of the next fifty years hundreds of ships and thousands of seamen from northwestern Europe crossed the Atlantic to explore, to fish, and to plunder the possessions of the king of Spain. Captains such as Cartier, Frobisher, Drake, and Davis laid open some of the navigational secrets of the New World. Norman and Breton fishermen and men of the West of England made annual voyages to Newfoundland's banks. Spain's would-be mare clausum, the Caribbean, was pierced time and again by corsairs from Dieppe, St.-Malo, and La Rochelle, by privateers from London, Southampton, and Plymouth, and by Dutch smugglers bearing European manufactures to Spanish colonists. Below the equator, Portuguese Brazil (from 1580 ruled by the king of Spain) was or seemed to be the helpless prey of any well-found fleet of marauders. The coast of West Africa, another Portuguese sphere of influence, lay open to all English or French traders who took sensible precautions. Everywhere in the Atlantic Spain's enemies swarmed. By 1600 the Iberian monopoly, never recognized by the rest of Europe, was an anachronism.

Yet, for all this maritime endeavor, no part of the New World was effectively occupied in 1600 save by subjects of the king of Spain. There were lodges in Newfoundland and on the St. Lawrence where French or English fishermen and fur gatherers sometimes passed an uncomfortable winter; a couple of little Dutch blockhouses stood on the Amazon; and on the Isle of Sables in the last year of the sixteenth century a handful of Frenchmen waited to be taken home and meanwhile died of cold and starvation. With these doubtful exceptions, not a colony, not even a garrison, had been planted by English, French, or Dutch: Spain's lead as the colonizer of America had stretched to a hundred years.

Spain had not merely been first in the field; it had also brought to its imperial mission in America experiences and colonizing techniques which northwestern Europe lacked.[1] In the Reconquest of Spain from the Moors

[1] J. H. Parry, *The Spanish Seaborne Empire* (London: Hutchinson, 1966), p. 100, discusses the transfer of Spanish institutions to the New World; Alexander Marchant, *From Barter to Slavery* (Baltimore: Johns Hopkins University Press, 1942), p. 16, does the same for

institutions had evolved which proved adaptable to America. The encomienda, for example, an efficient if crude method of exploiting a subject people, had been transplanted from the Peninsula to the Canaries in the fifteenth century, later to the Caribbean islands and to Central and South America. Slavery, a foundation stone of Spain's Atlantic empire by 1600 and of everyone else's by 1700, had been a familiar institution in the Mediterranean world of the Middle Ages: contacts with Africa and the Levant ensured its survival until the time came for its transfer to America. France (that part which faced the Atlantic), England, and the Netherlands did not have these advantages. It is true that about the middle of the sixteenth century England resumed the colonization of Ireland, started long before but laid aside; for the next fifty years Englishmen were apt to consider Ireland and America in the same light, experience of the first suggesting ways in which the second might be tackled.[2] No doubt what Englishmen tried to do in Ireland in the reign of Elizabeth I helped to spread the idea of expansion, and particularly the belief — the almost distinctively English belief — that a gentleman might advance his fortune by acquiring estates overseas. But what was performed in Ireland in the sixteenth century, as opposed to what was promised, was not enough to furnish many useful precedents for colonizing America. Some Englishmen thought that the Irish could and should be treated the way Spaniards treated Indians, as a people reduced by conquest; but this was not a universally held doctrine.[3] For one thing the Irish, with nowhere else to go, resisted better than the Indians; and for another, they were more or less Christians already which induced scruples whether they could be justly dispossessed and killed if they demurred. And if experience in Ireland accustomed Englishmen to living away from home, it may in other ways have held back the colonization of America. As long as the war with Spain lasted, Ireland for reasons of defense was much the more important of the two and may have consumed energy and resources which would otherwise have been devoted to the New World.

Portugal and Brazil. Charles Verlinden has written extensively on connections between colonization in the Mediterranean and Levant in the Middle Ages and post-Columbian colonization in America. His views are summarized in his *Les origines de la civilisation atlantique* (Paris: Michel, 1966), chapter 9.

[2] David B. Quinn, *The Elizabethans and the Irish* (Ithaca, N.Y.: Cornell University Press for Folger Shakespeare Library, 1966), especially chapter 9, "Ireland and America Intertwined."

[3] David B. Quinn, "Ireland and Sixteenth Century European Expansion," in T. D. Williams, ed., *Historical Studies* (London: Bowes & Bowes, 1958).

Both France and England tried to found colonies in America in the sixteenth century; not surprisingly these experiments lack the professional appearance of Spanish colonization. Aside from a *comptoir* in Brazil in 1530–31, French colonization was launched by Jacques Cartier and Jean François de la Roques, Sieur de Roberval, under patent from King Francis I dated January 15, 1541. Cartier — whose third voyage to the St. Lawrence this was — set out in May of the same year with five ships, some settlers, and livestock. The winter was passed at Cap Rouge, not far from Quebec, and the St. Lawrence reconnoitered as far as the Ottawa. A fine pilot, Cartier failed as colonizer; convinced that he had found gold he quitted the settlement and sailed for France with his people. Meanwhile Roberval was on his way with three ships and two hundred recruits, expecting to find the colony a going concern. The two little fleets met in Newfoundland in the summer of 1542. Cartier stuck to his gold samples and slipped away in the night for St.-Malo. Roberval went on, occupied Cartier's site, and in the following winter lost a quarter of his men by scurvy. In the spring he ascended the St. Lawrence but here the record ends. How his colony finally fell to pieces is not known. Some colonists, Roberval among them, got back to France. Cartier's gold proved false. A tradition had been founded and a claim laid to the St. Lawrence which was useful later on; but for the time being France got nothing.

Roberval intended to found a colony, not just a trading post. This is attested by the inclusion of women in his party, their presence or absence being a nearly infallible indication of the direction which Europeans meant their overseas interest to take, not only in North America but throughout the world. France's next attempt at a genuine colony was in Brazil.[4] Nicolas Durand — alias Villegagnon — planned a settlement to which Catholics and Protestants could withdraw from religious conflict in Europe: not a prefiguration of the Pilgrim Fathers whose strength was cohesion, but a naive expression of the belief that Old World antagonisms would melt away in the New. With Calvin's approval and with help from King Henry II, the colonists sailed from Le Havre in July 1555. They chose an island in the bay of Rio de Janeiro for their home, and more ships with more settlers came out in 1557. The French had only to stick together to survive; they could not. The Protestants shifted to the mainland where some died of disease, some deserted, some were picked off by the

[4] C.-A. Julien, *Les voyages de découverte et les premiers établissements* (Paris: Presses Universitaires de France, 1948).

Portuguese. Villegagnon went home, cured forever of his faith in a reconciling formula. The colony collapsed in 1560.

The French settlement in Florida (1562–65) was less utopian, more sectarian, and much more aggressive. Henry II was dead, his successor a boy. Great nobles did much as they liked, among them the Huguenot leader, Admiral Coligny, who determined to give substance to his vision of a Protestant France in the Atlantic, hammering Spanish communications from the Caribbean to Seville.[5] The choice of Florida was shrewd. The winds of the Caribbean blowing from east to west made the Florida channel one of the normal exits for sailing ships. A French privateering base there amounted to a declaration of war on the Spanish colonies. In 1562 Jean Ribaut, Protestant, sailed from Dieppe with two ships, wintered where South Carolina now is, and returned to France the next year. The main party, under René de Laudonnière, went out in 1564.

This colony, too, fell to pieces. Gold fever ran high; no agriculture was started; a mutiny broke out and the mutineers left to become pirates. Meanwhile Spain armed. With an overwhelming force Pedro Menéndez de Avilés — one of Spain's ablest representatives in America in this century — crossed the Atlantic to win a province for himself and destroy the heretics. Landing in Florida in September 1565 he annihilated the French in a style long remembered, a St. Bartholomew massacre in the New World. Perhaps a thousand colonists, mostly Huguenots, died in battle or were executed. Menéndez did not win another Mexico but he did fortify St. Augustine, setting a limit to the southward expansion of England's later colonies. The French revenged themselves by killing several hundred Spaniards in these parts in 1568, but there was no more colonizing. The Frenchmen who are reported in Florida between 1577 and 1580 were privateers not settlers; they too were mostly put to death. A land suitable for tropical agriculture was thus effectively sterilized: the Spaniards did little with Florida except defend it.

The colonizing of Canada was not quite forgotten during the French Wars of Religion. In 1577 La Roche, a Breton gentleman, got a patent from Henry III as viceroy of Terre-Neuve. He took his time developing it, embarking a hundred colonists in 1584 who were shipwrecked off the French coast. A new effort was made under a new patent in 1597. Sixty settlers were planted on the Isle of Sables a hundred miles off Acadia;

---

[5] A. W. Whitehead, *Gaspard de Coligny* (London: Methuen, 1904), chapter 18.

eleven survivors were taken off in 1603.[6] This little company was the nearest France, or for that matter northwestern Europe, had got to a colony-in-being in the first year of the seventeenth century.

England was behind France in the colonizing of America. Yet its first attempt was not ill-conceived. By 1550 the Newfoundland fisheries had become the resort of ships of several countries; the country that first founded a colony there might give the law to its competitors if not exclude them. Economically there were advantages in settlement: a longer season for fishing and better arrangements for drying and curing. These objects were in the view of Sir Humphrey Gilbert when he sailed to Newfoundland in 1583 with a patent from Queen Elizabeth giving him proprietorship of lands he found and occupied in America. Gilbert was drowned soon after taking possession and no more is heard of settlement. Had he lived, he would probably have run into trouble with the annual fishermen from West of England ports, quick to see the monopolist behind the colonist.

Gilbert was interested in many Atlantic projects, fishing, privateering, colonies, exploration. England's next attempt at planting, "Virginia," was connected with operations against Spain. Sir Walter Raleigh, Gilbert's heir in some of these schemes, got a new patent from the queen in 1584 and in 1585 settlers were landed on Roanoke Island, off the coast of present-day North Carolina. Without a good harbor, badly sited for an agricultural colony, Roanoke had only the virtue of being hard for an enemy to find. The Spaniards were expected. After one winter the survivors were glad when Drake arrived to take them off, but soon afterwards Raleigh's cousin, Sir Richard Grenville, landed a small holding party. Reinforcements came out in 1587 but their fate is not known; probably the Indians got them. When relief came in 1590 there was no one to relieve. Indians apart, Roanoke was not much of an advance on Roberval's venture. There was little concern for agriculture; no land grants to settlers are known to have been made. The colonists depended on supplies from England. This was inevitable at the start of a colony but all later history showed that self-sufficiency in food was the condition of survival. For one thing supplies from Europe might be interrupted, as they were to Roanoke in 1588 and 1589. And, further, financial backers at home soon lost interest when they found they were expected to pump money into a colony for years while waiting for something valuable to turn up. They

    [6] Julien, *Voyages de découverte*, pp. 283–284.

hoped for a gold mine; a good cash crop would do. Failing either, the colonists might at least feed themselves. No other English colony was planted in the sixteenth century, partly because privateering offered backers a better return with smaller overhead.

The economic reasons why English and French colonizing failed in the sixteenth century, and why the Dutch did not try, will come into view later in this chapter. Part of the explanation, however, was not economic at all but was connected with Spain's power of resistance. This power must not be underestimated. The treasure fleets were defended against English and French marauders with almost complete success, and well into the seventeenth century Spain was capable of organizing and delivering heavy counterstrokes.[7] Nevertheless, it does seem that toward the end of the sixteenth century and in the first two decades of the seventeenth century there was a time of Spanish enfeeblement. Compare Spain's reactions to foreign invaders in Florida (1565), on Roanoke (1585–90), in Virginia (1606–12), and in Bermuda (1611–15). Florida showed the Spanish empire at the height of its powers, capable of totally destroying its enemies. Twenty years later the Spaniards took the Englishmen in Carolina very seriously: "It was only by a series of mischances that they did not wipe out the Roanoke colony and themselves establish a strong, continuing fortress on Chesapeake Bay."[8] The expedition of destruction was timed for 1588, the year of the Armada; the troops to be sent from Old Spain were diverted to the enterprise against England. Other action was planned, and laid aside only when the frailty of the English colony was appreciated. Another twenty years later, when Virginia was the issue, some of Philip III's advisers thought that the English should be expelled, Florida-fashion, but others, and the king himself, preferred to wait and see, hoping that these intruders too would go away. Four years were consumed by reconnaissance. Then, in 1612, the Council of War in the Indies proposed that an expedition of 4000 men should be sent against the English colony. The king thought it over and decided to do nothing.[9]

Bermuda, occupied in 1612, looked even more dangerous than Virginia

[7] For example, the Dutch were evicted from Punta del Araya in 1605 and from Brazil in 1625 by fleets from Old Spain; the French and English were evicted from St. Kitts in 1629; the English from Providence in 1640; the English and after them the buccaneers from Tortuga more than once.

[8] David B. Quinn, "Some Spanish Reactions to Elizabethan Colonial Enterprises," *Transactions of the Royal Historical Society*, 5th series, 1:6 (1951).

[9] Irene A. Wright, "Spanish Policy towards Virginia," *American Historical Review*, 25:448–479 (1920).

because of its proximity to the homeward route of the treasure ships. "The day they establish a footing and fortify themselves there," Philip's Council wrote in 1613, "being to windward of all the Indies, they can do very great damage in proportion to the strength they may possess, even if this be not a fleet, but only four or six ships, even on the high seas, without a fixed rendezvous wherein to await the silver galleons and fleets, since these, not sighting land, endeavouring to keep far out, must nevertheless approach the altitude of Bermuda."[10] Again the king played down the threat, not only because he was pacifically inclined but also because of Spain's weakness. When he finally dismissed the matter in 1615 he still did not think the danger great but in any case had no funds for an expedition. It was not so much the cost of repelling intruders in the Caribbean that had emptied his treasury as Spain's military expenditure in the Mediterranean, Portugal, the Netherlands, France, Germany, and Ireland and against England over the previous forty years. Spain lost its American monopoly in Flanders and the English Channel. Not even the doubling of American silver shipments to Seville in the last thirty years of the sixteenth century could meet all the costs of Spain's chosen role as the Catholic policeman of Europe.[11] The New World became, not safe, but safer for Englishmen, Frenchmen, and Dutchmen to live in.

Reconnaissances

Northwestern Europe's first steps in colonizing lend more support to the view of the sixteenth century as an age of reconnaissance than to the conception of it as an age of expansion.[12] No colonies were firmly planted but there was a record of maritime achievement, both purposeful and random, on the part of English, French, and Dutch. From a consideration of this record we can learn something of what it was in America that pulled Spain's enemies across the Atlantic, and, equally, what it was in Europe that gave the necessary push. It is with these forces, the pull and the push, that any history of colonization must begin.

[10] [Irene A. Wright], "Spanish Intentions for Bermuda, 1603–1615," *Bermuda Historical Quarterly*, 7:65–66 (1950).

[11] A table of treasure imports is to be found in Earl J. Hamilton, *American Treasure and the Price Revolution in Spain, 1501–1650* (Cambridge, Mass.: Harvard University Press, 1934), p. 34.

[12] The phrase is J. H. Parry's. See his *Age of Reconnaissance* (Cleveland, Ohio: World, 1963).

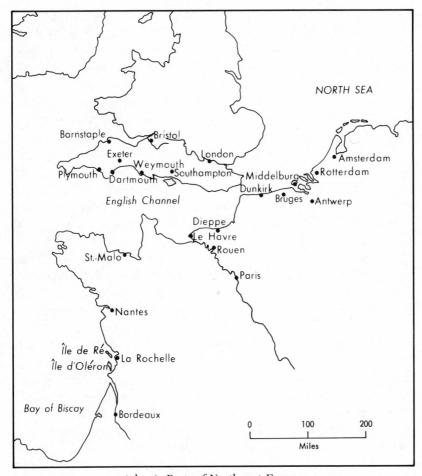

Atlantic Ports of Northwest Europe

   The first pull, and the longest and steadiest in the sixteenth century, was fish. In the northwestern waters of the Atlantic the Gulf Stream and the Arctic current meet, bringing an abundance of plankton. Infusions of warm and cold water mingle to cause local variations in temperature, enabling different kinds of marine life to flourish. The Banks themselves, underwater plateaus, contribute a hospitable seabed. It is because the small creatures are plentiful that the fish teem.[13] These Banks, lying off

   [13] Ralph G. Lounsbury, *The British Fishery at Newfoundland, 1634–1763* (New Haven, Conn.: Yale University Press, 1934), Introduction.

New England, Nova Scotia, Newfoundland, and southern Labrador, were one of Europe's great finds, perhaps the greatest. Properly pickled, wet or green fish could be got to Europe in reasonably appetizing condition; even the dry or cured fish was nutritious. Without the fisheries, few English sailors would have crossed the Atlantic before 1585.

Portugal claimed these waters in virtue of a papal grant and, soon after John Cabot's voyage, sent Corte-Real to reconnoiter; from this there descended an important Portuguese fishery lasting until at least the end of the sixteenth century.[14] Biscayans, Normans, and Bretons arrived about 1504, the French quickly taking the lead. The English came later; though there were English ships on the Banks in the first half of the century, it seems that regular voyages did not begin until about 1550. Evidence is fragmentary but the estimates made in 1578 by Anthony Parkhurst, an early propagandist for the annexation of Newfoundland, may be roughly right. After visiting the Banks, he told Richard Hakluyt that the French had 150 vessels in the fisheries, Spaniards 100, English and Portuguese 50 each.[15] By 1600, when the first Irish ship is thought to have sailed for Newfoundland, the whole Atlantic coastline of Europe had acquired an interest in New World fish.

Both the green and the dry fisheries needed salt: in the early seventeenth century nearly half the outward loading of English ships for Newfoundland was salt, not less than 7000 tons a year.[16] A good supply was a condition of success, and here French and Basque fishermen had the advantage. The Atlantic coast from La Rochelle and the Bay of Bourgneuf round to southern Portugal was one of the few parts of Europe with a conspicuous surplus.[17] New World fish raised demand for salt, exposing England's dependence on foreign supplies. Some Englishmen, like Sir George Peckham — one of Gilbert's backers — hoped to solve the problem in Newfoundland, "God granting that salt may be found there."[18] It

[14] Frédéric Mauro, Le Portugal et l'Atlantique au XVIIe siècle (Paris: S.E.V.P.E.N., 1960), pp. 287–289.

[15] Lounsbury, British Fishery, pp. 21, 23, 35.

[16] Harold A. Innis, The Cod Fisheries (rev. ed.; Toronto: University of Toronto Press, 1954), p. 60.

[17] J. H. Parry, "Transport and Trade Routes," in E. E. Rich and C. H. Wilson, eds., Cambridge Economic History of Europe, vol. IV (Cambridge: At the University Press, 1967), pp. 184–185. This essay is a valuable summary of the history of international trade in the sixteenth and seventeenth centuries.

[18] R. H. Tawney and Eileen Power, eds., Tudor Economic Documents, 3 vols. (New York: Longmans, 1924), III, 257.

was not, anyway not enough. England's dependence continued, constricting its Atlantic fishery particularly in times of war with France or Spain.

England's first steps in the Newfoundland fishery can be connected to hopes and frustrations elsewhere. In the fifteenth century, through its east coast ports as well as Bristol, England had an important fishing trade in Iceland. At its height about 1450, this trade was in difficulties toward 1500 as a result of England's domestic unruliness, competition from the Hanse towns of north Germany, and worsening diplomatic relations with Denmark. The discovery of the Atlantic fisheries, in which Bristol took a leading part through John Cabot, should have been a godsend to the West of England fishermen, if not exactly good news to the east coast ports. Cabot's crew reported that "they could bring thence so many fish that they would have no further need of Iceland."[19] The switch from an Icelandic fishery, worked by both east and west coast ports, to a Newfoundland fishery, worked mainly by the west, did not, however, take place at once. In 1528 there were still 149 ships, all from the east coast, in the Icelandic trade, and fifty years later Parkhurst wrote that "the trade that our nation hath to Island maketh that the English are not there [Newfoundland] in such numbers as other nations." [20] After 1580 Denmark enforced a more stringent system of licenses in the Icelandic fishery, accelerating the decline of English and particularly east coast interests there.

By 1600 the switch was well under way. Despite the late start, the West of England had caught up with Portugal and Spain, though not yet with Normandy and Brittany. War with Spain, open since 1585, helped more than hindered the English effort. True, Spain could hit back, as in 1594 when Spanish warships patrolled the entrance to the English Channel and put the returning Newfoundland fleet at risk. But the Spaniards took harder knocks. In 1585, Bernard Drake's fleet sailed to Newfoundland and captured 600 Spanish prisoners. Calls for men, ships, and material for war at sea drew Spanish fishermen and vessels away from peaceful pursuits. Both Iberian countries lost ground. As Catholics they needed fish, but the fish they ate in the seventeenth century was more and more

[19] Quoted by E. M. Carus Wilson in "The Iceland Trade," in Eileen Power and M. M. Postan, eds., *Studies in English Trade in the Fifteenth Century* (London: Routledge, 1933), p. 182. The facts above have been taken from this article and from Miss Carus Wilson's "The Overseas Trade of Bristol" in the same volume.

[20] Quoted in Innis, *Cod Fisheries*, pp. 13–14.

Dutch from the North Sea or English and French from Newfoundland.[21] Northern Europe won the initiative, fish being the first of the Atlantic staples to pass largely into northern hands.

France, like England, had an important fishery before the Discoveries. For Dieppe, Honfleur, St.-Malo, La Rochelle, St.-Jean-de-Luz, and dozens of smaller ports, fishing was as normal a way of earning a living as agriculture was for country dwellers. Nearly everywhere, small craft predominated. In the port of Dieppe, over a period of thirty years in the fifteenth century, 275 ships of less than thirty tons are recorded (in fishing and all other trades) to 51 of greater burden.[22] Toward 1500 larger ships became commoner, preparing the way for the Atlantic fisheries. Well before this, however, fish was big business at Dieppe. Even the small vessels, in aggregate, caught a lot: in 1475, for example, 530 tons of herring came into this port, besides the other Channel specialty, mackerel. Catches like these were not consumed locally; in Dieppe's case the market was Rouen. When Dieppois, with other Normans and Bretons, began to cross the Atlantic, they and their financial backers already knew how to handle relatively large quantities of fish. Some changes there must have been, bigger ships, more victuals, more salt, more capital and probably more sophisticated ways of raising it; but essentially the switch from European waters to the northwestern Atlantic was the extension of a well-established industry and the application of familiar techniques.

John Rut, an Englishman, counted eleven Norman ships, one Breton, and one Portuguese in Newfoundland in 1527. By 1543–45 the number of Atlantic fishing ships clearing from Rouen, Le Havre, Dieppe, and Honfleur (all Norman ports) is reckoned to have been two a day in January and February, the high season for departures. Evidence from Honfleur between 1574 and 1583 suggests that about fifty ships were employed in the fisheries from that port alone.[23] Here, as elsewhere in the early history of French overseas enterprise, provincial separateness was marked, the Bretons fishing in the Gulf of St. Lawrence as well as off Newfoundland, the Normans sticking to the southern Banks. Competition was sharp, the acts of hostility committed by one French group on

[21] Harold A. Innis, "The Rise and Fall of the Spanish Fishery in Newfoundland," *Proceedings and Transactions of the Royal Society of Canada*, 3rd series, 25:51–70 (1931).
[22] Michel Mollat, *Comptabilité du port de Dieppe au XV.ᵉ siècle* (Paris: Colin, 1951), pp. 31–35.
[23] For early French fishery, see Innis, *Cod Fisheries*, pp. 13, 25, 42; and P.-E. Renaud, *Les origines économiques du Canada* (Mamers: Enault, 1928), pp. 119–129.

another being more suggestive of collisions between men of different nationality than of encounters between compatriots.[24]

As in voyages of discovery, so in the financing of the fisheries risks had to be shared so that losses could be covered. In the setting out of a ship, the owner, master, and victualler might be one person or three different persons with separate financial interests; in many voyages there was another, entrepreneurial interest behind all three. Food for six months had to be found, salt, tackle for the ship and catch, advances in wages for the crew. Whether the sailors served for monthly pay, at piece rates, or for a share of the catch, they were entitled to clothing for the voyage and money to support their families. Capital for these purposes might be found locally but it is clear that many French voyages to Newfoundland were underwritten by monied men in the nearest big city: the Norman in Rouen, the Breton in La Rochelle, the Biscayan in Bayonne.

The key position in the Atlantic fisheries occupied by the financier — or more likely the syndicate — was described by an English pamphleteer in 1580:

There goethe out of Fraunce commonly fiue hundreth saile of shippes yearely in Marche to Newfoundlande, to fishe for Newlande fishe, and comes home againe in August. Amongest many of theim, this is the order, tenne or twelue Marryners doeth conferre with a Money man, who furnisheth them with money to buy Shippes, Victualls, Salte, Lines and Hookes, to be paied his money at the shippes returne, either in fishe or in money, with fiue and thirtie pounde vpon the hundreth pounde in money lent. Likewise here in Englande, in the West countrey the like order is vsed, the fishermen conferres with the money man, who furnisheth them with money to prouide victualls, salte, and all other needefull thinges, to be paied twentie fiue pounde at the shippes returne vpon the hundreth pound in money lent. And some of the same money men doth borrowe money vpon ten pounde in the hundreth pounde, and puts it forthe in this order to the Fishermen. And for to be assured of the money ventered, they will haue it assured, geuyng sixe pounde for the assuring of euery hundreth pound to hym that abides the venture of the Shippes returne, as thus: A shippe of Excester is gone to the Warde house, to fishe for Codd and Lyng, the venture of the Shippe, Salte and Victualls is three hundreth pounde; for eightene pownd all is assured. So that if the ship neuer returne, yet the money man gaineth *declaro* fortie and eight pound and his principall againe.[25]

[24] Robert Le Blant, "L'avitaillement du Port-Royal d'Acadie par Charles de Biencourt et les marchands Rochelais, 1615–1618," *Revue d'histoire des colonies*, 44:138–164 (1957).
[25] Tawney and Power, *Tudor Economic Documents*, III, 253.

These financial arrangements, highly sophisticated for sixteenth-century provincial ports, show how the Atlantic fisheries brought new opportunities to the French and English bourgeoisie.

The connection between the French fisheries and the planting of colonies is not a simple one. Ships from Normandy and Brittany found out the way for Cartier who, on his first voyage, "proceeded along a well-known route to well-known places."[26] And when the Roberval colony was given up and the Florida settlement came to nothing, it was through the fisheries alone that a French interest in the New World was kept alive. Moreover, it was from the dry fishery, in which the catch was salted and cured ashore, that the fur trade sprang. At first there were merely casual encounters between seamen and wandering Indians, but from about 1581 merchants of Rouen, Dieppe, and St.-Malo were sending ships to the St. Lawrence expressly for furs. By 1600 furs may even have overtaken fish, the first North Atlantic staple having engendered the second.[27] Fur collecting did not compel colonization, but it made it more likely.

This train of events was not, however, what the fishermen looked for, and not even what most fur gatherers wanted. What has been called "the new formula of colonization" devised for France at the end of the sixteenth century — monopolies of New World trade in return for the promotion of settlement — was hotly opposed by independent fishing and fur-trading interests. When, in January 1588, King Henry III gave Cartier's nephew a monopoly of the Canadian fur and copper trades with the requirement of transporting settlers, the Estates of Brittany responded by asserting free trade; in May the king explained that he intended to leave the fishery open; and in July he virtually destroyed his own patent by freeing the fur trade as well.[28] This was the first — but not the last — public clash between merchants seeking free trade and minimal settlement ashore and colonizers (some of whom might be rival merchants) seeking a trade monopoly and ready to pay for it by transporting settlers. The same conflict will be found in England's fishery. Gilbert's "annexation" of Newfoundland was the first episode in a struggle between

[26] Innis, *Cod Fisheries*, p. 23.
[27] "La fin du XVIe siècle marqua le triomphe de la tourrure sur la morue": Julien, *Voyages de découverte*, p. 283.
[28] Marcel Trudel, *Histoire de la Nouvelle-France*, vol. I: *Les Vaines Tentatives, 1524–1603* (Montreal: Éditions Fides, 1963), pp. 224–225, 276; Henry P. Biggar. *The Early Trading Companies of New France* (Toronto: University of Toronto Press, 1901), pp. 33–34.

"fishermen" and "colonizers" which was to last until the eighteenth century.

That Europe could find the money for speculative oceanic voyages in the sixteenth century is suggested not only by the fisheries but also by efforts to find a passage to the East that would be an alternative to the one pioneered by Vasco da Gama. Voyages to the northwest — the most favored of the alternatives — began with John Cabot who sailed from Bristol in May 1497, two months before da Gama set out from Lisbon. For the next 135 years, to the northwest (through Davis Strait), to the west (up the St. Lawrence, the Hudson, or any likely looking inlet), to the northeast (beyond Norway and through the straits of Nova Zembla), and to the southwest (Strait of Magellan), expeditions to Cathay were launched by English, French, and Dutch. Laid aside in 1632, the quest for a Northwest Passage was resumed in the eighteenth century.

Most of these voyages were commercially abortive as well as failures in their main purpose. Yet the search went on. To the west, Verrazano (1524), Cartier (1534–35, 1541–42), and Champlain (from 1603) sought Cathay for France; further north, on behalf of England, Frobisher (1576–78), Davis (1585–87), Waymouth (1602), Hudson (1610–11), Button (1612), Bylot and Baffin (1615–16), Fox (1631), and James (1632). Meanwhile the Dutch looked for a Northeast Passage; between 1594 and 1597 they sent three fleets in this direction, the last of which entered the Kara Sea before being stopped by ice.[29] The English, too, were interested in the northeast from 1555 when the Muscovy Company was formed to seek lands "northwards, northeastwards, or northwestwards."[30] In 1607, though the Cape of Good Hope route had by then been shown to be usable by northern Europeans, this company sent Henry Hudson to find a northeastern passage to China. Two years later the same navigator set out on the same mission in Dutch service. His crew's unwillingness to face arctic cold forced him to go west instead of east, so adding Hudson River to the list of possible routes to Cathay.[31] Earlier, Francis Drake (1577–80)

[29] Charles T. Beke, ed., A True Description of Three Voyages by the North-East towards Cathay and China, undertaken by the Dutch in the Years 1594, 1595, and 1596 by Gerrit De Veer (London: Hakluyt Society, 1853).

[30] Quoted in T. S. Willan, The Muscovy Merchants of 1555 (Manchester: University of Manchester Press, 1953), p. 9.

[31] J. Franklin Jameson, ed., Narratives of New Netherland, 1609–1664 (New York: Scribner, 1909), pp. 13–28.

and Thomas Cavendish (1586–88) had reconnoitered the southwestern passage, as Verrazano had meant to do on his second voyage. They at least showed a profit but, equally, proved that the route round Cape Horn and across the Pacific was too long and too dangerous for trade.

From these voyages of exploration there followed the hesitant beginnings of a French empire in Canada. For the Dutch the outcome of their random discovery of the Hudson River was an entrée to the fur trade and the beginning of their tenuous hold on New Netherland. The English had to be satisfied with greatly increasing Europe's geographical knowledge (Davis Strait, Baffin Bay, Baffin Island, Hudson Bay), and for the time being little else; not till 1670, nearly forty years after the quest for a Northwest Passage had been laid aside, was an English company formed to exploit the fur-bearing regions of Hudson Bay.

The question of how these voyagers attracted financial support is an important one. Part of the answer lies in royal or public backing. Queen Elizabeth put money into Martin Frobisher's second voyage, though this was more a hunt for gold than a hunt for China. The Dutch expedition to the northeast in 1595 was backed by the States-General of the United Provinces and by Prince Maurice; that of 1596–97 by the city of Amsterdam. Jens Munk's voyage to Hudson Bay, when he spent the winter of 1619–20 at Churchill River and lost nearly all his men by scurvy, was a royal enterprise paid for by King Christian IV of Denmark. Rulers had much to hope for: the prosperity of their own country, the weakening of Spain and Portugal, a rise in returns from customs. This last point was clearly put by Samuel Champlain in his petition to Louis XIII in 1618. New France's revenues, once the route to Cathay was found, would "surpass in value at least ten times all those levied in France, inasmuch as all the merchants of Christendom would pass through the passage sought by the Sieur de Champlain, if it please the King to grant them leave to do so, in order to shorten the said journey by more than a year and a half."[32]

Despite such ground bait, investment by rulers in discovery was seldom enough to cover costs. Money had to be raised from merchants, courtiers, or syndicates of both. The most obvious source was the merchants already interested in the Eastern trade who stood to gain most by a

[32] Beke, *Voyages by the North-East*, pp. 40–42, 70; Thorkild Hansen, *North West to Hudson Bay: Life and Times of Jens Munk* (London: Collins, 1970), pp. 187, 203–204; Henry P. Biggar, ed., *The Works of Samuel Champlain*, vol. II (Toronto: Champlain Society, 1925), p. 331.

shorter route. There is some reason to think that Verrazano's voyages in 1524 and 1528 were sponsored by merchants of Lyons, a city remote from the Atlantic but linked to Italy and the Mediterranean. The explanation may be that Mediterranean spice traders in the 1520s were feeling the effect of Portugal's discovery of the Cape route and were looking for another for themselves.[33] Much later, the English East India Company, while using the Cape route, showed interest in the Northwest Passage, beginning with the voyage of George Waymouth in 1602. The funds for this expedition, which was to "light Hudson into his Streights" came from a 5 percent call on the company's shareholders. In 1614 Sir Thomas Smith, governor of the East India Company as well as treasurer of the Virginia Company, claimed that £300 a year for three years had been spent "towardes the discovery of the Norwest passage." Results were nil, but the directors decided to try again "considering that it were dishonorable for such a bodie to withdrawe their hand from so worthie a worke for a small matter of charge, which will not exceede a noble a man." [34] It was the Dutch East India Company that paid Henry Hudson in 1609; and it was an English partnership, including Thomas Smith and others concerned in the Eastern trade, that sent him on his last voyage in 1610.

By the time these voyages were undertaken, both English and Dutch had a formed interest in the East. Money for earlier expeditions to find the Northwest Passage, Frobisher's and Davis's, had to be conjured into existence in a less formal way. Quite a lot is known about the business side of Frobisher's first voyage in 1576, a tiny affair of two ships of twenty and twenty-five tons with a pinnace of ten.[35] The sum raised was £875, though more was spent. A list of adventurers, probably imperfect, shows that it was subscribed by eighteen persons, none putting in more than £100.[36] One is struck, first, by the continuity between this voyage, opening a new

[33] Julien, *Voyages de découverte*, pp. 80, 88; Charles de la Roncière, *Histoire de la marine française*, vol. III (Paris: Plon, 1923), p. 258; Fernand Braudel, *La Méditerranée et le monde méditerranéen à l'époque de Philippe II* (Paris: Colin, 1949), pp. 422–423.

[34] R. Collinson, ed., *The Three Voyages of Martin Frobisher* (London: Hakluyt Society, 1867); Thomas Rundall, ed., *Narrative of Voyages towards the North-West* (London: Hakluyt Society, 1849), pp. 57–58, 96.

[35] See the two works cited in note 34 and David B. Quinn, *The Voyages and Colonising Enterprises of Sir Humphrey Gilbert*, Hakluyt Society Publications, 2nd series, vol. 73 (London: Hakluyt Society, 1938), where Gilbert's "A New Passage to Cataia" (1576) is printed.

[36] W. N. Sainsbury, ed., *Calendar of State Papers*, Colonial Series, East Indies, 1513–1616 (London: Longmans, 1860), no. 24, p. 11.

series of attempts to find the Northwest Passage, and earlier expeditions to Guinea and Muscovy in the 1550s. The moving spirit in the voyage of 1576, apart from Frobisher himself, was Michael Lok whose father had been a promoter of the Guinea voyage of 1554 and a founder-member of the Muscovy Company. Michael Lok had lived in Spain and Portugal — the European terminus of the Cape route to the East — and had traveled widely. It was he who secured the credit on which funds beyond the £ 875 were raised for Frobisher. Another much-traveled partner in the enterprise was Anthony Jenkinson, Turkey and Russia merchant, who had seen Suleiman the Magnificent enter Aleppo in 1553, had been received by Ivan the Terrible in 1557, and had called on the king of Bokhara in 1558. Such men could think in global terms.

Other subscribers were Lionel Duckett, Alderman William Bond, and (probably, though his name is not in the list of adventurers) George Barne. Duckett had been a founder-member of the Muscovy Company and its governor in 1575 and 1577; he had also been lord mayor of London. Bond, another founder-member, had later fallen out with the Muscovy Company and traded to Narva on his own account. Barne's father had backed the expedition of Willoughby and Chancellor to find a Northeast Passage in 1553; the son was governor of the Muscovy Company and brother-in-law of Francis Walsingham, Elizabeth's secretary of state. What these leading City men put into Frobisher's voyage (Bond, £ 100) was a very small fraction of what they were worth, a kind of side bet. Altogether there were nine investors of £ 25 each, five of £ 50, and four of £ 100, a reflection not of the poverty of the adventurers but of the risks of the adventure. Not all the money came from the City. Lord Treasurer Burghley and the Earls of Sussex, Warwick, and Leicester put up £50 each, Philip Sidney and Walsingham — drawn in perhaps by Barne — £ 25. This easy amalgamation of court and City, now and later, was a distinctive feature of English Atlantic enterprises. Nobody thought any worse of courtiers for dabbling in trade, so long as they used their own money; and the merchants loved it, if not for the social cachet, then for the privileges a courtier could attract to the enterprise.

When Frobisher came back in October 1576 with news of gold (false of course, like Cartier's), more backers were ready to come in. A Cathay Company was formed with Lok as treasurer, and a charter obtained.[37]

---

[37] William R. Scott, *The Constitution and Finance of English, Scottish and Irish Joint-Stock Companies to 1720*, vol. II (Cambridge: At the University Press, 1910), pp. 78–79.

The queen put in money and plans were laid for a bigger expedition in
1577. Yet, even with gold in the air, the new list of subscribers reveals the
same fragmentation: seventeen contributed £ 25, sixteen £ 50, and only
four more than £ 100.[38] The same blend of court and City is there, with
the interesting appearance of four Bristol merchants who put in £ 25 each.
For the third voyage in 1578 the balance shifted somewhat: there were
twenty-three shareholders "of the court" and only fourteen "of the City,"
a shift confirmed by plans for a fourth voyage which never took place. One
big ship was to be set out by a City alderman and his cousin, a smaller one
by the Earl of Shrewsbury, and two others by a partnership consisting
almost entirely of courtiers and noblemen.[39] Probably the City men were
losing interest after so much promise and so little performance.

Frobisher's voyages have been discussed at some length because they
show the presence in English society, well before the age of colonization,
of the initiative and resources to organize and pay for Atlantic ventures. In
France, too, there were courtiers and merchants with eyes on the Atlantic
but they came together less easily. English courtiers at Greenwich could
watch ships dropping down the Thames on voyages to distant lands or
returning on the tide, bringing novelties and news. The French court, in
Paris or along the pleasant middle reaches of the Loire, was another world
from the Norman ports where merchants risked their fortunes and seamen their lives.

Fish and furs were sober business; the Northwest Passage was more
romantic. Romance there had to be, to overcome the disappointment of
finding continental masses blocking the way to Asia and to ignite a flame
of popular interest and make men write and talk and dream of America.
No tale was too tall to find believers. Canada had its race of men with but
one leg, its men who drank but did not eat, with skins as white as the
French. Africa had its shy men with lower lips that covered their bosoms,
salted to stop putrefaction. Guiana had its men with eyes in their shoulders and mouths in the middle of their breasts, the headless men who
caught Shakespeare's fancy; and its warrior women, visited by men for
one month each year, who killed their sons and raised only daughters.[40]

[38] Great Britain, Public Record Office, *Calendar of State Papers*, Colonial Series, East
Indies, China, and Japan, 1513–1616 (London: H.M.S.O., 1862), nos. 33, 45.
[39] *Ibid.*, no. 105, pp. 43–44; Rundall, *Voyages towards North-West*, p. 33.
[40] Trudel, *Nouvelle-France*, I, 109; Richard Jobson, *The Golden Trade* (1623; reprinted,
London: Penguin Press, 1932), pp. 140–141; Robert H. Schomburgk, ed., *The Discovery of
the Large, Rich and Beautiful Empire of Guiana by Sir W. Ralegh* (London: Hakluyt Society, 1848), pp. lvi–lxi, 85–86.

Such stories were, and were meant to be, publicity for the New World, but more was needed to hold Europe's interest. What else but gold and silver? Spain's empire was formed by the plundering of the treasure hoards of Mexico and Peru, and no less by the finding of silver mines at Potosí. "By the abundant treasure of that countrey," Sir Walter Raleigh wrote, "the Spanish King vexeth all the Princes of Europe, and is become in a fewe yeares from a poore king of Castile the greatest monarke of this part of the worlde."[41] Raleigh was right: one should not be so obsessed with the harm American treasure did to Spain's economy as to miss the good it did to Spain's striking power. Philip II's failures, of which much is made, were more of his own contriving than the consequences of inflation. He tried to do too many things.

The age of the conquistadores soon came and went. For a time imitators of Cortes and Pizarro roamed new lands, seeking gold: De Soto (1539–41) through Florida to the Mississippi, Coronado (1541) across the Rio Grande, Gonzalo Pizarro (1541–42) east of the Andes toward the Amazon. They found nothing. Most of Spanish America then settled down to working the silver mines that did exist and to humdrum occupations like cattle ranching. Only in one quarter were hopes still alive. Arguing that the Inca empire must have originated in the East, Spaniards tried in expedition after expedition for sixty years to penetrate the lands between the Amazon and the Orinoco. Here the legends accumulated of the golden city of Manoa with its palace so extensive that it took a day and a half to walk round, its garden of golden trees, golden flowers, and golden birds, and its ruler, *el hombre dorado* who smeared himself with turpentine, rolled in gold dust, and plunged into the lake of Manoa.[42] In the sixteenth century the location of El Dorado was pushed steadily eastwards by Spanish exploration; by 1600 it had reached Guiana, "a Countrey that hath yet her Maydenhead,"[43] and could be pushed no further. It had to be there.

Meanwhile the northern Europeans had joined the hunt. On Cartier's second voyage to the St. Lawrence he was told of the Kingdom of Saguenay north of the great river where "il y a infiny or, rubiz et aultres

[41] Schomburgk, *Discovery*, p. 15. There are other modern editions of Raleigh's work, notably that edited by Vincent T. Harlow and entitled *The Discoverie of the large and bewtifull Empire of Guiana* (London: Argonaut Press, 1928) which has a useful introduction and important evidence of Spanish explorations in Guiana.

[42] Harlow, *Discoverie*, pp. l–li.

[43] Raleigh's phrase; see *ibid.*, p. 73.

richesses."[44] Probably it was these reports that induced Francis I to invest heavily in Cartier's third voyage and in Roberval's colony: gold was "l'objectif essentiel."[45] Certainly it was gold that drew English and French traders to loosen Portugal's hold on the West African coast long before they were interested in slaves. Gold was much in the minds of the Florida colonists in 1562; it was the target of Frobisher's second and third voyages in 1577 and 1578, his first having yielded an ore that looked promising; and it was one of the objectives, and perhaps one of the causes of failure, of the Roanoke settlement.

The northern Europeans got a little gold from Africa, dearly bought, but their prospecting in North America yielded nothing. As hopes faded, interest switched to South America and the fabulous golden man, now conveniently cornered in Guiana within striking distance of the sea. Raleigh's expedition in 1595 is one of the great treasure hunts of all time, if only because *The Discoverie of the large and bewtifull Empire of Guiana* is a classic and deservedly became a best seller. Raleigh had already tried planting in Ireland, the quest for the Northwest Passage, and colonization at Roanoke. Now, England's nearest approach to a conquistador, he was looking for a ready-made empire to conquer or annex according as its ruler proved amenable. *El dorado* was to be told about Spanish atrocities committed on Indians, shown Las Casas's "booke of the Spanish crueltyes with fayr pictures," and promised Queen Elizabeth's protection.

Raleigh sailed from Plymouth on February 6, 1595. Landing in Trinidad, he was lucky enough to take prisoner a Spaniard who had spent years of his life and much money looking for the golden man. Thus briefed, he began the ascent of the Orinoco toward the golden city of Manoa 600 miles distant. Frequently complaining of discomfort in a most unconquistadorlike fashion, he made about 250 miles, decided that he was two-thirds of the way to his goal, and turned back in order, as he explained, to obtain the queen's sanction and sponsorship.[46] Home again, he wrote the *Discoverie* to attract royal and popular support, to defend

[44] Henry P. Biggar, ed., *The Voyages of Jacques Cartier*, Publications of Public Archives of Canada, no. 11 (Ottawa, 1924), p. 221.

[45] Trudel, *Nouvelle-France*, I, 147.

[46] Perhaps he was made apprehensive by Robert Dudley, on a privateering cruise, who was nosing around Trinidad a little while before Raleigh arrived. For Dudley's interest in Manoa, see George F. Warner, ed., *The Voyage of Robert Dudley* (London: Hakluyt Society, 1899), pp. 74–75, 88–89.

the quality of his gold samples, and to rebut the canard that he had lain hidden in Devon throughout the expedition. The *Discoverie* was a publishing success but Raleigh did not see his greater objectives achieved. He sent ships to Guiana in 1596 and 1597 which did nothing notable; Charles Leigh (1604) and Robert Harcourt (1609) tried to found colonies on the Wild Coast between the Amazon and the Orinoco; Thomas Roe, a gentleman-adventurer, went up the Amazon in 1609; and Raleigh was back in 1617, looking this time for a mine not a man. Gold was in all their minds. Harcourt, for instance, sent his cousin to explore the uplands and find the way to Manoa. When the search failed, "our greedy desire of Gold being thus made frustrate, divers unconstant persons of my vnruly company began to murmure, to bee discontented, to kindle discords and discusions and to stirre up mutiny . . . only because they were deceived of their golden hopes and expectations." [47] The golden city continued to inspire occasional believers for a long time after Harcourt. In 1714 the Dutch West India Company sent secret orders to its agent in Guiana to collect information concerning such a city, and in 1772 a Spanish officer set out with a party of soldiers to occupy it. [48] But neither here nor anywhere else did gold or even the lure of it make a major contribution to the planting of permanent colonies by northwestern Europe. Charles M. Andrews, reflecting on the history of early English settlement, observed that "gold, trade, tillage represent the three stages in the history of colonization, and the greatest of these, because fundamentally essential to permanence, is tillage." [49] Gold made America news, but it hindered more than it helped the formation of English, French, and Dutch territorial empires.

War at Sea

In the eighteenth century, when the *ancien régime colonial* was at its height, European countries expected to fight one another in the Carib-

---

[47] C. Alexander Harris, ed., *A Relation of a Voyage to Guiana by Robert Harcourt, 1613*, Hakluyt Society Publications, 2nd series, vol. 60 (London: Hakluyt Society, 1928), pp. 106–107.

[48] C. R. Markham, ed., *Expeditions into the Valley of the Amazons* (London: Hakluyt Society, 1859), pp. 78–79; C. A. Harris and J. A. J. de Villiers, eds., *Storm Van's Gravesande: The Rise of British Guiana*, Hakluyt Society Publications, 2nd series, vol. 26 (London: Hakluyt Society, 1911), p. 186; Harlow, *Discoverie*, p. xcv.

[49] Charles M. Andrews, *The Colonial Period of American History*, 4 vols. (New Haven, Conn.: Yale University Press, 1934–38; reprinted, 1964), I, 49. Compare Francis Bacon's advice in his essay "Of Plantations" — "moile not too much under Ground."

bean. The instruments were powerful fleets sent from Europe, the prizes sugar colonies. The elder Pitt adopted this strategy and extended it to take in Canada, India, and West Africa. War became, for England at least, a means of acquiring colonial possessions and enlarging its trade; the affairs of Europe could never be altogether set aside but they were sometimes relegated to second place. When and how did the Atlantic first enter the serious considerations of European statesmen and commanders, when and how did blue-water strategy begin?

Spain was attacked in the Atlantic from early in the sixteenth century. The French led the way for the good reason that France and Spain were so often at war. English diplomacy until 1558 continued mainly on traditional lines, backing France's enemy and staying on good terms with the ruler of the Netherlands, since 1516 the king of Spain. French strategy at sea was that later tried by Elizabethan captains: prowling between Cape St. Vincent and the Azores, hoping to pick off Spanish galleons and Portuguese carracks. Both the scale and the style of this warfare are suggested by the operations of Jean d'Ango of Dieppe who obtained letters of marque from Francis I in 1531 and then allowed the Portuguese to buy immunity from his privateers for 60,000 ducats. Some remarkable successes were won both in West Africa and in the Caribbean. In 1537 d'Ango's privateers fought a Spanish fleet, took nine ships, and looted towns in Hispaniola. Cartagena fell to corsairs in 1543, Santiago in 1553, Havana in 1555. In time the defenses of the greater Spanish-American cities were strengthened, though never to the point of complete security. Smaller towns remained virtually open, the people flying at the approach of a foreign fleet. Punctuating these depredations came a series of acknowledgments by the French king, partial or complete, of the Iberian colonial monopolies: in 1531, 1540, 1545, 1547, 1554, and 1556. How seriously they should be taken, and whether the king could stop his subjects from sailing into Spanish and Portuguese Atlantic zones even if he really wanted to, is not clear. The Peace of Cateau-Cambrésis (1559) did not put an end to French privateering; on the contrary, the Huguenot colony in Florida in 1562 should be seen as the culmination of earlier raiding. More effective in checking the French was the thorough destruction of that colony by Menéndez, and perhaps most effective of all the involvement of western and northwestern France in the religious wars that consumed the rest of the sixteenth century.

The English took up the running, modestly to begin with. The French had traded as well as plundered; and it was toward peaceful if not exactly legitimate trade that the voyages of Sir John Hawkins (1562–68) were directed, with a show of force to give the Spanish colonists the necessary excuse for doing business with him.[50] Hawkins's calculations were optimistic but not unreasonably so. The market was there and he had the right cargo: slaves. Not all the colonists were pure-blooded, loyal Spaniards. Not all their wants were met by Seville's monopoly of the American trade. *Rescatadores* (traders with the enemy) were always to be found in thinly populated places like western Cuba or Jamaica. "They are," a Spanish official wrote to the king in 1606 of the colonists in Hispaniola, "the most disloyal and rebellious vassals that any king or prince in this world ever had, and if your highness were to appear among them, they would sell your highness for three yards of Rouen silk or even for nothing."[51]

Hawkins went to the market once too often and a little too blatantly; he was also unlucky. On his third voyage, in 1568, he was blown toward the mainland and cornered in San Juan de Ulúa by a Spanish fleet — he lost most of his ships and crew, some killed, some starved, the rest captured. Eighteen of these prisoners were brought to trial by the Spanish Inquisition and, six years after the event, collected among them one death sentence, 130 years in the galleys, and 3300 lashes.[52] San Juan de Ulúa coincided with an Anglo-Spanish quarrel in Europe but did not cause it. It was not serious enough. Drake's appearance in the Pacific ten years later was another matter, a rare and nicely calculated piece of daring on the part of the English queen which gave rise to loud Spanish protests but still no war. English hit-and-run raids went on, but when open war finally came it was at Philip's initiative, not Elizabeth's or Drake's. In May 1585 he caused a large number of English, French, and Dutch ships in Spanish ports to be confiscated, some of them grain ships having the king's safe-conduct. England's responses were to attack Spanish fishing vessels in Newfoundland, to dispatch the Roanoke colony, and most important of all to launch a wave of privateers.

Put like this, the war between England and Spain can be made to

[50] J. W. Blake, *European Beginnings in West Africa, 1454–1578* (London: Longmans, 1937); J. A. Williamson, *Hawkins of Plymouth* (London: Black, 1949).

[51] Irene A. Wright, "Rescates: with Special Reference to Cuba," *Hispanic American Historical Review*, 3:337–338, 352, 354 (1920).

[52] Williamson, *Hawkins of Plymouth*, pp. 154–155.

appear as the first European struggle to dominate the Atlantic; and the way the war was fought lends some support to this view. New ways for England to act offensively were tried, not only by privateers but by the queen's ships and by mixed fleets, part royal, part private. The favored plan was to blockade Spain and Portugal and so cut the flow of silver from America to Seville. Convincing enough on a map, it proved too ambitious. The seas were too wide, the Spanish convoys too efficient. Blockade of a sort might be maintained for a few months in summer but not longer — the ships and crews of the day were not up to it. Further, England itself was too vulnerable to Spanish counterstrokes to rely for defense on naval patrols ranging far out in the Atlantic. It was too easy to miss a second Armada, as the Earl of Essex did in 1597.

The Atlantic and the Caribbean were not unimportant in the history of worsening relations between England and Spain to 1585 or in the history of the war that followed. But, after many years in which these events have been represented as the beginning of a predominantly blue-water strategy on England's part to which Spain was compelled to respond, recent scholarship has tacked in the other direction. To Garrett Mattingly the struggle was not about "the command of the ocean seas and the opportunity to exploit the newly discovered route to Asia and the Americas" but about "conflicting systems of ideas": "the clash of the English and Spanish fleets in the Channel was the beginning of Armageddon, of a final struggle to the death between the forces of light and the forces of darkness."[53] A more sober view is that the war was brought on by events in the Netherlands and France. Philip did not launch his Armada against England to stop privateering in the Caribbean but to crush heresy and rebellion in the Netherlands, to which Elizabeth sent covert help.[54]

These opinions are valuable correctives to earlier exaggerations of the role and achievements of the Elizabethan seadogs, both in bringing on the war and in fighting it. It is manifestly true that the queen and her advisers worried more about the Netherlands, Ireland, and home defense than they did about the Atlantic. Nevertheless, the English privateers were facts. An average of something like a hundred ships set out each year throughout the war to prey on Spanish and Portuguese trade and territory. Whatever the official strategy, there were plenty of private citizens,

[53] Garrett Mattingly, *The Defeat of the Spanish Armada* (London: Cape, 1959), p. 15.
[54] R. B. Wernham, *Before the Armada* (London: Cape, 1966), pp. 354, 367–368.

nobles, gentlemen, merchants, and captains who waged their own wars in the Atlantic, not to please the queen, not as a game, not as a religious exercise, but as a business.

London was predominant in this war-trade, though especially in the first years of the war every English port of any size from Chichester round to Bristol took a hand. Privateers went alone; in twos and threes; or in large squadrons. The bigger fleets might include some royal ships and have strategic as well as economic objectives; such was Drake's force of twenty-one vessels in 1585–86. His official task was to free Englishmen and goods detained in Spain, but once he had made sure that this could not be done he sailed away to Madeira and the Caribbean to plunder.[55]

Who were the privateers? There were "wild men" like Sir Anthony Sherley who took and ransomed Jamaica's chief town but failed to make a living and died a pauper; or John Chidley whose expedition in 1589 cost £10,000 and brought no profit. There was George Clifford, 3rd Earl of Cumberland, who sent out fleet after fleet "bound for no other harbour but the port of honour though touching at the port of profit." In 1592 Cumberland's ships took the Portuguese *Madre de Dios*, worth half a million pounds, and in 1594 burned the *Cinco Chagas*, which was carrying 2 million ducats, when they failed to carry her by boarding. On balance he did badly, partly because he was too ambitious and partly because he was too conspicuous. When he took the *Madre de Dios* the queen's hand was instantly on the loot and Cumberland's take-home booty was reduced to a mere £36,000, not enough to make good his losses elsewhere.[56]

Yet there were gentlemen who did well: Sir John Gilbert, Sir George Somers, and George Popham who turned to colonizing when privateering ended; William Parker of Plymouth; and Ferdinando Gorges who stopped at home and served as commissioner of prizes, looking after the queen's share and no doubt his own as well.[57] There were professionals like Captain Christopher Newport who sailed most years to the Caribbean, lost an arm off Cuba, but survived to take a leading part in the founding of Virginia. There were merchants like Thomas Watts, Paul Bayning, and Thomas Myddelton, all of London, who prospered and later joined in

---

[55] Julian S. Corbett, ed., *The Spanish War, 1585–1587* ([London]: Navy Records Society, 1898), pp. 1–27.

[56] Most of the facts given above and those following are taken from Kenneth R. Andrews, *Elizabethan Privateering* (Cambridge: At the University Press, 1964), pp. 4, 15, 63ff.

[57] James P. Baxter, *Sir Ferdinando Gorges and His Province of Maine*, 3 vols. (Boston: Prince Society, 1890), I, 16.

promoting the East India and Virginia companies. Privateering was always a gamble but hundreds of prizes were taken: during nearly twenty years of war prize goods worth between £ 100,000 and £ 200,000 came into England annually, not big money having regard to costs but something to set against the decay of normal trade in the 1590s. About seven-tenths of the booty came from America or American waters; Africa, the Canaries, and the Azores each provided one-tenth.

Besides yielding profits to some, privateering lit the way for colonization. Merchants grew accustomed to investing in Atlantic ventures, seamen were familiarized with Atlantic navigation. Spanish colonists, if not Spanish governors, were demoralized. "For the last four years," an official at Hispaniola wrote in 1595, "corsairs are as numerous and as assiduous as though these were ports of their own countries. They lie in wait on all the sailing routes to the Indies, particularly the courses converging on this city of Santo Domingo. Coming or going, we always have a corsair in sight. Not a ship coming up from the outside escapes them; nor does any which leaves the harbour get past them."[58] Spain could still hit a stationary target. The strength of the privateers lay in their being always on the move, too strong for the naval forces Spain kept in the Indies, too quick for a fleet summoned from Europe.

The Dutch were late arrivals in the Caribbean.[59] They had seafaring traditions at least as old as Normandy's, and from the start of their revolt against Spain (1568) they had no reason to expect a negotiated entry into the trade of America, Africa, or Asia, and, one might suppose, every reason to attack their enemy wherever he was vulnerable. Yet they held back, committing little to the Atlantic until 1585 and not much more until 1595. The relative lateness of the Dutch move in the direction of America may have some connection with the urgency of their fight for existence in the Netherlands against the strongest army in Europe, but it is also a caution against the easy assumption that European merchants saw and grasped every new opportunity of profit that came along. Some did; others had to be pushed. England's fishermen, it has been suggested,

[58] Quoted in Kenneth R. Andrews, ed., *English Privateering Voyages to the West Indies*, Hakluyt Society Publications, 2nd series, vol. 111 (Cambridge: At the University Press for Hakluyt Society, 1959), p. 37.
[59] See Engel Sluiter, "Dutch-Spanish Rivalry in the Caribbean Area, 1594–1609," *Hispanic American Historical Review*, 28:171 (1948); G. Edmundson, "The Dutch on the Amazon and Negro in the Seventeenth Century," *English Historical Review*, 18:642–663 (1903), 19:1–25 (1904).

were pushed into Newfoundland by difficulties in their old grounds off Iceland; England's merchants were pushed into the Muscovy and African trades in the 1550s by the collapse of their favorite cloth market, Antwerp.[60] So with the Dutch: they lacked incentives to go to Newfoundland, catching fish nearer home, and for many years they lacked incentives to go to the Caribbean. Trade to Old Spain was important to them, their market for north German corn, Baltic timber and naval stores, cloth and other manufactures; from Spain they took wine, sugar, dried fruit, silver, and Biscayan salt, vital for their herring industry. None of this came to an end when the Netherlands revolted in 1568. Philip II hoped to buy naval stores from the German Hanse merchants and grain from Danzigers and English instead of from the Dutch; but they were unable to meet Spain's needs. If anything, the volume of trade between the Dutch and Old Spain rose in the early years of the Netherlands Revolt.[61]

The first interruption, the first push, came in 1585 when about a hundred Dutch ships were seized in Spanish ports including thirty from the town of Hoorn. Soon after, four ships from Hoorn sailed to the Cape Verde Islands to fetch salt. Dutch-Spanish trade in Europe soon recovered, surviving a second arrest of ships in Iberian ports in 1595. Now at last the Dutch began to make a mark in the Caribbean but it took a third arrest in 1598 — this time two hundred ships — to send them there in great numbers. The European salt trade was badly hit by this Spanish action, compelling the Dutch to turn to the New World. There, on a tongue of land projecting from Venezuela known as the Punta del Araya, was probably the finest salt pan in the world. In 1599 the first Dutch salt ships arrived: 611, according to Spanish reports, gathered salt there between 1600 and 1605. Local officials could do nothing but watch and wonder if it was possible to destroy the pan by flooding it. At last, in 1605, a Spanish fleet came from Europe and took nine Dutch ships at Araya. The masters and pilots were hanged, their crews sent to the galleys. The Dutch-Spanish truce of 1609 restored normal trade in Europe but the Dutch were back at Araya with the resumption of war in 1621. Again they were evicted, but by this time they had found salt elsewhere in the Caribbean and had also developed an illicit trade in manufactures with the Spanish colonists.[62]

---

[60] Such is the classic argument of F. J. Fisher, "Commercial Trends and Policies in the Sixteenth Century," *Economic History Review*, 10:95–117 (1940).

[61] Sluiter, "Dutch-Spanish Rivalry," pp. 166–167.

[62] *Ibid.*, pp. 176–189, and the same author's "Dutch Maritime Power and the Colonial Status Quo," *Pacific Historical Review*, 11:30 (1942).

Until the formation of the West India Company in 1621 the Dutch in the Caribbean were salt gatherers and traders first, privateers second. Of course they took prizes when they could: in 1606, 130 privateers set out to take revenge for the Araya incident.[63] But what interested them most, besides salt, were hides from Cuba and Hispaniola, tobacco, and dyewood from the Indians of Venezuela and Guiana. As early as 1599 Flushingers had two little forts on the lower Amazon, sited for the Indian trade.[64] Similar posts were planted in the seventeenth century on the Negro and Essequibo rivers, not colonies but *comptoirs* with a few traders and a handful of soldiers. The Dutch preferred taking over going concerns to building colonies of their own. For thirty years (1624–54), while England and France founded a string of colonies in the Antilles, the Dutch labored to conquer a going concern in Brazil. Their failure to do so was a worse setback than any they inflicted on Spain.

Atlantic Ships

No one thing explains why America and the sea route to India were discovered at the end of the fifteenth century instead of earlier or later. It is possible, however, to distinguish certain technical changes in shipbuilding without which it is hard to imagine the Discoveries taking place and harder still to imagine their being commercially exploited. A fanatic like Columbus would probably have tried to cross the Atlantic in anything that floated but working seamen with families to support needed reasonably safe and versatile ships which would stand up to Atlantic gales and sail approximately the course the navigator intended, ships that could carry as well as cargo enough food and water to subsist the number of men required to hoist the main yard. By 1500 such ships could be built.

Until about 1400 ship design and shipbuilding in northern Europe and the Mediterranean were to some extent independent of one another. The standard northern vessel was the cog, a "round" ship, broad in the beam, single-masted with one square sail, not handy but having a good cargo capacity for transporting grain and timber. In the Mediterranean the long-oared galley was still in use, fast and reliable but with a big crew and a small payload, fit to carry passengers or valuables but of little use for bulky staples. The Mediterranean sailing ship had two or more masts and carried a lateen sail, triangular not square, which hung along the ship, not

---

[63] Sluiter, "Dutch Maritime Power," p. 34.
[64] Edmundson, "Dutch on the Amazon and Negro," pp. 642–643.

across it, and received the wind on one side or the other according to which quarter it was coming from. These styles were already merging before 1400: both regions, for example, had adopted the sternrudder. By 1450 what has been called "the vital marriage between square-rig and lateen" was virtually complete, bringing forth the ships which, with later improvements, sailed the world and supported the Atlantic empires of England, France, and the Dutch. Northern European ships became longer. Masts increased from one to three, sometimes more. For the foremast and mainmast the square sail was retained: these drove the ship before the wind. For the mizzenmast the lateen was introduced: this helped maneuvering. The result, the full-rigged ship, was a long way from perfect but handier than its northern predecessors because sails could be adjusted to changing conditions.[65]

Size is another matter. Big ships were built in the fifteenth century, sometimes with royal encouragement for prestige reasons. Henry V ordered a ship 186 feet long and 46 feet in the beam, probably never finished. The *Peter* of La Rochelle in 1462 was 150 feet long overall. Henry VIII built the *Great Harry* of more than 1000 tons, and Francis I built a ship of 2000 tons with a private chapel, tennis court, and windmill.[66] These monsters were anachronisms and often met untimely ends. Far more important was the development in the sixteenth century of a specialized fighting ship — the galleon. This was around 500 tons, big but not a monster, full-rigged and heavily armed. Crack Spanish ships of this class brought the American treasure to Seville each year and could show a fine record in protecting it from marauders. In the confines of the English Channel Spanish galleons could be beaten by English galleons in 1588, but they were safe against a Caribbean privateer of 100 or 150 tons.

[65] T. C. Lethbridge, "Shipbuilding," in Charles Singer et al., eds., *A History of Technology*, vol. II (Oxford: Clarendon Press, 1956), pp. 583–585; R. and R. C. Anderson, *The Sailing Ship* (London: Harrap, 1926), pp. 85–90; Parry, *Age of Reconnaissance*, p. 78, and for excellent accounts of all developments in shipbuilding, navigation, and chart making in the period of the Discoveries, see chapters 3–7 of the same book.

[66] Jean De La Varende, *Cherish the Sea* (London: Sidgwick, 1955), pp. 195–198, 227. The "ton" at this time was a very rough measurement denoting the carrying capacity of a ship when loaded with some standard commodity such as wine or grain. It was probably estimated by eye, and a ship's tonnage will often be found stated differently at different times. Much learned discussion of this subject has taken place. See for example papers by P. Chaunu and P. Gille in Michel Mollat, ed., *Le navire et l'économie maritime du XVe au XVIIIe siècles* (Paris: S.E.V.P.E.N., 1957); a note by J. H. Parry in *Cambridge Economic History of Europe*, IV, 218–219; Ralph Davis, *Rise of the English Shipping Industry* (London: Macmillan, 1962); etc. These authorities agree that stated tonnages are approximations and that countries measured differently.

Some big merchantmen, or more accurately cargo-carrying ships of force, were built in the sixteenth century. One was the *Madre de Dios*, Portuguese, carrack-built, 1600 tons, 165 feet overall, with a crew of 600–700, meant to look after herself but falling to privateers in 1592.[67] Great ships like this had no place in the Atlantic trades of France, England, or the Netherlands. The typical merchantman plying between Europe and America in the seventeenth century was between about 60 tons and about 250 tons; a few were bigger, more were smaller, some were mere cockleshells. Frobisher had a pinnace of 10 tons in 1576, Davis a similar one in 1596, to attend fleets searching for the Northwest Passage. Harcourt set out to colonize Guiana in 1609 with one ship of 80 tons, one of 36 tons, and one (with a crew of four) of 9 tons. Generally these small craft ran messages and collected wood and water for the bigger ships but sometimes, by design or accident, they operated independently. Witness the *John* of London, coming home from a privateering cruise in the Caribbean in 1575, with 15 men alive out of a crew of 25: her burden was 18 tons.[68] The *Mayflower*, of ten times that burden and with a crew of 41 and a passenger list of 101, was not exactly an ocean liner and must certainly have been crowded; but she was probably bigger than most English Atlantic ships of that time.

The most notable development in merchant-ship building in the later sixteenth century was the evolution of the *fluyt* or flyboat. Turned out in thousands by the Dutch shipyards, the *fluyt* largely accounts for Dutch supremacy in the carrying trade. Flat-bottomed, long in proportion to beam, broader below than above the waterline, and with plenty of cargo space, it was slow and usually undefended. Perfect for peacetime trading in the Baltic or North Sea, the *fluyt*'s unhandiness made it less than ideal for the Mediterranean and Atlantic; but low operating cost was the decisive consideration. The Dutch built more cheaply than other Europeans: they had easy access to Scandinavian timber and Baltic naval stores, low interest rates, and mass production.[69] Cheapness in use was probably even more important than cheapness in building. Contrasting English and Dutch freight rates out of Danzig in 1620, an English observer thought the Dutch "do serve the Merchant better cheap by one hundred

[67] G. P. B. Naish, "Ships and Shipbuilding," in Charles Singer et al., eds., *A History of Technology*, vol. III (Oxford: Clarendon Press, 1957), p. 481.

[68] Williamson, *Hawkins of Plymouth*, p. 203.

[69] Violet Barbour, *Capitalism in Amsterdam in the Seventeenth Century* (Baltimore: Johns Hopkins University Press, 1950).

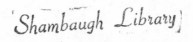

pounds in his freight than we can, by reason he hath but nine or ten Marriners, and we near thirty; thus he saveth twenty mens meat and wages in a voyage."[70] In the Atlantic the Dutch may not have held quite such an advantage; in any case their rivals could and did buy Dutch ships or use captured ones. Even so, Dutch freight rates appear to have been highly competitive; hence English and French laws in the seventeenth century compelling their colonists to use English and French ships. These laws were not merely designed to benefit the mother country economically. They were also intended to force up reserves of trained seamen, ready for pressing into the navy in time of war. This consideration goes far toward explaining the interest northwestern European governments continued to take in the Atlantic long after dreams of gold had faded away.

[70] Quoted by Violet Barbour, "Dutch and English Merchant Shipping in the Seventeenth Century," *Economic History Review*, 2:282 (1929–30).

CHAPTER 2

PLANTING

The Founding of Colonies

About 1600 peace overtook Europe. France, Spain, and England came under new rulers. Philip II made the Treaty of Vervins with France in 1598 and died a few weeks later. Henry IV put an end to the French Wars of Religion, extending toleration to the Huguenots in the Edict of Nantes (1598). Elizabeth I died in 1603; her successor, James, made peace with Spain in 1604. Even the war *à l'outrance* in the Netherlands was halted by the Twelve Years Truce of 1609. For a few years there was an interruption to the raising of troops, the taxation for war, the billeting of soldiers on civilians, the spreading of diseases by marching armies, the commandeering of ships, and the pressing of sailors, as well as an interruption to the more theatrical miseries of war depicted in the engravings of Jacques Callot. When, in 1618, this extraordinary lull was ended by the Bohemian Revolt, the seat of the new fighting was remote from the Atlantic. Spain was involved in Germany from the start; so, from 1621, were the Dutch; so from 1635, after years of shadowboxing by Cardinal Richelieu, was France. England was not. James's wish to support his son-in-law's claim to the Palatinate and the Bohemian crown by diplomacy was rejected by his Parliament; his Parliament's wish to reopen maritime war with Spain was rejected by James. Apart from an absurd and halfhearted attempt to take on France and Spain together between 1626 and 1629, England kept out of war in Europe. As a colonizing power this was to its advantage, though part of the advantage was forgone when England's own civil wars began in 1642.

Peace was a spur to the planting of colonies. Long wars become encrusted with interests which have done well out of the fighting or out of providing for armies and navies; they also breed people who become accustomed to a state of war and find it hard to imagine anything else. By 1600 there were thousands of Englishmen whose adult lives had been spent at war with Spain, fighting on land in the Low Countries and Ireland (Spain sent help to the Irish "rebels"), serving in royal fleets both defensive and offensive, or privateering in the Caribbean. What were they to do? Richard Hakluyt supplied an answer. In the dedication of the second volume in the second edition of the *Principal Navigations*, published in 1599, he wrote: "And here by the way if any man shall think, that an universall peace with our Christian neighbours will cut off the emploiment of the couragious increasing youth of this realme, he is much deceived. For there are other most convenient emploiments for all the superfluitie of every profession in this realme. For, not to meddle with the state of Ireland, nor that of Guiana, there is under our noses the great & ample countrey of Virginia. . . ." [1] No time was to be lost. France since 1565 had thrown away the lead in the harrying of Spain at sea and in the promotion of colonies in America; England had swept into a commanding position. But in 1600 that position needed to be strengthened by firmly planted colonies which would finally expose the hollowness of the king of Spain's claim to the New World.

On this subject, Spain's title to America by papal donation and prior discovery, the peace that came to Europe about 1600 was less than explicit. In negotiating the Treaty of London the English asserted the principle of effective occupation, i.e., that they were free to trade to or settle in any part of the New World not yet occupied by another European power. The Spaniards, aware that a papal grant more than a hundred years old no longer impressed the heretics, replied with the claim of prior discovery. Neither side gave up its stance; the treaty left the question thoroughly unanswered. On location in America, Spanish attitudes toward rival colonies stayed much the same: they were to be removed if possible. What was changing, as we have already seen, was Spain's capacity to effect the removal. In the Dutch-Spanish truce of 1609, a small step was taken

[1] *Voyages*, Everyman ed., 8 vols. (London: Dent, n.d.), I, 39.

toward realities. Spain recognized the right of the Dutch to trade with any part of the world willing to trade with them, at the same time taking promises from the Dutch that they would not visit the Spanish Indies and giving promises that Spanish subjects there would not be allowed to do business with foreigners. In this guarded fashion the claim that the seas of the world outside Europe were Iberian maria clausa was breached.[2]

These seas, by 1600, had become known in broad outline to the mariners and cartographers of all western European countries. Discovery for the time being was laid aside; exploitation in earnest took its place. The quest for a Northwest Passage went on for a few more years; but this and lesser details apart, Europe's stock of knowledge concerning the oceans of the world was not to be greatly enlarged until the charting of the Pacific in the second half of the eighteenth century. The Age of Reconnaissance, in which England had played a part but by no means the preeminent one, was over; the Age of Settlement, in which England excelled all others, began.

Any kind of categorizing is likely to do violence to the varied efforts which went into the founding of colonies by northwestern Europe in the seventeenth century. This variety, economic, political, and social, is the main theme of this book and will be developed in later chapters. Here, all that is intended by way of introduction is a brief chronology of the planting of colonies, a roll call of English, French, and Dutch achievements in the Atlantic.

England's continuous colonization of America began on April 26, 1607, when the first settlers sent by the Virginia Company of London sailed into Chesapeake Bay.[3] After many hardships and the spending of much more money than at first envisaged, Virginia was a going concern by about 1615. Old soldiers like Sir Thomas Gates and Sir Thomas Dale supplied the harsh discipline, for want of which colonies had fallen to pieces before and would do so again. In 1612 the cultivation of tobacco was started and the colony moved toward self-sufficiency. A terrible setback occurred in 1622 when local Indians killed a third of the settlers, but the colony

[2] Max Savelle, with M. A. Fisher, *The Origins of American Diplomacy: The International History of Angloamerica, 1492–1763* (New York: Macmillan, 1967), pp. 24–32.

[3] At the head of all histories of the English colonization of America in the seventeenth century clearly stands Charles M. Andrews, *The Colonial Period of American History*, 4 vols. (New Haven, Conn.: Yale University Press, 1934–38; reprinted 1964). Among the many virtues of this work is the attention given to the Caribbean colonies, equal or nearly so to that given to the mainland.

survived. Meanwhile, under much the same management, Bermuda was being colonized.[4] Sir George Somers on his way to Virginia in 1609 had been shipwrecked there, bringing the island into the news; three men who stayed on when the other survivors got away found an enormous lump of ambergris worth thousands of pounds; systematic settlement began in 1613. Back on the mainland, a few years later, a new colony was fashioned to the north of Virginia for George Calvert, 1st Baron Baltimore.[5] A charter was issued in 1632, granting palatine powers — like those enjoyed by the bishop of Durham — to the Calverts; the first settlers landed in March 1634. Thus was created, on the tobacco-growing western shore of Chesapeake Bay, an infelicitous division between two unlike-minded colonial governments.

Attempts by the Plymouth Company, contemporary with the Virginia Company, to found settlements in what was later New England failed, partly for want of a Gates or a Dale to deal with the lack of discipline among the colonists. The survivors and successors of this Plymouth Company turned themselves into the Council of New England, chartered in 1620. Their purpose was to negotiate agreements with individuals or groups wishing to settle in America rather than to plant settlers themselves; they were more a land company than a colonizing company.[6] Their first clients were the Pilgrims, English refugees mostly living in Holland, who wanted to be left alone to live peacefully and separately from the Church of England. Intending to settle in Virginia, the Pilgrims changed their minds when they anchored in Cape Cod Bay in November 1620. They had a hard time for a few years but survival was never much in doubt: they did not expect to get rich quickly and probably asked less of their environment than any other group of colonists crossing the Atlantic in the seventeenth century. Doctrinal accord meant that most of the discipline necessary in a young colony was self-imposed. Plymouth Colony continued in unspectacular style until 1691 when it was swallowed by Massachusetts.[7]

[4] Wesley Frank Craven, "An Introduction to the History of Bermuda," *William and Mary Quarterly*, 2nd series, 17:176–215, 317–362, 437–465 (1937), 18:40–63 (1938), where good use is made of the Manchester Papers.

[5] Newton D. Mereness, *Maryland as a Proprietary Province* (New York: Macmillan, 1901).

[6] James P. Baxter, *Sir Ferdinando Gorges and His Province of Maine*, 3 vols. (Boston: Prince Society, 1890), I, 115 et seq.

[7] George D. Langdon, *Pilgrim Colony: A History of New Plymouth, 1620–1691* (New Haven, Conn.: Yale University Press, 1966).

The Council of New England found other clients in the 1620s, including the West of England Dorchester Company which began a not particularly successful fishery colony at Cape Ann in 1623.[8] The council failed, however, to get the greatest exponents of planting in New England as its lessees: the Massachusetts Bay Company went over the council's head and obtained a charter directly from the king. Its first settlers arrived at Salem on June 29, 1629, and no fewer than seventeen shiploads followed in 1630. Few colonies have made such a convincing start. The Puritans were better led than the Pilgrims, having brought their own squirearchy with them as well as some highly educated divines; but they were less coherent in their ideology. To hold the colony together, strict discipline was imposed by the minority on the majority; but even this did not always work well. To some extent this incoherence was responsible for extending New England. Partly as transplants, partly as breakaways from Massachusetts, new colonies came into being in Connecticut (1635, royal charter 1662), Rhode Island (1636, royal charter 1663), New Haven (1637–38, incorporated in Connecticut in 1664–65), and New Hampshire (made a royal province in 1679).

In the Caribbean English colonization began with unsuccessful attempts to settle on the Wild Coast between the Orinoco and the Amazon and with brief landings on some of the Lesser Antilles. This was before 1623; ten years of highly successful planting followed. Backed by London merchants who at last perceived that tobacco was a crop from which quick profits could be taken, and bedeviled by English noblemen trying to get something for nothing, colonies were founded on St. Kitts (1624), Barbados (1625), Nevis (1628), Antigua (1632), and Montserrat (1650).[9] Similar attempts were made on Tobago and St. Lucia but failed, the latter because of Carib hostility. All these were colonies of settlement, meant to grow crops, not particularly well sited for commerce raiding and no good for expeditions against the Spanish Main. Providence Island (Santa Catalina) and Association Island (Tortuga), settled in 1631, were different, daggers pointed at Spain's trade and cities. They were owned and run by

[8] For Dorchester Company, see Carl Bridenbaugh, *Vexed and Troubled Englishmen, 1590–1642* (New York: Oxford University Press, 1968), pp. 436–437.

[9] J. H. Parry and P. M. Sherlock's *A Short History of the West Indies* (rev. ed.; London: Macmillan, 1971) does very well what it sets out to do, i.e., to present the history of the Caribbean as a region. See also Clarence H. Haring, *The Buccaneers in the West Indies in the XVII Century* (London: Methuen, 1910), and Vincent T. Harlow, *A History of Barbados, 1625–1685* (Oxford: Clarendon Press, 1926).

Puritan political leaders in England who banded themselves into the Providence Island Company, chartered in 1630.[10] Providence and Association were Puritan colonies, just as much as Massachusetts; the same Calvinist morals and observances were enforced. But this was another Puritanism, more militantly anti-Spanish and more acquisitive, an important historical link between Elizabethan privateering and Oliver Cromwell's Western Design against Spain in the 1650s. Both islands proved too vulnerable to attack by an enemy still far from finished. The Tortuga colonists were massacred in 1635, those at Providence expelled in 1641.

Discounting tiny islands like Barbuda, twelve English colonies had been planted in the New World by 1634, too hot a pace to keep up. The tobacco boom ended; the supply of emigrants from England was not inexhaustible; and the supply of slaves from Africa had not yet begun. New England continued to extend itself but, except for Surinam founded from Barbados in 1650 and lost to the Dutch in 1665, no more new colonies were planted until after the restoration of Charles II. On the other hand, two important colonies developed by rival Europeans were acquired by conquest, one by the Protectorate, the other by the restored monarchy. Cromwell's acquisition was Jamaica, a Spanish colony, taken in 1655 by the Penn-Venables expedition from England.[11] Hispaniola, the force's objective, proved too strong: Jamaica was the consolation prize, disappointing at the moment but good in the long run. Jamaica gave the English what none of their other Caribbean colonies had — space: enough to last well into the eighteenth century. It was also handily sited for trade, licit and illicit, with the Spanish colonies and a good base for buccaneering, well forward but several hundred miles nearer to safety (i.e., to windward) than Providence. The other capture was New Netherland (1664), from which were fashioned the colonies of New York and New Jersey, first fruits of a swing from Cromwell's anti-Spanish Western De-

[10] Arthur P. Newton, *The Colonising Activities of the English Puritans* (New Haven, Conn.: Yale University Press, 1914). On pp. 59–78 of this book there is an interesting discussion of the investors in the Providence Island Company, which may be compared with the mention above (pp. 19–21) of the financing of Frobisher's voyages. The same mixture of court and City is apparent, but there were more plain country gentlemen in 1630. No one investor risked much in either venture; the intention in the Providence Island Company was that each subscriber should put up £200.

[11] For the conquest, C. H. Firth, ed., *The Narrative of General Venables* (London: Camden Society, 1900). The writing of Jamaica's history is now proceeding under the auspices of the University of the West Indies, but there is as yet no book both handy and reliable on the early settlement and exploitation of the island.

sign to the vigorous prosecution of anti-Dutch policies by James, Duke of York, Anthony Ashley Cooper, later Earl of Shaftesbury, Sir George Downing, and others of Charles II's courtiers and ministers.[12] These policies also found expression in new laws to exclude the Dutch from England's Atlantic trade and in a more systematic and aggressive participation in the slave trade than anything yet attempted.

Territorially, the planting of colonies for the rest of the seventeenth century was in-filling. Shaftesbury's group of courtiers and City merchants brought Carolina into being, took a grant from Charles II of the Bahamas, and formed the Hudson's Bay Company to win a share in the fur trade by outflanking the French.[13] All this happened in one year, 1670, recapturing some of the spirit of the earlier colonizing boom. The last English colony to be planted in the seventeenth century was Pennsylvania (chartered in 1681), a felicitous blend of the religious refuge for the persecuted — in the New World as well as the Old — and the proprietary colony intended to advance the fortunes of the family lucky enough to get the king's ear.[14]

Whereas Massachusetts and Pennsylvania came into existence with the swiftness of a curtain rising on a play, and whereas other colonies like Plymouth and Maryland had particular days on which they may be said to have been planted, the beginnings of New France were stretched not over months or even years but over decades, a series of tentative moves and checks, a history of neglect matched with heroism. Certain dates can be recited: 1608, founding of Quebec; 1634, founding of Three Rivers; 1642, founding of Montreal. Each started as a *comptoir*, not a *colonie*, answering the needs of the fur trade, to which were soon added Champlain's need of a base for his journeys into the west and the need of the Récollets (1615) and the Jesuits (1625) for headquarters from which to convert the heathen. Population was absurdly small, 52 at Quebec in the winter of 1624–25, 240 in all New France in 1641.[15] Agriculture was

[12] Wesley Frank Craven, *The Colonies in Transition, 1660–1713* (New York: Harper & Row, 1968), pp. 56ff. See also the same author's *New Jersey and the English Colonization of North America* (Princeton, N.J.: Van Nostrand, 1964). New York has been less fortunate in her historians: one can do worse than return to E. B. O'Callaghan, *History of New Netherland; or New York under the Dutch*, 2 vols. (New York: Appleton, 1846–48), or consult Andrews, *Colonial Period*, vol. III.

[13] E. E. Rich, "The First Earl of Shaftesbury's Colonial Policy," *Transactions of the Royal Historical Society*, 5th series, 7:47–70 (1957).

[14] Catherine O. Peare, *William Penn* (Philadelphia and New York: Lippincott, 1957).

[15] Marcel Trudel, *Histoire de la Nouvelle-France*, vol. II: *Le comptoir, 1604–1627* (Montreal: Editions Fides, 1966), p. 486. See below, p. 77.

scarcely contemplated despite the arrival at Quebec in 1617 of Canada's first farmer, Louis Hébert, an apothecary from Paris. Seldom since Cortes's conquest of Mexico had so much been done by so few as by the handful who pioneered New France, but self-sufficiency and self-defense eluded them. The Kirkes, English privateers, easily took Quebec in 1629 and might have kept it had Charles I not been anxious to see his French wife's dowry paid in full. New France was restored to its owners but cannot be deemed a going concern much before 1660.

Acadia (later Nova Scotia) followed the same path. Port Royal was founded in 1606 by Biencourt de Poutrincourt, a noble courtier keen enough on colonization to cross the Atlantic in person.[16] Abandoned in 1607, it was resettled by de Poutrincourt in 1610, burned by Samuel Argall, deputy governor of Virginia, in 1613, taken again by the English in 1629, and restored at the same time as Quebec. Acadia continued, with vicissitudes, to be a French colony until 1713, by which year it boasted a population of fewer than fifteen hundred.

No evaluation of France's status as a colonizing power, certainly no verdict pronouncing France's inferiority to England, should be based on evidence of North America alone. The contrast between New France's beginnings and New England's is a caricature, not a true representation of the two styles. In the Caribbean France's style and record are more like England's. Where New France, considered as a colony of settlement, was for so long a top that needed to be whipped by the mother country, the French in the Antilles displayed much of the initiative and vitality found in English planting.[17] Pierre Belain d'Esnambuc, a disappointed privateer, landed on the island of St. Kitts or St. Christopher in 1625, found the English already there, helped them beat off an attack by Caribs, went home to raise men and money, and came back in 1627 with more than 500 Norman and Breton colonists. On May 13, 1627, a partition treaty was signed, dividing the island into St. Kitts (English) and St.

[16] Robert Le Blant, "L'avitaillement du Port-Royal d'Acadie par Charles de Biencourt et les marchands Rochelais," *Revue d'histoire des colonies*, 44:138–164 (1957); and the same author's "La compagnie de la Nouvelle France et la restitution de l'Acadie," *ibid.*, 42:69–93 (1955).

[17] Parry and Sherlock, *Short History of the West Indies*; Nellis M. Crouse, *French Pioneers in the West Indies* (New York: Columbia University Press, 1940); Auguste Lacour, *Histoire de la Guadeloupe*, 4 vols. (Paris: Besson & Chantemorle, 1960), a reprint of an important work of reference first published in 1855–60; M. Satineau, *Histoire de la Guadeloupe, 1635–1789* (Paris: Payot, 1928); C.-A. Banbuck, *Histoire politique, économique et sociale de la Martinique sous l'ancien régime* (Paris: Rivière, 1930).

Christophe (French). This treaty was often broken and often renewed. The French, though inferior in numbers, more than once overran the whole island, held on until 1702, finally losing it by the Treaty of Utrecht (1713).

Guadeloupe was settled by emigrants from France in 1635 and Martinique by colonists from St. Christophe in the same year. More offshoots followed: on St. Martin (jointly with the Dutch), St. Bartholomew, St. Croix, Marie-Galante, Grenada, and St. Lucia. Comprehensively neglected by the French government from France's entry into the Thirty Years War (1635) to the Peace of the Pyrenees (1659), and less thickly populated than the neighboring English colonies, the French Antilles were nevertheless going concerns when Colbert first turned toward them.

Martinique and Guadeloupe were big islands as the Lesser Antilles go but the best land was soon taken up. Newcomers had to look elsewhere. Frenchmen, like Englishmen, wanted a base for privateering nearer the Spanish shipping lanes; Tortuga, vacated by the Providence Island Company, supplied it. This island may be regarded as a French colony from 1665 when Bertrand d'Ogeron was made governor. He, at the same time, encouraged French settlement on the western end of Hispaniola and began step by step what the Penn-Venables expedition had failed to achieve. From these beginnings came, in the eighteenth century, the apotheosis of all Caribbean planting, the French colony of St.-Domingue. Here, on the eve of the French Revolution, half a million slaves were to labor to support not merely a few thousand owners but the shippers and shipowners of western France and much of France's reexport business with the rest of Europe.

Louisiana (1699) was the last colony to be founded by Europeans in the seventeenth century. Canada was the springboard, gold (still) the incentive, though the attraction of a warm-water port for New France and the glimpsed possibility of fencing in the English were additional considerations. Pierre Le Moyne d'Iberville, a Canadian, built the first fort at Biloxi in 1699. Mobile was founded early in the eighteenth century. The best of the early immigrants were Canadians; predictably there was no rush of settlers from Old France. By 1714 there were some 380 French in the colony of whom 170 were on the king's payroll, a proportion fairly indicating the role assumed by the crown in nursing along the new settlement. Louisiana, however, proved expensive. In 1712, the crown while continuing to rule the colony ceded a monopoly of its trade and mineral rights for fifteen years to Antoine Crozat, a Parisian *officier*, who undertook to transport settlers and eventually to take over financial responsibility for running and defending the colony.[18] Thus, well into the eighteenth century, the "new formula for colonization" — monopoly in return for the provision of settlers — continued to be the recourse of an impoverished monarch.

Dutch colonizing in the Caribbean and the North Atlantic is a story quickly told. The Dutch planted, not colonies, but factories, small lightly defended structures, garrisoned by a few soldiers and worked by a few traders, sited wherever profitable trade was expected — Spitsbergen, the Gold Coast, Guiana, the North (Hudson) and South (Delaware) rivers, and on rocks in the Caribbean. Settlers, if not actively encouraged, were not discouraged from grouping themselves round these posts, not too much notice being taken of their country of origin. So long as they did not interfere with the West India Company's trade, they could make themselves useful by supplying fresher and cheaper food to the posts than that which was sent from Europe. In 1664, when the English conquered it, New Netherland was just turning into a colony of settlement, but this was fifty years after the first *comptoir* was built. Henry Hudson had found Manhattan Island in 1609. Adriaen Block sailed up the North River in 1613 and established Fort Orange near where Albany now is. In 1624 a few settlers were sent there, a few more to Fort Nassau on the South River. In 1625–26 New Amsterdam was built on Manhattan Island. Slowly people accumulated. It was New France again, minus the high purpose of the priests and the heroic deeds of the explorers.[19]

In the Caribbean, in the first phase of northern European colonization, the Dutch showed even less interest in planting settlers than they did on the Hudson and Delaware. They took St. Eustatius from its Anglo-French occupants in 1632, an island of little value for growing crops but useful as a trading center from which to work the Spanish, French, and English colonies from the Mona Passage right down to Barbados. In 1634 they took Curaçao from Spain, wanting it for its salt and as a forward base for

[18] Marcel Giraud, *Histoire de la Louisiane française*, vol. I: *Le règne de Louis XIV (1698–1715)* (Paris: Presses Universitaires de France, 1953), pp. 229 et seq.

[19] Andrews, *Colonial Period*, vol. III, chapter 3; J. Franklin Jameson, ed., *Narratives of New Netherland, 1609–1664* (New York: Scribner, 1909); Charles R. Boxer, *The Dutch Seaborne Empire, 1600–1800* (London: Hutchinson, 1965); C. de Lannoy and H. Van der Linden, *Histoire de l'expansion coloniale des peuples européens: Néerlande et Danemark* (Brussels: Lamertin, 1911).

privateering and illicit trade with the Spanish colonies, much as the English wanted Providence and had to be satisfied with Jamaica, and much as the French wanted and got Tortuga. Other specks of Caribbean rock which became Dutch were Bonaire (95 square miles), half St. Martin (18 square miles), and Saba (5 square miles).

Yet the Dutch could found colonies when they chose to do so. Their long fight to conquer and hold Brazil (1624–54) brought many Dutchmen across the Atlantic, releasing them, when it failed, to become settlers in the Caribbean. In 1665 they took Surinam from the English, kept it at the Peace of Breda (1667), and slowly turned it into an orthodox tropical colony. No one interfered with them in Surinam; no one interfered with them at the Cape of Good Hope (1652). Both colonies were gradual evolutions without the drama of mass migrations.

The total number of colonies founded in America by English, Dutch, and French during the seventeenth century depends on the definition of a colony and whether Massachusetts and Saba count equal. Ignoring dependencies, very small islands, and colonies which had failed or been absorbed by others, a total of twenty-eight more or less independent establishments would be somewhere near the mark for 1700: three Dutch, eight French (more if St.-Domingue and Tortuga are reckoned as two or if some of the Lesser Antilles are counted), and seventeen English.[20] Even this bare recital has suggested the magnitude of the work performed. In less than a hundred years, immovable foundations of European dominance had been laid. How was it done?

Sections

Colonies were not founded by the French, Dutch, and English *nations* but by sections, usually geographical, sometimes religious, of those countries. One must indeed question the aptness of the term *nation* to describe any western European country in the seventeenth century, particularly such a random bundle of interests as the United Provinces. Historically the Dutch Republic was a detached segment of the Low Countries, its southern boundary fixed at the line reached by the Spanish

[20] Dutch: Curaçao, St. Eustatius (Statia), Surinam. French: New France, Acadia, Louisiana, St. Christophe (soon to be lost), Martinique, Guadeloupe, Cayenne, Tortuga–St.-Domingue, to which number might be added several of the smaller Antilles. English: Newfoundland, New Hampshire, Massachusetts, Rhode Island, Connecticut, New York, New Jersey, Pennsylvania, Maryland, Virginia, Carolina, St. Kitts, Nevis, Montserrat, Antigua, Barbados, Jamaica, to which might be added smaller islands and Hudson Bay.

general Alexander Farnese in 1590 when he was called from reconquering rebels to fight the heretical French king. Religiously, the seven provinces were divided into a Protestant majority and a Catholic minority; economically, into seaward provinces with traditional trading and fishing interests and landward provinces which lived by agriculture. These diversities were enhanced by a miraculously preserved political system, a museum piece of medieval liberties which gave virtual self-government to every city'and representative institutions to every province. From time to time ambassadors of the provinces met at The Hague and transacted business as the States-General. This, politically speaking, was the Dutch "nation."

Except in Brazil, where the United Provinces had to fight a war, few signs of public direction can be found in the Dutch Atlantic effort. By charter dated June 3, 1621, Dutch interests in West Africa, the Americas, and the Atlantic islands were granted to the West India Company, a copy of the already successful East India Company of 1602.[21] Like the Dutch Republic itself, the West India Company was a federation, the interests of its components guaranteed by the charter much as the interests of towns and provinces were guaranteed by the Dutch constitution. Any Dutchman could subscribe to the company's capital of 7 million florins; a general account was to be made every six years and profits distributed in proportion to stock held. As regards ownership, therefore, the West India Company was a recognizable corporate enterprise. It was into the management of the trade that Dutch sectionalism was built, underlining the fact that there was more to the company's business than making profits and distributing them to shareholders. There were ships to be built or hired, jobs to be filled, seamen to be recruited, trade goods to be contracted for, imports to be sold. All these activities were beneficial to a community; the charter required that they should be distributed among the leading seaports and not monopolized by one. Management, accordingly, was committed to five chambers (kamers), Amsterdam, Zeeland, Maas, North Quarter, and Friesland with Groningen. These did not correspond exactly to the seven provinces, being weighted toward the seaports; on the other hand, chambers could recruit directors from anywhere they liked. Among directors of the Amsterdam chamber in the first fifteen years of the West India Company are found men from Utrecht, Leiden, Gelderland, and Overijssel; in the Zeeland chamber, men from Middelburg and Flushing; in the Maas chamber, men from Delft and Dordrecht as well as men from

---

[21] There is an English translation of the West India Company's charter in O'Callaghan, *History of New Netherland*, vol. I, appendix A.

Rotterdam. To this extent management was more diffused than the charter suggests.

The division of trade was unequal: to the Amsterdam chamber was allotted four-ninths, to Zeeland two-ninths, to the others one-ninth each. Thus, in theory, when the West India Company sent a fleet of nine ships to Africa to buy slaves, four would be found and equipped, their crews recruited and paid, and their cargoes furnished by the Amsterdam chamber, two by Zeeland, and one by each of the other three. Under Article XXV of the charter, ships were to return to the port from which they set out. If forced by weather to enter another port (i.e., within the province of another chamber) "each chamber shall nevertheless have the direction and management of the vessels and goods it sent out." Article XXVI recognized that sugar refiners, tobacco workers, and others who set up near ports were dependent on regular supplies of raw materials. "If any chamber has got any goods or returns from the places included within the limits of this charter, with which another is not provided, it shall be held to send such goods to the chamber which is unprovided."

Central management was not entirely forgotten. There were to be meetings "so often as it shall be necessary" of a committee of nineteen, the Heeren XIX, eight of whom were appointed by the Amsterdam chamber, four by Zeeland, two each by Maas, North Quarter, and Friesland, and one by the States-General of the United Provinces. This committee may be seen as the equivalent in the West India Company of the Dutch States-General, meant to override sectional interests where necessary. In practice, the bad effects which this clumsy constitution might have had on the Dutch Atlantic effort were mitigated by other things than the Heeren XIX. Just as, politically, the States-General of the United Provinces was dominated by Holland, the strongest and richest province, and Holland by Amsterdam, the strongest and richest city, so the India companies, East and West, were subordinated to that same city. Of the West India Company's initial capital of 7 million florins, 3 million were owned in Amsterdam; by 1670 more than half was, with other chambers in debt to Amsterdam.[22]

[22] On the Dutch West India Company, see J. Franklin Jameson, *Willem Usselinx*, Papers of the American Historical Association, vol. 2, no. 3 (New York: A.H.A., 1889); W. Van Hoboken, "The West India Company," in J. S. Bromley and E. H. Kossmann, eds., *Britain and the Netherlands* (London: Chatto, 1960); J. Postma, "The Dimension of the Dutch Slave Trade from Western Africa," *Journal of African History*, 13:237–248 (1972); Charles R. Boxer, *The Dutch in Brazil* (Oxford: Clarendon Press, 1957); Violet Barbour, *Capitalism in Amsterdam in the Seventeenth Century* (Baltimore: Johns Hopkins University Press, 1950). There is still no adequate history of the company.

Secondly, instead of each fleet sent out by the West India Company consisting of contributions from each chamber, particular chambers ran particular trades without interference from the others. Thus Zeeland merchants had traded on the coast of Guiana twenty years before the West India Company was founded. In 1621 this trade was subsumed into the operations of the Zeeland chamber, which claimed to exclude not just foreigners but all other Dutchmen. In 1635 the Zeelanders sent a deputation to the Heeren XIX "to insist on the trade on the Wild Coast, and that nobody navigate there save those who have a contract to that effect from this chamber with the approval of the Council of Nineteen."[23] By the 1650s the Zeeland chamber had grown tired of bearing the cost of Guiana and transferred its interest to three towns, Middelburg, Flushing, and Veere. Exactly the same happened in New Netherland. Within a few years the fur trade and the little colonies of Manhattan and Fort Orange were being run, not by the Heeren XIX (which served more as a court of appeal), but by the New Netherland subcommittee of the Amsterdam chamber. In 1657 part of Delaware was sold to the city of Amsterdam, in 1663 the remainder. In West Africa the chamber of North Quarter managed the trade of the Gambia, the chamber of Maas that of Sierra Leone.[24]

The third modification of the West India Company's charter came with the abandonment step by step of trading on a common stock. The trade of Brazil, New Netherland, Curaçao, and finally in 1734 West Africa was opened to all Dutchmen, at first on payment of a license fee, then without charge. The company's territorial responsibilities were reduced by the loss of Brazil in 1654 and of New Netherland in 1664. It survived in the later seventeenth century as the administrator of the Dutch Caribbean islands and as a slave-trading company of some importance. In 1730 its African monopoly was cut back to the Gold Coast and four years later abolished altogether.

In France central government was stronger, becoming more so from 1624, the coming to power of Cardinal Richelieu. Institutions were less particularized than in the Dutch Republic, the crown far more powerful and endowed with far greater prestige than any central authority in the

[23] G. Edmundson, "The Dutch in Western Guiana," *English Historical Review*, 16:669–670 (1901).

[24] Christopher Ward, *The Dutch and Swedes on the Delaware, 1609–1664* (Philadelphia: University of Pennsylvania Press, 1930), pp. 246–247; Walter Rodney, *A History of the Upper Guinea Coast* (Oxford: Clarendon Press, 1970), p. 127.

United Provinces. Bit by bit, under the stress of war and urgent needs to raise money and troops and to beat down the opposition thereby engendered, royal agents (intendants) took over the administration of the French provinces. Yet there were still provincial assemblies in the *pays d'états* in the seventeenth century; Brittany in particular kept many marks of independence to prove its recent attachment to the crown of France. Local codes of law (*coutumes*) were still in force, guarded by provincial courts (*parlements*). Under stress, as in the Wars of Religion or the Fronde (1648–52), France was still disposed *se cantonner*, to form cantons, to rebel by localities, to assert not a national opposition but sectional independence against a weak or untrustworthy central authority.[25] The country was too big, given seventeenth-century communications, to be economically unified or for merchants, farmers, and artisans to think in national terms. There was not one French metropolis but several.[26] Mediterranean France and Atlantic France had economic interests which were broadly distinct, if not entirely separate. The two seas were not linked by the Canal des Deux Mers until 1681.

Sectional interests at home profoundly affected France's colonial and commercial efforts in the seventeenth century. Can France indeed be said to have founded colonies in the seventeenth century? Should not these communities in Canada and the Caribbean be regarded in the first place as detached portions of Normandy, Brittany, Aunis, and Saintonge? Most of the settlers came from those provinces and, abroad, did not give up their clannishness.[27] Canada and Martinique were Norman colonies: four-fifths of the people of New France as late as 1680 had been born in Normandy, had been born in Canada of Norman parents, or were married to Normans.[28] When St.-Domingue was being settled toward the end of

[25] R. Doucet, *Les institutions de la France au XVI ᵉ siècle*, 2 vols. (Paris: Picard, 1948), especially vol. I, part II, chapters 1, 6, and 8; E. Esmonin, *Études sur la France des XVII ᵉ et XVIII ᵉ siècles* (Paris: Presses Universitaires de France, 1964), especially part I which studies intendants; H. Frèville, *L'intendance de Bretagne*, vol. I (Rennes: Plihon, 1953), pp. 17–30, which discusses special characteristics of this province; G. Pagès, *La monarchie de l'ancien régime en France* (Paris: Colin, 1928), especially the sections on French Wars of Religion.

[26] Abbott P. Usher, *History of the Grain Trade in France, 1400–1700* (Cambridge, Mass.: Harvard University Press, 1913), pp. 48 et seq., for the conflict between Paris and Rouen leading to establishment of defined metropolitan areas from which each drew its food supplies.

[27] Gabriel Debien, "Les engagés pour les Antilles (1634–1715)," *Revue d'histoire des colonies*, 38:55 (1951): "The colonies and the colonial market were divided into districts as precisely defined as the divisions among the captains of the different ports of France."

[28] William B. Munro, *The Seigniorial System in Canada* (New York: Longmans, 1907), p. 10.

the seventeenth century Normans occupied the northern part, Poitevins and Angevins the western end.[29] Father du Tertre, Dominican missionary and author of one of the classics of early colonization, thought that life in a new colony was so much like that of a beleaguered garrison that old distinctions, local as well as social, soon disappeared. Yet the same author tells us that the faction fights that nearly destroyed Martinique in the 1650s were between "Normands" and "Parisiens."[30]

At home, France's Atlantic trade and colonies, instead of fostering a new national interest with benefits diffused through the whole country, served in the first place to sharpen old divisions. Guadeloupe and western St.-Domingue were predominantly La Rochelle's colonies, Martinique Dieppe's, northern St.-Domingue Dieppe's and Le Havre's, Acadia La Rochelle's.[31] There was nothing inefficient or harmful about those links; on the contrary they worked well. The trouble began when kings or ministers, sometimes to satisfy expectant courtiers, sometimes at the instance of merchants, sometimes for reasons of state, entered the field and upset the course of trade. For example, to develop trade with Africa, Richelieu gave a monopoly to a firm based in Rouen and Dieppe in 1631; to another in St.-Malo in 1634; and to a third in Paris in 1635.[32] Other ports or firms able to engage in that trade were excluded or at least disadvantaged by having to buy licenses from the monopolist. When, in 1664, the crown tried to tie together the interests of different ports in Atlantic trade and colonization into a giant company modeled on the Dutch West India Company clumsy devices were built into it to safeguard local interests. The Compagnie des Indes Occidentales was run mostly from Colbert's office but with boards of directors, like Dutch chambers, at Rouen and La Rochelle and agents at Honfleur, Le Havre, Dieppe, St.-Malo, Nantes, and Bordeaux.[33] Like so much of Colbert's work, this company initiated little or nothing; it was a Parisian harness cast over the Atlantic ports, constricting not stimulating them.

France's weakness in the Atlantic was Paris, not a port or a major domestic entrepôt, but nevertheless a financial center, the seat of gov-

[29] Debien, "Engagés pour les Antilles," pp. 151–152.
[30] [J.-B.] du Tertre, Histoire générale des Antilles, 4 vols. in 3 (Paris, 1667), I, 535.
[31] Debien, "Engagés pour les Antilles," pp. 148, 151; M. Delafosse, "La Rochelle et les îles au XVIIe siècle," Revue d'histoire des colonies, 36:238–281 (1949); R. Le Blant, articles cited in footnote 16 above.
[32] Abdoulaye Ly, La compagnie du Sénégal ([Paris]: Présence Africaine, 1958), p. 67.
[33] Stewart L. Mims, Colbert's West Indian Policy (New Haven, Conn.: Yale University Press, 1912), p. 94.

ernment, and the home of the court: too influential to be left out of account. Trade in Colbert's eyes was too important to be run by traders. If Normans and Bretons and Rochellais were allowed to get on with making money "French" interests would suffer; i.e., the traders would do only what they were good at, not what Colbert wanted them to do. Hence interference from Paris, often ineffective, sometimes disastrous. The Compagnie du Sénégal, when it passed into Parisian ownership in 1684, became hopelessly entangled with the tax-farming activities of Parisian *officiers* and slid into insolvency. From Colbert's time onwards, there was a growing awareness of the benefits of freedom (that is, freedom from Paris) in the Atlantic trade. But there were still the old sectional interests of the ports to contend with; as late as 1717 a royal edict confined the privilege of trading with the French colonies to thirteen named ports.[34]

Considered emotionally or considered practically England was more of a "nation" in 1600 than any other European country. There was a special self-consciousness, heightened by the Reformation and toughened by the war with Spain, a consciousness met time and time again in Elizabethan literature but above all in Foxe's *Book of Martyrs* and Hakluyt's *Principal Navigations, Voyages, Traffiques and Discoveries of the English Nation.* The first appeared in English in 1563, was enlarged and reissued in 1570, and reprinted three more times in the sixteenth century and four more times in the seventeenth.[35] Nearly every literate Englishman must have read it, and for the illiterate there were fifty-six woodcuts in the edition of 1563, more in the edition of 1570. Foxe's original purpose was to keep green the memory of the Protestant martyrs put to death in Queen Mary's reign (1553–58); but "the book," especially in the 1570 edition, did more than that. Foxe plunged far back into history to discover and chronicle instances of God's special care and mercy toward Englishmen throughout recorded time. A past was constructed in which Christ struggled with Anti-Christ, the former bravely supported by his English auxiliaries, the latter generally sustained by the pope. Often the battle was a close-run thing, as it was to be in 1588, a renewed mercy which along with deliverance from Guy Fawkes found its way into the edition of 1632. If it was possible between 1560 and 1660 for Englishmen to be Puritans and pa-

[34] Richard Pares, *Merchants and Planters, Economic History Review* Supplement no. 4 (Cambridge: Economic History Society, 1959), p. 27.

[35] William Haller, *Foxe's "Book of Martyrs" and the Elect Nation* (London: Cape, 1963), p. 13.

52   THE NORTH ATLANTIC WORLD

triots (and the life of Oliver Cromwell is proof that it was) instead of Puritans and international conspirators, this was in large measure owing to Foxe. No better intellectual food for privateers and colonizers could have been found. Drake took a copy round the world, read bits aloud to Spanish prisoners, and passed time coloring the pictures.[36]

Hakluyt's book began to appear in 1589. The first complete edition came out in three folio volumes in 1598–1600, and more of Hakluyt's manuscripts were published in 1625 by Samuel Purchas in *Purchas His Pilgrimes*.[37] Hakluyt, like Foxe, roamed back in time to fulfill his purpose, into chronicles which told of the voyages of Ochther and Edgar and showed that London was "a Citie of great traffike and Marchandize not long after the beginning of the Saxons reigne."[38] Discoveries by foreigners were admitted, of necessity because Hakluyt wanted his work to be useful, but it was the achievements of his own people that loomed largest. "So," he wrote, "though not in wax, yet in record of writing have I presented to the noble courages of this English Monarchie, the like images of their famous predecessors, with hope of like effect in their posteritie."[39]

It is relevant to recall '88 and the unity of England at a time of external danger, relevant too to recall that there was one Parliament for all England, not seven local and one central as in the United Provinces, and that there was one law common to all Englishmen, not as in France several local codes with Roman law predominating in the south. Those are some of the things that distinguished England from other countries, but they are not the whole story. Socially and economically, England was not a single homogeneous community but a federation of local communities with separate, often jarring, interests. For most purposes, town and county came before nation. When a man spoke of his "country" he nearly always meant his "county."[40] This sense of locality, this regional patriotism, has been found in many aspects of English history in the seven-

[36] *Ibid.*, p. 221.
[37] *Hakluytus Posthumus, or Purchas His Pilgrimes*, 20 vols. (Glasgow: MacLehose, 1903–4).
[38] *Voyages*, Everyman ed., I, 104.
[39] *Ibid.*, p. 39.
[40] Austin Woolrych, "The English Revolution: An Introduction," in E. W. Ives, ed., *The English Revolution, 1600–1660* (London: Arnold, 1968), p. 2. Examples of studies of English local communities are William B. Willcox, *Gloucestershire: A Study in Local Government, 1590–1640* (New Haven, Conn.: Yale University Press, 1940), and Thomas G. Barnes, *Somerset, 1625–1640* (London: Oxford University Press, 1961).

teenth century: in the county commissions of peace which ran the country
subject to the occasional and not always effective interference of the Privy
Council; in the military organization of the realm through the county
militia; in the conduct of members of Parliament inside and outside the
House of Commons; and in the county committees which organized
Parliament's resistance to the king in the Civil War. It would be surprising indeed if this geographical sectionalism had failed to leave its mark on
England's colonizing activities. The wonder is that in more formally divided countries like the Netherlands and France any collective authority
or stamp at all was imposed on the doings of the separate sections.

The first moves toward English colonization exhibit signs of sectional
divergencies as deep as the French or Dutch. In the petition for incorporation of the Virginia Company distinct regional interests are visible:
London's represented by George Popham, those of Plymouth, Bristol,
and Exeter by Ferdinando Gorges. The resultant charter of April 10,
1606, created not one Virginia Company but two — the London and the
Plymouth — with separate parts of America to settle and a neutral zone
between them. The next fifteen years showed which was the stronger.
London merchants, courtiers, the City authorities, even the crown,
poured money into southern Virginia;[41] and more, financed the Bermuda
Company and (for £ 60,000) colonized Londonderry at the same time.[42]
The West of England simply could not match this investment. The
Plymouth Company's colony of Sagadahoc in New England failed; settle-
ment dwindled to summer resorts for fishermen. The West could easily
finance fisheries, it could even afford a shot at the Northwest Passage, but
it could not make a go of colonization. The best the Council of New
England could do was invite settlers within its jurisdiction; it could not
itself found colonies. And the first settlers to accept the invitation, the
Pilgrims, got their financial backing in London.[43]

Frequently in the sixteenth and seventeenth centuries the outports
complained that the metropolis sucked up the wealth of England and
reduced them to poverty, and in times of economic distress Stuart gov-

[41] The Virginia Company raised about £ 200,000. See William R. Scott, *The Constitution
and Finance of English, Scottish and Irish Joint-Stock Companies to 1720*, 3 vols. (Cambridge: At the University Press, 1910–12), II, 246–297.

[42] T. W. Moody, *The Londonderry Plantation, 1609–41* (Belfast: Mullan, 1939), a book of
great relevance to early English colonization.

[43] Bernard Bailyn, *The New England Merchants in the Seventeenth Century* (Cambridge,
Mass.: Harvard University Press, 1958), p. 23.

ernments — no lovers of London — were disposed to attend to those grievances.[44] London did not have everything its own way. Bristol got into the tobacco trade, the emigrant business, later into sugar. The West Country ports fought a running battle with London over the Newfoundland fisheries and did not always get the worst of it. But London's domination cannot be questioned. In 1700, 69 percent of all English exports, 80 percent of imports, 80 percent of reexports, were handled by London.[45] In specifically colonial trades this preponderance was a little less marked, but two-thirds of the tobacco and five-sixths of the sugar coming into the country did so through London. The chartered monopolies, East India, Royal African, and Hudson's Bay companies, did not have and were not made to have provincial chambers like the Dutch or French. They were London-based, working easily with government and court.

London in 1600 was La Rochelle, Dieppe, Rouen, and Paris in one. Had English colonization begun a century earlier the story might have been different. Bristol, with traditions of trade to Ireland, Iceland, and Spain, and with the natural advantage of facing the Atlantic, might have become England's first city for trade and planting in America. In the course of the sixteenth century, however, London rose to an unassailable position, not only in exports and imports but also in the internal trade of the kingdom in foodstuffs, textiles, and coal. Riches were concentrated where power was; that was an important asset when English colonization began. Sectional interests were never banished from colonizing. In one respect they were more pronounced than in other empires. Only the English planted colonies in America for persons of religious beliefs different from those of the "national" church at home, Plymouth, Massachusetts, Maryland, Pennsylvania, all looking in some degree not to the English "nation" but to that section of the English people which thought as they did. Such exclusiveness was certain to be divisive. Happily, in most instances it was relaxed. As the colonies prospered, most of those which had not been founded on London's money entered London's commercial net.

Ingredients and Styles

Kings could not compel colonies into life. A characteristic of European monarchy, arguably its hallmark, was the wide gulf separating theoretical

[44] B. E. Supple, *Commercial Crisis and Change in England, 1600–1642* (Cambridge: At the University Press, 1959), p. 69.

[45] From Elizabeth B. Schumpeter, *English Overseas Trade Statistics, 1697–1808* (London: Oxford University Press, 1960).

and legal claims from administrative resources, a gulf that was not narrowing and may have been widening until about 1620. While there might be less and less that a king of France or Spain was legally restrained from doing, there was no corresponding advance in the sixteenth century in the sophistication or effectiveness of government machinery. Much administration continued to rest on contracts or bargains struck between the ruler and one or a group of his subjects. Lack of money on the king's part was as cogent a reason for this as lack of a civil service: the king hoped to harness private resources to his own purposes while the subject hoped to harness the king's legal powers to his private interests. In Spanish history one particular contract, the *asiento*, is remembered above all others but the term has no necessary association with the slave trade; it denotes any contract for any purpose between the crown and *adelantande* or adventurer.[46] Every country had its *asientos*. Tax farming was probably the commonest type, the farmer advancing a lump sum to the king and extracting rather more from the subject later. But comparable contracts were made for other purposes: raising and equipping armies and fleets, starting new industries, draining land, exploring and founding colonies.[47]

Many trading and most colonizing ventures launched from northwestern Europe in the sixteenth and seventeenth centuries began with some kind of bargain between crown and adventurers, the terms defined by charter; and it is thus or chiefly thus that European rulers made their initial impact on expansion. Direct financing by government was hardly to be expected. Wholly or predominantly royal foundations are rare; on the other hand, most colonies through their charters bore some stamp of government. Reciprocal advantage was the foundation of these bargains. The crown had privileges which it alone could bestow; by careful distribution it could also benefit itself. First was incorporation, the right which the king granted to cities and guilds and without which enterprises like the Virginia and East India companies could not have gone into business. Second were exemptions, sometimes the freedom to do what everyone

[46] Georges Scelle, "The Slave-Trade in the Spanish Colonies of America: The Assiento," *American Journal of International Law*, 4:614–615 (1910).

[47] Two interesting books on tax farming and contracting are Robert Ashton, *The Crown and the Money Market, 1603–1640* (Oxford: Clarendon Press, 1960), and A. D. Lublinskaya, *French Absolutism: The Crucial Phase* (Cambridge: At the University Press, 1968). Studies of great contractors in the seventeenth century include A. V. Judges, "Philip Burlamachi: Financier of the Thirty Years War," *Economica*, 6:286–300 (1926); and Raymond Carr, "Two Swedish Financiers: Louis De Geer and Joel Gripenstierna," in H. E. Bell and R. L. Ollard, eds., *Historical Essays Presented to David Ogg* (London: Black, 1963). See also R. H. Tawney, *Business and Politics under James I* (Cambridge: At the University Press, 1958).

else was forbidden to do, such as the privilege of exporting undyed wool-
ens given to the English Merchant Adventurers, sometimes freedom
from customs duties such as was given for seven years to the Virginia and
Bermuda companies.[48] Third, monopolies, in France more or less without legal restriction, in England more or less subject to common law. The
English act of Parliament of 1624 forbidding grants of monopolies to
individuals allowed them to be given to companies, thus enhancing the
royal gift of incorporation.

It was by manipulating grants of these privileges, sometimes purpose-
fully and beneficially, sometimes willfully and deleteriously, that French
and English kings influenced if they could not initiate early colonization.
In return they hoped for riches, preferably mines like the king of Spain's.
When a second Peru ceased to be even a dream, there were still solid
benefits to be expected: increased customs revenue, more and bigger
ships, more trained seamen to fight naval wars, more employment and
hence less discontent, more taxable capacity.

Colonies needed the support of government; mercantile capital and
management; leaders for the new community; farmers, artisans, laborers,
and servants to make them self-supporting. Success depended on the art
or the luck with which these four ingredients were blended. Probably no
two blends were exactly alike. Different European countries were richer
in one ingredient, poorer in another; it is by the blends that distinctive
styles of French, Dutch, and English colonizing can be recognized.

French colonization in the early seventeenth century owed little to
government stimulus and subvention. In the Antilles colonies came into
being of which the French crown seemed scarcely aware and about which
it cared next to nothing. In New France the *comptoirs* of fur gatherers and
fishermen were supplemented after 1600 by mission stations for work
with the Indians. The crown, in its many charters, defined a policy of
settlement on the St. Lawrence but could not implement it. Cardinal
Richelieu, always prone to believe that he could succeed where others
had failed, set out to coerce Frenchmen into being colonists and colonists
into being Frenchmen. He, too, failed. Mazarin, his successor, did not
even try. By 1660 French colonies had been firmly planted in the Caribbean but were run by private interests; New France, with fewer than
2500 residents, was also largely in private hands.

Colbert changed this, and changed too the style of the French colonial

---

[48] As recommended by Francis Bacon, "Of Plantations," in *Essays*.

empire. True, his success was qualified. Government's intervention was intermittent not continuous. Support lavished on New France between 1660 and 1670 was not sustained. Moreover, help given to the colonies in one way was partly nullified in another, for example, by treating them as counters in peace settlements. Louis XIV spent more on his European clients such as Bavaria and Sweden than on New France.[49] It is nevertheless from 1660 that the colonies were subordinated to the French crown and that the distinctively royal style of France overseas began to appear.

Neither New France nor Old lacked men of spirit to lead new communities. From frequent wars France was rich in leaders, most of them poor and all of them barred by the rules and conventions of their caste from earning a living in trade. D'Esnambuc, founder of St. Christophe, is an example of the French hidalgo; from a respectable but bankrupt Norman family, he sold what was left of his lands and went privateering as his ancestors might have gone on crusade. D'Ogeron, an Angevin, did like service in St.-Domingue and before the end of the seventeenth century New France produced in d'Iberville a colonial version of the same type.[50]

France was far less successful in furnishing colonies with mercantile capital or rank-and-file settlers. Repeatedly the distinction must be made between organizing a fishing, privateering, or commercial voyage across the Atlantic and planting a colony. The first was an extension, in every way riskier but still an extension, of established maritime practices; the second called for new techniques and a new style. French merchants in the Atlantic ports willingly found money for fishing and privateering; they would also, though more cautiously, advance cash to infant colonies as Le Havre sponsored St. Christophe in 1626 and Dieppe backed Guadeloupe in 1635. What they were unwilling to do was to sustain a colony, as Virginia and Bermuda were sustained, over a period of years, or invest liberally in long-term projects like Colbert's East and West India companies. As for settlers, the French Antilles always needed more whites than they received from the mother country while New France throughout the seventeenth century attracted too few to be either economically viable or secure from external threats. Leaders like d'Esnambuc could collect personal followings, though not necessarily the right kind of col-

[49] Louis André, *Louis XIV et l'Europe* (Paris: Michel, 1950), pp. 131, 135, 213. To break up the Triple Alliance Louis made a treaty with England costing 800,000 livres a year and another with Sweden costing 400,000 crowns a year in peace and 600,000 crowns in war. In 1682 he bought a Bavarian alliance for 400,000 livres.

[50] Nellis M. Crouse, *Lemoyne d'Iberville: Soldier of New France* (Ithaca, N.Y.: Cornell University Press, 1954).

onists. Peasants and swordsmen were not enough. You must send, Jacques Dyel du Parquet, d'Esnambuc's nephew and eventual successor, wrote from St. Christophe in 1635, "masons, bricklayers, stone cutters, limeworkers, carpenters, joiners, locksmiths, toolmakers, nailsmiths, tilers, and other workmen furnished with the tools of their trade."[51] Even peasants were often hard to get, whether because of the inadequacy of French colonizing propaganda or simply because of the reluctance of Frenchmen to leave home. The Antilles' manpower problem was solved by slaves; New France's not at all.

Parkman's epigram "New France was all head"[52] does less than justice to the tenacity of the *habitants* and the boldness of the *coureurs de bois*. Nor does it have application to the Antilles. Yet France by 1700 had a colonial style which more reflected the purposes of the government in Europe than either England or the Dutch Republic. This was not merely because Versailles intervened minutely in colonial affairs from 1660. It was also because the French church was strong in the colonies and generally on the crown's side, and even more because no elective institutions were permitted to develop overseas. The French style of colonization by 1700 embodied the assumption by the monarchy of an initiative which in England and Holland came from below.

The Dutch style was different but it had at least one characteristic in common with the French: shortage of people. There was nothing, it seems, to stop Dutchmen becoming very good colonists, as they later proved themselves to be in Surinam and South Africa. De la Court, a seventeenth-century Dutch businessman and writer on colonial affairs, claimed that "the ingenious, frugal and industrious Hollanders, by those virtues which are most peculiar to them, are more fit than any other nation in the world to erect colonies and to live on them."[53] Yet the Dutch planted no colony in the Caribbean to compare with Barbados or Martinique; they failed to supplant the Portuguese in Brazil; and they lost New Netherland for want of Dutchmen to defend it. In 1650 a representative body in New Netherland lamented: "we have neglected to populate the land . . . we have, out of regard for our own profit, wished to scrape all the fat into one or more pots, and thus secure the trade and neglect

[51] Du Tertre, *Histoire générale des Antilles*, I, 110.
[52] Francis Parkman, *Pioneers of France in the New World* (Boston: Little, Brown, 1897), p. xx.
[53] Quoted in Boxer, *Dutch Seaborne Empire*, p. 220.

population."[54] It is not enough to point to the small number of Dutchmen at home or to the preoccupation of many of them with seafaring and manufacture, not the best training for pioneer agriculture. There were plenty of peasants in the landward provinces of Gelderland, Overijssel, and Drente; and if they did not want to go to America themselves the Dutch could have recruited foreigners. They had connections everywhere in north Germany and Scandinavia; that there were people there wanting to settle in the New World is suggested by the story of 140 Finns who, without any encouragement and apparently without the knowledge of either the Swedish or the Dutch government, made their way to Amsterdam in 1664 and camped there hoping for a ship.[55]

The Dutch government cannot be blamed for this failure to find colonists. The West India Company was responsible, particularly in its early years; it did not want to plant colonies of settlement. The charter contained only one reference to colonization, permitted not required. Later, gestures were made toward the transporting of people but they came too late. Just as the French style of colonizing after 1660 owed rather too much to the crown, so the Dutch especially in the early years was formed rather too much by merchants.

England's style in the Atlantic was more versatile than that of any other European country. Englishmen planted Dutch-type trading posts in Hudson Bay and on the West African coast; privateering colonies; colonies based on African slave labor; colonies of refuge for religious exiles; a colony of ex-servicemen; and colonies for no purpose other than to live by agriculture and make the land valuable. The only current type of colony England failed to plant in the seventeenth century was that reared on the backs of Indians such as Spain achieved and such as Raleigh doubtless had in mind in Guiana.

That so much was done in so many directions did not result in the first place from initiatives by the crown. Elizabeth I's interest in the Atlantic was a sensitive plant, opening when Drake came home with treasure, closing when she was afraid of provoking Spain. She distributed charters sensibly and occasionally risked a few pounds in the hope of getting back more; her attitude to planting was not unlike that of her merchants, interested but noncommittal. King James approved of the Virginia project

[54] Jameson, *Narratives of New Netherland*, p. 306.
[55] Ward, *Dutch and Swedes on the Delaware*, pp. 230–231.

and gave it moral support, though he too was frightened of offending Spain and sacrificed Raleigh to prove it. Money problems made him look on America, as on much else, as a cow to be milked. To his death (1625) the colonizing record of the English crown was neither particularly good nor particularly bad; it had done the obvious things, but no more.

With the accession of Charles I policy swung from mild encouragement to active discouragement of certain colonial enterprises and baneful meddling in others. The planting of colonies became, for the only time in English history, more an opposition program than a government policy, with the Massachusetts Bay and Providence Island companies taking the lead. Archbishop Laud's only interest in America was to stop it from becoming a refuge for his victims. Emigration was hindered and in 1634 forbidden except for certified members of the Church of England.[56] The charter of Massachusetts was brought to court and declared forfeit in 1637. Elsewhere, in the West Indies, Newfoundland, and the East India trade, the crown caused confusion by the grant of conflicting charters to favorites or high bidders. One example must suffice: the Leeward and Windward islands. Barbados and other small islands in the eastern Caribbean were tobacco colonies planted by competing groups of London merchants led by Ralph Merrifield, Sir William Courteen, and Marmaduke Rawdon. Naturally the groups tried to strengthen their positions: Courteen found a noble protector in Herbert, Earl of Pembroke, Rawdon the same in James Hay, Earl of Carlisle. A patent war ensued. Carlisle obtained from the king a grant of the "Caribee Islands" on July 2, 1627; Pembroke one of "Trinidado, Tabago, Barbudos and Fonseca" on February 25, 1628. Carlisle got a confirmation of Barbados on April 7, 1629, and his governor succeeded in ousting Pembroke's. The wrong side was allowed to win. No one was in it for love but Courteen had at least supplied his settlers regularly with food. Under Carlisle the island had a starving time.[57] The best that can be said of Charles I's government in the colonial field is that it was not efficient enough to stop the "swarming of the English." The Commonwealth and Protectorate did better and the restored monarchy in some ways better still. James, Duke of York, later James II, in his heavy-handed way was more aware of America and indeed of the Atlantic as a whole than any other European king in the seven-

[56] H. R. Trevor-Roper, *Archbishop Laud* (London: Macmillan, 1940), pp. 258–262.
[57] Harlow, *History of Barbados*, pp. 7–13. Also J. A. Williamson, *The Caribee Islands under the Proprietary Patents* (London: Oxford University Press, 1926).

teenth century. His hand can be seen in the refashioning of New York after the conquest, in the Dominion of New England, in the founding of companies for the fur and slave trades, and in the emergence of central institutions to govern the colonies. Had he had his way, the English colonies might have been brought into almost as close subjection as the French; but the Revolution of 1688 redressed the balance. England's style of colonization settled to one that was not independent of the crown but rested chiefly on other initiatives.

English merchants were readier than French to invest in long-term projects: industrial ventures, schemes for drainage and water supply, trading companies and colonies. Hence the greater importance of the joint-stock company in English history in the seventeenth century than in French particularly for purposes of trade.[58] The Virginia Company from this point of view was something of a fluke: merchants put large sums into colonization with no suspicion that the return to capital would be as slow or as disappointing as it turned out to be. They burned their fingers. After Virginia, Bermuda, and Londonderry, this method of financing was not much used for planting colonies; but it was used and was decisive in the promotion of trading companies. The contrast between Colbert's failure to attract private capital to his grand *compagnies* and the ease with which the East India Company raised funds or the oversubscription in five weeks of the English Royal African Company (1672) is too obvious to need laboring.[59]

In every western European country there were nobles and gentlemen who saw America as an extension of royal patronage for which they might compete. It was a special feature of English colonizing that, as well as favorites hungry for monopolies and patents and out-of-work swordsmen looking for patrons, there were courtiers and countrymen, not bankrupts, who were ready to use their influence, give up their time, and even invest their money in planting and nursing colonies:[60] the Earl of Southampton

[58] Scott, *Joint-Stock Companies*, especially vol. I. Also Eli F. Heckscher, *Mercantilism*, 2 vols. (London: Allen & Unwin, 1935), I, 366 et seq.

[59] Mims, *Colbert's West India Policy*, pp. 80–81. Also K. G. Davies, *The Royal African Company* (London: Longmans, 1957), p. 59.

[60] T. K. Rabb's "Investment in English Overseas Enterprises," *Economic History Review*, 2nd series, 19:70–81 (1966), is perhaps more remarkable for its methods than for its conclusions but furnishes the useful figure that, of 3800 classifiable investors between 1575 and 1630, 23 percent were gentry or nobles. These two classes were naturally more interested in colonizing and land schemes than in purely trading ventures; they formed nearly half of all investors in the Virginia Company.

and Sir Edwin Sandys in Virginia; Sir Ferdinando Gorges in New England; the Calverts in Maryland; Robert Rich, Earl of Warwick, in Bermuda, Providence Island, and other schemes between 1620 and 1640; John Pym in Providence; Anthony Ashley Cooper, Earl of Shaftesbury, William, Earl of Craven, and their associates in Carolina, the Bahamas, the African and Hudson's Bay companies. They all wanted something back but they were willing to work for it, in Parliament, in the King's Council, on boards of directors. Some did well, Calverts, Fairfaxes, Penns, proof that the dreams of Elizabethan gentlemen of valuable estates in the New World could in the long run be realized. Many got nothing. The best work of these promoters was done at home: only a few crossed the Atlantic. But a little lower in the social scale there were country gentlemen, leaders of local communities, who went with the colonists, pioneered like d'Esnambuc though not compelled by poverty to do so, and became leaders of new communities in the New World: John Winthrop in Massachusetts, John Winthrop, Jr., and William Pynchon in Connecticut, Calverts in Maryland, Draxes and Walronds in Barbados, Christopher Jeaffreson in St. Kitts. Here, in the social composition of backers and colonists, we come closer to an English "national" interest than anywhere else.

Finally, people, the "Gardners, Plough-men, Labourers, Smiths, Carpenters, Joyners, Fisher-men, Fowlers, with some few Apothecaries, Surgeons, Cookes, and Bakers" that Francis Bacon thought needful for a plantation.[61] Without followers, no leaders; without people, no colonies. That which above all else distinguished England's empire in America in the seventeenth century was the readiness of the English to go to it, whether because the prospect pleased them or because they were repelled by what they were leaving behind. England overcame first the Dutch, then the French, in the Atlantic by superiority of numbers. How that superiority was achieved is the subject to which we now turn.

[61] Francis Bacon, "Of Plantations" in *Essays*.

CHAPTER 3

PEOPLE

Population

By about 1660, when it was clear that the Europeans had come to stay, the North American colonies of England and the Netherlands contained between 60,000 and 70,000 people, exclusive of Indians who were already manifesting a disposition to retreat from the jurisdiction of the whites. The white population was distributed as follows: New England (Massachusetts, Plymouth, Connecticut, Rhode Island, New Haven) 25,000–30,000; New Netherland, 5000 (not all Dutch); southern colonies (Virginia and Maryland), 36,000–38,000. Well over half, perhaps two-thirds, of these people must have been born in Europe. Forty years later, at the end of the century, the picture was very different. Pioneering, except on the frontier and for those who chose that kind of life, was virtually over; and despite continued immigration probably a majority of the population was American-born. There were then about a quarter million people living in the following sections: New England, 92,000; southern colonies (with the Carolinas added), 104,000; middle colonies (New York, New Jersey, Pennsylvania), 53,000. These figures now include black slaves who constituted something less than 10 percent of the total.[1]

No parallel can be found in the colonial histories of other European

[1] Wesley Frank Craven, *The Colonies in Transition, 1660–1713* (New York: Harper & Row, 1968), pp. 15–16, 288–291.

63

powers to this multiplication of Anglo-Americans. Yet almost everywhere they were thin on the ground by prevailing European standards. About 1700, the British Isles, France, and the Netherlands had a combined population of about 30 million, suggesting an average density of between 75 and 100 to the square mile.[2] It is not possible to make any general statement regarding the density of population in the American colonies: in the tidewater lands of Virginia and Maryland, a relatively thickly populated region, there are thought to have been as many as 6 persons to the square mile at the start of the eighteenth century.[3] Here and perhaps in one or two other places the most crowded zones of North America had overtaken the emptiest zones of Europe: Scandinavia, for example, with an average of only 3.3 to the square mile. But in general the contrast was still between a crowded western Europe, with a population too big to be adequately supported by primitive farming and industrial techniques, and an America it was impossible to imagine full; between a population that could not be much further increased without far-reaching technological improvements, and one that could.

Growth toward this total of a quarter of a million in what were to be the thirteen colonies did not proceed uniformly or at an even rate in the first century of settlement. Populations in different sections grew untidily at different speeds at different times. Massachusetts, for example, was highly successful in attracting immigrants in the first dozen years: by 1642 the population is believed to have been approaching 20,000 as a result of this immigration and of a high birthrate. Then came a pause, so that the 20,000 mark appears not to have been finally passed until about 1660.[4] Several reasons can be suggested for this flattening of the curve of growth: economic recession in the colony, emigration from it to better land or a more congenial religious establishment, changed conditions in England — Parliament's victory over the king — so that fewer people wanted to go, or needed to go, to Massachusetts and some who wanted to return home were able to do so. It is also possible that by 1645 many of the young first settlers had had their children, and these children were not themselves yet old enough to procreate. If, as often was the case, settlers in a

---

[2] G. N. Clark, *The Seventeenth Century* (Oxford: Clarendon Press, 1929), pp. 7–9.

[3] Stella H. Sutherland, *Population Distribution in Colonial America* (New York: Columbia University Press, 1936), p. 193. At the end of the colonial period Rhode Island counted 45 to the square mile, Connecticut 39, Massachusetts 35, New Hampshire 8.7, and Maine 1.5. *Ibid.*, p. 37.

[4] Kenneth A. Lockridge, "The Population of Dedham, Massachusetts, 1636–1736," *Economic History Review*, 2nd series, 19:321 (1966).

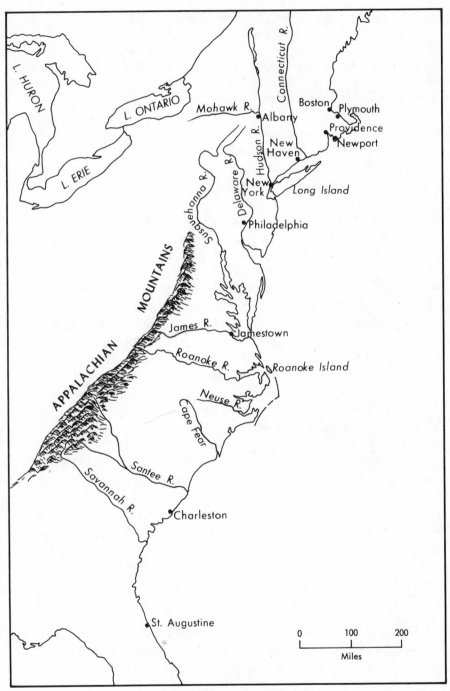

English Colonies in North America

new colony arrived in waves, and if a majority of them were young, some kind of corresponding wave patterns might be expected to occur in the later demographical history of that colony. At all events, growth in the population of Massachusetts was resumed after 1660: by 1700 the colony had passed 50,000 and was entering upon a time of even swifter increase. The growth of Pennsylvania's population, which rose from a few hundreds in 1682 to 18,000 in 1700, matched the speed of takeoff in early Massachusetts. Both were colonies to which immigrants were drawn by religious and political as well as economic considerations, one formula for laying a sound demographic foundation.

Virginia made a bad start, demographically speaking. It had no inflow of refugees keen to fill a Promised Land with witnesses to the Lord's mercy to his chosen people. Beset by Indians, bedeviled by inexperience and by disease, Virginia killed more people than it saved. John Smith, the colony's first chronicler, believed that by 1625, when the population was 1232, 8000 had been buried.[5] After 1625 growth began. In 1642 Virginia was probably still lagging behind Massachusetts, despite a start of more than twenty years, but by 1660 it was ahead. Indeed the combined population of Virginia and Maryland, 38,000, exceeded that of the New England colonies, the period of slowest growth in Massachusetts (1642–60) appearing to have approximately coincided with the period of Virginia's fastest. In the last forty years of the seventeenth century the positions changed again, at least as regards white population. By 1700, despite the foundation of new settlements in the Carolinas, New England probably had a slightly larger number of whites than the southern colonies. Here we are comparing regions with different climatic conditions, different agricultural organizations, and different social structures. Adjacent colonies with similar social arrangements can also be found moving at different speeds. Plymouth's 300 inhabitants in 1630 had increased to 3000 by 1660, a more than respectable rate of growth but not enough to guarantee the colony's independence. Plymouth in those early days did not promote immigration in the way Massachusetts did, and so failed to lay the foundations of a population at the end of the century large enough to resist absorption by her greater neighbor. Another example of adjacent colonies developing at different speeds is supplied by North and South Carolina, the former remaining a backward and thinly populated colony until well into the eighteenth century.

[5] Sutherland, *Population Distribution*, pp. 184–185.

The explanations of these different experiences are complex and local, defying generalization. Clearly rapid growth of a colony's population in the first fifty or hundred years could come about only as the result of a sustained high level of immigration or of conspicuous natural increase or of both; conversely, a slow growth was the result of a low level of immigration or of a surplus of deaths over births. There is no reason to assume that these two determinants always worked at the same time and in the same direction. A high level of immigration could be negatived by natural decrease, a low level — once a reasonable foundation had been laid — made good by natural increase. The problem is to know which determinant was preponderant in what North American colonies, and when; it would be wrong to pretend that wholly convincing answers to these questions have been found.[6]

The present state of the evidence regarding the population of the English colonies in North America about 1700 suggests that New England's already depended a good deal on natural increase, that is, on a surplus of births over deaths producing population growth independent of immigration, either white or black. This pattern seems strongest for Massachusetts and Plymouth, but it is quite likely that seventy years after first settlement demographic differences that initially may have existed between one New England colony and another were tending to disappear. The region as a whole was not the destination of large numbers of immigrants in the second half of the century; on the contrary it supplied settlers to New York and Pennsylvania. Yet its population grew apace. One community which has been carefully investigated is Dedham, Mass., population 410 in 1648, 750 in 1700.[7] Here, after 1650, immigration was of no statistical importance: the increase of population was natural, at the rate of 1 percent per annum 1648–78, 1½ percent 1678–95, and 5 percent 1695–1709. In these last fifteen years the population of Dedham almost doubled, though in the next fifteen years it scarcely increased at all. The explanation of this puzzling demographic phenomenon is by no means obvious, but at least it is clear that for sixty years after the mid-seventeenth century a regular annual natural increase of population was in progress. Dedham's history was not unique and its demographic record

[6] Philip J. Greven, "Historical Demography and Colonial America," *William and Mary Quarterly*, 3rd series, 24:438–454 (1967).
[7] Lockridge, "The Population of Dedham," from which all references to Dedham have been taken.

to 1700 is broadly compatible with that of the colony of which it formed part.

Western Europe in the seventeenth century appears to have known no such surplus of births over deaths, or only a small one, or one which might accrue over a few famine-free, plague-free years, only to be wiped out by demographic catastrophes. In societies without efficient birth control, a major regulator of the birthrate is the age at marriage and particularly the age of brides: the earlier the bridal age the more children are likely to be born to the marriage. In seventeenth-century England the common age at marriage seems to have been 27 for men and 26 for women, and in France 27 for men and 24 for women, with the proviso that visitations of plague or famine could, temporarily or even for decades, raise the age of brides by several years. The evidence at present available suggests that in New England in the second half of the seventeenth century the age of men at marriage was a little lower and the age of women significantly lower than in Europe, as shown in the tabulation. The Plymouth figures, showing a

	Men	Women
Dedham, Mass., 1640–90[8]	25.5	22.5
Andover, Mass., late seventeenth century[9]	27.1	22.8
Plymouth, seventeenth century[10]	27 falling to 24.6	20.6 rising to 22.3

high age for bridegrooms and low age for brides in the early years, may be typical of a pioneer society in which men outnumber women: there were twenty boys on the *Mayflower* but only eleven girls. As settlement was consolidated and children born in the colony came to marriageable age, the age at marriage of the two sexes moved closer to one another. Pioneer Plymouth apart, the bridal ages in these three communities are remarkably similar, arguing for a longer period of childbearing by about four years than in Old England. This would produce at least two more children per marriage, other things being equal. More emphatic figures have emerged from a study of Bristol, R.I., earlier part of Plymouth Colony.[11] Here, before

[8] *Ibid.*

[9] Philip J. Greven, "Family Structure in Seventeenth-Century Andover, Mass.," *William and Mary Quarterly*, 3rd series, 23:234–256 (1966).

[10] John Demos, "Notes on Life in Plymouth Colony," *William and Mary Quarterly*, 3rd series, 22:264–286 (1965).

[11] John Demos, "Families in Colonial Bristol, Rhode Island," *William and Mary Quarterly*, 3rd series, 25:40–57 (1968).

1750, the mean age of men at marriage was 23.9 years and of women 20.5, lower by two years than in the three other communities. One may either regard Bristol's figures as exceptional or suppose that they refer more to the eighteenth than to the seventeenth century.

At Dedham, at Andover, and in Plymouth Colony, men in the seventeenth century continued to marry at or only a little below the European norm, as if in this important social matter old traditions died hard. It is possible that more complex social considerations were at work in some New England communities. On a New England farm the labor force was the family and the work of grown-up sons was needed: parental influence, not negligible in a Puritan society, may have operated against the early marriage of males. Additionally, in a settlement such as Andover, most of the cultivable land was distributed to first settlers, leaving none for children except by inheritance. The alternative to waiting for an inheritance, emigration without capital, was bleak. Hence a high age at marriage for men, imposed by parents rather than chosen by the bridegrooms themselves. Such restraint would not, however, affect the number of children born to the family nearly as much as the age at marriage of women.

This is the theory: that New England women married earlier than European women and bore more children, contributing thereby to a natural increase of population. On this point, however, the number of children born to each marriage, the evidence divides disconcertingly. At Dedham, only 4.8 children were born per family in 1636–68, 4.1 in 1669–1703, 5 in 1704–36, giving an average of 4.6 for the whole century, figures on the low side even by European standards. At Andover and in Plymouth Colony, on the other hand, the legend of large families in early American life is amply confirmed.[12] There were 8.2 recorded births per family of second-generation settlers at Andover, with 7.2 children per family surviving to the age of twenty-one. Ninety couples in Plymouth Colony also produced families of about this size. That two New England communities should have apparently procreated twice as many children per marriage as a third community is a warning against easy generalization. All that can be regarded as proved is that high birthrates existed but not everywhere, that they probably contributed to New England's natural increase of population but were not the only agent in it.

[12] A notable exemplar of the legend is Mary Buell née Loomis, b. Windsor, Conn., 1680; m. 1696; d. Litchfield, Conn., 1768. At the time of her death she had 336 living descendants; 74 more had predeceased her. Her history was considered remarkable enough to be reported to the secretary of state for the American Department. Public Record Office, London, C.O. 5/1285, fos. 116–136d.

It is probable that more children born in New England survived to adulthood than in Europe. Seven out of eight at Andover (omitting those who died before registration) lived to be twenty-one. And at twenty-one the chances of a long life in New England were excellent. In this same community the average age at death of thirty of the first settlers was 71.8 years. Their children did not live quite so long, but the average age at death of 138 second-generation males was 65.2 years, with females a little lower. In Plymouth Colony the expectation of life at twenty-one was 69.2 years for men, 62.4 for women, the lower age for women reflecting the hazards of pioneer obstetrics. Once a woman was safely past childbearing, she could expect to live almost as long as a man. Dedham's death rate looks to have been 24 per 1000, well below anything we should expect to find in Europe. Beyond any reasonable doubt New England about 1700 offered better prospects of longevity than Europe. Until it has been established whether Dedham's low birthrate or Andover's high birthrate is the more typical of New England as a whole, we are on surer ground in seeing lower mortality rates as the chief reason why New England's population was growing and at times growing rapidly while Europe's grew little or not at all in the second half of the seventeenth century.

Diseases, the plague especially, were less virulent in America: it would be surprising indeed to find a demographic catastrophe in New England similar to that which struck the village of Colyton in Old England in 1645–46 when plague carried off 392 persons in twelve months, about one-fifth of the total population.[13] New England's "famines" were less serious than French, once the starving times were over. This relative immunity from severe demographic crises helps to explain not only the lower death rate but also a higher birthrate, should one eventually be found to exist over the region as a whole. In Europe a crisis resulting from plague or famine reduced the number of live births in succeeding years, by lowering the chances of conception, by increasing the proportion of stillbirths, or by forcing up the age of marriage for women. New England in the second half of the seventeenth century certainly knew years in which more died than were born, but these natural decreases were too slight to have serious long-term effects. They were not crises of a European order. With luck they might hold off for a long time — between 1686 and 1712 there was no year in which more deaths than births were re-

[13] E. A. Wrigley, "Family Limitation in Pre-Industrial England," *Economic History Review*, 2nd series, 19:85 (1966).

corded at Dedham — with a consequent leap forward in the size of population.

Whether anything like the New England "demographic way" existed elsewhere in North America in the seventeenth century is an open question. It seems unlikely. The fastest growing section from 1675 to 1700 was that collectively known as the middle colonies. Here, until 1640, the Dutch had made little effort to colonize New Netherland either with their own people or with prospective settlers from other parts of Europe. Insofar as the West India Company was interested in the Hudson River, it aimed to win by means of trading posts as large a share of the fur trade as possible. After 1640 more Dutchmen, with some Swedes and Finns, settled in this region but by then it was too late. At the time of the English conquest in 1664 there were still only about 5000 (higher estimates have been given) where forty years later the combined populations of New York, Pennsylvania, and the Jerseys had risen to 50,000.[14] A large part of this increase resulted from immigration, particularly into Pennsylvania. New York itself continued to grow fairly slowly, probably because of the practice of granting large blocks of land to a handful of people, and perhaps also because during the greater part of the proprietorship of the Duke of York (1664–85) there were no representative institutions. Of the Jerseys, East had reached 10,000 by 1700, West only 3500.[15]

Not all the immigrants into the middle colonies came from the British Isles. Some came from other colonies, others from continental Europe. There were Germans in New York and Pennsylvania before 1700, and French (chiefly Huguenots) in New England, Carolina, and Virginia as well as New York. As yet, however, their numbers were small: 68 percent of Pennsylvania's settlers to 1700 were English, 20 percent Welsh or Irish, and only 5 percent Dutch or German.[16] The flow of immigrants from continental Europe to British North America was a feature of the eighteenth not of the seventeenth century. The few who were there before 1700, and the handful of Dutch and Swedes who had been absorbed into New York and other colonies after 1664, were important not for their numbers but as symbols of a broadly favorable attitude on the part of governments, both British and colonial, and on the part of the

[14] Craven, *Colonies in Transition*, p. 60 and n. 72.

[15] Wesley Frank Craven, *New Jersey and the English Colonization of North America* (Princeton, N.J.: Van Nostrand, 1964), p. 78.

[16] Catherine Owens Peare, *William Penn* (Philadelphia and New York: Lippincott, 1957), p. 272.

settlers themselves toward alien immigrants, at least toward Protestant immigrants of non-British origins. New England, with its emphasis upon religious and moral qualifications for acceptance into the community, might have contributed toward the establishment of this tradition in American life, but did not. It was the middle colonies that received Europe's poor and persecuted after 1700, with the Carolinas and Georgia following their example.

The growth of population in Virginia and Maryland to 1660, and probably beyond, is likely to have been connected more with a high and apparently fairly steady intake of immigrants than with natural increase. The number of white indentured servants reaching Maryland about 1670 has been estimated at 500 a year, and for Virginia in the later seventeenth century 1500 a year. In all, according to one authority, "considerably more than 100,000" whites arrived in Virginia between first settlement and 1700.[17] Many died before they could contribute to future population growth. Much is recorded, even after the first two deadly decades, of the effects of Virginia's diseases, of yellow fever, plague, and scurvy, especially on newcomers. The epidemic of 1623 is supposed to have carried off 500 people. When a Dutch observer landed in Virginia in 1635, he found thirty-six English ships loading tobacco: fifteen of their captains were dead "in consequence of their coming too early in the unhealthy season, and not having been before in the country."[18] Later in the century things improved. Governor Berkeley's statement in 1671 concerning mortality among immigrants has often been cited, less often given in full: "All new plantacons are for an age or two unhealthy till they are thoroughly cleared of wood but unlesse wee had a perticuler register office for the denoting all that dye I cannot give a perticuler answer to this query only this I can say that there is not often unseasoned hands (as wee terme them) that dye Whereas heretofore not one of Five scaped the first yeare."[19] Berkeley's notorious four dead in five, therefore, referred to a state of affairs which he believed had already passed away. The indications are, however, that he spoke too soon. Virginia's population growth from 30,000 in 1660 to about 60,000 in 1700, having regard to the volume of

[17] Maryland: Abbot E. Smith, *Colonists in Bondage* (Chapel Hill: University of North Carolina Press, 1947), p. 299. Virginia: Thomas J. Wertenbaker, *The Planters of Colonial Virginia* (Princeton, N.J.: Princeton University Press, 1922), pp. 35–36.

[18] J. Franklin Jameson, ed., *Narratives of New Netherland, 1609–1664* (New York, 1909), p. 195.

[19] The document is in Public Record Office, London, C.O. 1/26, fo. 198. Sutherland in *Population Distribution in Colonial America*, pp. 184–185, reverses the proportions and makes one-fifth succumb to the fevers of seasoning time.

white immigration (say, 1500 a year) and to the number of slaves already in the colony by the end of the century (about 6000), is unimpressive and no argument for the presence of natural increase. On the other hand, if a considerable proportion of newcomers (*pace* Berkeley) continued to die soon after arrival, and if of those who survived some left to find land or living in another colony and others returned to England, it remains a possibility that there may have been some natural increase of population among Virginia's permanent residents, compensating a little for the failure of indentured servants to make a more positive impression on the colony's demographic history.

By 1700 the population figures of New York as well as of the Carolinas, Virginia, and Maryland were beginning to be affected by a new class of immigrant, slaves. Negligible in numbers in 1660, they may have increased to as many as 16,000 in English America by the end of the century, one-third in Virginia and perhaps one-quarter in Maryland. Thousands more were to follow in the early eighteenth century with the establishment of freer trade for Englishmen, including colonials, on the African coast. In this as in other respects the later demographic characteristics of the United States were beginning to show themselves. Virginia's population, which in the seventeenth century had owed so much to annual infusions of white servants, now began to include a larger and larger proportion of blacks.

Much less work has been done on the demography of the English Caribbean than on that of the mainland colonies. The evidence is scantier, the picture more complicated. It is complicated, first, by the history of Barbados which, in the seventeenth century, was not only unlike any continental American colony but in many respects untypical of the Caribbean itself. First settled in 1625, Barbados was reported to have 1800 inhabitants in 1630. In the next ten years, and perhaps for longer, there was a rush of settlers and servants from England which equaled if it did not surpass the movement toward Massachusetts. That Englishmen in the same decade should have set out for the New World in such numbers with two such different goals is an indication of the complexity of migratory drives. Those who went to Barbados, at least those who knew what they were doing, went to get rich quickly or anyway to make a living; probably most of them expected to come home one day.[20] The island, with an area

[20] Carl Bridenbaugh, *Vexed and Troubled Englishmen, 1590–1642* (New York: Oxford University Press, 1968), chapters 11 and 12, has an excellent discussion of these contemporary but contrasting flows of emigration.

of 166 square miles, was cleared and brought under cultivation before the arrival of large numbers of slaves, the only Caribbean colony to have been brought anywhere near its full productive capacity by the labor of whites. The result was a white population at mid-century at least equal to that of any mainland English colony. Richard Ligon, the island's first historian, guessed in 1657 that there were 50,000 whites in Barbados.[21] This is scarcely credible, but even a population of half that size would put the colony on terms with Virginia or Massachusetts. Underneath this white population there were then crammed in the 1650s and 1660s more slaves than were to be found in any other English colony at any time before 1700. In 1673 Barbados counted 33,184 blacks, and in 1680, 38,782; both figures are more likely to be understatements than overstatements.[22]

Black slave labor thus ousted white indentured labor, as in time it did everywhere in the Caribbean, in Virginia, and in Maryland. The unique characteristic of Barbados was to have acquired a full complement of whites before the blacks took over. Some whites stayed on, as smallholders or wage earners, but for many there was nothing to do but reemigrate. From the 1640s Barbados was furnishing people to other colonies as well as large numbers of volunteers for the conquest of Jamaica (1655) and for the French wars in the Leeward Islands (1664–67). Probably this white population reached its peak between 1650 and 1660, thirty years or so after first settlement. By 1680, when there were 23,624 whites, a decline had set in, which continued until 1712 by which time Barbados had lost nearly half of its 1680 white population.

Barbados is *not* the Caribbean archetype in the seventeenth century. No other island, French or English, developed at anything like the same pace. The four principal English Leeward colonies were St. Kitts (first settled in 1624), Nevis (1628), Antigua (1632), and Montserrat (1650). Their combined area was about 225 square miles. According to a census of 1678 these islands, with minor offshore dependencies, had a white population of 11,132 with 8560 slaves. Fewer than two-thirds of the whites were English, more than a quarter Irish, with a sprinkling of Scots, Dutch, and French. These islands, despite the displacement caused by destructive Anglo-French wars especially in St. Kitts, suffered no collec-

[21] Richard Ligon, *True and Exact History of the Island of Barbadoes* (2nd ed.; London, 1673).
[22] Vincent T. Harlow, *History of Barbados, 1625–1685* (Oxford: Clarendon Press, 1926), Appendix B; Richard S. Dunn, "The Barbados Census of 1680: Profile of the Richest Colony in English America," in *William and Mary Quarterly*, 3rd series, 26:3–30 (1969).

tive decrease of white population in the later seventeenth and early eighteenth centuries such as occurred in Barbados. In 1724 the Leewards counted 12,420 whites, suggesting a virtually stationary population over nearly fifty years; the blacks in the meantime had increased fivefold and numbered 44,030.[23]

Jamaica's population in the seventeenth century, white and black, is still an unexplored subject. Estimates published in 1774 hazard a total of 8564 whites and 9504 blacks in 1673. Over the next forty years and perhaps over the next eighty years, if these guesses are anything like accurate, the white population remained about the same while the blacks increased rapidly to an estimated 45,000 in 1703 and 75,000 in 1730.[24] None of these figures will bear looking at too closely, but we may reasonably conclude that the aggregate population of the English West Indies about 1680 was on the order of 40,000–45,000 whites and 60,000 blacks, one-half of these whites and two-thirds of these blacks residing in one colony, Barbados. Comparing the density of the Barbadian population (360 to the square mile in 1680) with the density already given for tidewater Virginia and Maryland twenty years later (6 to the square mile) or that for Jamaica about 1680 (perhaps 4 or 5) serves to emphasize the uniqueness of Barbados. Was there any predominantly agricultural community in Europe, let alone in America, with so many people living and working in so confined a space? Jamaica by contrast was a frontier colony and remained one well into the eighteenth century. Apart from great tracts of mountain land unfit for plantation farming, Jamaica as late as 1752 had 600,000 acres of plantable land not yet granted as well as 1 million acres patented but not brought under cultivation.[25]

In the light of what has already been said, it is almost superfluous to raise the question how the English Caribbean colonies were peopled in the seventeenth century. They owed their growth to immigration, white and black, not to natural increase. On the contrary, there is some reason to think that the white population of Barbados suffered a natural decrease, perhaps a big one, quite apart from the loss of people by reemigration. Richard S. Dunn's study of a Barbados census of 1680 illustrates the

[23] Leewards in 1678: C. S. S. Higham, *The Development of the Leeward Islands under the Restoration, 1660–1688* (Cambridge: At the University Press, 1921), p. 148. In 1724: Frank Wesley Pitman, *The Development of the British West Indies, 1700–1763* (New Haven, Conn.: Yale University Press, 1917), p. 379.

[24] Pitman, *British West Indies*, pp. 373–374.

[25] *Ibid.*, p. 125.

divide which separated the social and demographical history of this colony from New England's.[26] In Bridgetown, Barbados, there were 351 householders in 1680: 89 were single men, 98 were married men without children, a state of affairs inconceivable in a New England town. The mean number of children present in these Bridgetown households was just under one per family. This must be regarded as something of a caricature of life in a tropical colony; Bridgetown was not typical of Barbados, nor Barbados of the West Indies. Some children belonging to these families may have been out of town, others undergoing education in England. Nevertheless, a natural decrease of the white Barbadian population is more plausible than the reverse. In eighteen months (March 1678–September 1679) white burials exceeded white baptisms by 506; in the year 1683 the excess was 655. These are the only figures available for the seventeenth century, and it is possible to argue that they are unrepresentative. Certainly things were better in the eighteenth century. Between 1710 and 1760 comparable figures of white baptisms and burials have survived for twenty-two years: eight show a surplus of burials over baptisms, fourteen show the reverse. Over all twenty-two years there is a small balance in favor of baptisms.[27] By then, however, fewer "unseasoned" whites were arriving in the colony from England to contribute to these annual totals of burials. The balance of probabilities remains that the white population of Barbados throughout the seventeenth century suffered a natural decrease.

Slave demography in the seventeenth century is another unexplored subject. Provisionally, there seems no compelling reason to reject the belief in a natural decrease. Whether Edward Lyttelton's claim, made in 1689, that the owner of a hundred slaves needed to buy six a year merely in order to keep up numbers is anything like an accurate measure of this decrease cannot at present be confirmed. The experience of Barbados between 1680 and 1712, when more than 70,000 slaves were delivered (some were reexported but Barbados was not such an important slave mart as Jamaica) without significantly increasing the black population, argues that Lyttelton may have been exaggerating, but not much.[28]

[26] "Barbados Census of 1680."
[27] Pitman, British West Indies, p. 385.
[28] [Edward Lyttelton], Groans of the Plantations (London, 1689), p. 18. G. Debien, Plantations et esclaves à Saint-Domingue (Dakar: Université de Dakar, 1962), pp. 50–51, discusses a plantation of about 150 slaves where at least 129 new slaves were bought between 1765 and 1778 in order to keep up numbers.

The conclusion must be that, counting whites and blacks but not Indians, the English colonies in North America and the Caribbean taken together were consumers of people in the seventeenth century. New England's naturally increasing white population was probably more than balanced by a natural decrease among the blacks of Virginia, Maryland, and the West Indies. Add to this the likelihood that in some Caribbean islands and in the mainland colonies south of the Chesapeake there were in the whole course of the seventeenth century more deaths than births among the whites, and the melancholy picture is complete. For this picture to be significantly altered, the demographic history of the southern colonies and the West Indies will have to turn out very different from what at present seems likely.

The experience of the French was different. In Canada they faced physical conditions comparable to those confronting the English in New England (if more severe); in the Caribbean conditions were much the same in the colonies of both countries. Yet by 1700 the outcome was very different in North America, and noticeably different even in the West Indies. No major English colony started as slowly as New France. For thirty or forty years after the foundation of Quebec, its population was negligible. In 1641 it was stated to be 240 and in 1663 about 2500, of whom 800 lived in the city of Quebec. Under Colbert's eye a serious attempt was made not only to enlarge this population but also to count it. Frequent censuses were taken, and there is evidence that some care was used to make them accurate.[29] Looking first at totals we find the situation as shown in the accompanying tabulation. These returns argue that the total

New France		*Acadia*	
1667............ 3,918		1671 441	
1679............ 9,400		1703 1,244	
1685............10,725 (and 1,538 Indians)			
1688............10,303 (and 1,259 Indians)		*Terre-Neuve*	
1695............12,786 (and 853 Indians)		1691 155	
1706............16,417		1705 520	

number of Frenchmen in North America at the beginning of the eighteenth century was well below 20,000, that is to say was no more than Pennsylvania's population two decades after first settlement.

[29] *Censuses of Canada, 1665–1871: Statistics of Canada*, vol. IV (Ottawa, 1876). For a discussion of methods of census taking, see A. J. Pelletier, "Canadian Censuses of the Seventeenth Century," in *Papers and Proceedings of the Annual Meeting of the Canadian Political Science Association*, vol. II (Ottawa: Canadian Political Science Association, 1930), pp. 35–47.

The main point of contrast with New England is of course in immigration. Only in the late 1660s and early 1670s did New France receive relatively large numbers of recruits from the mother country. For the whole period of 150 years of French rule in Canada, the total of immigrants has been put at no more than 10,000, roughly what Virginia expected to receive in half a dozen good years.[30] After Colbert, New France was forced to rely for population growth mainly on her own natural increase, and this in the later seventeenth century was checked by the shortage of marriageable women. In 1681, for example, there were 5375 males of all ages and 4302 females in New France. This disparity, serious enough, was worse than it looks because naturally concentrated in the adult population. There were then 1339 unmarried men of sixteen years of age or over to 406 unmarried women; in the age group twenty-one to forty years, the age group of most marriages, there were 715 bachelors to 99 spinsters. Jesuits and officials in New and Old France might attribute the wanderlust of the *coureurs de bois* and their sexual adventures with Indian women to original sin, social indiscipline, covetousness, or plain perversity; but these figures prove that there was nothing to keep many of them at home. Such a disparity between the sexes can only echo a predominantly male immigration in preceding years. The authorities in New France and at home were aware of the need for brides, organizing cargoes of women for Quebec and supplying them with dowries. Needless to say, they quickly found husbands.[31] Even so, too few arrived and the growth of New France was correspondingly stunted. If between 1670 and 1760 the Canadian population doubled every thirty years, the brides sent by Colbert should have averaged at least sixteen living descendants apiece by the time of the Seven Years War. Another thousand brides in the 1660s might even have kept Canada French. Toward 1700, with the colony depending for population less on immigration and more on the approach to marriageable age of Canadian-born children, the disparity between the sexes was reduced; but as late as 1706 there were still only 1227 unmarried females of fifteen years or more to 1828 unmarried males.

This scarcity of women was probably responsible for forcing down the age at marriage of women, at least in the early years. An investigation of

[30] Jacques Henrepin, "From Acceptance of Nature to Control: The Demography of French Canadians since the Seventeenth Century," *Canadian Journal of Economic and Political Science*, 23:11 (1957).

[31] G. Lanctôt, *Filles de joie ou filles du roi* (Montreal: Chantecler, 1952), pp. 112–113, gives annual totals of *filles du roi* for 1663–73: in all, 961 reached New France in these years.

eighty-five marriages at Montreal between 1642 and 1663 shows the average age of brides to have been 20.9 years, younger by about three years than in France. Correspondingly, the age of bridegrooms was high, 29.2 years.[32] Mid-seventeenth-century Montreal probably gives an exaggerated picture of pioneer life: six of these brides were only twelve years old. Later, in more settled conditions, the age of brides and bridegrooms moved closer together: 22.4 years for spinsters, 26.9 for bachelors in the first thirty years of the eighteenth century, not so different from European averages.[33] If these figures are approximately correct, they afford an interesting instance (comparable to Plymouth's) of the reassertion of something approaching a European social habit after its temporary abandonment in the early days of the colony, and this despite inducements to early marriage offered by the government of New France.

A woman who married at fifteen and survived to the end of childbearing might expect to have twelve or thirteen children; marriage at twenty-two would reduce this total by at least three. The evidence suggests that in the early eighteenth century Canadian mothers bore eight or nine children, which would cause the population to double every generation, allowing for infant mortality.[34] Certainly there were plenty of children in New France's population as there must have been in New England's. In 1667, 41 percent of Canadians were fifteen years old or younger, 34 percent ten years old or younger. The census for 1698, which includes some "Sauvages Établis près des Français" and is not therefore strictly comparable to that of 1667, records 42 percent of the population as under fifteen years. At the same time the expectation of life was probably better than in metropolitan France; in Canada as in New England departure from Europe's demographic norms was more conspicuous on the side of mortality than it was in either age or fertility of marriages. Canada's death rate (1700–30) has been computed at 26 per 1000, compared to Dedham's 24 (1636–1736) and to much higher figures for Europe. The early Canadian censuses record the number of males (not females) in the population of fifty years of age or over: they show a small but steady rise census by census from 4.2 percent of the total in 1667 to 6.4 percent in 1698. Here, as in New England, a lower mortality rate than western Europe's is attributable to the relative mildness of *crises de subsistance* caused by

[32] Marcel Trudel, "Les débuts d'une société: Montréal 1642–1663," *Revue d'histoire de l'Amérique française*, 23:186–206 (1969).
[33] Henrepin, "Demography of French Canadians," p. 12.
[34] *Ibid.*, pp. 12–13.

famine or plague. These checks to population were not entirely absent; one notices a fall in New France's population between 1685 and 1688. But as killers neither the Canadian winter nor the Iroquois had the virulent effects of a famine in the Beauvaisis.[35] All in all, Canada's demographic prospects about 1700 were bright, but the leeway between New France and New England could never be made up. Demographically, the domination of North America by English-speaking people had already been decided by the end of the seventeenth century.

In the Caribbean the advantage of numbers gained by the English in North America (a quarter million to 20,000 in 1700) was less overwhelming but still marked. About 1680 there were roughly twice as many whites in the English islands, owning about three times as many slaves, as in the French. The French inferiority sprang in the first place from the familiar cause: the flow of *engagés* from France to the Caribbean between 1630 and 1660 came nowhere near matching the flow of indentured servants from England. France had no Barbados. Secondly, from 1660 to 1700, despite (or perhaps because of) repeated efforts on the part of the French government, no satisfactory solution was found to the problem of furnishing France's Caribbean plantations with enough slaves. By the end of the seventeenth century French numerical inferiority was serious. It was not, however, as serious in the Caribbean as in North America, and it was redeemable. In the eighteenth century France solved the problem of a sufficient supply of slaves and, thanks above all to the growth of St.-Domingue, caught up to Britain.

A census of 1683 of all the French Caribbean islands except St.-Domingue reveals a white population of 12,737, a black population of 19,346, and a handful of mulattoes and Indians (350).[36] At this date St.-Domingue's development had scarcely begun: an estimate of 1681 gives 4546 whites and 2102 slaves.[37] Putting these figures together, we can infer a total population for the French West Indies in the early 1680s of approximately 17,000 whites and 21,000 slaves. It is necessary to insist on these figures, such as they are, as evidence that in the Lesser Antilles

[35] The fall in population of New France in the 1680s is probably to be associated with epidemic sickness in 1685. In 1701 smallpox is said to have caused 1000 deaths. See W. J. Eccles, *Canada under Louis XIV, 1663–1701* (Toronto: McClelland and Stewart, 1964), p. 251.

[36] Printed in Abdoulaye Ly, *La compagnie du Sénégal* ([Paris]: Présence Africaine, 1958), p. 51.

[37] Stewart L. Mims, *Colbert's West India Policy* (New Haven, Conn.: Yale University Press, 1912), p. 336.

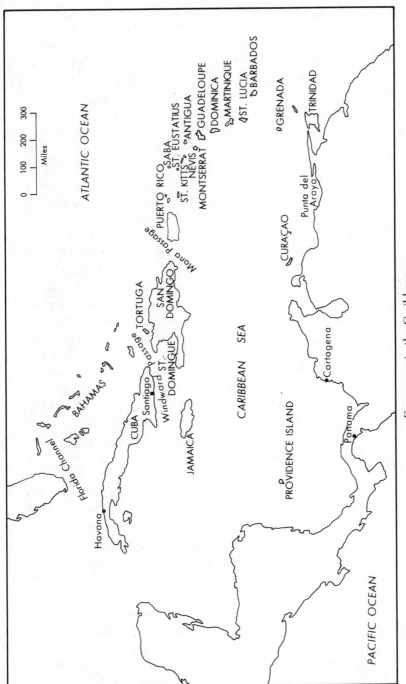

Europeans in the Caribbean

the so-called sugar revolution was not an overnight event, with dramatically shrinking white population and the appearance in quick time of vast numbers of slaves. The white population of the English Leewards, we have already seen, remained stationary between 1678 and 1724 despite the growth of sugar cultivation. St. Christophe (the French part of St. Kitts), Martinique, and Guadeloupe all began to grow sugar in or soon after the 1640s; yet in none of those islands, forty years later, were there as many as two blacks for each white. St. Christophe, with 4301 slaves in 1683, was probably the most intensively cultivated. Martinique, a big island for the Lesser Antilles, fifty miles long and thirteen broad, had 9364 slaves in 1683 — that is, nearly half of all French-owned slaves in the Caribbean — but was still far from being fully settled. As for Guadeloupe, in 1683 and for long afterwards, it was a frontier colony with a white population increasing almost as quickly as that of a New England community, though very likely for different reasons. Here in 1683 there were 2998 whites and 4109 blacks. Settlement was concentrated mainly in the western portion, Basse-Terre, though the census of that year takes in Grande-Terre and the offshore Saintes, a total area of more than 600 square miles. In the whole of Guadeloupe there were fewer than 7 slaves to the square mile compared to 241 to the square mile in Barbados in 1680. Sixteen years later, by the time of the census of 1699, whites in Guadeloupe had increased by 30 percent to 3921 and blacks by 50 percent to 6185. More rapid growth now set in. By 1730 Guadeloupe had 7374 whites, an increase of 86 percent in thirty-one years, while the black population had approximately quadrupled.[38]

The demographic history of Guadeloupe in the late seventeenth and early eighteenth centuries thus lends no support to the theory of the sudden and catastrophic effects of the introduction of sugar on the white population of a Caribbean colony. On the contrary, the number of whites increased there by 140 percent in less than fifty years, from 1683 to 1730. It is at present impossible to say what part was played by immigration in this growth. Debien's study of the departure of engagés from La Rochelle reveals a marked falling-off of interest in Guadeloupe after 1685; most engagés were heading for St.-Domingue.[39] On the other hand, no systematic record was kept of the migration from France of free settlers as

[38] The 1683 census is in Ly, Compagnie du Sénégal; 1699 and 1730 censuses are in Maurice Satineau, Histoire de la Guadeloupe, 1635–1789 (Paris: Peyot, 1928), pp. 380–383.

[39] G. Debien, "Les engagés pour les Antilles (1634–1715)," Revue d'histoire des colonies, 38:7–257 (1951).

opposed to *engagés*; and there is also the possibility of immigrants to Guadeloupe arriving from other French colonies, particularly St. Christophe from which the French were finally evicted in the War of Spanish Succession. With so much uncertainty about, the possibility of some natural increase in Guadeloupe's white population cannot be discounted. True, there are complaints of a "famine of white women," but in the censuses under consideration it was slightly less acute than in the early Canadian population: the ratio between the sexes of all ages in Guadeloupe was about 60 to 40 in 1683, 54 to 46 in 1699 and about the same in 1730. As printed, only the census of 1699 allows the computation of the proportion of children to the whole white population: 37 percent of Guadeloupe's whites were then under twelve years of age, a figure not strikingly different from the figures already given for New France.

Martinique's white population also continued to rise well into the eighteenth century.[40] Between 4000 and 5000 in the 1670s and early 1680s, it passed 6000 in the 1690s and reached 8000 in the decade 1710–20. Between 1720 and 1740 it nearly doubled, reaching a peak in 1742 when it was at least five times greater than it had been at the time sugar was first introduced. As in the case of Guadeloupe there is uncertainty about the cause of this growth, whether immigration or natural increase. We know that in 1683 there was a serious disproportion between the sexes — 1806 males to 941 females — but this was partly rectified by the arrival of at least seven cargoes of brides from France in the next three or four years. Here, no more than in Guadeloupe, can the possibility of natural increase in the white population be ruled out. Martinique's black population, like Guadeloupe's, increased fairly slowly until about 1710. Then, with a freer French slave trade, it doubled in ten years and nearly doubled again between 1720 and 1742, reaching 68,469 in 1742. For both these colonies, the years between the Treaty of Utrecht (1713) and the beginning of the War of Jenkins' Ear (1739) were times of tremendous growth, a growth shared in by the white population; one can see why the British government in the 1730s was alarmed about French competition in the Caribbean.

The history of St.-Domingue belongs to the eighteenth century, when it eclipsed all other Caribbean colonies. By 1753 it had 12,799 whites, 4732 *gens de couleur*, and 164,859 slaves, in other words thirteen slaves to

[40] Louis-Philippe May, *Histoire économique de la Martinique* (Paris: Rivière, 1930), p. 322.

every white inhabitant. There were two white males to each white female, but even here it would be wrong to think of a diminishing white population. Between 1753 and 1775 both whites and blacks increased by about 60 percent. Curiously, the *gens de couleur* who might be expected to have the fastest growth rate had the slowest, only 25 percent in twenty-two years, an apt reminder of the complex unpredictabilities of Caribbean demographic history.[41]

One region with a critical contribution to make to the North Atlantic trade and empires of England, France, and the United Provinces has not yet been mentioned in the demographic context: West Africa, the deadliest place for a European to be in the seventeenth century. All three countries had trading posts there, run by companies and staffed in quasi-military fashion by men who signed on for a definite tour of duty, intending if they survived to return home. Very few European women accompanied their husbands to these posts, and those who did mostly came straight home or died soon after arrival. These establishments varied in size a good deal from time to time, depending on the incidence of mortality and the supply of new recruits, but they were never large. Probably at no time in the period under consideration were there more than a few hundred English, French, and Dutch employees on the coast. In addition there were permanent residents, some of them time-expired company servants, some not, who made a living by trading as middlemen between Europeans and Africans. Most of these "settlers" were Portuguese; in the commerce of Senegal, Gambia, and Sierra Leone, they and their descendants of mixed race played an important part. The number of English, Dutch, and French following this example is not known but appears to have been very small indeed.

About the "settlers" there is no information; but the records of the companies make it possible to get a glimpse of the fate of men coming to West Africa from Europe. Their life expectancy on landing was poor, worse than that facing Europeans anywhere else in the Atlantic and almost certainly worse than that of a slave arriving in a Caribbean colony. Consider three shiploads of passengers sent by the Royal African Company to its headquarters, Cape Coast Castle, in 1695–96. In all, eighty-four persons were enrolled: twelve officers, nineteen tradesmen, five sailors, forty-seven soldiers, and one woman. Five deserted before sail-

[41] P. de Vaissière, *Saint-Domingue* (Paris: Perrin, 1909), p. 116.

ing; six died on the voyage; seventy-three landed. Of those who landed, twenty-four were dead by the end of the first six months, ten more by the end of the first year, five more (for certain) by the end of the second year. Because of defects in the records the fate of the remainder has not been precisely ascertained: nine lived at least six years (one of them for seventeen), but only three are known to have been discharged from the company's service.[42] Comparable evidence of shiploads of passengers arriving at other English stations suggests that the Gold Coast was not the sickliest but the healthiest region and that these consignments of 1695–96 were among the luckier ones. Whydah was certainly a deadlier place; here, of fifty-one passengers landing on May 27, 1721, exactly two-thirds, thirty-four, were dead by the end of the second month. The Gambia, in the wet season, was almost as bad. These figures are of course quite without significance in an overall statistical picture of the population of the North Atlantic; their importance is simply as a token of the incidence of mortality which Europeans were prepared to accept or rather to inflict upon each other in order to further the slave trade.

The Logistics of Settlement

From the previous section it appears that by the end of the seventeenth century the king of England had perhaps 350,000 to 400,000 subjects, including slaves, in the New World; and that the king of France had about 70,000, also including slaves. What proportion had been born in the New World is anyone's guess. All we can be certain of is that this proportion would not be uniform from colony to colony or from region to region; it would be high in New France and New England, lower in the southern colonies, low too in the middle colonies because of their recent establishment, and probably lowest of all in the Caribbean. It is also anyone's guess how many Europeans and Africans had been transported across the Atlantic in the first hundred years of colonization in order to achieve this Anglo-French population of between 400,000 and 500,000. How many, white and black, died without issue, contributing nothing to the total?

[42] These and the figures in the following paragraph are taken from the service records of the Royal African Company, Public Record Office, London, T.70/1441–1448. These records are not perfect but they strongly suggest that out of every ten Englishmen going to West Africa in the late seventeenth and early eighteenth centuries, six died in the first year, two more died later, and one was discharged home; the fate of the tenth must be left in doubt because of imperfections in the evidence. See below, pp. 250–252.

How many founded families and multiplied more prolifically than those they left behind in Europe? We do not know. But, whether the number crossing the Atlantic in the seventeenth century was a quarter million (it cannot have been less) or a half million (it may have been more), it represents a problem in maritime logistics more formidable than any faced by Europe before the Discoveries.

To begin with, the peopling of the New World was a confused affair. Only after experiment and some failures were winning formulas evolved. In part this confusion sprang from inexperience, in part from the mixed purposes with which different interests approached and evaluated the new lands. Putting aside those who merely sought refuge from Europe and clergy wanting mission stations as a springboard for converting the heathen, two principal and to some extent conflicting purposes have been discerned among the supporters of early overseas ventures. There were, first, those who hoped to exploit the new lands in a wholly or mainly commercial way, who were prepared to invest money in order to obtain supplies of fish, fur, pepper, or dyewood but who were apt to cut their losses if such supplies were not soon forthcoming. And, secondly, there were those who looked to the colonies for land on which well-peopled estates could be erected as nearly as possible like manorial or seignorial properties at home. The crown, in France and to a lesser extent in England, more often exerted itself on behalf of settlers than merchants but not always consistently and not always intelligently.

In retrospect we can see that certain styles of European establishment suited certain geographic and physical environments in the New World and not others; that the North American continent could be, and if it was to be fully exploited had to be, lived in by Europeans; that India and Indonesia could be exploited in a commercial way by tiny enclaves of Europeans defended by strong naval forces; and that Africa, though unlike either, more resembled East than West. We know that the land and climate of New England and New France were hospitable to Europeans and their families, and that West Africa was deadly. We know that Europeans were physically capable of laboring in tropical and subtropical fields, as in Virginia or the Caribbean, but did so reluctantly, needing strict discipline.

None of these things was understood at the beginning of the seventeenth century, and not all of them were fully appreciated at the end. Aberrations, or what appear to us to be aberrations, could still be contemplated. Thus, one might suppose that well before the end of the seventeenth century it would have become obvious that the only way to exploit West Africa was by visiting ships supported by a regime of trading posts. The climate, or what Europeans continued for centuries to call the "climate," was too hostile for a regime of settlement. Yet we find an agent of the French Compagnie du Sénégal, Chambonneau, arguing vigorously in 1693 for a colony of settlement in the valley of the Senegal River to grow tobacco, cotton, indigo, and sugar.[43] Its Frenchness was to be preserved by a strict ban on marriage with Africans and the furnishing of enough Frenchwomen to give every man a wife. Fortunately the colony was never planted; one can be quite sure that it would not have survived six months.

A regime of trading posts, as opposed to a regime of colonization, was cheaper in the short run: throughout the seventeenth century there were Anglo-French efforts to establish such regimes on the other side of the Atlantic, not wholly without success. Remarkably successful, for example, was the Hudson's Bay Company chartered in 1670. In the far north, just as in West Africa but in much healthier conditions, handfuls of men lived in stockaded "forts," buying furs gathered by Indians, working out their tours of duty, and returning to their homes in England, Scotland, or the Orkneys. It is not perfectly clear why no colony of settlement was formed on the shores of Hudson Bay; women from the British Isles could have lived there as well as men, and some did. The charter of 1670, evoking earlier charters granted to the Virginia and Massachusetts Bay companies and a contemporary charter to the proprietors of Carolina, "must, from an analysis of its terms, be considered as the charter of a colony, Rupert's Land, as much as the charter of a trading company."[44] Presumably the company feared that permanent residents, free of its control, would infringe the fur-trade monopoly, as indeed the Dutch West India Company's monopoly was impaired in New Netherland.

In some instances, colonization was accepted reluctantly and only after the insufficiency of a regime of trading posts had been conclusively proved. For many years the French settlements at Quebec and in Acadia were *comptoirs* not *colonies*. In 1627, for example, there were twenty Frenchmen in Acadia. At Quebec that same winter there were about

---

[43] The argument is summarized by Ly, *Compagnie du Sénégal*, pp. 257–263.

[44] E. E. Rich, *History of the Hudson's Bay Company*, vol. I (London: Hudson's Bay Record Society, 1958), pp. 54–55.

seventy persons including only three families with children,[45] a poor result for twenty years of struggle by Champlain and a pitiful challenge to the wilderness, if one were to see Quebec as a colony of settlement, but a reasonably thriving trading post if one sees it as a stage for the collection and dispatch to France of furs collected by Indians. Quebec's weakness, the most serious flaw in any regime of trading posts, was its defenseless condition, exposed by David Kirke in 1629; though the French got Quebec back by treaty, it became clear that a *comptoir* in the St. Lawrence had to be either guarded by costly fortifications and troops from Europe or turned into a colony of settlement capable of defending itself. Slowly in the next thirty years *comptoir* became *colonie*, agriculture providing the foundation for settled habitation which the fur trade could never supply.

The leading exponents of the regime of trading posts, in the East, in Africa, and in America, were the Dutch; such a regime consorted best with their commercial purposes. The thrust toward colonies of settlement, which in England came from nobles and gentlemen and in France from kings and ministers, was weaker if not altogether absent in the Netherlands, especially in the dominant provinces of Holland and Zeeland. Willem Usselinx, propagandist from 1607 for a Dutch West India Company, argued strongly for colonies of settlement, even if it meant recruiting colonists from outside the United Provinces; but he argued to little effect.[46] When the West India Company at length materialized in 1621, its charter permitted but did not require the founding of colonies. From the start the company was too busy with privateering to bother with the less rewarding burden of transporting settlers to America. Nor was this, in the short run, an error of judgment. For a time the war against Spain and Portugal went well and the West India Company paid dividends. Small Caribbean islands — St. Eustatius, taken from the French and English in 1632, and Curaçao, taken from the Spaniards in 1634 — served as depots for trade with settlers of other countries and were by no means ruined when France and England later initiated exclusive commercial policies. In Guiana a regime of trading posts was transformed in the course of the eighteenth century into a Dutch colony of settlement.

The West India Company's two major defeats in the New World were

[45] Marcel Trudel, *Histoire de la Nouvelle-France*, vol. II: *Le comptoir, 1604–1627* (Montreal: Éditions Fides, 1966), pp. 486, 489.

[46] J. Franklin Jameson, *Willem Usselinx*, Papers of the American Historical Association, vol. III, no. 2 (New York: A.H.A., 1887), pp. 32 et seq.

Brazil and New Netherland. With the first we are not concerned; the second is an instance of a regime of trading posts failing to complete in time its transformation into a colony of settlement, which here as on the St. Lawrence was necessary for the purpose of defense. The Dutch came to the Hudson for the fur trade. The Company of New Netherland (1614–18) was granted a monopoly for only four voyages and so had no incentive to promote settlement. So far as is known, it built no establishment on Manhattan Island; its American headquarters, Fort Orange at Albany, was a fur-trading post in all essentials resembling a Dutch slaving post on the coast of West Africa. This was the situation when the West India Company took over in 1621, and its main concern was to keep the fur trade in its own hands. Toward colonization it was neither consistently encouraging nor actively hostile. Plans were produced for patroonships in 1628, and after 1640 more was done to get Dutchmen to New Netherland. The West India Company's failure, however, was less in peopling America with Dutchmen — probably no one could have done that — and more in neglecting Usselinx's advice to transport other north Europeans under the Dutch flag. No one was more aware of the vulnerable position of New Netherland, sited between two regions of major English settlement, than Pieter Stuyvesant, the last Dutch governor. If, as appeared to be the case, neither the company nor the city of Amsterdam could entice Dutch settlers to America, then Stuyvesant thought "homeless Polish, Lithuanian, Prussian, Jutlandish or Flemish families . . . are soon and easily to be found during this Eastern and Northern War."[47] Stuyvesant might have lengthened his list to include Swedes and Finns, some of whom were already living under Dutch rule on the Delaware, but he might equally well have kept quiet for all the effect achieved. Ironically, at the time of the English conquest in 1664, there were more Englishmen than Scandinavians or Germans living in New Netherland, an apt comment on the Dutch failure to found a true colony of settlement in a part of America to which the regime of trading posts had no lasting relevance.

From the beginning of the seventeenth century, if not earlier, there were more Englishmen than Frenchmen or Dutchmen determined to plant people instead of instituting a regime of trading posts. Plainly a colonizing policy was going to cost more, though how much more was not apparent for some years. Free settlers might be in a position to transport

---

[47] Quoted in Henry H. Kessler and Eugene Rachlis, *Peter Stuyvesant and His New York* (New York: Random House, 1959), p. 198.

themselves and families to a new colony, bringing provisions, tools, seeds and money; their chief needs were good land titles and good laws, protection from Indians and Spaniards, and the possibility of regular trade with the mother country. But emigrants from Europe with this degree of substance were never plentiful; if they were doing well enough at home to be able to pay the costs of emigration, there was no compelling reason, persecution apart, why they should emigrate at all. Moreover, if there were to be landlords and substantial farmers in America there had also to be tenants and laborers who could be expected neither to pay their fares across the Atlantic nor to subsist themselves when they arrived. To get large numbers to the colonies, to make the plantations defensible, and to raise land values, some kind of scheme for assisted passages was the first necessity. Where was this assistance to come from? Three ways of financing the transport of emigrants from Europe to America were practiced in the seventeenth century. The cost might be met in whole or in part by a European government. Emigration might be organized and financed by European companies. Or it might be turned into a business and run by private merchants like any other business or like the slave trade, according to laws of supply and demand.

We can quickly dispose of government-sponsored emigration in the first half of the seventeenth century. There was hardly any: kings were pleased enough to confer privileges on corporations that said they intended to transport colonists to America, and even to call such corporations into being specifically for that purpose, but there was not much direct royal subvention. After about 1650, when the use of permanent colonies was plainer to see, both French and English rulers began to promote settlement more actively. They did so in several ways. There are, first, two examples of the peopling of colonies in the Roman style by discharged soldiers. When the English regiments sent to conquer Jamaica in 1655 had done their work, officers and men were encouraged by Cromwell to stay there, turn themselves into farmers, and become the first settlers of the island. In like manner, 400 men of the Carignan-Salières regiment, sent to New France to fight the Iroquois, were demobilized there in 1668, given grants of land, provisions and gratuities, and invited to become *habitants*. Neither of these experiments was particularly successful.

Royal support in the second half of the seventeenth century also took the form of a cash payment to meet the cost of the emigrant's passage to the colony. Under Colbert's scheme to colonize Canada the crown paid 100 livres per emigrant, recovering 30 from the employer; brides were carried free and given a dowry. But neither form of subsidy lasted for many years. The English government found no necessity to give comparable subsidies to bona fide emigrants (as opposed to the transportation of undesirables) until sufficiently alarmed by the supposed shortage of Englishmen at home to begin paying for the shipment of foreigners; in 1710 £5 10s. a head was paid by the government for the transportation of 3200 Germans to New York.[48] This encouragement to poor foreign Protestants to colonize English America continued down to the War of Independence, costs being met either by the British government or by the governments of colonies who wished to attract settlers.

Both the English and the French governments from the mid-seventeenth century permitted or required the transportation to the colonies of convicted criminals, defeated rebels, and certain other unwanted persons; it was in this way that the kings of England made their greatest direct contribution to the peopling of America. Transportation was not a sentence ordinarily imposed by English law courts but rather an exercise of the king's prerogative to mitigate the law's undiscriminating severity. As early as 1615 a royal commission was set up to commute sentences to servitude in "parts abroade" for a prescribed term and from 1634 the same function was exercised by the king. It was not until after the Restoration, however, that the transportation of convicts became statistically important in the English colonies, the policy of meeting colonial needs for manpower out of the worst elements in the mother country being another token of growing concern in England at the loss of population by bona fide emigration. Between 1660 and 1700 at least 4500 persons sentenced to death by the courts were shown royal mercy and reprieved for transportation to the colonies, though probably nothing like that number arrived at their destinations, some being pardoned, others dying in the white Middle Passage. This was still only a trickle compared to shipments in the eighteenth century, when in just over sixty years 17,000 felons were transported to America from London and the Home Counties alone; but the precedent had been firmly established.[49]

[48] Walter A. Knittle, *The Early Eighteenth Century Palatine Emigration* (Philadelphia: University of Pennsylvania Press, 1936), pp. 143–144.

[49] All figures in this and the following paragraph have been taken from Smith, *Colonists in Bondage*, chapters 8 and 9.

Roundups of undesirables, vagrants, prostitutes, and the like for consignment to the colonies were occasionally undertaken, as in 1619 for Virginia's benefit, but were rare and of doubtful legality. Far more important were mass deportations of prisoners taken in the civil wars and rebellions of the second half of the seventeenth century. Many of the victims were Scots or Irish: 150 Scots were sent to America after the Battle of Dunbar (1650) and sold in Boston at £ 20 to £ 30 a head, more after the Battle of Worcester (1651). Later in the 1650s, when the civil war moved to Ireland, perhaps 1000 Irish (fragments of greater deportations to continental Europe) were dispatched across the Atlantic, many to the Leeward Islands, where Montserrat became a predominantly Irish colony; 400 Irish children were sent to New England. More Scots were transported in 1666; and in 1685, after the failure of Argyll's rebellion, 177 of his followers were sent to Jamaica, 100 to New Jersey. Nor was banishment to the colonies a fate which the English reserved for other people. Englishmen were transported to the West Indies after Penruddock's rising against Cromwell in 1655; and of Monmouth's supporters 306 were sent to Barbados in 1686 and 159 more to Jamaica. The list is a long one; scarcely a civil commotion took place in the British Isles between 1650 and 1700 that did not deposit some human sediment on the other side of the Atlantic. It is not a record to be proud of. But there is no reason to think that these reluctant emigrants necessarily made bad colonists; on the contrary, those who survived and stayed in America were probably as good as orthodox indentured servants, if not better.

Transportation in seventeenth-century France was seldom inflicted as a punishment by the courts; it would have reduced the number of convicts needed for the Mediterranean galleys. On the other hand, more as an administrative than as a judicial act, intendants from time to time rounded up rogues and vagabonds and sent them to the colonies.[50] Transportation was also used as a threat to force Huguenots to conform or fly the country, and in the years following the Revocation of the Edict of Nantes (1685) a number of obdurates were actually shipped to the Antilles. In 1686–88 twelve ships bore about a thousand Huguenots from Marseilles to Martinique.[51] This was the most conspicuous example of enforced emigration to the French colonies in the seventeenth century; in general

[50] G. Debien, Le peuplement des Antilles françaises au XVII e siècle: les engagés partis de La Rochelle (1683–1715) (Cairo: Institut Français, 1942), p. 71.

[51] Debien, "Engagés pour les Antilles," p. 192.

Huguenot colonists were not wanted, and this kind of conscription contributed little to the peopling of either New France or the Antilles. Of the party sent to Martinique, many got away to more congenial English colonies or returned to live in other parts of Europe.

These transfusions of lawbreakers into colonial life were not wholly pleasing to respectable elements already established in the New World. New England could fairly easily absorb some morally substandard residents, but the disorderliness of the Caribbean in the seventeenth century may have owed something to the system of transportation. On the other hand, the Caribbean would probably have been disorderly without the presence of reprieved criminals, and on the whole it is remarkable what little trace they and their counterparts left on the societies of which they became part. In the long run, convicts, vagabonds, defeated Irish and Scots, royalists and prostitutes, because their servitude was seldom perpetual, because their children were free, and because they were white, merged into the colonial communities in much the same way as indentured servants who had served their time.

Remembering the bargains with their subjects which kings commonly struck when some task needed to be done beyond the administrative resources of their governments, we should not expect to find that in every case of banishment or deportation in the seventeenth century the transports were organized and the prisoners delivered to America by public authority. Often they were not, and in many of the instances just mentioned the active role of government ceased when the prisoners were taken from jail and handed over to contractors, who furnished shipping and such food as it was deemed advisable to give the passengers in order to ensure that enough of them reached their destination in vendible condition. Private enterprise, in other words, was called in to do what government wanted. Turning now from government-initiated or government-sponsored emigration to emigration organized or enabled by chartered companies, we find the same disposition at work further down the scale. Just as kings, by conferring privileges on corporations, tried to induce them to people the colonies, so those corporations, when they bothered to meet their obligations, often did so by getting rid of them to individual contractors or merchants. Nearly every chartered company in the seventeenth century turned into, if it did not begin as, a holding company for individual enterprise, in trade as well as in the promotion of colonization.

Only a small fraction of white immigrants reached the New World directly under the aegis and at the expense of chartered companies. This can be shown by reference to Dutch, French, and English examples. The failure of the Dutch West India Company to people New Netherland has already been discussed: in 1628 it launched a scheme, modified in 1629, to stimulate others to do what it could not or would not do itself. Patroons were to receive large grants of land and other privileges on condition *inter alia* of settling fifty families in New Netherland within the space of four years. Rensserlaerswyck (population in 1643 about 100) came into existence on these terms, but other projected patroonships were abandoned or never begun.[52]

French companies did better though not much better. The Compagnie de la Nouvelle France (1627), despite the obligation laid on it by Richelieu to settle colonists, did not give Canada enough men to defend itself. The *seigneuries*, of which this company created about sixty and which were granted with the requirement that the *seigneur* should people his land, might have served the purpose intended by the patroonship; but the metropolitan connections necessary for recruiting settlers appear to have been lacking.[53] Canadian *seigneurs*, recruiting in the colony, merely competed against each other for the few men available. Under the Compagnie de Saint-Christophe (1627) and the Compagnie des Îles d'Amérique (1635) Normans and Bretons were recruited for the Antilles, but much of the organization and financial responsibility for emigration seems to have been passed by these companies to private contractors. Colbert's creation, the Compagnie des Indes Occidentales (1664), organized emigration only for the first few months of its life. All added together the companies which had a hand in French America achieved little: of Debien's 6200 *engagés* passing through the port of La Rochelle between 1634 and 1715, fewer than 600 traveled in the service of companies.[54]

Lastly, England. The Virginia Company certainly intended to undertake the peopling of its colony and at first did so. But the strain on its resources became too great: from 1617 it called in private enterprise and began to constitute "societies of adventurers" to which large grants of land

[52] Terms of patroonships are printed in Jameson, *Narratives of New Netherland*, pp. 90–96.

[53] William B. Munro, *The Seigniorial System in Canada* (New York: Longmans, 1907), pp. 23, 25, 28, 42–50.

[54] Debien, "Engagés pour les Antilles," pp. 153–154.

were made on condition of transporting complete "colonies" — governor, gentlemen, tenants, and servants. Between 1619 and 1623, forty-four such grants of "particular plantations" were made; though not all were taken up, it is clear that the promotion of settlement in the company's last years was largely left to these groups. Thus in 1619, of 811 servants brought to the colony only 151 were on the Virginia Company's account, the remainder being transported by private effort for the "particular plantations."[55] In Bermuda, colonized by the Somers Island Company, the element of company-promoted emigration was even smaller. As early as 1615 the majority of settlers had come on private account, and when this company was reorganized in 1618 the corporate role was reduced still further.[56] In Bermuda units of settlement called "tribes" corresponded to the "hundreds" granted to "societies of adventurers" in Virginia; both bear some resemblance to the intentions of the Dutch scheme for patroonships in New Netherland; all are witnesses of the failure of chartered companies to keep up out of their own resources the sustained flow of immigrants which new colonies needed.

To this rather dismal record, there is in the first half of the seventeenth century one remarkable exception, the Massachusetts Bay Company, which organized the dispatch of seventeen ships in 1630 carrying 1500 settlers and which by 1635 had ensured the arrival of 8000, enough to make the colony a going concern.[57] The reasons why it succeeded where others failed are many and well known; they need not be rehearsed in detail. For one thing, both climate and Indians were more tolerant of white men in New England than they were in Virginia: each settler transported by the company was, demographically, a better investment. Secondly, many who came to New England came in family units, some in even larger community groups formed by the following of a particular preacher at home; this gave them cohesion and something familiar to hold onto in strange conditions. Thirdly, they had leaders, one might say natural leaders, men who commanded respect in England in virtue of their social status, and who retained that leadership and respect in the vital early years of the colony. Some, if not rich, were comfortably off;

[55] Philip A. Bruce, *Economic History of Virginia*, 2 vols. (New York: Macmillan, 1896), I, 589.
[56] Wesley Frank Craven, "An Introduction to the History of Bermuda," *William and Mary Quarterly*, 2nd series, 17:176–215, 317–362, 437–465 (1937), 18:40–63 (1938).
[57] Charles M. Andrews, *The Colonial Period of American History*, 4 vols. (New Haven, Conn.: Yale University Press, 1934–38; reprinted, 1964), I, 395–396.

instead of being mouths for the company to feed and hands to be set on work, they brought assets with them and started work on their own account. And, finally, there was Puritanism itself, fissiparous in so many of its effects, but of critical importance not only in prompting emigration in the first place but also in shaping the attitude of the colonists to their new home. They believed they were doing God's work; there was no better formula in the seventeenth century for planting a colony.

The age of company-promoted white emigration from Europe was short, over with a few exceptions by the middle of the seventeenth century. That does not mean that the chartered companies had finished with peopling the New World by 1650; on the contrary their greatest contribution, the transportation of African slaves, was still to come. To this subject we shall presently return; but, first, the matter of white colonization must be concluded by considering the achievements of private enterprise, the private merchants and small partnerships of men with money, who turned the supply of indentured servants and *engagés* to the colonies into a business and so did more to people America than either kings or companies. Thus and thus only was the merchants' fear of a regime of colonization finally dispelled: by creating a trade in men, there was harnessed to imperial purpose what Colbert called "the innate longing men have for profit and to make themselves comfortable."[58]

Indentured Servants and Engagés

England's success in peopling her colonies faster than France was largely, though not entirely, achieved by fuller use of the device of indentured labor. New England, as so often, was the exception, receiving some indentured servants but few in proportion to population: an economy of family farms, fisheries, and shipbuilding engendered less demand for bondsmen than an economy of plantations. It is also possible that New Englanders eschewed the common sort of servant out of fear of contamination, at least until the growth of Boston modified attitudes toward the outside world. The export of servants from England and France, moreover, tended to follow established trade routes, Norman ports sending *engagés* to Canada, Bristol sending men to Virginia, Barbados, and Nevis, because these were

[58] Quoted in May, *Histoire économique de la Martinique*, p. 51.

the colonies with which they dealt for fur, tobacco, or sugar.[59] Since New England produced no comparable cash crop for the metropolitan market, direct sailings between Boston and the English ports must have been rarer.

Available statistics are, it must be admitted, imperfect; but the leading authority on indentured service in the English colonies has estimated that at any time in the 1670s there were between 12,000 and 15,000 white servants at work in the plantations, distributed as follows: Virginia, 6000; Maryland, Barbados, and Jamaica, 2000 each; the rest shared among the Leewards, middle colonies, and New England.[60] To maintain a working force of this size, 3000–4000 recruits would be needed annually, making no allowance for mortality during service. If that number is approximately correct, it follows that, despite the growing use of African labor in the Caribbean, down to the end of the third quarter of the seventeenth century more white servants than black slaves were crossing the Atlantic to work in the English colonies. Throughout the century, indentured labor was of prime importance in the economies of Virginia and Maryland. In 1624–25, out of a population of 1227 in Virginia, 487 were servants, survivors of hundreds more who had perished from disease or at the hands of Indians. Of 2675 recorded immigrants into this colony between 1623 and 1637, at least 2094 were servants. Down to 1666, probably as many as three-quarters of all immigrants to Virginia were servants; and in the later seventeenth century they were still arriving at the rate of 1500 a year.[61] Maryland's history of settlement was much the same, on a smaller scale: 21,000 white servants arrived there between 1633 and 1680, that is,

---

[59] The relationship between trade and emigration from La Rochelle and other ports is discussed at length by Debien, especially in "Les engagés pour les Antilles." Regarding Bristol, 27 ships from North America and 50 from the West Indies discharged cargoes there in 1678–79 (one year); 25 of the 27 North Americans were from Virginia, and 37 of the 50 West Indiamen from Barbados and Nevis. In 1699–1700 (one year) 24 ships from North America and 50 from the West Indies discharged cargoes in Bristol; 12 of the 24 North Americans were from Virginia and 26 of the 50 West Indiamen were from Barbados and Nevis. These figures are taken from P. V. McGrath, *Merchants and Merchandise in Seventeenth Century Bristol*, Bristol Record Society Publications, vol. XIX (Bristol: B. R. S., 1955), pp. 281, 295. They point to a large measure of specialization in Bristol's Atlantic trade and a heavy concentration on three colonies. It is therefore to be expected that indentured servants from Bristol would be moving in the same direction, and in fact 85 percent of the 10,394 registered emigrants between 1654 and 1686 were destined for these same three colonies. See Smith, *Colonists in Bondage*, p. 309.

[60] Smith, *Colonists in Bondage*, p. 336.

[61] *Ibid.*, pp. 31–33; Wertenbaker, *Planters of Colonial Virginia*, pp. 35, 80.

about 500 a year.[62] As late as 1707 there were 3000 indentured servants in Maryland, compared to 4657 slaves. Slave labor came earlier to the Caribbean than to the southern colonies, but in 1680 Barbados still had 2317 white servants with hundreds arriving annually.[63] One reason for this was fear that a shrinking white population would render Barbados indefensible against foreign attack or slave rebellion. Here and elsewhere statutory encouragements were offered to the import of white servants eligible for militia service. In Jamaica (1672), Antigua (1677), and St. Kitts (1679), deficiency laws were enacted, prescribing the proportion to be maintained between white and black labor.[64] They were not particularly effective, turning into a method of raising money by fines; everywhere in the Caribbean the conquest of indentured service by slavery can be seen as a matter of time.

No computation of the total number of *engagés* in the French colonies has been made that is comparable to Abbot E. Smith's estimate of English indentured servants; but clearly it was much lower. Bristol recorded the departure of 10,394 servants to the colonies in thirty-three years between 1654 and 1686; La Rochelle, an approximately comparable port, sent 6200 in 82 years between 1634 and 1715.[65] Down to about 1680 the great majority of these La Rochelle *engagés* went to St. Christophe, Martinique, and Guadeloupe, thereafter to St.-Domingue. Few went to Canada: 231 between 1656 and 1659, 126 in 1664–65, but only 105 between 1670 and 1689.[66] La Rochelle was not the leading French port for the Canadian trade; undoubtedly the Norman ports sent more servants there, for in the (incomplete) Canadian census of 1665–66, 401 out of 763 persons classified by occupation were *engagés*.[67] But these servants soon worked out their three-year contracts and, though others went to Canada in the 1670s, the flow was reduced to a trickle. Here, more than anywhere else, the inadequacy of the French effort is exposed. In the Caribbean, Colbert's policies appear to have been only a little more efficacious. Concern for defense led him in the 1660s to prefer white *engagés* to black slaves,[68] but it is not clear that the results achieved owed much to his

[62] Smith, *Colonists in Bondage*, p. 324.
[63] Dunn, "Barbados Census of 1680," pp. 10, 39.
[64] Smith, *Colonists in Bondage*, pp. 31–33.
[65] *Ibid.*, pp. 308–309; Debien, "Engagés pour les Antilles."
[66] G. Debien, "Les engagés pour le Canada au XVIIe siècle vus de La Rochelle," *Revue d'histoire de l'Amérique française*, 6:177–220 (1952–53).
[67] *Censuses of Canada*, p. 3.
[68] May, *Histoire économique de la Martinique*, p. 35. In 1686 Seignelay ordered a reduc-

ministrations. Martinique, which early on had received 600 *engagés* from Honfleur, got virtually none from there after 1680. Guadeloupe, where La Rochelle sent 340 between 1638 and 1667, received only 33 from that port between 1683 and 1715. The French, as we have already seen, were fairly successful in keeping up their white populations in the Lesser Antilles, but they do not seem to have done so by means of *engagés*. If La Rochelle reflects the general pattern of emigrations, all routes by the beginning of the eighteenth century led to St.-Domingue.

Indentured service was the means whereby, with no cost to themselves, young men (seldom single women or families) were transported to the colonies and maintained for a term of years by the master to whom they were bound. In return they worked sometimes as artisans but more commonly as field hands, normally receiving wages only at the conclusion of service. In some respects the arrangement resembled military service or engagement as a sailor. The *engagé* or servant was a volunteer; but by signing on, he submitted to laws and customs which put him at the disposal of his master. This element of unfreedom in colonial servitude was neither particularly novel nor necessarily rebarbative: liberty to withdraw labor was not general in seventeenth-century Europe, and there were certain compensating restraints on the master's freedom to dismiss his employees. Formally, the servant's position in the colonies was like that of an apprentice in Europe, but with less prospect of learning a trade and probably less hope of redress if ill-treated. In practice, his lot depended on his luck, the kind of master he served.

Some servants were recruited by persons acting on behalf of a prospective employer in the colonies; in these cases they might know a little about their masters-to-be. More commonly the recruiter, often a ship's captain, signed on such servants as he thought he could sell in the plantations, much as captains bought slaves in the Calabar River or on the Windward Coast of Guinea. Indentures were drawn at the seaport before sailing and were assignable by the captain. Many English servants received no indentures; their terms and conditions of service were regulated by the "custom of the country" to which they were going. The French were more formal: few *engagés* appear to have left La Rochelle without a proper contract of engagement, though the same term, *coutume du pays*, was used in the French colonies to define mutual obligations of

tion in the number of slaves to be delivered to the Antilles; see Ly, *Compagnie du Sénégal*, p. 54.

master and servant. On arrival, the captain or supercargo found a buyer to whom the indentures were transferred, perhaps to be reassigned once or more than once before expiry. In these assignments the servant had no voice, save in Pennsylvania and New York where his consent was needed. "The servant had rights but while he was in servitude these rarely conflicted with the conception of him as private property." [69]

Such a system was open to abuse, in the colonies as it was in Europe. Young men were shanghaied as expertly for America as they were for service at sea. On the other hand, there are cases of servants falsely claiming to have been kidnapped and seeking damages from recruiters. Pressure for public regulation of the trade came from the merchants concerned in it. There were attempts to set up a registry office in London in the seventeenth century, and in Bristol registration was undertaken by the city authorities; hence the Tolzey Book, 1654–86, one of the most complete records of indentured emigrants to have survived in Europe. In 1682 and 1686, Orders in Council were issued requiring intending servants to be taken before a magistrate, but it was not until 1717 that the organizers of the English servant trade got what they wanted: statutory relief from the charge of enticement once an emigrant had registered for service. [70] In France indentures for colonial service were concluded in front of a notary, as were indentures of apprenticeship for service at home, and in much the same form.

The term of service of an *engagé*, whether written into the contract or determined by the *coutume du pays*, was almost without exception three years. Colbert in a misconceived attempt to make service more attractive lowered it in 1670 to eighteen months but his decree had no effect and was rescinded two years later. [71] Enforced, it would have made the system unworkable, a year or so being needed for an "unseasoned hand" to become acclimatized and thoroughly useful. In the English colonies four or five years was normal, with longer terms for youths below the ages of eighteen and nineteen. The effect of Virginia's legislation on this subject in the second half of the seventeenth century was to ensure that a servant remained in bondage until he was twenty-four, the age favored by the English Statute of Artificers of 1563 to mark the attainment of years of discretion; released younger, it was feared, some would lead a "licen-

[69] Smith, *Colonists in Bondage*, pp. 233, 279.

[70] See *ibid.*, chapter 5, for a full discussion of government and public attitudes toward the servant trade.

[71] Debien, "Engagés pour les Antilles," pp. 64, 209.

tiouse and ryotouse life," marrying and begetting children, while others
would "falle to choppinge, chaunginge and making of many unadvised
bargaynes."[72]

When he signed on, the La Rochelle *engagé* was given clothing for the
voyage and a small cash payment, and was fed and lodged until the ship
sailed. English arrangements were more haphazard but included maintenance in the waiting period. Once in the colony, the master was bound to
feed and clothe his servant, but exactly how he did so was largely up to
him. In the eighteenth century there was room for debate among plantation owners whether to work and starve their slaves to death, replacing
the whole stock every few years, or to treat them well and make them last.
About indentured servants there could be no such argument: the interest
of the master was to get everything possible from them before their term
was up. If the servant survived an experience which some compared
unfavorably to the condition of slavery, he became eligible for freedom
dues, that is, wages in cash or kind which represented the reward for the
whole period of service. In Canada a craftsman got up to 200 livres in
money, a laborer only 70, just enough to get him back to France.[73] In the
Antilles, time-expired *garçons* got 300 livres (weight) of tobacco or sugar
which, if actually paid in kind, must have declined in purchasing power
throughout most of the century. In Barbados, Nevis, and Antigua, freedom dues were 400 pounds of tobacco or sugar, and in Jamaica (where
cash was generally more plentiful) 40s. Maryland supplied an outfit of
clothes, three barrels of corn, tools, and a gun, suggesting at least the
possibility that a time-expired servant could set up as a smallholder on the
fifty acres of land which in that colony, until 1683, he could claim.[74]

The return fare to Europe was not as such part of the contract; in the
1680s when sugar prices were low it is not clear that 400 pounds of sugar
would buy an Atlantic crossing.[75] If an ex-servant stayed, by necessity or
choice, his hope of acquiring land depended not on his indentures but on
the law of the colony in which he found himself. In the early years of the
West Indian colonies a freed servant might expect to get land and within a
year raise a crop of tobacco and so hoist himself to independence. These

[72] Bruce, *Economic History of Virginia*, II, 3–5; R. H. Tawney and Eileen Power, *Tudor
Economic Documents*, 3 vols. (New York: Longmans, 1921), I, 355–356.
[73] Debien, "Engagés pour le Canada," p. 212.
[74] Smith, *Colonists in Bondage*, pp. 238–240, has a table of freedom dues in the English
colonies.
[75] One hundred pounds of muscovado sugar ex-Barbados fetched about 15s. or 16s. in
1686 in London, less in the island.

favorable conditions soon disappeared. Tobacco was ousted by sugar, a crop not within the very small cultivator's capacity; and where, as in most Caribbean islands, there continued to be unoccupied land fit for cultivation, the work of clearing it was too heavy for one man with scarcely any capital. Ex-servants who stayed in the sugar colonies mostly became wage earners, the *petits blancs* of the eighteenth century. In Canada, on the other hand, a former *engagé* with an aptitude for farming could easily attach himself to a *seigneurie* and become a *censitaire* (customary tenant) on favorable terms. That so many French *engagés* headed for St.-Domingue and so few for Canada argues ignorance on their part or the absence of choice or some kind of belief that the Caribbean was the place that offered the one chance in a thousand of striking it rich.

Not all indentured servants aspired to be colonial farmers, and of those who did only a fraction succeeded. Maryland supplies the evidence for this, one of the few colonies where land grants were made to ex-servants over any considerable period of time. Of 5000 servants entering that colony in the 1670s, 1249 (probably quite a high proportion of the survivors) proved their right to fifty acres; but 869 of them sold that right as soon as proved, and only 241 — fewer than one in twenty of arrivals — are known to have taken up their lots in person. Smith's conclusion is that one in ten of all servants going to the English colonies took land, one in ten became artisans or overseers, and the other eight died, went home, or became poor whites.[76] To men with no capital and no habit of saving, free or cheap land did not mean much.

What kept this flow of white servants moving westwards, particularly to Virginia, Maryland, and St.-Domingue? Three separate interests were involved: the merchant's, the employer's, and the emigrant's. To the first, the supply of servants to the colonies was a business, a specialized business probably for only a few, but a sideline for many. Capital was needed. Debien has estimated that it cost 100–120 livres to put an *engagé* ashore in the French colonies, about half of this sum being attributable to the cost of passage, the remainder to outfitting and maintenance before embarkation.[77] An English servant's passage cost £ 5–£ 6, about the same as the transportation charge for an African slave to Jamaica. Prices at which *engagés* and servants were sold in the colonies have not been firmly established, but a rough idea is deducible from inventories of effects of

[76] Smith, *Colonists in Bondage*, pp. 299–300.
[77] Debien, "Engagés pour les Antilles," pp. 73–75.

deceased masters in Virginia, their servants being appraised like other possessions. With only one year of service to run, a servant was valued at £ 2–£ 4; with two years, £ 6–£ 8; and so on up to £ 13–£ 17 where six years were still to be worked.[78] If these valuations correspond to prices, there was certainly money to be made in bringing servants from Europe.

The employer's first consideration was to acquire a disciplined labor force as cheaply as possible, and in some colonies this was his only consideration. In Virginia, however, there was the additional benefit for the employer of headright, probably the cheapest and certainly one of the commonest ways of acquiring land. The adoption of headright — fifty acres granted, not to the time-expired servant as in Maryland, but to the importer — was an acknowledgment of the Virginia Company's failure to people the colony; it passed responsibility for recruitment to the planters and gave them the necessary inducement. Headright's influence on the colony's history was far-reaching and pervasive. It explains why Virginia was the leading continental colony for indentured servants, if not indeed the leading English or French colony anywhere. It helps to explain how the southern colonies, before slaves arrived in large numbers, managed to keep abreast of New England in population. Finally, headright — a devastatingly simple and effective application of the rule "to him that hath shall be given" — contributed to the appearance of social and economic inequalities, fostering the great estate in Virginia, never to the exclusion of smaller holdings but on a scale big enough to influence the style of life in the eighteenth century. In the middle colonies, headright was less significant but still a useful device to enable late-starting colonies to make up leeway. In the Caribbean it was of no lasting importance.

Of the motives of the emigrants themselves, less is known. Some, the convicted criminals or defeated rebels, we have already seen, were given no option; but the majority were volunteers, at least at the moment of engagement, who must have made some calculation of self-interest, however uninformed. Why? A few went for high wages, a skilled man in the Antilles earning five or six times what he could make in France. These were the carpenters, coopers, masons, and stone workers, above all the sugar refiners — *les princes des engagés* — badly wanted in the Caribbean.[79] The majority, however, had no such skills; all that can be said of their wages is that they were better than no wages at all. Did they

[78] Bruce, *Economic History of Virginia*, II, 51–52.
[79] Debien, "Engagés pour les Antilles," pp. 115, 158.

know that their chances of survival in Virginia or Martinique were in all probability less than at home? that their chances of becoming landowners were small? that they were to be subject to a rigorous disciplinary code, for breaking which their servitude could be extended? It seems unlikely. The "spirits" (recruiting agents) of Bristol and London and the *rabatteurs* who held forth at fairs in northwestern France could be relied upon to put the best appearance on what awaited a young man in the colonies. Probably the ground had to be prepared by some dislocation, personal or general, of normal life: "a large family, death of a mother or father, the example of a brother or kinsman already settled in the colonies,"[80] or by bad harvests, high prices and rents, plague, increased taxation, unemployment in the textile or other industries, the billeting of troops, or any of the other scourges of Europe's poor. Probably one should not insist on wholly rational explanations for engagement. Christopher Jeaffreson, a St. Kitts planter, was aware of this: "How many broken traders, miserable debtors, penniless spendthrifts, discontented persons, travelling heads and scatter-brains would joyfully embrace such offers: — the first, to shun their greedy creditors and loathesome goales . . . the third, to fill their bellies, though with the bread of affliction; the fourth, to leave an unkinde mistress or dishonest wife, or something worse; the fifth to satisfie fond curiosity; sixth, he knows not why, unless to cross his friends and seek his fortune. These and the like humours first peopled the [West] Indies, and made them a kinde of Bedlam for a short tyme. But from such brain-sick humours have come many solid and sober men, as these modern tymes testify."[81]

Poverty was widespread in the seventeenth century, ignorance scarcely less so, yet the recruitment of servants for the colonies was largely a local matter with nothing to show that it was the poorest or most ignorant regions of England and France that supplied the most emigrants. For engagement to be the solution to a young man's problems he needed, first, to have met a recruiter, and secondly, to be able to travel to a port where ships sailed for America. Neither was impossible for a young man from Lancashire or Lincolnshire, Provence or Burgundy; both were easier for young men from Gloucestershire, Somerset, Normandy, Aunis, Saintonge, or Poitou.[82] That the flow of servants and *engagés* to the

[80] *Ibid.*, p. 110.
[81] Quoted in Higham, *Development of the Leeward Islands*, pp. 169–170.
[82] For a discussion of the geographical origins of English emigrants, see Mildred Campbell, "Social Origins of Some Early Americans," in James M. Smith, ed.,

colonies can be correlated with short-term or long-term prospects of employment at home is indeed possible, though no one has yet performed it except in the most general way; it must, however, also reflect the efficiency of recruiters and the effectiveness of propaganda. That English colonies received so many more servants than French from the mother country need not be taken as a sign that conditions of life were worse in England than in France; if taxes are anything to go by, they were better. It may rather denote that English propaganda was better, the servant trade freer and better organized, with more ships going from English ports to more colonies, and a bigger proportion of the population within walking distance of those ports.

Differences in the conditions of employment of servants and *engagés* do not explain the massive numerical advantage of English over French. In the colonies of both countries servants formed a distinct class, the object of much suspicion and of much special legislation intended to restrain the trouble-making propensities they were assumed to have. In the Caribbean and the southern colonies master-and-servant codes were enacted. In New England, the smaller number of indentured servants from the mother country was balanced by a greater awareness on the part of lawmakers of their capacity for sin; here too they were the subject of special legislation. These codes were various but their principal purposes can be reduced to three: to keep the servant at work and in obedience, to deny him a sexual life, and to restrain fraud and ill-treatment on the part of the master.

In Maryland between 1639 and 1650 the statutory punishment for a servant who ran away was death. It was replaced in the latter year by the doubling of the period of service, but helping a fugitive servant continued to be a felony.[83] There is no evidence that these pieces of savagery were ever enforced; their enactment is important only as a recognition of the extreme necessity of keeping servants in obedience in societies where the traditional European sanctions were lacking. Commonly, the statutory penalty for desertion or absence was an extension of the term of service. In the French Antilles runaways had their terms doubled and were

Seventeenth-Century America (Chapel Hill: University of North Carolina Press, 1959), pp. 78–80. For the origins of La Rochelle emigrants, see Debien, "Engagés pour les Antilles," pp. 99–109.

[83] Eugene J. McCormac, *White Servitude in Maryland, 1634–1820*, Johns Hopkins Studies in Historical and Political Science, series 22, nos. 3–4 (Baltimore: Johns Hopkins University Press, 1904), pp. 51–52.

whipped.[84] Heavy penalties in colonial laws frequently denote nonenforcement, and servants certainly did escape. In Virginia they could be pursued, like criminals in England, by hue-and-cry.[85] Obviously it was harder to get away from servitude on an island: hence the readiness of indentured servants of Barbados to volunteer for warlike ventures. The recruiting officers of the Penn-Venables expedition in 1655 promised not to enroll servants, but "ther indentures not being writt in there foreheads, they were by some ignorantly and by others wilfully received."[86]

Marriage was everywhere forbidden without the master's consent. In Virginia it was punished by one year's extra service, a light penalty compared to Pennsylvania where the marriage of servants, even if lawfully contracted in other respects, was invalid, the offspring deemed illegitimate, and the couple punished for fornication.[87] Apart from a generalized feeling, brought over from Europe, that the state of apprenticeship and the state of marriage should be distinct, the second restraint beginning when the first ended and both deterring idleness and irresponsibility, the main fear was of servants begetting children for whom they could not provide. Fornication among servants in all English colonies was punishable by the whipping of both men and women, and there were extra penalties in some colonies for miscegenation. Under a Maryland statute of 1664 "freeborne English women forgetful of their free condition and to the disgrace of the Nation" who married black slaves were to remain servants for the lifetime of the husband; their children to be slaves for life.[88] In Guadeloupe an engagé who debauched a black woman received twenty lashes for the first offense, forty for the second, fifty and branding for the third.[89]

Not every piece of legislation affecting the servant was meant to restrain him. Where there were master-servant codes, the masters were forbidden to ill-treat servants and, while no doubt many cases of brutality

[84] Debien, "Engagés pour les Antilles," pp. 205–206. To attempt to fly to a foreign colony, on the third offense, was punishable by death.

[85] Bruce, Economic History of Virginia, II, 25.

[86] Harlow, History of Barbados, p. 108.

[87] Bruce, Economic History of Virginia, II, 38; Smith, Colonists in Bondage, p. 271.

[88] McCormac, White Servitude, pp. 67–68. The enactment of a law does not imply its execution. It might lie unenforced for years, either because there was no sufficient administrative machinery to do otherwise or because the fit of pique which gave rise to it had passed. Colonial laws are not a good guide to the humanity or lack of it in rulers.

[89] Satineau, Guadeloupe, p. 74.

went unregarded, the courts were open to complaint and can be shown to have extended some protection to victims. One action, that taken by John Thomas of Barbados in 1640, must serve to illustrate both the barbarity of which masters were capable and the possibilities of redress. Thomas was hung up by his wrists and lighted matches placed between his fingers. He complained to the governor and council of the island who ordered that he be freed from servitude and given 5000 pounds of cotton as damages; the master was required to pay for medical treatment and also to suffer imprisonment, a judgment comprehensive enough to suggest strong public disapproval of such conduct.[90] Numerous cases in the courts of Maryland show that trouble was taken to get at the truth of charges of ill-treatment; at least one master was executed for causing the death of a servant.[91]

Servants had no political rights. Statements that white servitude was indistinguishable from slavery, though often made, should not, however, be taken too seriously.[92] There were resemblances: servants and slaves might work side by side in the fields; both were heavily punished for running away; both could be whipped without an order of court; both were forbidden to trade, the presumption being that what they sold was stolen. But the differences were obvious: whites, if they survived, became free, as did their children; whites could apply to the courts; whites in the English colonies were assumed to be Christians, slaves not to be Christians; all whites served in the militia, bearing arms, slaves only exceptionally. What may well be true is that the arrival of more and more black slaves toward the end of the seventeenth century led to a worsening of the position of the white servant. Such at least is Debien's belief respecting the French Caribbean colonies. When the *engagés* were a majority, slaves were treated more like *engagés*; when the positions were reversed, the *engagés* were treated more like slaves.[93] To this is perhaps attributable the fear of loss of status among the poorest members of the white community in the eighteenth century. Debien thinks that this was more noticeable in the French than in the English Caribbean colonies; but a

[90] Harlow, *History of Barbados*, pp. 303–304.
[91] McCormac, *White Servitude*, p. 65.
[92] Governor Du Lion of Guadeloupe to Colbert in 1669: "This contract of service for three years is a form of slavery, indeed somewhat worse than slavery." Quoted in Debien, "Engagés pour les Antilles," pp. 207–208. Compare Intendant Robert's "Mémoires sur les engagés," quoted in Satineau, *Guadeloupe*, p. 73.
[93] Debien, "Engagés pour les Antilles," chapter 13, especially pp. 256–257, discusses the coexistence of white servants and slaves.

comparable decline in the status of white servants in Maryland has been observed, the result of the importation into the colony of numerous convicts and slaves.[94]

The Slave Trade

Slavery and the slave trade, relatively unimportant in 1600, developed in the course of the seventeenth century into one of the most powerful influences, if not the most powerful, shaping the European presence in South and Central America and in the Caribbean. Without African slaves and the Atlantic slave trade, Spain and Portugal might have contrived to rear empires of exploitation on the backs of South American Indians; but neither Spaniards nor English nor French could have done so in the Caribbean. The pre-Columbian Indians of Hispaniola, Cuba, and Jamaica had a complete answer to Spanish plans to conscript them: they died, leaving empty lands with which little could be done but ranching. In the Lesser Antilles the Caribs were equally uncooperative in a different way: they fought, and with enough success to compel the English and French to leave them certain islands as in effect reservations. In North America a few Indians were enslaved but they were found to be unapt for most of the tasks the whites wanted done. Where the enslavement of the indigenous people failed through lack of aptitude, lack of docility, or simply lack of physical strength and stamina, a stark choice was left: white peasant farming, as in New England and along the shores of the St. Lawrence, and unambitious planting of tobacco with white servants as in early Virginia and Barbados; or the importing of slaves from Africa. We do not have to assume that all Europeans adopted this alternative with relish. "It is not possible," concluded Prince Johan Maurits, "to effect anything in Brazil without slaves . . . and they cannot be dispensed with upon any consideration whatsoever: if anyone feels that this is wrong, it is a futile scruple."[95] Johan Maurits was not an insensitive boor but a cultivated man, the highest ranking European and one of the least self-interested to cross the Atlantic in the seventeenth century; his is the voice of such enlightenment as Europe had. There were scruples and they were voiced, by Dutchmen, Portuguese, Spaniards, and others.[96] But in almost

[94] McCormac, *White Servitude*, pp. 74–78.

[95] Quoted in Charles R. Boxer, *The Dutch in Brazil, 1624–1654* (Oxford: Clarendon Press, 1957), p. 83.

[96] *Ibid.*, pp. 83–84; Walter Rodney, *A History of the Upper Guinea Coast, 1545–1800* (Oxford: Clarendon Press, 1970), pp. 119–121.

every instance scruples yielded to the force of economic logic, and yielded as comprehensively in the empires of Spain and Portugal, the supposedly easygoing "feudal" countries of Europe, as in the empires of England and France, the supposedly "capitalist" countries. Tropical and subtropical America could be most profitably exploited by agriculture on a large scale: large-scale agriculture necessitated, as it had always done in Europe, some element of unfreedom in the working population. White servants were not the answer. They might have been able to stand the heat of the sun and the hard labor of sugar cultivation; what they could not be brought to accept was the necessary element of continuous unfreedom. In young colonies, with little or no police force, there was no possibility of con- scripting and retaining anything like enough of them to form the labor brigades needed on large estates.

The taking of slaves from West and Central Africa began before the discovery of America. Some reached Europe across the Sahara in the Middle Ages; with captives from other sources, enough were forthcoming to keep alive the institution of slavery in Spain and Portugal. From the mid-fifteenth century the Portuguese were on the west coast of Africa, and although slaves were not the main objective of their voyages they quickly found in the slave trade an adjunct to the business in gold and pepper they hoped to develop. By capture at first, then almost entirely by purchase, they obtained slaves for shipment to São Tomé where a colony of settlement was founded, to Madeira and the Azores to work on the sugar plantations, and to southern Europe. The number taken to Europe was never great: Lisbon, the chief port of entry, received some 500 a year at the beginning of the sixteenth century.[97] Later the supply fell away, though a trickle continued even in the seventeenth century, long after America had become the normal venue. More than once the French toyed with the notion of using African slaves in their Mediterranean galleys. It is unlikely that much regard was paid to a mid-seventeenth- century *ordonnance* of the French Marine requiring all ships trading on the African coast to bring back a certain number of slaves to the mother country, but in Louis XIV's reign a more serious attempt was made to meet the galleys' needs. In 1678–79, years of exceptional activity in the early French slave trade, the Compagnie du Sénégal dispatched sixteen ships to Africa, four of them destined to deliver their cargoes to the galleys

---

[97] Philip D. Curtin, *The Atlantic Slave Trade: A Census* (Madison: University of Wiscon- sin Press, 1969), p. 18.

at Marseilles. The plan miscarried. A consignment of seventy-three slaves was got away from Cape Verde, but six died on the way to Normandy, eleven more soon after reaching France, and twenty were rejected as medically unfit, leaving fewer than half the original cargo to be put to work.[98]

Employment of slaves in this kind of work was unusual in Europe. In the sixteenth century blacks were used in Spain and Portugal for manual labor but in the northern countries most of the handful of slaves who arrived came in the character of personal servants. Their position in law was ambiguous. In England, Lord Mansfield's ruling in Somersett's Case (1771) that "the black must go free" was neither wholly novel nor wholly effectual. The legality of slavery had been questioned before in the English courts. In 1693, for example, in an action in King's Bench, chattel slavery was declared legal, but in another case in 1696 involving a baptized black an opposite decision was reached. In a third case, Holt, the greatest legal authority of his time, held that "as soon as a negro comes into England, he is free."[99] This seems clear enough, but in practice the ambiguity remained and was not entirely removed by Mansfield. Certainly there were slaves in England after Mansfield, regarded by the law as voluntary slaves who were entitled to run away and establish freedom but who chose not to do so. A comparable ambiguity surrounded the status of slaves in France which an edict of 1716 sought, not altogether satisfactorily, to dispel.

The want of a clear definition of slave status in England may be connected with the disappearance of bondmen a little while before the appearance of black slaves. In the mid-sixteenth century there were still a few left in the country; hence the demand of Kett's rebels in 1549 "that all bond men may be made free, for God made all free with his precious blood-shedding."[100] William Harrison, writing in the reign of Elizabeth I, claimed: "As for slaves and bondmen, we have none," though this may not have been strictly true; it was only a few years earlier that an English government had enacted enslavement as the punishment for

[98] Gaston-Martin, *Histoire de l'esclavage dans les colonies françaises* (Paris: Presses Universitaires de France, 1948), p. 4; Ly, *Compagnie du Sénégal*, p. 164.

[99] David Ogg, *England in the Reigns of James II and William III* (Oxford: Clarendon Press, 1955), pp. 73–74.

[100] A. E. Bland, P. A. Brown, R. H. Tawney, eds., *English Economic History: Select Documents* (London: Bell, 1914), p. 249.

vagabondage.[101] By the time that the colonization of America began, however, bondage in England had become too dim a memory to furnish a working definition of slavery fit to be transferred to the New World and applied to blacks. At home the law remained ambiguous; abroad, colonies like Virginia and Jamaica were left with a large measure of freedom to compose slave laws of their own. In France, too, enslavement had either disappeared before the Discoveries or been modified out of recognition; hence the claim of the Parlement of Guienne in 1571, "France, the mother of liberty, allows no slavery."[102] Because of the centralizing purposes of the French crown and the greater influence of the church, French colonies were not accorded the same freedom to draft their own slave laws as the English. In 1685 there was proclaimed one single definition of slave status and one single declaration of the responsibilities of slave owners, applicable to all French colonies. The Code Noir, however, though drawn up in the mother country, was founded more on practices and precedents already existing in the Antilles than on metropolitan law, so that the difference between English and French colonies was more apparent than real.

By contrast, it has been urged, the slave laws of the Spanish empire were founded on thirteenth-century Castilian codifications, envisaging a form of European enslavement different from and milder than the chattel slavery of the North American plantation. These laws, if not transferred in entirety to the colonies, at least molded metropolitan attitudes toward slavery in the colonies. Crown and church together are represented as having accomplished what was only hinted at in the Code Noir: a measure of legal protection for the slave and a measure of humanization of his living and working conditions. Such at least is the view of those who hold that the slavery instituted in the Americas by countries whose metropolitan societies in the seventeenth and eighteenth centuries were becoming more competitive (England, France) was more oppressive than the slavery emanating from countries (Spain, Portugal) whose societies still retained organic traits. This theory has its own weaknesses: doubts on how far Spanish colonial laws were administered in practice, doubts whether the existence of an "organic" society in Portugal was of much help to

[101] William Harrison, *Elizabethan England* (London: Walter Scott, n.d.), p. 13. The statute is 1 Edw. VI, c. 3, repealed in 1550.
[102] Charles Verlinden, *L'esclavage dans l'Europe mediévale*, vol. I (Bruges: Rijksuniversiteit te Gent, 1955), p. 851.

slaves in Brazil, doubts about the value of legal attitudes which failed to stop heavy mortality among slaves.[103] But it cannot be dismissed. Crown and church *did* intervene on behalf of slaves more effectively in the Spanish than in the English colonies, though countervailing forces were often too strong for them. We are, therefore, left with the paradox that the relatively early demise of bondage in England, though preparing the way for such dicta as Holt's and Mansfield's,[104] ensured that the slave laws in the English colonies would be drafted and enforced mainly by slave owners.

From soon after 1500 the Americas began to compete with Europe for African slaves; by 1550 they were the chief markets; and for the next 250 years the Atlantic slave trade, though passing through many vicissitudes, marched onwards, bringing to the American continents and the Caribbean islands many more black immigrants than the most generous estimate of whites. This vast movement of people was the greatest act of conscription performed in history previous to the twentieth century; yet until recently its proportions have not been methodically studied. Because the evidence ranges in quality from precise records of sales of slaves to contemporary guesses of little credibility, and because the trade was more often studied nation by nation than as a whole, estimates of the aggregate size of the slave trade were allowed to circulate which, it now appears, were far wide of the mark. The outcome of Philip D. Curtin's convincing research is the suggestion that those historians (many) who accepted the traditional total of 15 million slaves delivered alive in the Americas throughout the entire period of the trade exaggerated by between 30 and about 45 percent. Curtin proposes, with more authority than anyone else has hitherto commanded, that "it is extremely unlikely that the ultimate total will turn out to be less than 8,000,000 or more than 10,500,000."[105]

This estimate is not meant by its author to create a new myth. It needs

---

[103] See, for example, Elsa Goveia, "The West Indians Slave Laws of the Eighteenth Century," in Laura Foner and Eugene D. Genovese, eds., *Slavery in the New World* (Englewood Cliffs, N.J.: Prentice-Hall, 1969); and Herbert S. Klein, *Slavery in the Americas* (London: Oxford University Press, 1967), for the view of Spanish colonial slavery as more humane than French or English. For criticism of this view, see David B. Davis, *The Problem of Slavery in Western Culture* (Ithaca, N.Y.: Cornell University Press, 1966), pp. 223 et seq.

[104] R. H. Tawney, *The Agrarian Problem in the Sixteenth Century* (London: Longmans, 1912), p. 44n, shows what arguments used in Somersett's Case were derived from English villeinage and its disappearance.

[105] Curtin, *Atlantic Slave Trade*, p. 87.

some qualification. It is, in the first place, a computation of arrivals in America not departures from Africa. For the purpose of gauging the impact of the slave trade on Africa, additions must be made for mortality in the Middle Passage. This varied enormously from voyage to voyage and perhaps also from nation to nation engaged in the trade. In the seventeenth and eighteenth centuries it may have accounted for 20 or even 25 percent of those shipped off the African coast.[106] And, taking an even broader view, the number of slaves shipped from Africa must always have been smaller than the number designed for shipment. Mortality occurring between the enslavement of Africans by Africans and their purchase by Europeans cannot be computed, but it is likely to have been statistically significant.[107] As well as deaths on the march to the sea, there were unfit slaves rejected by white buyers whose expectation of life thereafter may not have been good; and there were slaves who looked healthy but mysteriously died before the ship sailed.[108] Finally, there were slaves bought by Europeans to be kept in Africa for work in forts and factories.[109] All these additions swell the volume and impact of the slave trade, viewed as it must first be from Africa, though they do not come near to justifying some of the wilder pronouncements about numbers that have been made.[110]

The slave trade reached its apogee in the eighteenth century when, it appears, 6 million slaves landed in the Americas: 80 percent or thereabouts of all those crossing the Atlantic from the beginning to the end of the trade did so after 1700. This must be stated, in order to put into perspective the volume of the slave trade in the seventeenth century. Deliveries to all parts of the New World for the years 1601–1700 are estimated by

[106] See below, p. 129.

[107] The majority of slaves shipped from West Africa, it is now thought, came from coastal regions; those shipped from Angola had traveled greater distances.

[108] Journal of the *Arthur*, slaving at Calabar in 1678: "wee have made Choice of negroes to the Best of our skill and Judgm'tt and as likely negroes as a man should see yett wee finde that some of them doe decay and grow Leane and some are sicke." Elizabeth B. Donnan, ed., *Documents Illustrative of the History of the Slave Trade to America*, 4 vols. (Washington, D.C.: Carnegie Institution, 1930), I, 228.

[109] The Dutch employed 409 castle slaves in 1645; the Danes "over 200" in the eighteenth century. See A. W. Lawrence, *Trade Castles and Forts of West Africa* (London: Cape, 1963), pp. 46–47. The English and French also staffed their forts and factories with slaves, and many more must have been owned by Portuguese and mulattoes who resided in the country.

[110] Basil Davidson, *Black Mother* (London: Gollancz, 1961), p. 104, writes of the "removing of fifty million souls from Africa."

Curtin at 1,341,100 or 13 percent of the aggregate for the whole period of the trade. Some 368,000 are thought to have arrived in the third quarter of the seventeenth century and 600,000 in the last quarter.[111] Of the total of 1.3 million, therefore, 75 percent is attributable to the years 1651–1700, so demonstrating the order of acceleration that took place in mid-century, generated by demand in Brazil and in the newly founded plantation colonies of France and England. In the course of the seventeenth century, the trade changed from a modest affair largely in Portuguese hands to a competitive international business involving traders of many countries.

The spread of slavery in the Americas requires a geographical as well as a chronological perspective. Nearly two-thirds of all the slaves brought to the New World from the beginning to the end of the trade were delivered to Brazil and the Spanish-American colonies, the remainder to English, French, and Dutch colonies in the Caribbean, with only a small fraction going to North America. In the seventeenth century the balance in favor of Latin America was somewhat less marked. The northern countries were catching up from a later start, but the speed of their progress must not be exaggerated. Even in the last quarter of the seventeenth century Brazil, according to Curtin, received more slaves than Jamaica, Barbados, and the Leewards added together. In this perspective, Virginia, Maryland, and Carolina were negligible importers, certainly until 1713 mere peripheral consumers in a trade heavily concentrated upon the Caribbean and the South Atlantic.

The extent of England's participation in the slave trade before about 1650 is obscure. That some interest existed is not in question. Van den Broeck, a Dutch trader, met an English ship off Cape Verde in 1606 and was invited to join in seizing a Lubeck vessel carrying slaves to Lisbon; the English insisted on the slaves as their share of the booty. In 1629, the ship *Benediction*, property of a London partnership, was taken by a French privateer off Senegal: she carried slaves. In 1651 the successors of this partnership ordered a ship to the Gambia to buy slaves for Barbados and instructed the captain of another vessel to bring fifteen or twenty blacks to London. There is a suggestion, too, of an early beginning of transatlantic interest in the trade: in 1643 a New England ship transported slaves to Barbados from the Isle of May, presumably bought from Portuguese there. This scattering of evidence is enough for us to reject

[111] Curtin, *Atlantic Slave Trade*, p. 119.

Richard Jobson's claim in 1620 that Englishmen had moral objections to slaving and did not "buy or sell one another or any that had our owne shape."[112] Nevertheless, and despite the early voyages of Hawkins, we can be fairly confident that the slave trade had a low priority in English calculations before about 1640. Until then, England's main concern was with other African products, gold, ivory, dyewood; and was focused more on Upper Guinea (Gambia, Sierra Leone) than on the Gold Coast or the slave markets further east. From about 1630 more interest began to be shown in the Gold Coast; the English had a factory at Winneba in 1632 and began to build their first fort at Cormantin in 1638.[113] Even this does not by itself prove a major interest in slaving; the main business of the Gold Coast was gold.

For most of the first half of the seventeenth century English trade with West Africa was in the hands of privileged companies. The Senegal Adventurers got a ten-year monopoly in 1588, as did the Company of Adventurers of London to "Gynney and Bynney" in 1618. The privileges of the latter were suspended in 1624 during parliamentary agitation against monopolies, but appear to have been reestablished. In 1631 and again in 1651 this company was reorganized and its monopoly renewed. New patentees were brought in on each occasion, but the driving force in English African trade from 1627 to 1660 was supplied by one London merchant, Sir Nicholas Crispe. How profitable the connection was to him is not known for certain; in 1644 he claimed that he had brought gold worth half a million pounds into the country, which suggests considerable profits from the African trade in the preslave era.

The Restoration in 1660 was the turning point. The Cavaliers came back from exile, looking for quick riches and hopeful of beating the Dutch; their interest in Africa did not last long but it gave a boost to the English slave trade. The Company of Royal Adventurers, headed by the Duke of York and including a number of prominent courtiers, was formed in 1660. Though, formally, it was another gold-seeking enterprise, with no mention of slaves in its charter, in fact the company began at once to deal in slaves. Reorganized and rechartered in 1663, with more merchants and

[112] Donnan, *Documents*, I, 122, 126–136; R. Porter, "The Crispe Family and the African Trade in the Seventeenth Century," *Journal of African History*, 9:60–61 (1968); Bernard Bailyn, *The New England Merchants in the Seventeenth Century* (Cambridge, Mass.: Harvard University Press, 1958), p. 84; Richard Jobson, *The Golden Trade* (1623; reprinted Teignmouth, England: E. E. Speight and R. H. Walpole, 1904), p. 112.

[113] Porter, "Crispe Family," pp. 63–64.

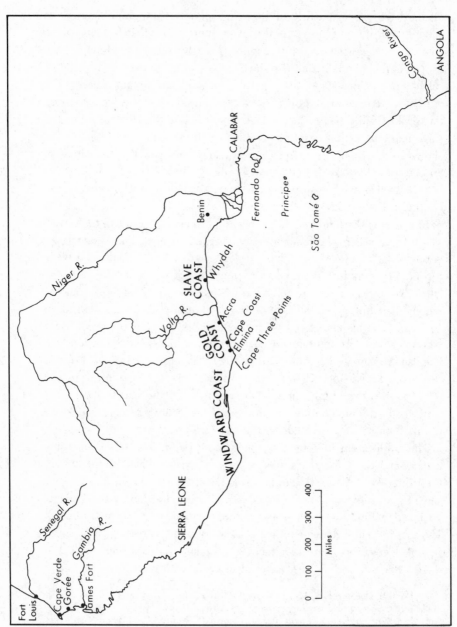

Europeans in West Africa

fewer courtiers and slaving at last made into a declared purpose, it looked to have a fair chance of competing with the Dutch.[114] In the event it failed more comprehensively than most African companies. In Africa its one permanent success was the capture of Cape Coast Castle, originally built by Swedes but later falling into Dutch hands. The English took it in 1664; the next year the company lost all its other possessions to a Dutch fleet under de Ruyter. From this blow there was no recovery. The company adopted the practice of selling licenses to private merchants (often the harbinger of bankruptcy in seventeenth-century corporations) and leased Upper Guinea to a subsidiary for a rent of £1000 a year. In the West Indies it had difficulty in getting the planters to pay for the slaves they had bought: some, delivered in 1665, were still not paid for ten years later. In 1670 liquidation began.

The Royal Adventurers were succeeded by the Royal African Company, chartered in 1672, the strongest and most effective of all European companies formed exclusively for the African trade.[115] With a capital of £110,000 and the probability of being able to raise more by borrowing, with a monopoly against English competitors on the African coast and a monopoly against all comers in the English colonies, and with warm support from Charles II and the Duke of York, the company set about furnishing Jamaica, Barbados, and the Leewards with blacks at controlled prices, and winning a share, not as yet a big one, in the supply of slaves to the Spanish colonies. Until 1689 fair results were achieved, though the colonists were never satisfied with the number of blacks brought to them and kept up nearly continuous sniping at the monopoly. The company paid dividends; its stock stood above par; and between 1680 and 1688 it delivered about 45,000 slaves to the colonies. These achievements were not, however, soundly based. Heavy investment had to be made in building and keeping up forts in West Africa; the company's servants were for the most part of poor quality, embezzling goods, trading with interlopers, and neglecting the corporate interest. In the West Indies debts owed by the planters for slaves bought on credit proved difficult or impossible to collect, and a sharp fall in sugar prices in the 1680s made matters worse. The English Revolution of 1688 brought into question the king's prerogative to grant monopolies in overseas trade. With the expulsion of James II the

---

[114] George F. Zook, "The Company of Royal Adventurers Trading to Africa," *Journal of Negro History*, 4:124–231 (1919).
[115] K. G. Davies, *The Royal African Company* (London: Longmans, 1957).

company lost its powerful friends. Even before this the monopoly, like all others in the African trade, had proved hard to enforce: the coast was too long to be effectively policed. After 1688 interlopers flooded into the trade with no one to stop them. In 1698 they got parliamentary recognition of their position, paying to the company 10 percent of what they exported from England as a contribution to the upkeep of the forts which they were now entitled to use. In 1712 this act expired, the duty ceased, and the last vestige of monopoly disappeared from the English slave trade.

From the planters' point of view, and having regard to the growing importance of tropical products in the European economy, monopoly by 1700 was obsolete. The separate traders to Africa proved it in the first years of the eighteenth century. Between 1672 and 1713 the African Company delivered about 100,000 slaves to the colonies, nearly half of them to Barbados, more than a third to Jamaica, and the rest to the Leewards and Virginia. Deliveries by interlopers before 1698 are not known for certain, but ran into thousands before the Revolution (including some hundreds from Madagascar) and probably many more in the 1690s. After the passing of the act of 1698 the rival systems of joint-stock company and private merchants competed on roughly equal terms, enabling their performances to be compared. The outcome was a defeat for large-scale trading. Between 1698 and 1708 the company delivered about 18,000 slaves to Barbados and Jamaica, their opponents about 75,000.[116] Free trade thus showed itself more efficient than monopoly, and incidentally permitted the ports of Bristol and Liverpool to enter in the eighteenth century what until then had been London's preserve. Yet monopoly had served some purpose in fostering an English slaving tradition and in accumulating the knowledge needed for a trade which more than most demanded skill and experience. At least the English slave companies were more effective than the French, and the English colonists, notwithstanding their complaints, were saved from the "fearful shortage" of labor which afflicted seventeenth-century Martinique and Guadeloupe.[117]

France's entry into the slave trade was slower and more tentative. Curtin, extrapolating from slave populations of the French Caribbean islands, credits them with 28,000 deliveries in the third quarter of the

[116] *Ibid.*, p. 143.
[117] Gaston-Martin, *Histoire de l'esclavage*, p. 24.

seventeenth century and 124,000 in the fourth quarter, but believes that these figures may be a little high. They are certainly not a correct reflection of the achievements of French slave traders; ships to carry such numbers were not sent to Africa during this period. In the later seventeenth century Le Havre and La Rochelle were the leading French ports for the slave trade, with the second growing faster than the first. Nantes did not become a major slaving port until about 1700; St.-Malo and Bordeaux were in the second rank. If France had been deeply engaged in the slave trade, La Rochelle would be the place to find the evidence. Yet between 1671 and 1693 only 45 ships left La Rochelle for Africa, and this total includes vessels intended to buy Guinea products other than slaves.[118] However generous an allowance were to be made for the other Atlantic and Channel ports with a lesser interest than La Rochelle in the slave trade, French participation would still fall far behind that of England, with the Royal African Company dispatching 249 ships from London to Africa between 1680 and 1688. Despite the efforts of Colbert and despite the "depressing procession" of French African companies, France did not become a major slaving power in the seventeenth century.[119] If Curtin's projections of deliveries in the Antilles and St.-Domingue are correct, many of those slaves must have been brought by foreigners, or in French ships from other parts of the Caribbean.

As with the English, French trade in the ivory, gum, and dyewood of Upper Guinea preceded a serious interest in slaving. Richelieu awarded monopolies to a number of private companies in Rouen, Dieppe, St.-Malo, and Paris, but no major corporation was formed until 1664. Lonvilliers de Poincy, who was made governor general of the Antilles in 1638, is said to have had 300 slaves on his plantation in St. Christophe; he probably got them from the Dutch or, less likely, through contracts like one of 1643 between the Compagnie des Îles d'Amérique and the Rouen-Dieppe firm of Rozée & Co.[120] In 1664 the successors of the Norman companies were bought out and the Compagnie des Indes Occidentales given a monopoly of French trade in both America and Africa.

[118] M. Delafosse, "La Rochelle et les îles au XVIIᵉ siècle," Revue d'histoire des colonies, 36:238–281 (1949).

[119] The phrase "morne succession" is Robert Mandrou's in "Français hors de France aux XVIᵉ et XVIIᵉ siècles," Annales-économies-societés-civilisations, October–December 1959, p. 657.

[120] Donnan, Documents, I, 97; Nellis M. Crouse, French Pioneers in the West Indies (New York: Columbia University Press, 1940), pp. 73–74.

On paper such a conjunction probably looked sound enough, but in practice it did not work. In the African trade it was possible to make a case for monopoly, at least until private traders were forthcoming to replace it; in the trade of the Caribbean the case for monopoly was weaker; but for yoking the two together in one giant corporation, there was no case at all. Efficient integration on such a scale, devoid of the personal connections which enabled smaller firms to sustain far-flung trade, was beyond the competence of Colbert's top-heavy creation.

Until 1664 the French Antilles got most of their slaves from the Dutch, who also purchased their tobacco, sugar, and indigo.[121] Colbert's intervention was meant to win both trades for France. Partly through the early efforts of the Compagnie des Indes Occidentales, which were not negligible, but even more by its eventual and resounding failure, which put an end to monopoly in the French Caribbean trade and gave a fillip to private enterprise, Frenchmen by 1670 had largely ousted Dutchmen from the main import-export business of their own colonies; but not from the slave trade. When the company could trade no more and began instead to grant licenses to private enterprise, something of a boom occurred in the French Atlantic economy.[122] But when monopoly in the slave trade was relaxed, as between 1672 and 1675 when the trade of Lower Guinea was opened to all Frenchmen, there was no corresponding growth. Colbert's medicine for getting rid of the Dutch, a monopoly corporation quickly giving way to private French traders, failed conclusively in West Africa. Here, as elsewhere, his policies were susceptible of swift modification in the light of experience; that he should have returned to a regime of companies in the African trade can probably be taken to mean that there was no practicable alternative.

None of the French African companies formed from 1673 to the end of the century succeeded in making money or in stilling the complaints of the *colons* about lack of labor. On the other hand, they contributed to the creation of a French interest in the slave trade. They were necessary because private capital was not yet disposed to enter the business, and they may be seen as in some sense investments for the future, the returns on which came after 1713 in the *ère des négriers*. From time to time, special efforts were put forth: in 1670 for instance when 753 slaves arrived in the Antilles in two ships, and in 1678–79 when eight ships were dis-

---

[121] Mims, *Colbert's West India Policy*, p. 47.
[122] *Ibid.*, p. 236. Delafosse, "La Rochelle et les îles," shows more growth in the 1680s.

patched from France to buy slaves for the plantations.[123] These efforts, so far as the evidence goes, were exceptional. Moreover, the spurt of 1678–79 led (and this is characteristic of undercapitalized seventeenth-century companies) not to profits but to liquidation of the company, "for having overextended its trade."[124] The greater the investment made, the greater the danger of financial collapse.

Besides creating and, after a fashion, sustaining a tradition of French participation in the slave trade (which made the taking of the *asiento* in 1701 at least plausible), the regime of the companies established permanent French settlements in Africa for the first time. The island of Gorée was taken from the Dutch in 1677, Fort Louis was built in the Senegal, and the foundations were laid by André La Brue for France's distant colonial future in Upper Guinea. In 1688 an attempt was made to settle further south, at Assinie, at the eastern end of the Ivory Coast, but neither this nor a later attempt (1698–1703) succeeded. Forced to get more slaves by having accepted the *asiento*, the French built a fort in 1704 at the great slave market of Whydah in Dahomey, but they never established a foothold on the Gold Coast.[125]

Once the development of St.-Domingue got under way, that is, in the last twenty years of the seventeenth century, the French needed as many slaves as the English — perhaps more, because they had a greater area to cultivate. They did not get them immediately, and their sugar trade was correspondingly retarded. The French *asiento* of 1702 must, to begin with, have made things worse for the *colons*: if French traders were taking more slaves from Africa than ever before, they had far greater demands to meet — at least 5000 slaves a year to be delivered to the Spanish colonies for ten years on top of the requirements of their own colonies.[126] Symptomatic of the shortage of slaves in the French colonies is the adoption of vigorous slave raiding as a major part of French Caribbean strategy in the wars of 1689–97 and 1702–13. In 1693, for example, 350 slaves were carried off from Jamaica, and the next year du Casse's fleet visited the same island, landed in Morant Bay, devastated the countryside, and took away 1200 slaves, perhaps the main purpose of the attack. Later, the

---

[123] Ly, *Compagnie du Sénégal*, pp. 153–154.
[124] *Ibid.*, p. 176.
[125] John D. Hargreaves, ed., *France and West Africa* (London: Macmillan, 1969), pp. 55 et seq.; Simone Berbain, *Le comptoir français de Juda (Ouidah) au XVIIIe siècle*, Memoires de l'Institut Français d'Afrique Nord, no. 3 (Paris: L'Institut Français d'Afrique Nord, 1942).
[126] Gaston-Martin, *Histoire de l'esclavage*, p. 30.

Compagnie du Sénégal contracted to supply 1000 slaves to St.-Domingue; these were to be plundered from Cartagena, though the venture failed. D'Iberville in the War of Spanish Succession took up this special branch of the *guerre de corse*: his raids on St. Kitts and Nevis in 1706 yielded 3500 slaves, making him one of the greatest French slave traders up to that time.[127] After the war, supplies from Africa improved. Like the English, the French in practice abandoned company trading in slaves early in the eighteenth century: the *ère des négriers* in both countries was an age of private traders, in hot competition with one another and with rivals of other countries. With the vanishing of the companies went a good deal of the public control of the slave trade exercised in France by Colbert and in England by the Privy Council. Planters at last got what they wanted — at a price. The French made up lost ground and became formidable competitors to the English. It was because of their slower start, the result of an insufficient supply of slaves, that the French Caribbean colonies were still developing rapidly in the early eighteenth century while the English (Jamaica excepted) were leveling off.

The Dutch share in the slave trade until the last quarter of the seventeenth century is, like the English and French, largely a matter of conjecture. Curtin's figures record deliveries in the Americas region by region and period by period, but they give little help in identifying carriers. And this is what the Dutch primarily were. Although the truth of it cannot be demonstrated statistically, they were in all probability runners-up to the Portuguese in the seventeenth-century African slave trade, and at times actually in front. Two of their own possessions, Curaçao and Surinam, became colonies of settlement with slave-worked plantations in the course of the eighteenth century, but this development had not gone far by 1700: Curtin credits these colonies with 40,000 slaves delivered in the seventeenth century, all in the second half.[128] Curaçao, that "cursed little barren island" as a Jamaican called it in 1664, was more important as a trading base and depot for slaves destined for the Spanish colonies than as an agricultural colony, more like Providence Island than like Barbados.[129]

[127] Donnan, *Documents*, I, 103; Ly, *Compagnie du Sénégal*, pp. 33–34; Nellis M. Crouse, *The French Struggle for the West Indies* (New York: Columbia University Press, 1943), pp. 299, 306.

[128] Curtin, *Atlantic Slave Trade*, p. 119. Note the warning on p. 117 that "any conclusion must be tentative until the records of the Dutch West India Company are more fully exploited."

[129] Great Britain, Public Record Office, *Calendar of State Papers*, Colonial Series, America and West Indies, 1661–68 (London: H.M.S.O., 1880), no. 744.

Slaves no more drew the first Dutch to Africa than they did the other northern traders. The attractions were pepper to start with, ivory, gold, and later on cotton cloth from the Benin region for resale to other parts of Africa. The gold trade was of special importance to the Dutch if we are to believe the claim that by 1621 almost the whole of the gold coinage of the United Provinces was minted from Guinea gold.[130] Gold continued to be an important objective throughout the century. Willem Bosman, who worked for the Dutch West India Company on the Gold Coast, thought that about 1700 they were still the masters of that trade.[131] The English African Company provided the royal mint with gold for half a million guineas in the last quarter of the seventeenth century; if Bosman was right the Dutch must have taken more than that.

Regarding slaves, the Dutch had early evinced a distaste for enslavement paralleling that of others who had as yet no plantations in America. In 1596 a hundred slaves, brought to Middelburg (perhaps a privateer's booty), were promptly freed by the rulers of the town, and when Willem Usselinx was promoting a West India Company in 1608 he argued that free white labor was preferable to slaves.[132] No doubt Dutch privateers acquired slaves from captured Portuguese ships in the early seventeenth century, and no doubt they sold them to the Spaniards or back to the Portuguese; but there seems to be little evidence of serious Dutch slaving in Africa before about 1630. Factories were established on the Gold Coast before 1600 and a fort of sorts built about 1612 at Mouri; the island of Gorée was acquired in 1617 (and lost to the French in 1677); and in 1625 an attempt was made to take Elmina, the oldest and strongest European fort in Africa. This assault was the counterpart of the Dutch attack on Brazil in the previous year; both were repulsed, signs that the Portuguese empire was weathering the battering of the northern privateers. Another and more successful campaign to conquer Brazil was begun in 1630, which forced the Dutch to extend their interests in Africa and enter wholeheartedly into the slave trade. Elmina was taken in 1638 and Axim in 1642, but Brazil's requirements could not be met from the Gold Coast alone. Hence the attack in 1641 on the Portuguese city of Luanda which controlled the slave trade of Angola. For a few years the Dutch dominated

---

[130] Charles R. Boxer, *The Dutch Seaborne Empire* (London: Hutchinson, 1965), p. 21.
[131] W. Bosman, *A New and Accurate Description of the Coast of Guinea* (2nd English ed.; London, 1721), p. 77.
[132] Boxer, *Dutch in Brazil*, p. 4.

West Africa and Angola. Even so the number of slaves brought to Brazil during their occupation seems not to have been enormous: 23,163 in the ten years 1636–45 were landed at Pernambuco, with a marked upward swing in the years after the taking of Luanda.[133] A Dutch survey of the economic and fiscal resources of Africa, made in 1644, appears to confirm that the Dutch trade at this date was of fairly modest proportions; 1200 slaves a year were expected from Angola and 2000 from Calabar (Nigeria).[134]

In 1621 Dutch trade in the Atlantic was placed under the monopoly of the West India Company. In Brazil, New Netherland, and the Caribbean, this monopoly was abandoned step by step in the first thirty years of the company's existence; free or freer trade had been conceded almost everywhere well before Colbert chartered his Compagnie des Indes Occidentales on principles which the Dutch themselves had by then recognized as obsolete in the American trade. Only in the Dutch slave trade was company monopoly allowed to continue, even surviving the reorganization of the West India Company in 1674, brought on by bankruptcy. The long life of the West India Company is evidence of the confidence reposed by the Dutch in the privileged company for meeting the special requirements of the African trade.

With Brazil lost — the Dutch were finally expelled in 1654 — the principal customers for Dutch slave traders became the recently established English and French islands and the Spanish colonies. That many, perhaps most, of the slaves landed in Barbados and the Leewards before 1660 were brought by Dutch merchants is likely enough. It is also clear that from 1660, if not before, the English government was set on driving the Dutch out of England's colonial trade including the slave trade, and that in the 1660s and 1670s a large measure of success was achieved. Clandestine deliveries may have continued to the English colonies, but the repeated complaints of the planters that they were deprived of a free trade in slaves argue that such deliveries were comparatively rare. In the French islands the same process of extrusion took place somewhat later and may have been less complete.[135] When war began in 1689, slaves became so scarce in the French colonies that the Dutch may have been

[133] Frédéric Mauro, *Le Portugal et l'Atlantique au XVII*ᵉ *siècle (1570–1670)* (Paris: S.E.V.P.E.N., 1960), p. 178.

[134] Summarized in Boxer, *Dutch in Brazil*, pp. 278–279.

[135] Mims, *Colbert's West India Policy*, p. 300.

able to win back something of what they had lost. In general, however, the Dutch predominance in the furnishing of slaves to the English and French colonies was a brief one, starting not earlier than about 1640 when the cultivation of sugar was introduced and passing its zenith by the decade 1660–70.

Dutch participation in the slave trade of the Spanish colonies lasted longer. Until 1640 the Spaniards, who failed to develop a serious slave trade of their own, depended on contractors (*asentistas*) of their own nation, or Portuguese, who purchased from the crown the right to license the shipping of blacks to the Indies. This privilege was much sought after, particularly in the early eighteenth century, though it is far from clear that big profits were made by those who held it. The *asentista*, in the first place, paid dearly for his privilege, the contract being regarded by the Spanish crown as above all a source of revenue. The trade itself was carefully regulated and controlled by Spanish officials to ensure that the blacks were of the prescribed quality. Contractors were obliged to furnish not slaves but piezas d'India, the correspondence between the two being a matter for negotiation depending on the physical condition of the blacks. Old, young, female, and sick slaves were accepted only at the rate of three for two piezas, two for one, or worse.[136]

When Portugal revolted from Spain in 1640 the current *asiento* lapsed and for two decades there was no official supply of slaves to the Spanish colonies. This gave the Dutch their chance, and there is evidence in published letters and papers from Curaçao between 1657 and 1660 that they took it. Trade was clandestine, connived at by Spanish officials in the colonies because there was no alternative but unacknowledged by the Spanish government in Europe, and feared by Spanish churchmen who apprehended the infection of heresy. Dutch interest was to keep it so. Thus the vice-director of the West India Company at Curaçao wrote to his principals in 1660: "I have witnessed with pleasure your honors' diligence in providing us here from time to time with negroes. That will be the only

[136] On the *asiento*, see Donnan, *Documents*, I, 104–121, and on pp. 342–346 there is a useful contemporary summary of its history. See also Georges Scelle, *Histoire politique de la traite négrière aux Indes de Castille*, 2 vols. (Paris: Librairie de la Societé du Receuil, 1906); and a summary of Scelle's views in "The Slave-Trade in the Spanish Colonies of America: The Assiento," *American Journal of International Law*, 4:614–660 (1910). Also Curtis P. Nettels, "England and the Spanish-American Trade, 1680–1715," *Journal of Modern History*, 3:1–32 (1931).

bait to allure hither the Spanish nation, as well from the Main as from
other parts, to carry on trade of any importance. But the more subtly and
quietly the trade to and on this island can be carried on, the better will it
be for this place and yours . . ."[137] From this unofficial trade the Dutch
probably made money, more perhaps than could have been made from
occupying officially the position of *asentistas*. And the Spanish colonists, it
seems, were better furnished without an *asiento* than with one; certainly
they complained less.[138] Meanwhile the Dutch drew to themselves the
incidental benefits which, more than the slave trade itself, explain the
international competition to win the *asiento*. These were two. First, the
Spanish in America were better endowed with silver currency than other
Caribbean colonies. Shortage of cash was continuous and pervasive in the
Atlantic economy in the seventeenth century, inhibiting domestic business and international trade alike. Winning it from the Spaniards was a
strong argument for entering the slave trade; when privateering in the
Caribbean came to an end this was virtually the only way to get
specie.[139] Secondly, the Dutchmen who sold slaves clandestinely to the
Spanish colonies could hardly be stopped from selling them other goods. It
is true that Spanish colonial needs for manufactures, beyond the capacity
of Spain's industry to satisfy, were to a large extent met by traders of other
countries who sent their goods to America via Seville in the name of a
Spanish merchant.[140] Nevertheless there remained, or was thought to
remain, a big market for northern European manufactures introduced
directly to Spanish America.

In 1662, after twenty years in abeyance, the *asiento* was revived and
given to two Genoese who undertook to deliver 24,000 piezas d'India in
seven years.[141] Neither this nor subsequent contracts of 1671 and 1679
excluded the Dutch. On the contrary, the *asentistas* were authorized to
subcontract and did so, with the English African companies as well as the
Dutch. Antonio Garcia's contract of 1671 was backed by the Amsterdam
firm of Balthazar Coymans, and in 1685 the Spanish crown swallowed its
dislike of dealing directly with the Dutch and sold the contract to

[137] Donnan, *Documents*, I, 151.
[138] Scelle, *Traite négrière*, I, 481, 490.
[139] Nettels, "England and the Spanish-American Trade."
[140] J. O. MacLachlan, *Trade and Peace with Old Spain, 1667–1750* (Cambridge: At the
University Press, 1940).
[141] Donnan, *Documents*, I, 106, n. 158.

Coymans for 200,000 crowns in cash.[142] Between 1662 and 1689 it is probable that most of the slaves delivered to the Spanish colonies came via Curaçao rather than via Barbados and Jamaica, though there were agents of the *asiento* in both those colonies from time to time.

Thanks to a recent investigation in the archives of the Dutch West India Company, a reasonably accurate picture can be formed of the number of slaves the company carried between 1675 and 1734. The estimated total for this whole period is 170,016 (two-thirds from Guinea, one-third from Angola), giving an annual average of 2790.[143] Such an average would make the Dutch very considerable slavers in the 1670s and 1680s but of diminishing account after 1700 when the English separate traders broke through the African Company's monopoly and the *traite negrière* of Nantes and Bordeaux began to flourish in relative freedom. The annual average of slaves shipped by the Dutch in the eighteenth century did not fall (as a matter of fact it rose) but it formed a dwindling proportion of the whole Atlantic slave trade. This was the true nature of the Dutch defeat: they stood still while others raced forward. Partly this stagnation is attributable to the loss of the *asiento* to Portugal in 1694, to France in 1701, and to England in 1713. Weakened by too much fighting and politically enfeebled by the War of Spanish Succession, the Dutch did not have the diplomatic weight to insist on the contract. Partly the Dutch were defeated by the exclusive colonial policies of France and England and by possessing too few colonies of their own. But they were also, to some extent, the authors of their own misfortune by allowing the West India Company to retain its monopoly (until 1734) long after England and France had given up this obsolete form of slave trading.

By the beginning of the eighteenth century there were clear indications that the privileged joint-stock company was no longer the best way to conduct the slave trade; in the next thirty years the countries principally concerned switched to competitive trading by private merchants and firms. Almost without exception, the profit-making record of these companies, English, French, and Dutch, had been bad or nonexistent; and few of them had performed their undertakings to deliver the slaves

---

[142] Violet Barbour, *Capitalism in Amsterdam in the Seventeenth Century* (Baltimore: Johns Hopkins University Press, 1950), p. 110.

[143] Johannes Postma, "The Dimension of the Dutch Slave Trade from Western Africa," *Journal of African History*, 13:241 (1972).

the planters insisted they must have. It has been argued above that companies were persisted in because there was no genuine alternative in the seventeenth century in what was undoubtedly a difficult and risky business, and that the companies served at least to lay the foundations of later growth. Nevertheless the seeming paradox must still be faced: why was so little profit forthcoming from a trade to which so many historians have applied the epithet *lucrative*? "By this triangular system," writes one of them, "three separate profits were taken, all high and all in Europe: the first profit was that of selling consumer goods to the slavers; the second derived from selling slaves to the planters and mineowners of the Americas; while the third (and biggest) was realised on the sale of American and West Indian cargoes in Europe. It was largely on the steady and often stupendous profits of this circuitous enterprise that France and England would ground their commercial supremacy." "Each transaction," claims another, "necessarily resulted in profit. Invariably the law of supply and demand worked to the advantage of the mother country."[144] Why then this record of failure on the part of slaving companies?

One suggested explanation is "the long depression of the seventeenth century" in Europe, signaled by falling prices, a probable slowing down of population growth which had animated the European economy in the sixteenth century, and a shortage of money resulting from the decline of shipments of silver from the Spanish American mines.[145] Some weight should be given to this theory, as we shall presently see; but, first, we need to look closely at the slave trade itself, and particularly at costs and overheads in the seventeenth century. There were, to begin with, the costs of building forts in Africa and of garrisoning them. Every country in the slave trade, including Denmark, Sweden, and Brandenburg, aspired to own forts and keep a permanent interest on the coast. It is true that opponents of privileged companies denied the utility of these forts; true also that the Portuguese, at a price, traded on the Gold Coast through English and Dutch middlemen, just as English and French often traded through Portuguese middlemen in Upper Guinea. The balance of advantage, however, was deemed to be with those countries that had settlements. Spain had no forts, and no African trade. And when the regime of companies was over, English, French, and Dutch all took steps to keep

---

[144] Davidson, *Black Mother*, p. 65; Gaston-Martin, *Nantes au XVIIIe siècle: l'ère des négriers (1714–1774)* (Paris: Alcan, 1931), p. 13.
[145] Mandrou, "Français hors de France," p. 667.

up their African establishments. These and the men in them cost money: perhaps £ 20,000 a year in the case of the Royal African Company at its height, one-half or two-thirds of which might be attributable as an over-head to the slave trade (the rest to the trade in gold, etc.), so adding at least £ 2–£ 3 to the cost of every slave sold in the West Indies.[146]

Then there were freight costs. Too much has been said of slaves bought for a handful of beads and sold for fancy prices on the other side of the Atlantic. Transport was expensive. Le Maire, after trading in the Senegal in 1682, observed that a good slave could be bought for four or five jars of *eau-de-vie* but "the cost is not so much in the purchase price as in trans-portation, because of the high charge for freight," an opinion fully confirmed by English evidence.[147] Till 1689 the English assumed, a little optimistically, that slaves cost £ 3 each in Africa, that is to say, were bought with trade goods for which £ 3 had been paid in England. Freight charges, covering the ship's voyage from London to the West Indies, were calculated at the rate of so much a head for slaves delivered alive in the plantations, an arrangement intended to provide captains with an incentive to look after their cargoes but in practice inducing them to cram into their ships more than could be safely accommodated. The rate for Barbados was £ 5 a head, a little more for Jamaica, a little less for the Leeward Islands. In war these could be doubled.[148]

Next came losses by the death of slaves in the Middle Passage, the nastiest part of a deplorable trade but also (and indignation must not cause this to be overlooked) bad business. Examples of appalling mortality rates are easily found: 110 dead out of 195 on the Dutch *St. Jan* from Calabar in 1659, 199 dead out of 267 on the English *Francis*, also from Calabar, in 1685. If these had been typical of the trade as a whole, however, there would have been no trade. Each voyage was unique, mortality varying according to the master's skill in rejecting sick slaves, the extent of over-crowding aboard ship, and the length of the voyage. The average in the seventeenth century is unlikely to have been less than one dead in four or one in five; on the African Company's ships between 1680 and 1688 it was 23½ percent. French losses for the Nantes trade between 1715 and 1775 were about the same.[149] Regarded as a comment upon European morality

[146] Davies, *Royal African Company*, p. 259.
[147] Donnan, *Documents*, I, 281.
[148] Davies, *Royal African Company*, pp. 198–199.
[149] *Ibid.*, p. 292; Donnan, *Documents*, I, 141–149; Gaston-Martin, *Nantes au XVIII siècle*, pp. 114–115.

these figures are shaming; regarded as overheads they add about 15s. per head to the cost of each slave who survived the experience.

We can now summarize the economics of the slave trade as it was conducted about 1680. Slaves, for sale in Barbados, cost, not "a handful of beads," but £ 3 (price in Africa) plus £ 5 (freight) plus £ 2 (share of cost of African establishment) plus 15s. (share of cost of mortality) — total, nearly £ 11. The price at which the African Company undertook to sell blacks in Barbados was £ 15 a head; if more was charged (until 1689) there were enraged complaints to the English government by the colonists. The average prices actually paid at Barbados between 1678 and 1688 were below £ 15.[150] Even so there remained a margin of profit of more than 30 percent and this ought to have been enough to enable a company to survive and go on trading; and so it would have been but for two facts, overlooked by the exponents of excess profits in the seventeenth-century slave trade but which more than any others explain the failure of the companies. The first is the reluctance or inability of West Indian and other planters to pay for all the slaves they bought, an international, almost a universal, phenomenon. We meet it in Brazil where by 1644 the planters' debts for slaves had risen to a point where the Dutch West India Company refused to sell any more except for ready money.[151] We meet it in the French Antilles where it was held to be "a fact well known" that the islands could afford only 1200 slaves a year and that more could be paid for only with the help of long credit.[152] And we meet it in the English Caribbean colonies, where the debt owing to the Royal African Company was estimated at £ 120,000 in 1680 and £ 170,000 in 1690, both sums in excess of the corporation's total share capital.[153] So much was credit part of the life of a sugar colony, where a plantation brought in nothing until the crop was sold, where debt laws were hostile to the interests of creditors, and where ready money was nearly always scarce, that very little could be done to reduce these planters' debts. They were one more overhead cost in the slave trade.

Planters, generally optimistic to the point of euphoria, overestimated their capacity to increase profits sufficiently to pay for the slaves they bought. Here, a second fact must be introduced, the crisis of overproduc-

---

[150] Davies, *Royal African Company*, p. 304.
[151] Boxer, *Dutch in Brazil*, p. 139.
[152] Ly, *Compagnie du Sénégal*, pp. 185, 190; Donnan, *Documents*, I, 101.
[153] Davies, *Royal African Company*, pp. 318–319.

tion that beset the Caribbean colonies (and Brazil) between 1670 and 1690, bringing prices of sugar in Europe close to, and at times even below, the cost of growing, transporting, and paying duty on the product. This crisis will be further discussed;[154] here it will be enough to note that in the 1680s when things were worst the third of the legendary profits earned by participants in the triangular slave trade — on Caribbean products shipped to Europe — was either very small or nonexistent. Hence the preference of slave dealers to be paid by planters not in sugar but in bills of exchange drawn in the West Indies and payable in Europe which, despite risks of their own, were a better form of remittance than sugar. Thus the regime of companies in the slave trade, at its height in the 1680s, coincided with a crisis that had nothing directly to do with inefficient company organization or the conditions of trade in Africa but a great deal to do with American supply of sugar temporarily outpacing European demand. By 1713, following a confused period of high sugar prices in Europe, offset by losses at sea, inflated freight charges, earthquake, hurricane, and war damage, the worst was over. Vicissitudes continued in the sugar trade, but it is doubtful if the private traders of the *ère des négriers* ever faced prices as low as those ruling in the years of company management. If falling prices of American products in the 1670s and 1680s are to be seen as a facet of "the long depression" in Europe, and not simply the result of overproduction, then it follows that that theory has some relevance to the failure of companies to take their chance in the slave trade.

Migrants

So far, we have considered only the founding and peopling of colonies from Europe and Africa; this was not the only way in which new colonies came into being or acquired inhabitants. Colonial people in general were much more mobile than those who stayed in Europe. There were exceptions: Dedham's seemingly immobile population over seventy years has already been mentioned, and there may have been other virtually closed communities among the early townships of Massachusetts. On the other hand, even in New England, there was a good deal of movement outwards from settled regions toward the frontier; and in the southern and Caribbean colonies, where the sense of community was weaker, reemi-

---

[154] See below, pp. 188–189.

gration was common. Indentured servants in particular were disposed to move on. Young, unmarried, and poor, they had on first engagement pulled up their roots in Europe; the conditions of service they met in the colonies were scarcely such as to encourage the formation of new ones. Free after three, four, or five years of servitude, they were ready for anything: for buccaneering in the Caribbean, for the life of a *coureur de bois* in Canada, for enlistment in an expeditionary force, for the founding of a new colony, or simply for drifting around the western shores of the Atlantic in search of a living.

New England's specialty in the seventeenth century was migration toward the frontier: despite Cromwell's encouragement to go somewhere useful like Ireland or the West Indies, many moved but few went far. The frontier, to begin with, offered better land than the sites chosen for first settlement: from 1634 there were good economic reasons for migration to the Connecticut Valley. What distinguished pioneering in New England, however, was that it was God's work too, a means of extending Israel's borders, of founding new churches, and of guaranteeing survival in a world that, in default of strong evidence to the contrary, had to be reckoned both corrupt and hostile. New England's imperialism was of a rare kind and by no means coherent or perfectly directed, but it was imperialism nonetheless.

The Puritan frontiersman was not, or was not intended to be, a solitary pioneer carving a farm from the wilderness. Efforts were made, by the government of Massachusetts in particular, to restrain the initiative of individuals and to make the township, with a working minimum of twenty families and a minister, into the unit of new settlement.[155] This precaution was sensible in view of the need for defense against Indians, but would probably have been imposed anyway: the nucleated community, with members keeping an eye on one another, was the Puritan town-planting style, not the isolated homestead. One of many tokens of the relaxation of Puritan ideals in the later seventeenth century is the appearance of straggling townships along the banks of the Connecticut River, farms stretching back from narrow river frontages, much as they did on the St. Lawrence, and much as they did, substituting sea for river frontages, in the British and French West Indies. In this respect new New England became a little more like other colonies.

[155] William Haller, Jr., *The Puritan Frontier: Town-Planting in New England Colonial Development, 1630–1660* (New York: Columbia University Press, 1951).

Good land and the prospect of enlarging the area of Puritan dominance are important explanations of the movement toward the frontier with its attendant dangers and hardships, and of the generally favorable attitude toward this migration taken by New England governments. They were not, however, the immediate causes of the most spectacular Puritan treks. These originated in the interior conflicts which, in New as in Old England, were the stuff of Puritanism and which so often made Puritan achievement more bitter than Puritan striving. About New England's first major expansion — Connecticut, projected in 1634, settlement begun in 1635 — there has been some argument. No less an authority than Charles M. Andrews found that "no question of religious freedom was involved and there was no intention of establishing a religious colony in any way different from that of Massachusetts."[156] Certainly there were economic reasons for seeking new land in Connecticut and some hope of the river turning out to be an entry to the fur trade. On the other hand, William Haller, Jr., a close student of the Puritan frontier, has seen in the founding of Connecticut "another example of the town-planting tendency ensuing from theological differences."[157] Perhaps these differences were more of a personal or political than a strictly theological nature: Thomas Hooker and John Haynes, leaders of the removal to Connecticut, wanted their own show. Governor Winthrop was as enthusiastic as anyone to extend New England's frontiers, but his preference was undoubtedly for unity under Massachusetts. That Connecticut became a separate government, with eventually a charter of its own, and that relations between "River" and "Bay" were often strained, can be explained without calling on doctrinal discord.

About the dramatic events leading to the foundation of the "colonies" of Providence (1635–36) and Portsmouth (1638), there is no room for doubt. They were religious conflicts of exactly the kind that conservatives in Europe had predicted would follow the casting down of traditional ecclesiastical sanctions, and they generated in Rhode Island the oddest, most un-European of all colonies, scarcely a colony at all, since from the grant of its charter in 1663 to the War of Independence it had no royal governor or council, virtually no royal scrutiny of its laws, hardly any correspondence with Whitehall, and only selective observance of British trade regulations. Its position was comparable perhaps to that of

---

[156] Andrews, *Colonial Period*, I, 82.
[157] Haller, *Puritan Frontier*, p. 80.

the Isle of Man before its annexation to the crown in 1763 but to that of no other British overseas possession. All this began with Roger Williams, a well-connected Cambridge graduate who arrived in America in 1631 and was put in charge of Salem Church in 1634, an excellent station from which to quarrel with the government of Massachusetts as publicly as possible.[158] Essentially, Williams's stand was over church government: he rejected an established colonial church as emphatically as he had already rejected the established Church of England, and asserted the right or rather necessity of congregational independence. There were other grounds of difference. Williams even questioned the validity of the Massachusetts Bay Company's charter. But above all he was a congregational separatist, and the colony's rulers reacted to him in the way men do who have pulled off any very difficult and (to them) desirable change and then see their achievement threatened by the outrageous claim that, after all, nothing has been altered. In 1635 Williams was banished. For a time he wandered among Indians, then formed the community of Providence, drawing to it other refugees and wanderers. Emphatically this was not a colony founded by a colony, but a settlement of exiles and dropouts who entered a plantation covenant to walk in the same way. They had no royal charter, no authorizing act from a parent colony, no proprietorial sponsor, and no mercantile backing. They were squatters, and their town, laid out on a two-mile stretch of the Great Salt River, was as different "from the lay-out of a Massachusetts town as the shapelessness of the Rhode Island religious organization differed from the orderliness of the Massachusetts system."[159] Not surprisingly Providence was poor and grew slowly; the surprise is that it survived.

Help (of a kind) was, however, on the way. The expulsion of Williams did not put all to rights in Massachusetts. One year later, the pretentiously named "Antinomian" crisis overtook the colony, producing a new quota of refugees and exiles. "Antinomianism" was another challenge to conservative authority, a rejection of the laws of Massachusetts which in religious matters placed, so their critics said, too much weight on formal observance and too little on inward conviction. At the heart of the storm was Mrs. Anne Hutchinson, a free-speaking and resourceful woman who had come to the colony in 1634. Like Williams, she took theological

[158] Perry Miller, *Roger Williams* (New York: Bobbs-Merrill, 1953).
[159] Andrews, *Colonial Period*, II, 6.

precepts and scriptural injunctions to their literal and logical conclusion, an uncomfortable stance in a community which above everything else wanted to survive. As much a New England Jansenist as a New England Ranter, she was a luxury Massachusetts could not afford. Sustained for a while by Governor Vane (1636–37), she was brought to trial soon after he was voted out of office, and sentenced to banishment. With other "Antinomians" she withdrew first to Providence, then to a new town, Portsmouth. Here, to remind us that in the search for purity whether in religion or politics there is no ending of refinement, the exiles quickly disagreed among themselves. One group stayed at Portsmouth, another founded Newport. Mrs. Hutchinson herself did neither, moving on to Long Island, then into New Netherland where she and her adherents were massacred by Indians. Her achievement, and Williams's, was not merely the forming of new communities which in time drew together (not too closely) to make the confederation of Rhode Island and even to gain the respectability of a royal charter, but the breaking up of a pattern of religious conformity which just possibly might have been New England's fate. Among later beneficiaries were Quakers. Some of the effect of persecuting them in Boston, even to the point of hanging four, was taken away by the presence of this dotty republic at the side door of Massachusetts.

Another Puritan colony which owed its existence to early dissensions in Massachusetts was New Haven on Long Island Sound.[160] Here the first settlers came directly from Europe, an instance of a whole congregation of like-minded Puritans moving under their minister. Led by John Davenport, some 250 of them arrived in Massachusetts in the summer of 1637, planning to stay there. They did not like what they saw. Davenport was in any case a Congregationalist who had crossed swords with Presbyterians before leaving home; like Williams, he found Massachusetts too far to go for too little. The group moved to Quinnipiac and there, by plantation covenant, formed New Haven with no more legal warranty than that conferred by Indian land titles. Recruiting from Massachusetts and Connecticut as well as from England, New Haven in its turn planted new townships, Southold on Long Island and Milford. Guilford was founded in 1639 on the New Haven plan by settlers from England. And here, too, there was town planting which proceeded from religious conflict. In 1644

[160] Isabel M. Calder, *The New Haven Colony* (New Haven, Conn.:Yale University Press, 1934).

Rev. Richard Dainton (well has it been said "every minister was the potential founder of a plantation")[161] withdrew his following, not only from New Haven but from the empire of England, founding Hempstead on Long Island within the jurisdiction of New Netherland.

After 1660, though New Haven founded Newark and contributed largely to the peopling of New Jersey, the fissiparous tendencies of Puritanism were less evident. The great age of the minister-founder passed, and with it migration for religion's sake. The last English colony to be founded in the seventeenth century, Pennsylvania, was of a different order. True, American Quakers had been subjected to disabilities, finding refuge in Rhode Island, later in New Jersey where the proprietorship fell largely into Quaker hands.[162] A new Quaker colony was sure to draw some such people together. But Penn's first concern was to recruit in the British Isles (New Wales was his own choice for the colony's name),[163] in Holland, and in Germany. His was a colony formed on initiative taken in Europe and peopled to a great extent by Europeans, a second Massachusetts in this respect more than a second Rhode Island.

Intercolonial migration in the Caribbean and between the Caribbean and the southern mainland had little to do with religion. There was a French Huguenot colony of brief duration on Tortuga where liberty of conscience was guaranteed; and Barbados received some Royalist (presumably Anglican or Presbyterian) refugees from the English Civil Wars. These were exceptions; in general, all movement to and within this region was economic in motivation, and there was a good deal of it.

France's first colony in the Antilles (1627) was on an island shared with the English. St. Kitts is small (sixty-eight square miles) and mountainous, so that the amount of land in the French quarter fit for planting was small and soon taken up. Later arrivals had to move on, St. Christophe becoming a springboard for the planting of new French colonies. In 1635 two new islands, Martinique and Guadeloupe, were settled, the first from St. Christophe, the second directly from France. Du Tertre contrasted the two styles, much to the advantage of the former.[164] Martinique was colonized by d'Esnambuc with 100 or 150 seasoned men "used to the air and to the hard work of the country"; Guadeloupe by 500 green engagés from

[161] *Ibid.*, p. 78.
[162] Craven, *New Jersey and English Colonization of North America*, chapter 3.
[163] Peare, *William Penn*, p. 215.
[164] [J.-B.] du Tertre, *Histoire générale des Antilles*, 4 vols. in 3 (Paris, 1667), I, 99–101.

Dieppe, financed by men who "having put up five sous in the hope of a profit of twenty by the end of the year" would give up if things did not at once go well. Guadeloupe's "starving time" lasted five years, but both colonies survived to become in time parents of new settlements. From St. Christophe colonies were planted on St. Martin, St. Bartholomew, and St. Croix; from Guadeloupe on Marie-Galante; from Martinique on Grenada and St. Lucia. Much of this activity occurred after Richelieu had spent his enthusiasm for colonies and before Colbert appeared on the scene. The contrast between the vitality of the French West Indies in the mid-seventeenth century and the apathy of the metropolitan government should not be lost on those who see France's early colonization as all head and no members.

Further west, close to the Spanish shipping lanes, the buccaneering settlement on Tortuga was peopled partly from St. Christophe, and later the founding and early development of St.-Domingue owed much to already established French colonies. The "real founder" of the western quarter of St.-Domingue was not Dieppe or Le Havre or La Rochelle but d'Ogeron, the governor (1665–75), who spent 40,000 livres of his own money turning buccaneers into colonists, and died poor.[165] In this way, most of the risk and some of the cost of founding a new colony were removed from the merchants and financiers of the French Atlantic ports, who came onto the St.-Domingue scene only when there was something worth selling.

Among the English colonies, Barbados performed the function of way station undertaken by St. Christophe, but on a far greater scale. Here, again, we return to the uniqueness of that small island with its dense and swiftly acquired white population, made increasingly redundant from soon after 1640 by the introduction of slave labor. Between 1650 and 1680, Barbados may have supplied to buccaneering, to expeditionary forces out from England, and to other colonies as many as 20,000 men — one authority says "nearly 30,000" — far more, certainly, than any other colony, English or French, in the seventeenth century.[166] For the Penn-Venables expedition against Jamaica, Barbados found 3000–4000,

[165] Richard Pares, *Merchants and Planters, Economic History Review* Supplement no. 4 (Cambridge: Economic History Society, 1959), p. 4.

[166] Alfred D. Chandler, "The Expansion of Barbados," *Journal of the Barbados Museum and Historical Society*, 13:106–134 (1946), from which all figures in this paragraph have been taken.

some of the survivors becoming the first settlers of that colony; 2000 more Barbadians are stated to have joined them in the early 1660s, including 1000 who migrated in 1664 with Sir Thomas Modyford, the first planter-governor of Barbados, now made governor of Jamaica. Another 2500 went to Jamaica in the late 1660s and 1670s. These are contemporary estimates; if they are roughly accurate, a large part of the population of early Jamaica must have come from Barbados, with smaller contingents from the Lee-wards and relatively few from England.

Nor was Jamaica the only destination of emigrants from Barbados. In the 1650s and 1660s, men went to Surinam, Trinidad, Tobago, St. Lucia, New England, New York (the Morrises, founders of Morrisania), the Dutch and French islands, and Carolina. Not all these endeavors were fruitful: the attempt on Tobago failed, the colonization of St. Lucia was blocked by Caribs, many Barbadians perished in Willoughby's expedition in 1666 to reconquer St. Kitts from the French, and Surinam was lost to the Dutch by the Treaty of Breda in 1667, most of the English there moving on to Jamaica. But with indentured servants still arriving in Barbados at the rate of some 500 a year, there were still men to spare. Hence the plan of the proprietors of Carolina, who received their first charter from Charles II in 1663, to draw Barbados into their scheme and make it a source of both men and capital for the new colony. The hope was that not merely servants but masters could be recruited, complete working units with provisions, tools, and seed. Ashley, one of the proprietors, wrote: "we find by deare experience that noe other are able to make a Plantation but such as are in a condition to stock and furnish themselves."[167] A group of 200 Barbadian adventurers was formed in 1663, with whom the proprietors in London made an agreement on the footing that each adventurer should, for every 1000 pounds of sugar subscribed, receive 500 acres of land whereon there was to be planted "an able man Armed with a good Firelocke boare twelve Bullets to the pound Tenn pounds of powder and twenty pounds of Bullets with six Monthes provision within one yeare";[168] each servant transported earned the master another 150 acres. It was the Barbadian group that reconnoitered sites for settlement and sent the first colonists to Carolina in 1665. Indeed most of what action there was appears to have been initiated in Barbados until 1669 when the

[167] Ibid., p. 129.
[168] Colonial Records of North Carolina, I, 77.

proprietors stirred themselves to send out settlers from England. More Barbadians went to Carolina in 1670–71, including masters and a few slaves; nearly half the early settlers on Ashley River came from the Caribbean.[169]

Intercolonial migration did not proceed on strictly national lines: Martinique's population included a few Dutch, English, Scots, Flemings, Portuguese, and eleven families of Jews. The Jews were expelled in 1683, but this seems to have been a rare instance of exclusiveness.[170] Most Caribbean colonies kept the door open to foreigners whatever the policy of the mother country might be, a tradition originating in the need of northern Europeans to stand together against Spain and the Caribs. Hence the arrangements for joint French-English occupation of St. Christophe/St. Kitts and joint French-Dutch occupation of St. Martin/St. Maarten. A few aliens came out as indentured servants, fifty-three to French colonies via La Rochelle;[171] and there were oddities like Heinrich von Uchteritz, captured by Cromwell's Ironsides at the battle of Worcester and shipped to Barbados where he was redeemed by Holsteiner merchants.[172] But most foreigners domiciled in the West Indies arrived from other colonies, forced out of their first homes by war or moving to better themselves. There were plenty of them if the cynical comment of an early eighteenth-century immigrant to Barbados is to be believed: "In short the first Setlers of this nation were a Babel of all Nations and Conditions of men English, Welch, Scotch, Irish, Dutch, Deans and French. The English they brought with them drunkness & swearing the Scotch Impudence & falsehood, The Welch Covetuousness & Revenge, The Irish Cruelty & perjury the Dutch & Deans Craft & Rusticity & the French Dissimulation & Infidelity and here they have Intermarr'd & blended together."[173] Of the emigrants from Barbados in the 1650s, 1300 are said to have gone to French and Dutch islands.[174] The reconquest of Brazil by the Portuguese caused something of a Dutch diaspora: some

[169] David D. Wallace, *South Carolina: A Short History* (Chapel Hill: University of North Carolina Press, 1951), p. 30.

[170] May, *Histoire économique de la Martinique*, p. 53.

[171] Debien, "Engagés pour les Antilles," p. 90.

[172] A. Gunkel and J. S. Handler, "A German Indentured Servant in Barbados in 1652," *Journal of the Barbados Museum and Historical Society*, 33:91–100 (1970).

[173] "T. Walduck's Letters from Barbados, 1710," *Journal of the Barbados Museum and Historical Society*, 15:50 (1947–48).

[174] Chandler, "Expansion of Barbados," p. 114.

went to other Dutch colonies, but 300 (including slaves) settled in Martinique in 1654 and 900 in Guadeloupe.[175] When Caribbean islands changed hands in the Anglo-French-Dutch wars of the later seventeenth century, there was more blending and shifting of population. Thus in 1666, when the French took St. Kitts, Antigua, and Montserrat, Englishmen and Irishmen were allowed to stay on condition of taking an oath of allegiance to Louis XIV; 500 Irishmen did.[176] Perhaps a less liberal attitude toward foreigners was taken by the end of the century: when the English conquered St. Christophe in 1690 many of the French were transported to St.-Domingue. The English West Indies, if anything, were moving in an opposite direction from the mainland colonies. In North America, the initial settlement was mainly on national lines, changing through the conquest and absorption of the Dutch, the reception of French Huguenots, and the German immigration of the eighteenth century into a population of multinational origins, some parts of which retained their distinctiveness; whereas in Barbados, diverse origins seem to have melted into the Englishness which many visitors to that island have noticed.

[175] Du Tertre, *Histoire générale des Antilles*, I, 460–465.
[176] Crouse, *French Struggle for the West Indies*, p. 60.

CHAPTER 4

PRODUCTS

Heading the list of products drawn by Europe from America in the sixteenth and seventeenth centuries must come silver and gold: silver from Spanish Mexico and Peru, gold from Portuguese Brazil, permeating and deeply affecting the European economy as well as making possible Europe's trade with the East. Except as the stuff of dreams of early colonists and the target of privateers American bullion does not, however, concern us; the northern Europeans found none. They, French, English, and Dutch, have been charged with exploiting people and places more efficiently and ruthlessly and in a more sordid style than the supposedly easygoing Iberians. Certainly they were more interested in American fish, furs, and crops than the Spaniards. They had to be; they had no income from bullion.

Viewed from Europe, the products of America can be put into three categories: those replacing or supplementing commodities already known; those which, originating in Asia and still produced there, were successfully transferred to and acclimatized in America; and those, indigenous and peculiar to America, not known to Europe until the Discoveries. The acquisition of products in the first category was, naturally, of greatest concern in early propaganda for colonization. In the *Discourse of Western Planting* (1584) Richard Hakluyt expressed the hope that "this westerne voyadge will yelde unto us all the commodities of Europe, Affrica and Asia, as farr as wee were wonte to travell, and supplye the wantes of all our decayed trades."[1] America, in other words, was to be an alternative to Europe both as market and as source of supply. Some Asiatic specialties, pepper, cloves, cinnamon, were included in Hakluyt's vision for good measure, but it was on substitutes for the products of the Baltic and Mediterranean, fish, furs, pitch, tar, potash, fruit, wine, silk, oil, and corn, that his attention was mainly fixed. To support the case for Western planting he dwelt at length on the lamentable state into which England's trading connections with Europe had fallen and showed how dependent what was left was on the whims of foreign rulers. England in America could, indeed must, build a new trading area as varied as the old and much more stable.

America's returns to Europe in this category were something of a disappointment. Out of Hakluyt's long shopping list only furs and fish came up to expectations in the first hundred and fifty years. Timber and its by-products were there for the taking but, because of high transport costs and want of skill, failed to replace Baltic supplies to any great extent. Also because of transport costs, American grain was too dear for Europe in the seventeenth and most of the eighteenth centuries. The grain deficiencies of southern and western Europe continued to be met, insofar as they were met at all, by Poland and the north German plain. Timber and corn were the principal products of the Baltic countries; those of the Mediterranean proved even more difficult to replace by American substitutes. No American dried fruit industry arose to displace Levantine currants and plums. American wine did not oust French and Spanish in America, let alone in Europe. American olive oil and American silk disappointed their many advocates by failing to appear in measurable amounts.

Few of these failures were for want of trying; some were for want of skill. Silk is a case in point. From Hakluyt ("silkewormes in marvelous nomber, a greate deale fairer and better than be our silkewormes")[2] to the end of the colonial period, Europeans entertained high hopes of an American silk industry which so often seemed on the verge of fulfillment, only to be cast down by a quirk in the climate or some technical flaw in the making. An act of Virginia in 1662 required landowners to plant ten mulberry trees for every 100 acres, and in 1668 King Charles II had a suit

[1] E. G. R. Taylor, ed., *The Original Writings and Correspondence of the Two Richard Hakluyts*, Hakluyt Society Publications, 2nd series, vol. 77 (London: Hakluyt Society, 1935), p. 222.
[2] *Ibid.*, p. 223.

made up of Virginian silk.[3] Mulberries were commended by Colbert and taken to Martinique in 1683, in 1700, and in 1716–17.[4] Much was expected from the specialized knowledge brought to the English colonies by Huguenots; little transpired.[5] The Georgia Society sent an Italian family of silk winders to Georgia in the 1730s to teach and practice their art; they did not succeed.[6] One of the few things Benjamin Franklin could find to say in favor of the Earl of Hillsborough as secretary of state for the American Department was that he was well disposed to the struggling silk industry of the southern colonies, obtaining a tiny public subsidy for it in 1771.[7] Two centuries had passed, and in this particular Hakluyt's prediction was scarcely closer to realization than when he made it.

Better results were got from acclimatized Asiatic crops though Hakluyt, looking for pepper, cloves, and cinnamon, picked losers. Grenada, one of the world's biggest producers of spices today, did not begin to grow nutmegs until the 1880s. Of the Asiatic crops which succeeded in early colonial times, sugar, grown in southern Europe and the eastern Atlantic islands before the Discoveries, was easily the most important transference. Indigo, coffee, rice, and cotton are further examples: none made much mark in the New World before 1700 but all were to become crops of first importance in the course of the next century. All continued to be grown in Asia, so that the prosperity of America within the Tropics and about 10 degrees outside was at Asia's expense once these things became marketable in Europe.[8]

America before the Discoveries was rich in products, particularly foodstuffs, unknown in Europe: maize, cassava, potatoes, artichokes, French beans, pineapples, cocoa, tobacco. None, except tobacco, found an important market in Europe in the seventeenth century. Nearly all proved

[3] Lewis C. Gray, *History of Agriculture in the Southern United States to 1860*, 2 vols. (Washington, D.C.: Carnegie Institution, 1933), I, 184–188. For Charles's suit, see Great Britain, Public Record Office, *Calendar of State Papers*, Colonial Series, America and West Indies, 1661–68 (London: H.M.S.O., 1880), no. 1878.

[4] Louis-Philippe May, *Histoire économique de la Martinique* (Paris: Rivière, 1930), p. 105.

[5] Gray, *Agriculture in Southern United States*, I, 184–188.

[6] Great Britain, Public Record Office, *Calendar of State Papers*, Colonial Series, America and West Indies, 1738 (London: H.M.S.O., 1969), p. 14.

[7] Public Record Office, London, C.O. 5/118, fo. 36d, Franklin to Thomas Cushing, January 13, 1772.

[8] There is a valuable discussion of Atlantic and Asiatic sugar in Europe in the seventeenth century in Kristof Glamann, *Dutch-Asiatic Trade 1620–1740* (The Hague: Nijhoff, 1958), pp. 157–167.

easily transferable to other parts of the world, maize and cassava to Africa, maize, potatoes, artichokes, beans, and pineapples to Europe.[9] From these transfers the colonists got little benefit. Even tobacco was being grown competitively in parts of Europe long before 1700, to the considerable detriment of colonial interests. Cocoa was not transferred to other continents until much later; it came nearest, especially after 1700, to being a uniquely American product for which a significant European demand emerged during the colonial period.

From these preliminary observations, the besetting economic problem of the colonial period emerges as one of costs, above all costs of labor and transportation. Almost everything Europe took from America in the seventeenth century was produced elsewhere in the world. To thrive, the colonists had to catch better or cheaper fish than the Dutch in the Baltic or North Sea, to trap or persuade the Indians to trap better or cheaper furs than the Russians, to grow better or cheaper sugar than the Javanese or Bengalis. Tobacco, briefly, was the exception. In 1600, when Englishmen, Normans, and Bretons first began to contemplate colonization, tobacco was still a uniquely American product; it was not grown in Europe to a significant extent much before 1650. This gave the first settlers a short period of grace, which was to be of critical importance in the history of the Caribbean, Virginia, and Maryland. It is therefore with tobacco that a survey of colonial products should begin.

Tobacco

In the infancy of the English and French settlements in the New World tobacco was the ruling colonial product. In the Caribbean islands as well as in Virginia and Maryland, bargains were struck, rents, wages, and taxes paid in it. In Bermuda in 1621 brides were sold for 100 pounds of tobacco apiece.[10] In Europe tobacco was the first American product to furnish important income to the governments of England and France, and one of the first to affect the lives and budgets of the common people. Compared to the slow penetration of potatoes into the European diet, the rise of

---

[9] Crop dispersal is discussed by G. B. Masefield in chapter 5 of E. E. Rich and C. H. Wilson, eds., *Cambridge Economic History of Europe*, vol. IV (Cambridge: At the University Press, 1967), and by Carl O. Sauer, *Agricultural Origins and Dispersals* (Cambridge, Mass.: M.I.T. Press, 1969).

[10] Wesley Frank Craven, "An Introduction to the History of Bermuda," *William and Mary Quarterly*, 2nd series, 17:449 (1937).

tobacco from the position of an exotic weed of supposed therapeutic virtue ("good for diseases of the chest and wasting of the lungs," was the opinion of one well-informed writer in 1571) to the status of poor man's luxury was truly remarkable. Observed and reported by the first Spaniards in America and by Cartier on the St. Lawrence in 1534, it made hardly any impact on Europe until about 1550 when claims for its health-giving properties began to be put forward.[11] While these were still in contention, smoking established itself as a fashionable social habit among the rich. In the later sixteenth century northern Europe received tobacco as part of the proceeds of privateering, but quantities were small and prices high, from 12s. to 90s. a pound in England in the 1590s.[12] When privateering ended, it is perhaps surprising that the northern Europeans showed no immediate interest in getting supplies for themselves. Among many objectives put forward in early English colonizing propaganda tobacco does not appear, possibly for fear of offending King James whose views on the subject had been made public in 1604. Once settlers were in Virginia, however, tobacco's possibilities were seen and, but for the colony's preoccupation with food gathering, would probably have been realized several years before John Rolfe's experiments in 1612.[13] A "tobacco rush" followed, somewhat restrained by Governor Dale's sensible ruling in 1616 that each planter must sow two acres of corn for himself and two more for each of his servants as a condition of growing tobacco.[14] Despite this decree, despite the misfortunes of the colony in 1622–23, and despite pressure from London to diversify the economy, tobacco carried all before it. Exports from Virginia to England rose from 60,000 pounds in 1619 to ½ million pounds in 1628 and to 1⅓ million pounds ten years later. By then, Bermuda, St. Kitts, Barbados, French St. Christophe, Nevis, Antigua, Maryland, Martinique, and Guadeloupe were also growing tobacco and growers everywhere had been introduced to the consequences of, but not the remedies for, overproduction.

After 1660 the West Indies began to drop out of contention, but the quantity of tobacco reaching Europe from the Americas continued to rise.

[11] Quoted in Charles M. MacInnes, *The Early English Tobacco Trade* (London: Kegan Paul, 1926), p. 16. Therapeutic properties continued to be claimed in eighteenth century, e.g., defense against plague, urged by William Byrd II in 1721; see Joseph C. Robert, *The Story of Tobacco in America* (Chapel Hill: University of North Carolina Press, 1967), p. 22.

[12] MacInnes, *Early English Tobacco Trade*, p. 35.

[13] Philip A. Bruce, *Economic History of Virginia in the Seventeenth Century*, 2 vols. (New York: Macmillan, 1896), I, pp. 194–195.

[14] Gray, *Agriculture in Southern United States*, I, 22.

In the year 1668–69, for example, London alone received 9 million pounds, nearly all from Virginia and Maryland; twenty years later London's annual average was 15 million pounds, besides what was shipped to other English ports, Bristol in particular.[15] By the opening decade of the eighteenth century, a hundred years after Englishmen first grew tobacco, gross imports into the country averaged about 26 million pounds a year. The greater part — about 16 million pounds — was reexported to Europe as far afield as Russia, leaving about 1½ pounds a head a year for every man, woman, and child in England and Wales.[16] Here, and to some extent in other European countries, tobacco had gone through the barrier which separated upper-class luxuries from articles of common consumption, and had done so ahead of sugar and well in front of tea, coffee, and chocolate.[17] This is the more remarkable because, of all the exotic products made available to Europe by the Discoveries, tobacco was the strangest. It had to make its way, not only against royal disapproval in England and Russia and an attempt by the French government in 1635 to restrict sales to apothecaries, but also, and much more important, against poverty. Most Europeans lived at no better than subsistence level; when bad harvests raised food prices many starved. To force its way into the tiny budgets of peasants and town laborers tobacco had to displace something else. It did so, and became the first luxury regularly enjoyed by the masses.

Despite this advance, sugar overtook tobacco in the Atlantic economies of France and England in the last quarter of the seventeenth century. From 1660 it gained ground in the principal Caribbean islands, and by the start of the eighteenth century the quantity imported into England and Wales was greater in bulk than tobacco and about twice as valuable.[18] For France, having no mainland colony equivalent to Virginia and Maryland, the eclipse of tobacco was even more absolute. About 1640 tobacco was the only product the French West Indies shipped to Europe; so complete was the transformation that between 1670 and 1675 nine-tenths of returns from the Antilles to the Atlantic port of La Rochelle were in the form of

[15] *Ibid.*, p. 213.

[16] The figures are from Elizabeth B. Schumpeter, *English Overseas Trade Statistics, 1697–1808* (Oxford: Clarendon Press, 1960), p. 61.

[17] Sir George Downing said in 1670 that "the common people love tobacco, as they do ale"; quoted in Jacob M. Price, *The Tobacco Adventure to Russia*, in *Transactions of American Philosophical Society*, new series, 51(part 1):7 (1961).

[18] Schumpeter, *English Trade Statistics*, p. 48.

sugar.[19] Everywhere in the French Caribbean, except St.-Domingue, sugar had overtaken tobacco before 1700.

Much of the history, economic, social, and to some extent political, of the first century of English and French colonization is enclosed in this progression from the cycle of tobacco to the cycle of sugar. Tobacco made possible the first settlements: none of those founded south of the Potomac before 1640 could have survived without it. By contrast, colonies established after 1650 owed little to it. Jamaica (1655) was a sugar colony from soon after its capture, with cocoa, indigo, and cattle raising secondary.[20] The Carolinas (1665) grew tobacco, but because of its low price in the 1670s and 1680s had no hope of thriving on it. For this and other reasons, North Carolina well into the eighteenth century was one of the most backward of the Atlantic communities, while South Carolina moved ahead on the profits of the Indian trade and, from about 1700, rice. St.-Domingue, the western end of Hispaniola, was an apparent exception: a new colony in the second half of the seventeenth century with an economy founded on tobacco. But the exception does not prove much. St.-Domingue at its inception was as much a privateering base as a tobacco colony, and failed to prosper until the adoption of sugar as its main crop. About 1690 the well-to-do planters there grew indigo; those who had not the capital to build an *indigoterie* grew tobacco and were objects of pity.[21] Only after 1700 did St.-Domingue begin to climb toward the position it was to occupy in the late eighteenth century as the most valuable European possession in the New World. To this rise tobacco contributed little.

Tobacco was a crop for pioneers. In Barbados the product proved so bad that the early settlers were obliged to turn to cotton and ginger;[22] but this was unusual. Quality certainly varied from colony to colony, but tobacco grew in different soils and under widely differing climatic conditions. Tropical heat and rain were not essential; had the colonization of America failed, tobacco would have become an important crop through-

[19] Stewart L. Mims, *Colbert's West India Policy* (New Haven, Conn.: Yale University Press, 1912), p. 250; M. Delafosse, "La Rochelle et les îles au XVIIe siècle," *Revue d'histoire des colonies*, 36:256–257 (1949).

[20] Hans Sloane, *A Voyage . . . to Jamaica* (London, 1707), reported tobacco grown only for local consumption.

[21] Mims, *Colbert's West India Policy*, p. 257.

[22] Vincent T. Harlow, *A History of Barbados, 1625–1685* (Oxford: Clarendon Press, 1926), p. 6.

out Europe. As it was, cultivation in England and France became sufficiently widespread to induce governments to ban it, partly to encourage the colonists overseas, partly because they found it easier to raise revenue on tobacco coming through the ports than on what was grown in the country. In England tobacco growing was at its height about 1650–60 when the Council of State was told (by the colonial interest) that the home crop was likely to exceed imports from Virginia.[23] Acts of Parliament of 1652, 1660, and 1663 placed heavy fines on native growers, but probably low prices in the 1660s and 1670s did more than legislation to check planting. Later in the century the Dutch, driven from the Atlantic tobacco trade by the exclusive policies of France and England, grew their own in Utrecht, Gelderland, and Overijssel, blending it with Virginian tobacco bought in London, and selling the results to the Baltic countries. About 1705 the combined tobacco production of the United Provinces and north Germany is said to have been as much as 37 million pounds, that is, more than shipments to England from Virginia and Maryland. The quality was lower than Virginian, but so was the price. Thereby the Dutch escaped some of the consequences of defeat in the Atlantic and kept, well into the eighteenth century, a hold on the tobacco trade of the Baltic.[24]

Tobacco's tolerance of different soils and climates is rare among noncereal crops. That it could be grown commercially in Gloucestershire, the Bordelais, Utrecht, Antigua, and Virginia, not to speak of Turkey, Africa, and China in later times, was a misfortune for the producers. But to the settlers under Thomas Warner who went ashore at St. Kitts in January 1624, to the passengers in the Ark who landed on St. Clement's Island in March 1634 to begin the settlement of Maryland, or to the hundred seasoned men d'Esnambuc took from St. Christophe to Martinique in 1635, this disadvantage was not yet apparent. For them, and for many others, it was on tobacco and tobacco alone that their hopes rested of earning enough to pay their debts, buy tools, acquire servants, afford wives and children, build churches, and rise in the world.

Fish and furs attracted European capital because of the promise of quick returns. Founding a colony was a longer term investment. Planting tobacco meant planting a colony, but tobacco could still give a quick enough return to be of interest to merchants. Through the support extended to colonization by merchants of London and Bristol, Dieppe, Le

[23] Gray, Agriculture in Southern United States, I, 236.
[24] Price, Tobacco Adventure to Russia, pp. 7, 88–89.

Havre, and La Rochelle, together with credit afforded by roving Dutchmen, tobacco gave a new turn to the history of the Caribbean between
1620 and 1630.[25] Islands long familiar from the deck of a privateer or as
ports of call for wood and water began to be viewed as potential colonies.
Tobacco made the difference, though not everyone liked the idea. There
is more than a hint of King James's disapproval in Lewis Hughes's address
to the colonizers of Bermuda (1621): "Your chiefe and merchantable
commodity for the present is Tobacco: pray to God to blesse you with
some other commodity, which may be more to his glory, and comfort of
his people than Tobacco is." [26] But pioneers could not really afford such
scruples.

Lands had to be cleared of bushes and trees for planting. Unless, as in
Virginia, maize fields could be annexed from the Indians, there was no
avoiding this backbreaking task, which proved too much for some green
settlers in Bermuda who "do sigh to see how many trees they have to fell,
and how their hands are blistered."[27] Once this was done, and a few acres
were enough, a crop of tobacco could be raised from sowing in nine
months. Thomas Glover's description (1676) is one of a number recorded
in the seventeenth century:

In the Twelve-daies they begin to sow their seed in beds of fine Mould,
and when the Plants be grown to the bredth of a shilling, they are fit to
replant into the Hills; for in their Plantations they make small hills about
four foot distant from each other, somewhat after the manner of our
Hop-yards; These hills being prepared against the plants be grown to the
forementioned bignes (which is about the beginning of May) they then in
moist weather draw the plants out of their beds, and replant them in the
hills, which afterwards they keep with diligent weedings. When the plant
hath put out so many Leaves as the ground will nourish to a substance and
largeness that will render them Merchantable, then they take off the top
of the plant; if the ground be very rich, they let a plant put out a dozen or
sixteen leaves before they top it; if mean, then not above nine or ten, and
so according to the strength of their soyl, the top being taken if the plant
grows no higher; but afterwards it will put out suckers between their
leaves, which they pluck away once a week, till the plant comes to perfec-
tion, which it doth in August. Then in dry weather, when there is a little
breez of wind, they cut down what is ripe, letting it lie about four hours

[25] Richard Pares, *Merchants and Planters, Economic History Review* Supplement no. 4
(Cambridge: Economic History Society, 1959), pp. 5 et seq.
[26] Wesley Frank Craven, "Lewis Hughes' 'Plaine and True Relation of the Goodnes of
God towards the Somer Islands,' " *William and Mary Quarterly*, 2nd series, 17:84 (1937).
[27] Pares, *Merchants and Planters*, p. 18.

on the ground, till such time as the leaves, that stood strutting out, fall down to the stalk, then they carry it on their shoulders into their Tobacco-houses, where other Servants taking of it, drive into the stalk of each plant a peg, and as fast as they are pegg'd, they hang them up by the pegs on Tobacco-sticks, so nigh each other that they just touch, much after the manner they hang Herrings in *Yarmouth*; thus they let them hang five or six weeks, till such time as the stem in the middle of the leaf will snap in the bending of it; then, when the Air hath so moistned the leaf as that it may be handled without breaking, they strike it down, strip it off the stalk, bind it up in bundles, and pack it into Hogsheads for use.[28]

Glover described a well-developed system; doubtless pioneers worked in a more hit-or-miss style, probably skimping the curing which counted for a lot in quality. The main point was that with hard work a crop could soon be won fit to sell in Europe; thus Warner was back in London in September 1625 with 9500 pounds of tobacco, only twenty months after his party went ashore at St. Kitts.

The tobacco boom lasted at most for the two decades in which so many English and French colonies were first established. By the end of the 1630s fear of glut had become the characteristic posture of growers. Virginia and Maryland must have benefited after the middle of the century by the abandonment of tobacco cultivation in the Caribbean, but the gain was a hollow one. They won, partly because their product was better; partly because tobacco exhausted land quickly and they had far more land than the Caribbean colonies; and most of all, because islands like Barbados and Martinique found an alternative in sugar and gladly withdrew from the ruinous tobacco race.[29] The decline of Caribbean tobacco was more than made good by continuing expansion on the mainland and by what Robert Beverley called "the Disease of planting Tobacco."[30] Each crop seemed bigger than the last: "our thriving is our undoing," Governor Culpeper of Virginia wrote in 1681, an epigram which could be attached to other colonial societies and to other products besides tobacco.[31]

[28] Thomas Glover, *An Account of Virginia* (1676; reprinted, Oxford: Blackwell, 1904), pp. 28–30.

[29] Pares, *Merchants and Planters*, pp. 20–21. The annual average of tobacco reaching London in 1637–40 was 1,395,063 pounds from Virginia and Maryland, 354,263 pounds from Barbados and St. Kitts. See Gray, *Agriculture in Southern United States*, I, 237–238.

[30] Robert Beverley, *The History and Present State of Virginia* (1705; reprinted, Chapel Hill: University of North Carolina Press, 1947, ed. Louis B. Wright), p. 71.

[31] Great Britain, Public Record Office, *Calendar of State Papers*, Colonial Series, America and West Indies, 1681–84 (London: H.M.S.O., 1898), no. 319.

The high prices of the 1590s vanished under the avalanche of tobacco produced by pioneer agriculture. As late as 1619 Virginian was fetching 5s. a pound but from 1620 to 1645 prices in Europe fell by 85 percent and continued in a downward direction until the 1680s.[32] Most of the second half of the seventeenth century was a bad time for growers, with periods of particular distress in 1662–67, in 1680–83, and in the war years after 1689 when privateers disturbed the Channel approaches and markets in Europe were spoiled by embargoes. These should not be seen as slumps alternating with booms but as intensifications of generally unfavorable market conditions.

Three remedies were open to the planter: restricting the supply; lowering the costs of production or marketing; and diversifying. The first came earliest. In Virginia efforts to limit production began with Governor Dale's stint of 1616, first adopted to ensure that enough food was produced for the colony's needs, later used as an expedient to support tobacco prices. In 1621, 1629, and 1630 the number of plants to be grown by each colonist was prescribed, and in 1639 came a more comprehensive attempt to confine annual output to 1,200,000 pounds for three years.[33] In the same year the English and French governors of the jointly occupied island of St. Kitts/St. Christophe agreed that no more tobacco should be planted there for the ensuing eighteen months. Hard enough to enforce locally, these restrictions were likely to harm more than help growers unless other colonies could be persuaded to cooperate. They seldom could. Liénard de l'Olive, governor of Guadeloupe, was invited to adhere to the St. Kitts plan but refused, pleading a contract with merchants of Dieppe.[34]

After the Restoration, Virginia and Maryland were better placed to concert restrictive policies. As a cure for the severe depression of the mid-1660s their governments agreed to plant no tobacco from February 1666 to February 1667. Little came of this: the agreement was made too late to affect planting for 1666; the proprietor of Maryland persuaded the Privy Council to veto the scheme; and in 1667 a great storm rendered it obsolete by destroying two-thirds of the crop. Legislative attempts to improve the quality of tobacco were in some instances thinly disguised ways of restricting output. In 1658, in the name of quality, planting was

[32] Pares, *Merchants and Planters*, p. 40; Gray, *Agriculture in Southern United States*, I, 259.

[33] Gray, *Agriculture in Southern United States*, I, 261.

[34] [J.-B.] du Tertre, *Histoire générale des Antilles*, 4 vols. in 3 (Paris, 1667), I, 143–144.

forbidden in Virginia after July 10, and in 1686 after June 30. The curing of suckers and ground leaves was also prohibited. None of these measures worked well because of the lack of effective machinery of inspection and enforcement. More might have been done, had not the Chesapeake region, geographically and economically a unity, been divided into the separate governments of Virginia and Maryland.[35]

Lowering costs was more difficult than limiting output. With no mechanization, the only possibilities were cheaper labor, economies of scale, and improved marketing. The second half of the seventeenth century saw the beginning of the substitution of slave labor for indentured servants in Virginia and Maryland, a change that had not gone far by 1690 but thereafter gained pace as private traders undermined the monopoly of the Royal African Company and began to make frequent shipments of blacks to the Chesapeake. Whether black labor was adopted out of a certainty or just a suspicion that slaves were cheaper than white servants is not clear; it has not been conclusively proved that they *were* cheaper, though the balance of probabilities lies in that direction.[36] Cheap labor was the need, and if planters bought slaves instead of white servants we have to suppose that they did so in the belief that they were in some way reducing costs, or at least preventing them from rising as the result of growing competition for white servants from Carolina and the middle colonies.

Economies of scale are another matter. Tobacco was versatile not only in its tolerance of different soils and climates but also in its adaptability to large or small units of cultivation. The identification of tobacco growing with great slave-worked plantations has no foundation in the pioneer days of Virginia and Maryland, and not a great deal by the end of the seventeenth century; even at the close of the colonial period the association is an imperfect one. Tobacco in the West Indies was more a free crop than a slave crop; in the period of transition to sugar, when those who could afford to do so were investing in the land, buildings, and slaves required for sugar planting, tobacco lingered as the poor man's specialty.[37] In

---

[35] Bruce, *Economic History of Virginia*, I, 393–394; Glover, *Account of Virginia*, p. 30; Gray, *Agriculture in Southern United States*, I, 224; Beverley, *History and Present State of Virginia*, p. 59; Arthur P. Middleton, *Tobacco Coast: A Maritime History of Chesapeake Bay in the Colonial Era* (Newport News, Va.: Mariners Museum, 1953), pp. 355–356.

[36] Bruce, *Economic History of Virginia*, II, 51–52, 59, 63. Pares, *Merchants and Planters*, p. 22, thought that slave labor was adopted in Virginia and Maryland "just because it then became available in sufficient quantities."

[37] Pares, *Merchants and Planters*, p. 21.

Virginia too, tobacco was grown by those who in Europe would have been called peasants. One man, Rolfe thought in 1619, could tend 1000 tobacco plants and four acres of maize, so making sure of subsistence and the wherewithal to buy European goods or a servant.[38]

Before 1700 there were great patents of land in Virginia but few great plantations. William Fitzhugh, Robert Carter, William Byrd, or Robert Beverley might acquire thousands of acres, but most of them lay unworked. Slaves made possible the organization of a larger scale of production, for they could be brigaded and disciplined where white servants could not; but the great plantation (such as it was about 1700) was probably more the result of natural accumulation in a society where landowning was the ordinary measure of social success than the outcome of a conscious attempt to lower costs. If there were economic pressures toward a bigger scale of production, they were less decisive than in the sugar colonies. Throughout colonial times, tobacco plantations with fewer than five slaves continued to exist in large numbers.[39]

In marketing the product, however, the rich grower may have had an advantage over the poor. Once the original sponsors of a colony, whether company, partnership, or sole merchant, had dropped from the scene, the greater part of the cash crop was sold as soon as ready to visiting traders or factors (including Dutch and New Englanders) who brought European goods in exchange. This method of disposing of sugar and tobacco ruled in the mid-seventeenth century and continued to be used by many planters in the eighteenth. It had disadvantages, the price in the colony being lower than that in Europe; planters frequently complained of being exploited or cheated by merchants. On the other hand, selling in the colony ensured the quick turnover vital to small or uncreditworthy producers. Later in the seventeenth century, in Virginia, Barbados, and some of the French colonies, an alternative system of marketing grew up alongside the first, whereby planters sent tobacco or sugar to Europe at their own expense and risk, consigned to an agent who sold it on commission and either remitted the proceeds or, more likely, held them as a fund on which bills of exchange could be drawn. The effect intended was the elimination of the middleman and his profit; and since we know that this system of marketing was widely used, we must believe that there was a balance of advantage in that direction. One effect of the commission

[38] Bruce, *Economic History of Virginia*, I, 252.
[39] Wertenbaker, *Planters of Colonial Virginia*, pp. 151–157.

system was the widespread indebtedness of planter to agent, who supplied on credit European goods and services not available in the colony; having an agent in Europe encouraged conspicuous consumption. By the beginning of the eighteenth century, it is probable that while most small planters continued to sell to merchants in the colony the bigger producers, with better credit and the resources to wait for returns, shipped to their agents in London, Bristol, or La Rochelle.[40]

The use of slaves on the plantations and direct selling in England thus helped to some extent to see Virginia and Maryland through the bad times between 1660 and 1713. Diversification of agriculture contributed more than either, and is the most convincing explanation of how these colonies survived without more serious social and political upheaval. Signs of tension were certainly not lacking. At the head of his list of causes of Bacon's Rebellion in Virginia (1676) Beverley put the "extream low Price of Tobacco, and the ill Usage of the Planters in the Exchange of Goods for it." [41] The same trouble was at work in Culpeper's Rebellion in Carolina (1677), and explicitly in the tobacco tumults in 1682 in Gloucester County, Virginia, when rioters imposed their own form of crop restriction by tearing up two-thirds of the tobacco plants, paying special attention to the sweet-scented variety favored by larger growers.[42] Planters, big and small, were apt to blame their misfortune on the Navigation Acts and on the Plantation Duty Act of 1673 which taxed commodities moving from colony to colony. This legislation made a bad situation worse; to hold it mainly responsible for the low price of tobacco, however, would be to exaggerate the effectiveness of seventeenth-century economic regulation and to ignore the low price of tobacco prevailing throughout Europe. Freedom to sell anywhere would have helped the grower in the 1670s and 1680s but not as much as he expected. His best remedy was to diversify.

Nothing had come of the Virginia Company's efforts to encourage glass and iron making; a few ships were built in Virginia but no industry of importance emerged in the seventeenth century, which is scarcely surprising in a province lacking towns. The Indian trade was taken more

[40] Middleton, *Tobacco Coast*, pp. 104–110; J. S. Bassett, "The Relations between the Virginia Planter and the London Merchant," *Annual Report of American Historical Association for 1901*, I, 553–575; Elizabeth Donnan, "An Eighteenth-Century English Merchant: Micajah Perry," *Journal of Economic and Business History*, 4:70 (1931–32).

[41] Beverley, *History and Present State of Virginia*, pp. 74–75.

[42] Robert, *Story of Tobacco*, pp. 12–14; Gray, *Agriculture in Southern United States*, I, 226.

seriously at the end of the century than at the beginning and contributed to the fortunes of some of the colony's leading families.[43] Growth of population created some demand for men skilled in the building trades and in rural crafts such as blacksmithing. Above all, a start was made in diversifying agriculture and the worst excesses of monoculture averted. Rice, vines, and mulberries were all tried in the seventeenth century without success, but the rearing of livestock and the production of grain not only freed Virginia from dependence on imported food (contrast Barbados) but generated a surplus of meat and corn for export to New England, Madeira, and the Caribbean. By the 1680s tobacco had ceased to be the major concern of Virginia's eastern shore, and elsewhere in the early eighteenth century there was some permanent movement out of tobacco into wheat.[44] Tobacco remained the staple. But this amount of diversification, together with cheap land for white yeomen on the frontier, a better balance between white and black population, and the rarity in Virginia's history of the absentee proprietor drawing an income from his estate and putting nothing back in the form of leadership, saved the colony from the moral, cultural, political, and ultimately economic stagnation which overtook the English and French Caribbean colonies. Virginia, Maryland, the Carolinas, and Georgia were slave societies at the end of the eighteenth century, but they were not sick societies like St.-Domingue, Antigua, or Jamaica.

William Fitzhugh's picture of his Virginian plantation in 1686, with its "choice crew of negroes at each plantation, most of them this country born, the remainder as likely as most in Virginia, there being twenty-nine in all," was complacent almost to the point of euphoria. He expected that "the yearly crops of corn and tobacco together with the surplusage of meat more than will serve the family's use, will amount annually to 60,000 lbs of tobacco, which at ten shillings per hundredweight is £300 per annum." An orchard of 2300 apple trees was to bring in the equivalent of 15,000 pounds of tobacco. With a "good stock of cattle, hogs, horses, mares, sheep" and a house with four rooms hung and nine plentifully furnished, Fitzhugh was living well in a young country. By the standards of his day, he was a big planter and slave owner; but the point to notice is that he

[43] See below, p. 170.
[44] Susie M. Ames, *Studies of the Virginia Eastern Shore in the Seventeenth Century* (Richmond, Va.: Dietz Press, 1940), pp. 51–54; Middleton, *Tobacco Coast*, pp. 178–179; Gray, *Agriculture in Southern United States*, I, 164–168, 232 et seq.

presided over an economy which contained important elements of diversification, not over a monoculture.[45]

Fish

The waters of the New World, both salt and fresh, impressed the first Europeans by the fish they contained. Some, like cod, were familiar; others, like the giant Mississippi catfish, were new and startling; yet others (the sturgeon is an example) were known, but grew in America to proportions rare in Europe. In many parts of the New World fish was a staple food of Indians; on the shores of the Gulf of Mexico and in Cuba it was virtually all they had. Except that they did not engage in deep-water fishing, they showed at least as much ingenuity in catching fish as the whites. As well as taking them with line and hook (bone or shell), they shot them with bows and arrows, speared them, trapped them in stone weirs with baskets, poisoned the water to force them to the surface, and swam underwater to capture them by surprise in nets.[46] Fish enabled some first settlers to survive when their European provisions were gone, though not all were quick to learn how to feed themselves in this way. Starving times in Virginia, Bermuda, Guadeloupe, and Plymouth could and should have been alleviated by more attention to fishing. Some early colonists relied on the Indians to sell them fish as well as corn. In West Africa, where the coastal people were expert fishermen, this dependence continued for a long time.

Although fish were obtainable almost everywhere in the Americas, only in the northwestern Atlantic did a fishing industry arise which made a major contribution to the European economy. Perhaps an exception should be made for whaling. Early in the seventeenth century the Dutch had important whaling interests at Spitsbergen and off the coasts of Iceland. Overfishing curtailed the Spitsbergen industry by 1640 and Europe's whalers were forced westwards into the Atlantic.[47] Many whales were taken off Newfoundland and New England, especially by Basques, but they were also hunted further south, from Bermuda, and further north, in Hudson Bay, where in 1686 a Hudson's Bay Company man saw

[45] Fitzhugh's letter to Dr. Ralph Smith, April 22, 1686, is in Bruce, *Economic History of Virginia*, II, 243n1.
[46] Harold E. Driver, *Indians of North America* (2nd ed.; Chicago: University of Chicago Press, 1969), pp. 87–88.
[47] Rich and Wilson, *Cambridge Economic History of Europe*, IV, 173.

"many 1000ds of white whales and soe tame that they were continually sporting round the sloope."[48] This report led to the first settlement at Churchill River and eventually to the building of the ambiguously named Fort Prince of Wales, the most northerly military or commercial establishment in North America in the eighteenth century. Whales were hunted partly for bone but chiefly for oil, used in making soap, in lamps, for oiling cloth in textile manufacture, and generally as a lubricant. Train oil could be extracted also from cod; in the seventeenth century probably more came from this source than from whales. That whales were nevertheless prized is suggested by the interest of the Dutch who controlled much of the supply of oil to northern Europe throughout the century, despite repeated but unsuccessful attempts by French and English to displace them. In the decade 1680–89, for example, the Dutch sent nearly 2000 whaling ships to Greenland alone, taking 10,000 whales. Even in wartime (1699–1708) the value of their catch averaged 2½ million florins (over £ 200,000 sterling) a year.[49]

Train oil was important to Europe: in 1569 the Spanish ambassador in London hoped that the English textile industry could be brought to a standstill by cutting off supplies of oil.[50] But cod was more important and bigger business. If Europe's demographic history in the seventeenth century was a melancholy one, and if as seems likely the recurring demographic crises proceeded from shortage of food more than from anything else, we can be sure that without "Newland" fish those crises would have been visibly worse. Statistical estimates of the fisheries before 1700 are rough-and-ready and often put together to support a case, but those compiled by officers of the Royal Navy in the eighteenth century appear at least to be objective. They show that in 1735, for example, the British "made" 419,075 quintals of fish at Newfoundland, all but 15,000 of which were shipped to foreign markets.[51] Taking a quintal as one hundredweight, this means 20,000 tons of fish from Newfoundland alone. The French at this time were catching as much or only a little less; and there must be added large quantities of fish taken off New England, much of

[48] E. E. Rich, *History of the Hudson's Bay Company*, vol. I (London: Hudson's Bay Record Society, 1958), p. 235.
[49] Charles M. Andrews, *The Colonial Period of American History*, 4 vols. (New Haven, Conn.: Yale University Press, 1934–38; reprinted, 1964), I, 302; J. T. Jenkins, *A History of the Whale Fisheries* (London: Witherby, 1921), pp. 166–167, 308.
[50] Jenkins, *History of the Whale Fisheries*, pp. 67–68.
[51] Great Britain, Public Record Office, *Calendar of State Papers*, Colonial Series, America and West Indies, 1735–36 (London: H.M.S.O., 1953), no. 119iii.

which went to Europe, particularly to Spain and other Mediterranean
countries short of grain. It is clear that by the eighteenth century the
North American fisheries were making a major contribution to keeping
Europe's poor alive. Cod's impact was less theatrical than that of sugar,
tobacco, and coffee, but greater in nutritional value.

The international appearance of the North Atlantic fisheries at the end
of the sixteenth century has already been described.[52] About 1600 there
were still Spaniards and Portuguese on the Newfoundland Banks disput-
ing the business with French and English. As late as 1625 one Spanish
port had forty-one ships and 1475 men in the fishery, and Basque whaling
voyages appear to have gone on throughout the seventeenth century.
Nevertheless, the Spaniards both before and after 1600 were losing
ground, a decline hastened by the imposition of a tax on salt, one more
example of the fiscal demands of the Spanish government destroying the
wealth it hoped to exploit. The Portuguese, too, surrendered to the English after 1600 in the supplying of cod to Madeira and Bahia as well as to
Lisbon.[53] By mid-century, with one or two exceptions, southern Europeans had given up the North Atlantic fisheries and become the passive
consumers of salted and dried cod sold them by French and English
skippers. From time to time Dutch ships sailed to Newfoundland to buy
fish caught by Englishmen, and in war (as in 1665 and 1676) their navy
inflicted losses on the French and English fishing fleets.[54] But on the
whole they stuck to their herring fishery in the North Sea and caught their
cod off Iceland or nearer home; the fear that they would one day apply to
the northwestern Atlantic the greater capital resources and the more
efficient methods which enabled them to dominate these nearer waters
was sometimes voiced by Englishmen, but was never realized. England
and France were left to fight it out, at first with economic weapons, then
at the close of the seventeenth century in King William's war.

The French had somewhat the better of the economic argument and
much the better of the war; the English had somewhat the better of the
Treaty of Utrecht. To begin with, the French had the advantage of a good

[52] See above, pp. 12–16.

[53] Harold A. Innis, "The Rise and Fall of the Spanish Fishery in Newfoundland,"
Proceedings and Transactions of the Royal Society of Canada, 3rd series, 25(section II):
62–65 (1931); Frédéric Mauro, *Le Portugal et l'Atlantique au XVIIe siècle* (Paris:
S.E.V.P.E.N., 1960), pp. 288–289.

[54] Violet Barbour, *Capitalism in Amsterdam in the Seventeenth Century* (Baltimore:
Johns Hopkins University Press, 1950), pp. 90–91; Charles B. Judah, *The North American
Fisheries and British Policy to 1713* (Urbana: University of Illinois Press, 1933), pp. 113, 141.

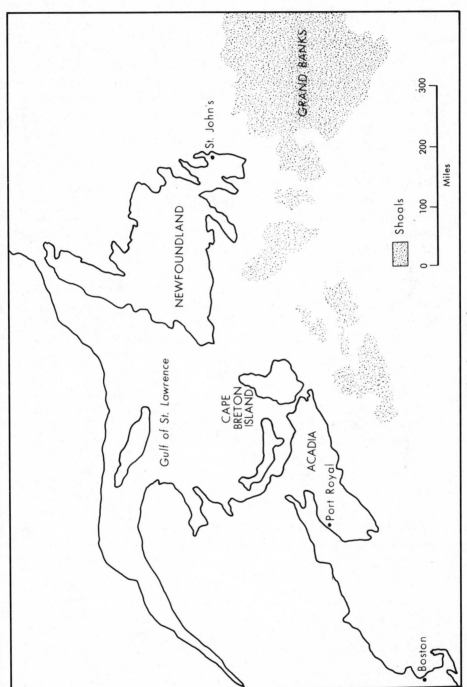

North Atlantic Fisheries

domestic supply of salt whereas England had to import or improvise. La Rochelle, a great fishing port, had ample salt three miles away on the Île de Ré. The French, too, had a bigger domestic market, with four times as many mouths to feed, most of them Roman Catholic. The revival of formal religious observance in France in the seventeenth century, at least among the upper classes, may have helped her fishermen. In England, though Queen Elizabeth's "political Lent" soon fell into disuse, fish was widely eaten; much more of it, however, was caught offshore (including North Sea herrings brought in by the Dutch) than was of Newfoundland origin. A large proportion of the English Atlantic catch, though probably not always as large as in the figures cited for 1735, must always have gone to foreign markets, either sold to foreign buyers at West Country ports such as Weymouth and Dartmouth or shipped directly from Newfoundland to Bilbao and Lisbon or through the Strait of Gibraltar. The first of these methods of disposal was the older and in the seventeenth century was probably that adopted by most small operators; the second method was developed by men with capital, particularly Londoners. Selling fish to foreigners to reexport from England in foreign ships was forbidden by the Navigation Act of 1651 (which in this respect was a victory for London interests over the West Country) but the ban was lifted in 1655 when the westerners were able to point to fish rotting in their harbors.[55] After the Restoration this trade was probably overtaken by direct shipments from Newfoundland to southern Europe. English fishing vessels, instead of bringing the catch to their home ports, sailed to Spain or Portugal and sold their fish for money or the products of those countries. This was the North Atlantic triangular trade, in full swing in the first half of the century, as can be seen from the instructions given by a Londoner, John de la Barre, to Thomas Breadcake, master of the *Faith*, in 1634. The *Faith* was a sack ship, that is, she did not catch fish but bought from those that did; Breadcake's orders were to be at Newfoundland by July 25 where 4000 quintals were to be purchased from three Dartmouth vessels at 11s. a quintal, paying with bills of exchange drawn on de la Barre. Cartagena, Alicante, Tarragona, and Barcelona were to be the ports of discharge, and the *Faith* was to be supplied with a return cargo by de la Barre's agent in Spain. This example, unearthed by Ralph Davis, reveals the use of London capital (£ 2200 for the fish alone) collaborating with Dartmouth exper-

---

[55] Judah, *North American Fisheries*, pp. 93, 101.

tise and cutting across the traditional rivalry between the metropolis and the West Country.[56] The voyage of the *Faith* also illustrates the penetration of the Spanish market by English merchants after 1604. In return for cod the English took wine, oil, fruit, and silver. Thus cod helped to finance purchases of Mediterranean products from a country where broadcloth, still England's major export, could command only limited sales.

The Spanish market was open to the French too, though war between 1635 and 1659 must have caused some interruptions. St.-Malo, Granville, Nantes, La Rochelle, and Bayonne were the French ports principally concerned, Bilbao, San Sebastian, Cádiz, Seville, Valencia, and the Balearic Islands the main Spanish ports of entry.[57] The French also sent cod to Italy though by the end of the seventeenth century they were complaining of being outtraded by the English. Probably the French Atlantic fishery reached a peak in the decade following the Treaty of Nijmwegen (1678). Certainly the English were made aware that there was something wrong with their own cod fishery and attributed the decline to French competition among other things. About 1680 the French were thought to have 300 ships in the Newfoundland trade, the English only 100.[58]

The wars which began in 1689 adversely affected the fisheries of both countries. Frenchmen claimed that by reason of the war the English had usurped their market for cod in the Iberian peninsula, while the English pointed to their losses at the hands of Breton privateers and the capture of St. John's, Newfoundland, by the French in 1696 and 1708.[59] Some of these complaints were special pleading, but there were genuine setbacks in both fisheries. Before the war St.-Malo was one of the major ports of Europe with a turnround of 2000 ships a year. There were then 100 Malouin ships in the Atlantic fisheries; in 1689 there were 47; in 1690, 6.[60] Fishermen on both sides were pressed into the navy, and it is one

---

[56] Ralph Davis, *The Rise of the English Shipping Industry* (London: Macmillan, 1962), pp. 236–238.

[57] Albert Girard, *Le commerce français à Séville et Cadix au temps des Hapsbourgs* (Paris: Boccard, 1932), pp. 388–390.

[58] Harold A. Innis, *The Cod Fisheries* (rev. ed.; Toronto: University of Toronto Press, 1954), p. 127.

[59] Girard, *Commerce français*, p. 389; Ralph G. Lounsbury, *The British Fishery at Newfoundland, 1634–1763* (New Haven, Conn.: Yale University Press, 1934), p. 228.

[60] Pierre Goubert, *Louis XIV and Twenty Million Frenchmen* (London: Penguin, 1970), pp. 186, 211.

historian's verdict on the effects of war that "all concerned were brought to the brink of ruin." [61] The Peace of Utrecht, respecting the fisheries, was a compromise, not a glittering English victory. True, Louis XIV was obliged to cede sovereignty over Newfoundland and Nova Scotia, but while Frenchmen were forbidden to fish anywhere within thirty leagues of Nova Scotia they were free to fish off Newfoundland and to use the coast from Cape Bonavista to Pointe Riche for drying and curing their catch. Above all, they kept Cape Breton Island which not only guarded their Canadian possessions but also left them well placed to renew competition in the fisheries. This, after 1713 they did, and by the 1730s the English were justly alarmed at the recovery of their rivals. [62] If, as has been claimed, 1713 was "the beginning of the end for the French American empire" the conclusion was not obvious to British fishermen. [63]

Neither country gave much attention to the colonization of these regions. From the first struggles to found a colony in Acadia in the last years of the sixteenth century down to 1713, the French failed to build up a population capable of defending itself. Few enough Frenchmen wanted to live in North America; most of those who did went to Canada to share in the fur trade. [64] The census of 1714 recorded a total of 1773 French in Acadia, of whom no fewer than 1179 were children. On the south coast of Newfoundland 60 French families were planted in 1662 with royal assistance. Fifteen years later there were said to be 250 French in the whole of Newfoundland, a total which by the time of the census of 1696 had advanced to only 293 *habitants*. [65] Despite some discouragement from home, the English managed to do a little better. In 1675, 1655 residents were reported there, responsible for nearly a third of the annual English catch; by 1712, there were 2017. [66]

One explanation of the slow increase in the number of Englishmen is to be found in the opposition of fishing interests in England to the planting of settlers and even to fortifying Newfoundland. In general, English col-

[61] Lounsbury, *British Fishery*, p. 227.

[62] Great Britain, Public Record Office, *Calendar of State Papers*, Colonial Series, America and West Indies, 1735–36 (London: H.M.S.O., 1953), nos. 9, 22, 119.

[63] Goubert, *Louis XIV*, p. 265.

[64] Innis, *Cod Fisheries*, pp. 129–137.

[65] *Censuses of Canada 1665–1871: Statistics of Canada*, vol. IV (Ottawa, 1876), pp. 38, 49.

[66] Innis, *Cod Fisheries*, p. 100; Lounsbury, *British Fishery*, pp. 161–162; Great Britain, Public Record Office, *Calendar of State Papers*, Colonial Series, America and West Indies, 1712–14 (London: H.M.S.O., 1926), no. 115i.

onization was less marked than French by provincial rivalries: the fisheries are an exception. For some years after the Discoveries, they were a West Country business. When, later, Londoners began to show interest, western merchants and fishermen claimed the right earned by prior discovery. The form taken by the dispute, which went on throughout the seventeenth century, was a debate upon the advantages (put by Londoners) and disadvantages (put by westerners) of colonizing Newfoundland. The westerners, visiting the Banks only in the summer months, accused the colonists of damaging drying stages, spoiling harbors by emptying ballast, poaching fishing berths, drunkenness, and immorality. What they most feared was that colonization would end in the institution of a colonial government, taxation, and interference with the customs of their trade. These customs accorded to the first ship arriving in each harbor the pick of the stages and drying grounds and made her skipper "admiral" for the season.[67] The Londoners, taking up the cause of colonization, argued that seasonal visitors were a disorderly and dissolute lot, completely uncontrolled by their "admirals," and needing to be brought under government, and that the fisheries should be defended against foreigners by forts.

The anticolonizers had rather the better of it. Gilbert did not get far with his colony in the sixteenth century; his imitators were not much more successful. One of the first was John Guy of Bristol, who in 1609 "intended a Plantation in the Newfoundland, and had gotten a Licence and Charter of the king for the same, having some Rich Merchants of London joyned with him for the better Fraying of the charge and bringing it to Pass: and likewise many of this city did put in their Moneys hoping to reap Benefitt thereby in the End, and so Mr. Guy with some other Young Merchants (having fitted themselves with Men and other things necessary) took shipping for Newfoundland to make a Triall of the Place by staying there all the winter."[68] Guy's venture, which struggled along for several years, shows that the West of England was not solid against colonization; Bristol interests more than once combined with London against the smaller West Country ports.[69] Until the English Civil War, however, the greatest threat to the anticolonizers came from royal paten-

[67] Judah, *North American Fisheries*, pp. 21–22.
[68] Patrick McGrath, ed., *Records Relating to the Society of Merchant Venturers of the City of Bristol in the Seventeenth Century* (Bristol: Bristol Record Society, 1952), p. 200.
[69] Judah, *North American Fisheries*, p. 114.

tees with London financial backing. Such a patentee was Sir George
Calvert to whom the king granted the land in Newfoundland called Avalon; such also was Sir William Alexander, given Nova Scotia by James I
in his capacity as king of Scotland. Meanwhile, the New England
fisheries had been discovered and had started to attract both western
fishermen and royal patentees. With Sir Ferdinando Gorges spending
years and money trying to found colonies on the New England coast, the
same conflict between "fishermen" and "settlers" broke out here.
Gorges's Council for New England was formed in 1620 and given a
monopoly of the New England fisheries, though this was later construed
to mean that all Englishmen were free to catch fish provided they did not
land. Gorges hoped to tax the fishermen in order to finance colonization,
and in 1623 five vessels of Plymouth and two of Dartmouth were arrested
for landing without license. To the westerners, already at odds with
patentees in Newfoundland, this was another monopoly "attempted of the
wind, and the sun."[70] Parliament, pressed by West Country M.P.'s and
the Virginia Company which hoped to get into the act, condemned the
New England Council's monopoly in 1624. Gorges went on trying for
some years. He did not succeed but he did enough to keep New England
open to colonization by others. If the westerners had had their way, New
England like Newfoundland would have been virtually sterilized as a zone
of settlement.

Alexander's plans to colonize Nova Scotia were ended when Charles I
acknowledged the French title to that country in 1632. But the westerners soon had to meet a new threat from a group of magnates, including
the Marquis of Hamilton, the Earls of Pembroke and Holland, and Sir
David Kirke, probably with London financial backing, who obtained
proprietary rights in 1637 over Cape Breton Island and Nova Scotia as
well as Newfoundland. Kirke himself went out as governor in 1638; but
for the Civil War, in which he was on the losing side, he might in time
have colonized Newfoundland. Instead he was evicted in 1651. At the
Restoration his claims and Calvert's, based on the Avalon patent, came
into collision, as did others founded on hastily drawn and ill-considered
royal charters. The Calvert group won but did nothing with their victory.
Proprietary colonization in this quarter petered out.

The confusion in Newfoundland's history caused by conflict between

[70] *Ibid.*, pp. 54, 56, 59.

fishermen and colonizers was thus heightened by the idiosyncratic behavior of Stuart kings. Down to 1640 the greatest dangers to the westerners came from courtiers, backed by London money and armed with royal patents. The westerners on their side tried to use Parliament to protect their rights, so involving Newfoundland in political clashes between crown and Commons. Several bills were originated by private members in the 1620s (none passed into law) to put free fishing on a statutory basis, which might suggest that the crown was hostile to the westerners' claims. Yet when the Privy Council inquired into the fisheries in 1633 the outcome was not a victory for courtiers and patentees but the "Western Charter" upholding most of the West Country customary practices.[71] The mayors of Southampton, Weymouth and Melcombe Regis, Lyme, Plymouth, Dartmouth, East Looe, Fowey, and Barnstaple were empowered to enforce the charter, a rare example of formal authority over America being vested in English municipal government. Four years later the Kirke group got their charter, contradicting the spirit if not the letter of the Western Charter. Thought-out policy thus favored the westerners but was negatived by the response of king or ministers to pressures on them, an example to be remembered when evaluating the contributions of monarchs to the expansion of Europe. After 1660, with the more rational rule of Louis XIV in France and the greater part assumed by Parliament in English government, colonies were less often treated as playgrounds where courtiers dreamed of rich estates and kings indulged in cheap acts of bounty.

The Western Charter was reissued in 1661 and 1676 and formed the basis of an act to encourage the Newfoundland trade in 1699 which guaranteed "free Trade and Traffick" to all the king's subjects.[72] Thus, it seems, the "fishermen" beat the "colonizers." Throughout the seventeenth century there was doubt whether Newfoundland was an English colony. In 1679 a special commissioner sent there held it to be a possession of the crown, but the customhouse ledgers for England and Wales which begin in 1697 list it as a foreign country.[73] The buildup of population was slow and of public institutions slower. There was no Anglican priest there until 1701, no grammar school till 1799. Justices of the peace

[71] Terms in *ibid.*, pp. 80–82.
[72] 10 and 11 William III, c. xxv.
[73] Judah, *North American Fisheries*, p. 145; Lounsbury, *British Fishery*, p. 202n—compare p. 94.

were first appointed in 1729. Until 1738 felons were brought to England for trial, together with the witnesses against them; only then was authority given for holding courts of oyer and terminer. All these things were slow to appear, but they came in the end and must be regarded as stages in the collapse of the western anticolonial formula. Newfoundland was too important and too vulnerable to be left empty and unruled. Parliamentary commissioners were sent there in 1651, the first instance of direct intervention by an English government; convoys were organized to defend the fishing fleet; officers of the Royal Navy inspected and reported on the fisheries and inhabitants. Bit by bit Newfoundland edged into England's empire. The formula of economic exploitation without colonization — the old aspiration of European merchants when they first contemplated America — lived longer here than on the St. Lawrence but it failed in the end.

If Newfoundland was a special case, so was fish. Sugar and tobacco could be shipped first to England, then reexported to Europe, however much the colonists hated it. Fish rotted. Cod was not, therefore, made an enumerated commodity by the Navigation Act of 1660; it could be sent directly from the Banks to southern Europe, and most of it was. Salt, a major component of exports to Newfoundland, was likewise left out of the Staple Act of 1663 which required that European manufactures should reach the colonies only via the English entrepôt. At the same time, the distinctive status of the fisheries as the nursery of seamen for the Royal Navy was recognized by special regulations. Privy Council orders required, and the act of 1699 confirmed, that fishing vessels must carry one "fresh" man in five, that is, one who had never been to sea before. By-boat keepers, who operated small craft in Newfoundland waters and sold their catch to sack ships, were required to carry two "fresh" men in six, one a novice, the other not having made more than one previous voyage.[74]

By the end of the seventeenth century, the fisheries of the northwestern Atlantic were beginning to provide American colonists with an economic life independent of the mother country. In the 1630s New Englanders were consumers of fish sold to them by fishermen from England, not competitors, but this did not last long. The Civil Wars interrupted English fishing, hastening what would have happened anyway. At

[74] 10 and 11 William III, c. xxv.

first the New Englanders caught their fish and marketed it in Europe as satellites of London. After 1660 they began to build their own ships and accumulate their own capital. Bernard Bailyn has given his opinion that "in no way" was New England's commerce independent of the mother country in the seventeenth century, but the fisheries seem to be an exception.[75] New England competed, within the Acts of Trade, by sending fish to southern Europe. By 1700 Boston was exporting 50,000 quintals, mostly to Bilbao. The West of England fishermen attributed the decline of their trade to this as well as French competition, and in 1671 the Lords of Trade accepted their view. At the same time New Englanders competed with Old in supplying provisions to Newfoundland, bringing tobacco, sugar, rum, bread, meat, and flour as well as stores such as tar and boards. By the end of the seventeenth century, New York, Maryland, and Pennsylvania were in the same business, partly at the expense of suppliers from the British Isles.[76]

All this was legitimate, and insofar as the New England fishery continued to be financed by London, some of the profits returned to England. But the New Englanders went further, using Newfoundland as an entrepôt for illegal trade with Europe. Sugar and tobacco, both enumerated commodities, were carried by New Englanders to Boston; thence to Newfoundland; thence to Holland or Scotland. Foreign manufactures returned by the same route. With no settled government in Newfoundland smuggling could not be stopped; a vice-admiralty court was set up there in 1708 but failed to curb what was by then a strong vested interest.[77] Another complaint by the mother country was the spiriting away of colonists and fishermen to New England — headed up in casks to escape discovery — impairing both England's economy and recruitment for her navy.

New England thus entered the business of smuggling, a momentous step. An independent stance could be taken up in the fisheries partly because the product was perishable, therefore less susceptible to regulation by the mother country; partly because the markets were in southern Europe, outside England's jurisdiction. Cod, moreover, was rare, if not unique, among New World products in not experiencing a dramatic fall in

[75] Bernard Bailyn, *The New England Merchants in the Seventeenth Century* (Cambridge, Mass.: Harvard University Press, 1955), pp. 79–80, 86, 90.
[76] Innis, *Cod Fisheries*, pp. 117–118; Lounsbury, *British Fishery*, pp. 141, 194 et seq.
[77] *Ibid.*, p. 225.

price as the result of overproduction. Instead of the lamentations of colonial producers of tobacco, sugar, and fur, we have Sir Josiah Child's complaint in 1694 that the price of Newfoundland fish in England had risen from 8s. 6d. to 12s. since the start of the century.[78] Despite the same author's injured protest that Spaniards were getting lax about fish eating, demand in southern Europe appears to have remained high. English skippers drank "to the Pope and ten shillings," the hoped-for price; but probably the shortage of cereals in the Mediterranean is a better explanation why Europe could absorb thousands of tons of protein food every year from the northwestern Atlantic without a collapse of prices. That was to New England's benefit, for falling prices would have compelled the English crown and Parliament to consider tougher measures against New England's competition.

Furs

Most of the principal fur-bearing animals of North America, beaver, fox, otter, marten, were familiar to Europeans before the Discoveries. The best furs came from Russia, and it was in that direction that England still looked in 1555 when the Muscovy Company was founded. Furs, like wine, oil, and silk, figured in colonizing propaganda as products to be got more cheaply and easily in the New World; unlike wine and the rest, they fulfilled the hopes pinned to them. Furs in the Middle Ages were for public display, worn by nobles, officials, and academic dignitaries as badges of rank or office. New World furs impaired this notion in the course of the seventeenth century, if not democratizing fur, at least changing it — especially in the form of the beaver hat — into a common bourgeois fashion. This hat was made not of skins but of fur fabric or felt, a composition produced from beaver wool. The animal's long guard hairs had to be removed to get at and cut the short hairs or wool, a skill at first known only to Russians but practiced in western Europe after 1600. Like other new industries depending on extra-European raw materials, felting had its headquarters at Amsterdam, with Paris and London (where the Company of Feltmakers was formed in 1629) providing the competition.[79]

Beaver was found almost everywhere in North America explored by

[78] Cited in Judah, *North American Fisheries*, p. 157.
[79] E. E. Rich, *The Fur Trade and the Northwest to 1857* (Toronto: McClelland and Stewart, 1967), pp. 7–8, 22.

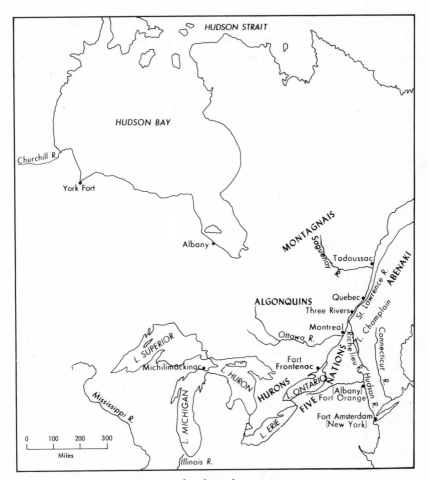

Fur Trade of North America

Europeans in the seventeenth century, including New England and the
southern colonies. Here the fur trade, though short-lived and negligible
compared to New York, New France, and Hudson Bay, was of considerable importance to the pioneers, furnishing a product, and sometimes the
only product, to sell in Europe. Without furs the Pilgrims and the Massachusetts Bay Company would have found it harder, perhaps impossible,
to get financial backing; like fish and tobacco, they supplied the quick
return desired by seventeenth-century capitalists. Nor were the backers
disappointed: for many years the Pilgrims depended on furs to pay their

creditors in London and bring over new settlers, and in Massachusetts fur trading for a time was quite big business. One man, William Pynchon, founder of Springfield, sent nearly 9000 skins to England between 1652 and 1657. As settlement spread and thickened, however, New England was soon trapped out.[80] Connecticut River proved not to be the hoped-for route to the Great Lakes, and New England's fur trade declined. On the whole it was better so. It is not easy to imagine a Puritan *coureur de bois*; in the long run the economy as well as the society of Massachusetts was sounder for not being based on the fur trade.

Virginia also had a fur trade and appears to have taken it more seriously at the end of the seventeenth century than at the beginning, exporting annually about 2000 beaver skins and in one exceptional year (1712) 40,000. South Carolina in the same period exported about a thousand a year. Both colonies traded extensively in deerskins, most Indians having nothing else to offer; in both, the Indian trade was an important diversifier of plantation agriculture, especially in times of low tobacco prices. The fortunes of William Byrd, Abraham Wood, Edward Bland, and Cadwallader Jones were raised by, if not on, Virginia's trade in furs and hides. For many years, from 1705, the principal support of William and Mary College was a tax on skins.[81]

In New England and the southern colonies the fur trade helped early settlement. Elsewhere it earned a reputation, which lasted until the nineteenth century, of hindering colonization. The conflict, already described, between fishermen and colonizers in Newfoundland was enacted on a larger scale between fur traders and colonizers in New France and New Netherland. In the St. Lawrence, fur trading began as the offspring of the French fishery, fitting comfortably into the routine of an annual fishing fleet leaving France in late spring or early summer and returning before the weather got too bad. At most, small shore stations or factories were needed where Indians could exchange furs for trade goods. Thus was the French fur trade run in the closing years of the sixteenth century, and thus it might have continued but for the intervention of the French crown and the persistence of Champlain. The new formula for Canada was monopoly, the monopolist being obliged to transport settlers, support

[80] Paul C. Phillips, *The Fur Trade*, 2 vols. (Norman: University of Oklahoma Press, 1961), I, 135; Samuel E. Morison, *Builders of the Bay Colony* (revised Sentry ed.; Boston: Houghton Mifflin, 1962), chapter 12.
[81] Phillips, *Fur Trade*, I, 173, 329, 331.

missionaries, and finance exploration: the fur trade was to be made to pay for colonization. Pierre Chauvin of Honfleur, given a monopoly of the fur trade of the St. Lawrence in 1600, was required to send out 50 settlers a year up to a total of 500. This grant was quickly and successfully contested by St.-Malo and Rouen. To meet such objections de Monts's monopoly in 1603 of the trade of Acadia and the Upper St. Lawrence contained provision for the participation (though only as sleeping partners) of the French fur-trading ports, including St.-Jean-de-Luz. De Monts was obliged to carry out 100 colonists a year. These stipulations were not fulfilled and were greatly reduced in later grants. The Duc de Condé (1612) had to transport only six families a year, and the Duc de Montmorenci (1620) — or rather his concessionaires, Guillaume and Emery de Caen — six families of three persons each and to maintain six missionaries.[82]

It is doubtful if even these modest requirements were met. With Richelieu's coming to power in 1624, sights were enormously raised, performance less so. The Compagnie des Cent Associés, subcontractors to Richelieu's Compagnie de la Nouvelle France, was made to undertake the settlement of no fewer than 1300 colonists a year for fifteen years.[83] Had this program been even half-completed, the fur trade would have been the true if unwilling parent of the colonization of New France. It was not. Champlain, looking at the anticolonizing interest in 1618, "saw that a greater fear held them; that if the country were settled their power would diminish, not making in this place all that they wished, and losing the greatest part of the furs which would fall into the hands of the settlers of the country who would hunt by themselves and who would be brought out at a heavy expense."[84] Only bit by bit did the fur-trading *comptoirs* turn into a *colonie*; and when by 1661 this could be said to have taken place, the antipathy between fur trade and colonization did not cease but took a new form.[85] As French explorers penetrated further into the West, the fur trade drew men away from farming, family life, and the influence of the church. There was of course a credit side. The fur trade paid, reluctantly, for the cost of running New France; gave the king at least in some years an income which encouraged him to subsidize the transporta-

[82] *Ibid.*, pp. 28–29, 32–33, 51, 58, 86.
[83] Rich, *Fur Trade*, pp. 15–17.
[84] Quoted in Harold A. Innis, *The Fur Trade in Canada* (New Haven, Conn.: Yale University Press, 1930), p. 36.
[85] W. J. Eccles, *Canada under Louis XIV* (Toronto: McClelland and Stewart, 1964), chapter 5.

tion of settlers and undertake public works; helped to pay for the church and the missionaries; made the fortunes of Aubert de la Chesnaye, Jacques Le Ber, and Charles Le Moyne, the first prosperous Canadians; and, not least, bred the *coureurs de bois* who in the wars with England did much to redress the balance of numbers against New France. But there was danger in spreading the colony's meager manpower over a vast territory, and Colbert saw it clearly. He aimed to check expansion, limit the fur trade, and organize a compact, defensible, agricultural community; but he was powerless three thousand miles away to influence more than the details of Canadian economic life. Versailles proposed, the fur trade dictated.

New Netherland offers many parallels. Furs, not colonization, were the business of the New Netherland Company; furs, not colonization, the reason for such interest as the West India Company took in the region. Like the merchants of St.-Malo, Rouen, and La Rochelle, the merchants of Holland and Zeeland looked for maximum trade with minimum settlement. Colonization was tolerated, not systematically undertaken; and when first the patroons, and later all colonists, were permitted to share in the fur trade the result in some cases was a neglect of farming, such as that of which Colbert complained in New France. Hence the breast-beating of the Dutch inhabitants in 1650 about the failure to people the colony, hence the easy conquest by the English in 1664.[86] No account of the remarkable history of the fur trade should gloss over the fate encountered by the two European colonies in North America whose economies were so largely dependent on it, New Netherland and New France.

Paradoxically, it was the English, the greatest exponents of colonization, who succeeded in applying to the fur trade the prescription of trade without settlement in its purest form. This was in Hudson Bay, the third of the great routes to the fur-bearing regions of the West used by Europeans and the last to be reconnoitered. Thither a small group of English noblemen and merchants, several of them prominent in contemporary Carolina and Africa ventures, sent the *Nonsuch* ketch, 43 tons, 36 feet long, in 1668; she returned the next year with furs which sold for £ 1379 6s. 10d. From this beginning arose the Hudson's Bay Company, chartered in 1670.[87] A few small forts were built at the bayside and an

---

[86] J. Franklin Jameson, ed., *Narratives of New Netherland, 1609–1664* (New York: Scribner, 1909), p. 306.

[87] On which see Rich, *Hudson's Bay Company*, I.

economical style of trading quickly evolved. No colonization ensued and few inland journeys were undertaken. The company's handful of men stayed by the Bay and waited for Indians to come to them. Sure enough they came, bringing more furs than the English or for that matter the European market could consume. From Charles II the company received a monopoly of Rupert's Land, with freedom but no compulsion to colonize. Parliament confirmed it, in 1690, but only for seven years; when that act expired the company had no monopoly, but was nevertheless left undisturbed by English competitors for many years. As in New Netherland and New France the critical problem for these trading posts was defense. Repeatedly between 1686 and 1709 the French attacked Hudson Bay by land and sea. By a hair the company survived, reduced in the War of Spanish Succession to a single post, Albany, and winning in the end not by its own efforts but by Marlborough's victories in Europe and Bolingbroke's diplomacy at Utrecht. In 1713 the French withdrew from Hudson Bay. The company recovered its earlier prosperity, remaining as a rare if not unique instance of the successful application to North America of the anticolonizing formula.

If the fur trade was often colonization's enemy, it was always exploration's friend, the equivalent for North America of gold and silver in South America. Furs took Breton and Norman fishermen up the St. Lawrence to trade with Montagnais and Ottawas at Tadoussac; furs paid for Champlain's probes to Lakes Huron and Ontario; furs took Radisson and Groseilliers and many other *coureurs de bois* beyond Sault Ste. Marie and Michilimackinac to trade with Foxes, Chippewas, and Sioux; furs inspired Frontenac's obstinate sponsorship, against the wishes of Versailles, of French trading and military posts in the Illinois and beyond; furs took Jolliet down the Mississippi in 1673 and La Salle to its mouth in 1682. Other considerations were present, not least a quest for experience and a self-indulgence in the freedom of the wilderness. Missionaries wanted converts; hopes of a waterway to the East lingered; Colbert and his successors looked for a warm-water port for New France; and by 1700 there were glimpses in Versailles of a mighty and prestigious empire in the West. But none of these could have worked without furs: even Jesuits needed capital.

Neither English nor Dutch matched this magnificent record. Yet it was to promote the fur trade, and for no other reason, that the English entered Hudson Bay in 1668. And it was to bring peace to the Indians, beaver to the Bayside, and profits to London that Henry Kelsey in 1690–92 made the only western journey by an Englishman comparable to the exploits of the *coureurs de bois*.[88] Starting from York Fort, he traveled at least as far as the Saskatchewan, making contact with Cree and Assiniboine Indians and recording his experiences in a rhymed journal. Kelsey had no imitators in the seventeenth century and few before 1763. Even less dramatic were the achievements of the Dutch at Fort Orange. The policy of the West India Company, like that of the Hudson's Bay Company, was to encourage Indians to come to the posts, meddle as little as possible in Indian affairs, and rely on better and cheaper goods to outtrade the French competition. The *bosch-loupers* (independent traders) of New Netherland may have penetrated some way into the interior, but if so their achievements went unrecorded. Yet even the West India Company's men at Fort Orange were not entirely firm-footed: they made the journey in 1634–35 to which we owe the earliest firsthand description of Iroquois life, a visit undertaken to investigate Mohawk and Oneida complaints that they were getting less for their furs than Indians who traded with the French.[89]

Finally, in the spur given to exploration by the fur trade, it was Indian trade in skins and slaves that drew frontiersmen from Carolina and Virginia round or through the Alleghenies. Toward 1700 the French were coming into the same territory down the Mississippi. Without the fur trade they would not have been there, nor the English to oppose them. From this rivalry arose the foundation of Louisiana (1699), the Anglo-French struggle for the Mississippi Valley in the eighteenth century, and the British nightmare of encirclement.

Exploration was one thing; selling the furs it made available to Europe quite another. What had been a trickle of beaver before 1600 became a stream by 1650 and a flood by 1700. From New Netherland the Dutch took 5758 skins in 1625, 8130 in 1626, 7890 in 1627, 7126 in 1631, and 15,174 in 1633, with a further if erratic increase in the 1640s and 1650s. In 1656 Fort Orange took 35,000 beaver, and in 1660, 25,000.[90] Naturally

---

[88] A. G. Doughty and C. Martin, eds., *The Kelsey Papers* (Ottawa: Public Archives of Canada and Public Record Office of Northern Ireland, 1929).

[89] Jameson, *Narratives of New Netherland*, p. 138.

[90] The figures are from E. B. O'Callaghan, *History of New Netherland; or New York under the Dutch*, 2 vols. (New York: Appleton, 1846–48), I, 103, 104, 110, 129, 139; Jean E. Murray, "The Early Fur Trade in New France and New Netherland," *Canadian Historical Review*, 19:377 (1938); Phillips, *Fur Trade*, I, 157.

the trade continued after the conquest, much of it remaining in the hands
of Dutchmen. From 1681 Pennsylvania took up and developed the fur
trade of the Delaware started by Swedes and Dutch. New France between 1615 and 1660 may have collected on the St. Lawrence about the
same number of furs as the Dutch on the Hudson; then westward expansion led to a huge and ultimately unwanted growth. In three years
(1675–77) the colony sent 223,000 livres (weight) of beaver to France; in
three more (1681–83) 266,000.[91] Worse was to come. In October 1693,
235,786 beaver skins were dispatched by New France to La Rochelle, a
quantity quite beyond France's capacity either to consume or to sell
elsewhere. England, since the founding of the Hudson's Bay Company
had satisfied its domestic needs, was also reexporting furs to Europe;
with 140,000 beaver skins reaching London in 1688–92 and 150,000 in
1693–94, it had to.[92]

An informed guess is that about 1700 the product of an average year's
hunt in the New World was around 300,000 beaver skins for the European market.[93] Beaver prices have not been systematically studied, but
enough is known to show that fur did not escape the common fate of New
World staples in the late seventeenth century. As early as 1610 a surplus
caused low prices in France. In the 1640s prices are said to have fallen in
one year from 10 to 6 livres. By inference they must have recovered in
order to fall again in the 1660s from 14 to 4 livres.[94] Intervention by
French planners made matters worse in the long run. When Jean
Oudiette took over the fiscal management of the French fur trade in 1675
he undertook to buy all Canadian beaver, irrespective of type or quality,
at 4 livres, 10 sous the livre (weight). Two years later a differential was
introduced between *castor gras* (5 livres, 10 sous) and *parchment* (3 livres,
10 sous).[95] The former was coat beaver trapped by Indians and sewn into
coats for their own use, the skins worn with the hairs inward. In a year or
two the guard hairs rubbed away, leaving the short hairs which meanwhile had absorbed natural grease from the body. Coat beaver was highly
prized in the 1670s. The immediate effects of these guaranteed prices in

[91] Phillips, *Fur Trade*, I, 216, 295–296.
[92] K. G. Davies, Introduction to E. E. Rich and A. M. Johnson, eds., *Hudson's Bay Copy Book of Letters Outward 1688–1696* (London: Hudson's Bay Record Society, 1957), p. xxxvii.
[93] Phillips, *Fur Trade*, I, 342.
[94] *Ibid.*, pp. 47, 96; Innis, *Fur Trade*, p. 63.
[95] Rich, *Hudson's Bay Company*, I, 403–408.

New France were good: Oudiette, who made money in the Antilles, lost it in Canada, thus subsidizing Canadian imports from Europe. But the long-term results were bad. "The beaver trade in France and Europe," it was observed in 1700, "is limited to a certain consumption beyond which there is no sale and the beaver remains a pure loss to those charged with the conduct of the trade."[96] *Castor gras* lost its preferred status; in 1698 the Hudson's Bay Company ordered its governor to burn coat beaver in the presence of Indians to convince them of its valuelessness and in 1706 the French farmers announced their intention of buying no more for six years.[97] The flood of furs continued: in three years (1702–4) 581,380 skins were brought to Montreal and Quebec, swamping the French market. Unsold beaver accumulated, went rotten, and was burned.[98] Worst of all, the economy of New France failed to grow in other directions fast enough to make good the damage done by overproduction of fur. As a French civil servant put it in 1704: the "Canadian colonists have never interested themselves in anything but fur-trading, and they are now falling into bankruptcy because of the low price that furs are bringing."[99]

Fear of overproduction was one reason, though not the only one, for persistent attempts to regulate the North American fur trade either by monopoly or by a system of licenses. Controls were imposed by colonial as well as by metropolitan governments and extended to the taking of furs in America as well as to their shipment from America to Europe. Every colony with an interest in the fur trade, French, Dutch, and English, made some attempt to restrict the sale of liquor, arms, and ammunition to Indians, more for reasons of self-preservation than out of concern for Indian welfare. This made licenses necessary in the fur trade. Massachusetts sold them from the first. Plymouth in 1649 issued licenses to five traders at £50 a year each for six years. Virginia experimented with free Indian trade in 1656, started licenses in 1661–62, reimposed them after Bacon's Rebellion in 1676, and gave them up in 1691. Carolina began to issue licenses in 1707.[100]

In all these colonies income from the sale of licenses was a further reason for controlling the fur trade. In New France the need for revenue was the dominant consideration, for fur had to pay for running the gov-

[96] Innis, *Fur Trade*, p. 73.
[97] Rich, *Hudson's Bay Company*, I, 370; Innis, *Fur Trade*, p. 70.
[98] Phillips, *Fur Trade*, I, 303.
[99] Quoted in Innis, *Cod Fisheries*, p. 136.
[100] Phillips, *Fur Trade*, I, 123, 137–138, 164–165, 175–177, 335.

ernment and if possible show a profit for the king. To a large extent the organizational history of the Canadian fur trade in the seventeenth century is a series of experiments in collecting the *droit du quart* — the tax of one beaver in four. As well as the fur-trading companies formed in France, Canadian companies were called into existence, given the sole right to buy beaver from the traders, and obliged to collect the *quart* and pay it or an equivalent to the government of New France. Such was the Compagnie des Habitans, a consortium of half-a-dozen Canadian merchants who ran the trade from 1645 to 1656. It was to this body that control was handed back in 1665 after the collapse of the Compagnie des Indes Occidentales, and to the Compagnie du Canada that it was returned in 1700. Between 1675 and 1700 the right to collect the *quart*, with the monopoly of shipping furs to France, was farmed to Jean Oudiette and (from 1685) Jean Fauconnet. The annual rent was 350,000 livres in 1675; it was raised to 500,000 in 1685 but lowered to the old figure in 1697 on account of the slump.[101]

The farmers and the companies were concerned only with the buying of furs at Montreal and Quebec. Some of these furs were brought in by Indians, most by *coureurs de bois*; regulating the latter acquired a history and a debate of its own. Colbert's policy of a compact colony required that their number should be limited. Royal edicts restraining them were issued in 1675, 1676, 1678, and 1681.[102] Governor d'Avaugour had two men shot in 1661, Governor Frontenac had one hanged in 1674, for breaking the rules.[103] No doubt many *coureurs* were free-livers: the church employed a few as *engagés* but on the whole disapproved of them. But the policy of suppression was not consistently applied. A system of *congés* enacted in 1681 provided for twenty-five a year to be issued, each to cover a party of three men, thus seventy-five men in all; the number out in the wilderness, after the decree as well as before, ran into several hundreds. Licenses in the fur trade, like most licenses in the seventeenth century, easily turned into either taxation or patronage. Governor Frontenac's *congés* became favors to be given to friends or deserving cases, and sold by them to the highest bidder. Many traders went out without licenses: the territory was too vast for effective control. If pushed

---

[101] Rich, *Hudson's Bay Company*, I, 403–408.
[102] Phillips, *Fur Trade*, I, 207.
[103] W. J. Eccles, *Frontenac, Courtier Governor* (Toronto: McClelland and Stewart, 1959), p. 37.

too hard, the *coureurs de bois* took their furs to Albany where there were English trade goods better and cheaper than those to be got at Montreal.[104]

Sugar

Sugarcane almost certainly was indigenous neither to Europe nor to America but to Asia. Moving westwards, it was in Persia by the sixth century A.D. and was brought to southern Europe by the Arabs and grown in Italy, Portugal, and Spain. Thence it was carried in the fifteenth century to the islands of the eastern Atlantic, Madeira, the Azores, the Canaries, Principe, and São Tomé, the nurseries of American colonization and of the Atlantic economy.[105] Here, by 1500, a flourishing sugar industry had arisen, based mainly on free labor in Madeira and on slave labor elsewhere. Till then sugar in Europe was a luxury comparable to spices, mainly used for mixing with wine. Now, with larger quantities arriving from the eastern Atlantic, prices collapsed. Between 1471 and 1540 the fall in England was from 1s. 2d. a pound or thereabouts for white sugar to 6d. a pound or less. In time cheapness stimulated the wider use of sugar as a preserve and as an ingredient in confectionery; after 1540 prices rose. This early, and not well-documented, slump and recovery adumbrates the later history of New World staples in general and of New World sugar in particular, supply moving ahead of European demand with consequential lowering of price.

The next step from the Atlantic islands was obvious: Columbus took cane from the Canaries to Hispaniola on his second voyage. Wild sugar growing in the Antilles a century or two later convinced some witnesses that the plant had a pre-Columbian history in America, but this is unlikely. The wild cane seen by Father Labat was probably planted by Caribs.[106] Columbus's canes did not prosper; sugar had to be reintroduced to Hispaniola about 1510. There followed a period of slow growth until the end of the sixteenth century, when production in Hispaniola dwindled to very little, with only token quantities grown in Puerto Rico, Cuba, and the Spanish mainland colonies. Spain thus had and muffed the chance to be first in the field as supplier of American sugar to Europe. The reasons for this failure are not clear. Lack of capital played

[104] *Ibid.*, pp. 90, 279, 297; Innis, *Fur Trade*, p. 67; Phillips, *Fur Trade*, I, 249.
[105] Noel Deerr, *The History of Sugar*, 2 vols. (London: Chapman & Hall, 1949), vol. I, chapters 9 and 10, II, 528.
[106] *Ibid.*, I, 17–19, for discussion of this question.

some part, for sugar's reputation from the beginning was that of a crop beyond the resources of most colonists. "And let it be said," wrote the Spanish historian of the Indies, Oviedo, "without repeating it many times that a large and well-equipped mill costs much money."[107] The Spanish colonial authorities made loans to help with the expenses but not enough. Restrictive controls, high duties, tithes, and the *deshonor de trabajo* have been suggested as further reasons for the failure of Spain's sugar industry. The Spaniards, one has to infer, came to the New World with other intentions: to fight, to plunder, to convert, to rule, to judge, to live on the labor of Indians, but not to manage sugar estates. Whatever the explanation, the fact is of first importance. The way was left clear for more profit-minded colonists of other countries to grow, make, and market a product which, properly managed, could have made fortunes for Spaniards and strengthened the economic base of Spain's empire.

The first to take advantage of Spain's lack of sustained interest were the Portuguese in Brazil, a reminder not to lump together the styles of colonization of the two Iberian countries. The Spaniards may have been too lazy or too gentlemanly to run sugar plantations; the Portuguese were not. By 1580 there were probably 60 *engenhos* (sugar works) in Brazil; by 1610 there were 230, a remarkable growth which coincides in time with the privateering assaults on Brazil by the northern Europeans, proof of the resilience of the Portuguese empire.[108] When privateering turned into the Dutch attempt to conquer Brazil, growth was indeed interrupted; but it seems to have been resumed after the Dutch were beaten and continued until the slump in sugar of the 1670s and 1680s. At the beginning of the eighteenth century Brazil had 528 *engenhos* and probably produced as much sugar as all the English Caribbean islands put together, and a great deal more than either French or Dutch. Deerr, in his world study of the history of sugar, estimated Brazil's production as follows: 1580, 4760 tons; 1600, 16,300 tons; 1650, 28,500 tons; 1710, 21,800 tons.[109] Sugar was indeed "le grand triomphe du xviie siècle au Brésil et du Brésil"; [110] it would be quite wrong to think of this industry collapsing like a house of cards at the first breath of English and French competition.

Sugarcane was introduced to Bermuda in 1612 with no effect. Not for

[107] Quoted in *ibid.*, I, 119.
[108] Frédéric Mauro, *Le Portugal et l'Atlantique au XVIIe siècle (1570–1670)* (Paris: S.E.V.P.E.N., 1960), p. 195.
[109] Deerr, *History of Sugar*, I, 112, 193–199.
[110] Mauro, *Portugal et l'Atlantique*, p. 183.

another twenty-five or thirty years were serious experiments made with it in the English and French islands. Traditionally the credit for spreading both the plant and the expertise is given to the Dutch. In 1637, according to a reporter thirty years later, Pieter Brower of North Holland brought sugar to Barbados from Brazil. And in 1639 the French Compagnie des Îles engaged Tréjel, a Fleming or Dutchman living in Rouen, to start sugar growing in Martinique. There is some evidence that Englishmen and Frenchmen went to Brazil to see for themselves, and in the 1640s and 1650s there were numerous Dutch refugees from Brazil in the Caribbean who helped to disseminate knowledge of cane cultivation and sugar making. Probably sugar came to the West Indies in a number of different ways, more or less independently. Certainly there were early failures. Tréjel appears to have accomplished little; and according to the island's first historian, Richard Ligon, it was not until the end of the 1640s that good sugar began to be made in Barbados.[111]

It is common to speak of the "sugar revolution" or "revolution de la canne" in the English and French colonies, denoting swift economic and social transformation: from tobacco, ginger, or cotton to sugar; from small holdings to large estates; from white indentured labor to slaves. This model has the virtue of simplicity to recommend it, but like most models is a better servant than master.

In the first place, the "sugar revolution" nearly everywhere was a matter not of years but of decades or scores of years. Barbados was the exception. Here between 1645 and 1660 sugar became the island's first concern. The speed with which a large slave population was accumulated in Barbados is itself evidence of the "revolution." A letter written in 1645 by George Downing, then teaching in Barbados, to his cousin, the younger Winthrop, catches the authentic note of boom: the Barbadians, he wrote, "have bought this year no lesse than a thousand negroes, and the more they buie, the more they are able to buye, for in a yeare and a halfe they will earne with God's blessing as much as they cost."[112] Ligon's *History*, published in 1657 but based on his residence in the island from 1647 to 1650, gives the same impression. Here indeed is the "sugar revolution." But where else? No other English or French island was so early conquered by sugar, and in few was the victory so swift or complete.

[111] Deerr, *History of Sugar*, I, 162–164; Charles R. Boxer, *The Dutch in Brazil* (Oxford: Clarendon Press, 1957), p. 143.
[112] Quoted in Harlow, *History of Barbados*, p. 44.

Nowhere was a colony so fully peopled *before* sugar; and no other island disposed of so many landless unemployed *after* sugar. Part of the historical importance of Barbados is to force us to ask why other colonies were different.

St. Kitts/St. Christophe might have been a rival, though smaller. Colonization began early and sugar was grown there in the 1640s. Joint Anglo-French occupation of the island, however, failed to work once the dangers from Caribs and Spaniards had passed. Friction turned into bitter and destructive war in 1666–67; the English were evicted. Their part of the island was restored by the Treaty of Breda but claims for damages were never settled. The island suffered again in the wars of 1689–1713 and was able to settle to peaceful growth only after the Treaty of Utrecht had made it wholly English.[113] Antigua, another of the English Leewards, was first settled in 1632 and made sugar in 1655 but progress was extremely slow until 1674 when Christopher Codrington brought slaves from Barbados and started a plantation there. In 1678 there were 2308 whites and 2172 blacks in this island of 108 square miles. Thereafter sugar was grown seriously. At the beginning of the eighteenth century Antigua was third (to Barbados and Jamaica) as English sugar producer. If this island may be said to have undergone a "revolution" it was in the closing not the middle decades of the seventeenth century.[114]

Martinique was something like a French Barbados, but not a very close approximation. Here, as in Barbados, there was a fair-sized population before sugar; here, too, tobacco was grown by indentured labor in the pioneer days. But in Martinique the "sugar revolution" was a far longer drawn out affair. The slave population mounted much more slowly; in 1683 it was only about 9000. Sugar progressed but did not for some time drive out other crops. In 1671 it occupied about three-eighths of the cultivated area, the remainder being devoted to tobacco and provisions. As late as 1717, on Deerr's estimates, Martinique made less sugar than Barbados, a much smaller island, had made in 1655.[115] In Guadeloupe growth was still slower, as may be inferred from the island's demographic history, already discussed. In 1699 Guadeloupe had 48 *sucreries* (sugar

---

[113] Richard Pares, *A West-India Fortune* (London: Longmans, 1950), p. 23.

[114] C. S. S. Higham, *The Development of the Leeward Islands under the Restoration, 1660–1688* (Cambridge: At the University Press, 1921).

[115] Abdoulaye Ly, *La compagnie du Sénégal* ([Paris]: Présence Africaine, 1958), pp. 49–51; May, *Histoire économique de la Martinique*, p. 88; Deerr, *History of Sugar*, I, 193, 235.

works); in 1730, 252.[116] Such appearances of a "sugar revolution" as can be found there locate it in the early eighteenth century not in the seventeenth, and after an overture lasting fifty years.

The Barbadian model has little relevance to the Greater Antilles, conquered from Spain. In Jamaica there was no tobacco period. Sugar began to be grown there soon after the Spaniards had left, making fairly slow progress until about 1690, speeding up in the eighteenth century, and in full spate after 1760. For a long time Jamaica had unpatented cultivable land, the government devising schemes to attract new settlers — a far cry from tiny, overpopulated Barbados shipping off its unemployed to other colonies. St.-Domingue, France's Jamaica, had a tobacco period, lasting until about 1700; the population then was still small. In 1701 there were thirty-five sugar mills in production there, but by 1720–22 output equaled that of Jamaica.[117] The "sugar revolution" here was an eighteenth-century phenomenon, different from Barbados in that it did not displace a large white labor force.

In the second half of the eighteenth century sugar largely dominated the Caribbean economy and almost entirely dominated Caribbean society. Why did it take so long, except in Barbados, to achieve this position? The answer to this question requires an examination of labor, capital, and marketing.

There were slaves in the French and English colonies before there was sugar. Whereas sugar was to close the planter's options, tobacco left them open: it could be grown by white labor or black, on small plots or on large estates. In pioneer Virginia and Maryland and in the first years of the Caribbean colonies, white labor was used because it was available and no alternative was in sight. Few tobacco planters then could afford slaves and few slaves were offered them. The Portuguese did not have enough for themselves and their Spanish clients; the Dutch did not take a grip on the sources of supply in West Africa until 1640; the English did not start systematic slave trading until 1650–60, the French later still.

Sugar needed slaves. Examples can be found in history of "free" sugar (Madeira in the fifteenth century) but they are rare. Compared to white indentured labor slaves were probably cheaper and certainly more

---

[116] Maurice Satineau, *Histoire de la Guadeloupe, 1635–1789* (Paris: Peyot, 1928), pp. 380–383.

[117] Deerr, *History of Sugar*, I, 238–240; Pierre de Vaissière, *Saint-Domingue: la société et la vie Créoles (1629–1789)* (Paris: Perrin, 1909).

efficient. The advantage in cost may not have been very great: £ 15–£ 20 for a prime slave in the decades 1670–90 against £ 10–£ 12 in Virginia for the services for five years of a white man.[118] But the advantage in efficiency was unquestionable. It did not spring from the physical superiority of blacks over whites, nor from their greater intelligence, nor to any great extent from their capacity to live and work in a warm climate. It sprang from their docility, and from the ease with which black labor could be organized into disciplined gangs for work in the cane fields. The work itself was hard but not skilled.[119] Ground was prepared for planting with no tool more sophisticated than the hoe; plows were rare in the seventeenth century and came in only slowly in the eighteenth. For each plant a hole was dug which might involve shifting up to twelve cubic feet of earth, 60–100 holes being a day's work. On good land ratooning was possible, that is, the last year's plants were left in the ground to give a further crop. On poor or exhausted land, ratooning was not advisable. No planter in Barbados by 1700, even on good land, ratooned for more than one year.[120] Hence the advantage in labor costs of new land, notably in St.-Domingue. Cutting the cane, which had to be done in the short time between ripening and overripening, was as hard labor as holing. Work in the boiling house, where the sugar was made, was more skilled but no less laborious. None of these tasks, however, was beyond the strength of white men; there is nothing to show that holing in the sun was harder than mining coal underground. It was rather that whites would not perform them than that they could not. Very high wages might have overcome objections, but after 1660 sugar could not pay very high wages. Perpetual enslavement for crimes or political offenses might have supplied some kind of conscript white labor force, but the cost of policing it would have been high and the formal enslavement of whites by whites did not fit comfortably into the ethical traditions of western Europe. Indentured laborers, sufficient for the pioneer days of tobacco, were too few to meet sugar's needs, too unamenable to regimentation and discipline, too de-

[118] See above, p. 103 (indentured servants). The contract price for a slave delivered to Virginia in the 1670s was £ 18; it went up after 1690. See K. G. Davies, *The Royal African Company* (London: Longmans, 1957), pp. 143, 295.

[119] There is a description of plantation work in Elsa Goveia, *Slave Society in the British Leeward Islands at the End of the Eighteenth Century* (New Haven, Conn.: Yale University Press, 1965), chapter 2. See also Orlando Patterson, *The Sociology of Slavery* (London: Macgibbon and Kee, 1967).

[120] Pares, *Merchants and Planters*, p. 42.

termined to be off as soon as their time was expired, if not sooner, and too hard to catch. Only people of another race could be subjected to the necessary degradation, only people of another color could be adequately policed; and until they were forthcoming in sufficient numbers the full development of sugar was held back.

Sugar needed capital, for buildings and machinery as well as land and slaves. "A sugar plantation was a factory set in a field."[121] In requiring so much fixed as opposed to circulating capital, sugar held a special position among colonial products. Cane passed through three main manufacturing stages and could be a marketable product at the conclusion of any one of them. The first stage was the production of *muscovado*, a Portuguese word meaning "less finished." Cane from the field was crushed by wooden rollers, the power supplied by wind, water, or cattle according to circumstances.[122] The juice from the rollers was run off into vats, lime added, and the solution boiled. If the boiling was successful, the liquid cooled into a mixture of crystals and molasses. This was *muscovado*, and in this form the planter might sell it in the island or ship it to Europe. Alternatively, he might work the *muscovado* into white or clayed sugar by covering it with layers of wet clay, the water from which seeped through and separated the sugar crystals from the molasses. This product was still a raw material but a higher priced one. Much of Brazil's output was clayed; so by the eighteenth century was nearly half the sugar exported from Martinique and Guadeloupe. The English colonies, however, stuck mainly to *muscovado*. An anonymous writer in 1670 claimed that "we have already beate out the Portugeize at Brazail from sending home any muscovadoes" but admitted that the English were behind in clayed sugar and needed help to get on terms. They did not get help, being further discouraged by the sugar duties imposed in 1685 which laid ¼d. a pound on *muscovado* and ¾d. on clayed. Habits formed in the early years of sugar appear to have lasted, perpetuating this difference between English and French colonial sugar making, important because eventually the French islands produced more and cheaper molasses to sell to the distillers of New England.[123]

[121] *Ibid.*, p. 23.

[122] In Barbados wind predominated: 409 windmills in 1709 against 76 driven by cattle. In Jamaica there were only 44 windmills in 1768 against 369 cattle and 235 water. Deerr, *History of Sugar*, I, 166, 176.

[123] Descriptions of sugar making in Pares, *West-India Fortune*, p. 15; Deerr, *History of Sugar*, I, 109n; Mauro, *Portugal et l'Atlantique*, pp. 203–210.

The last stage in sugar making was refining, in which the raw product was reheated, white of egg or bullock's blood added, the solution clarified by the removal of scum, reboiled, and cooled in molds with a layer of wet clay to separate the crystals.[124] Most refining was done in Europe, furnishing the best example of the working of the *pacte coloniale*. Colbert at first was keen to encourage refining in the Antilles: in 1679 there were five small refineries in Martinique and Guadeloupe. Five years later a metropolitan edict forbade further refineries, and in 1695 all refineries in the French colonies were ordered closed.[125] In the English islands no important refining industry developed, whether through reluctance to invest, lack of skilled labor, or merely from habit, it is difficult to say. Europe was the beneficiary, sugar refining being one of the fastest growing industries of the later seventeenth century. In Amsterdam there were fifty bakeries in 1662, the Dutch being the best customers for French and English reexports. On the whole the industry located itself at or near ports, London and Bristol, Rouen, Nantes, La Rochelle, and Bordeaux, which were themselves importers. In 1690 there were said to be 8000 workers in Hamburg's sugar industry. Sweden and Denmark had refineries; even Russia built one in 1702. Of the sugar countries only Portugal failed to develop a refining industry. By a quixotic reversal of the *pacte coloniale* sugar refining in Lisbon was forbidden in 1559: the intention was to benefit Brazil, the effect to benefit Amsterdam and Hamburg.[126]

Capital for refining was thus mainly found in Europe; but the capital costs of sugar making in the colonies had to be met by the planter, as well as the cost of land and slaves. It was a formidable requirement. Oviedo estimated 15,000 gold ducats for a plantation with 80–120 slaves and 1000–3000 cattle in sixteenth-century Hispaniola; Dalby Thomas, an English colonizing propagandist, valued a 100-acre sugar estate in the English colonies at £5625 in 1690.[127] These statements do not have to be taken literally, but they at least denote public awareness of sugar as a highly capitalized industry. The association of sugar and capital, sugar and

---

[124] Deerr, *History of Sugar*, vol. II, chapter 28. For a contemporary description of sugar making see Thomas Tryon, *Letters, Domestick and Foreign, to Several Persons of Quality* (London, 1700), letter XXXIV.

[125] Mims, *Colbert's West India Policy*, pp. 274, 278–279.

[126] Barbour, *Capitalism in Amsterdam*, p. 62; Deerr, *History of Sugar*, II, 454; Mauro, *Portugal et l'Atlantique*, p. 231.

[127] Pares, *Merchants and Planters*, p. 42; Deerr, *History of Sugar*, I, 119, II, 332.

the large estate, sugar and the rise of a "plantocracy" thus appears inevitable though not one achieved in a flash.

The aggregation of small holdings into large estates following the introduction of sugar is a tale too often told to bear repetition. It is a major constituent of the "sugar revolution." Undeniably it happened in Barbados and Martinique, and to some extent in other colonies where tobacco preceded sugar. One agent in the decline of the small cultivator was the ending of grants of land to time-expired servants: in Barbados by 1640, in Martinique, Guadeloupe, and St. Christophe in the 1660s, even in St.-Domingue in the 1680s. Another was the eclipse of Caribbean tobacco, manifestly inferior to Virginian. The West Indian tobacco growers, some of them tenants, were probably not hard to shift.

Even so, and even in Barbados, the great estate did not come like a thunderclap nor the small holding vanish overnight. Apart from a rather mysterious grant of 10,000 acres of land to the "London Merchants" made in 1628, and not subdivided until 1642, the average size of land grants in Barbados in the early years (1631–38) was seventy-two acres, not large but not exactly tiny plots.[128] Richard S. Dunn's investigation of the social and economic structure of the colony in 1680 (long after sugar's victory) shows that 175 planters then owned 53.4 percent of the cultivated land, 53.9 percent of the white servants, and 54.3 percent of the slaves. These great planters held ten out of twelve seats in the island's Council, twenty out of twenty-two seats in the Assembly, nineteen out of twenty-three judgeships.[129] This picture of precocious Barbados foreshadows the predominance of the "plantocracy" in the Caribbean generally in the eighteenth century. Yet, alongside these great planters, owning sixty or more slaves, there were 190 middling planters in Barbados in 1680, owning between twenty and sixty slaves and 1041 small planters owning fewer than twenty. There were still 1186 freemen in Barbados in 1680, some with one or two slaves, some with none, occupying less than ten acres each. The almost complete monopoly of political office held by the great men does not therefore imply an almost complete monopoly of the means of production. Elsewhere in the Caribbean small planters (or more accurately the owners of small numbers of slaves) survived well into the eighteenth century, though eclipsed in the end.

[128] Pares, *Merchants and Planters*, p. 57, n. 15.
[129] Richard S. Dunn, "The Barbados Census of 1680: Profile of the Richest Colony in English America," *William and Mary Quarterly*, 3rd series, 26:3–30 (1969).

There was no absolute overriding reason why these small planters should not have produced sugar, and in the seventeenth century it is likely that some did in the Portuguese style. In Brazil a sugar estate was divided, like a medieval manor, into the lands of the *senhor* and the lands of the *lavradores*. The *senhor* grew sugar and owned the *engenho*. His tenants also grew sugar, each cultivating perhaps fifteen acres and owning up to twenty slaves; they were obliged to bring their crop to the *engenho*. Thus they were neither peasants nor great planters but middling sugar farmers, dividing their produce with the *senhor* in the proportion two-fifths to three-fifths, or something like it.[130] Evidence that this style was not unknown in the Caribbean is furnished by du Tertre who records Governor Houel's bargain with a proprietor of sugar works whereby land was granted in Guadeloupe on condition that it should be held "à labrados" in the Brazil-style.[131] It is not clear why the Brazil-style failed to take root in the French and English colonies, but fail it apparently did. By 1700, according to Richard Pares, "it was beginning to be thought that every planter must have a mill and boiling house of his own."[132]

What else besides sugar could smallholders produce? The obvious answer was provisions. In Martinique in 1671, 107,000 *pas carrés* were devoted to provisions, 76,000 to sugar, 36,000 to tobacco. This sensible balance did not last long. By 1710, it is claimed, this island had become "a great factory, the workers in which obtained their provisions from outside in exchange for what they themselves produced." Provisions had yielded to cash crops, though not yet to sugar to the exclusion of all else.[133] Tobacco lingered a long time in the north of Martinique where the soil was unfit for cane. Cocoa was grown, at least until the earthquake of 1727: 6000 quintals were exported in 1710, 14,000 in 1722. Bananas were cultivated: 5 million plants in 1734, 8 million in 1753. Indigo was another alternative to sugar. Jamaica in 1670 had fifty-seven sugar works, forty-nine indigo works, and forty-seven cocoa walks.[134] Edward Cranfield's "Observations on the Present State of Jamaica" (1675) gives a picture of a mixed economy with cotton "very proffitable, especially to the middle sort of Planters, that cannot compasse a sugar-work" and "incredible

---

[130] Boxer, *Dutch in Brazil*, pp. 140–142; Mauro, *Portugal et l'Atlantique*, pp. 201–202; Deerr, *History of Sugar*, I, 108.
[131] Du Tertre, *Histoire générale des Antilles*, I, 464.
[132] Pares, *Merchants and Planters*, p. 25.
[133] May, *Histoire économique de la Martinique*, pp. 84, 88.
[134] Patterson, *Sociology of Slavery*, pp. 19–20.

nombers of cattle."[135] Pares's pronouncement that "every great planter turned to sugar sooner or later and, having turned to it, he hardly ever turned back to anything else" cannot be doubted. What can and should be emphasized is that not every planter was a great one.[136]

Where the small planters erred was in not continuing to specialize in provisions. Barbados, Winthrop was told as early as 1647, was "so intent upon planting sugar that they had rather buy foode at very deare rates than produce it by labour, soe infinite is the profitt of sugar workes after once accomplished."[137] Profits did not long remain "infinite," and the decline in the production of provisions in Martinique and elsewhere was a much longer drawn out affair than in Barbados. By the eighteenth century, however, the English West Indies were importing meat from Ireland, luxury foods from England, wine from Madeira, and fish and corn from New England. It was this insufficiency of food in the Caribbean that gave New England its special place in the Atlantic economy, trading surplus agricultural products, lumber and low-grade fish for sugar, molasses, and bills on London. Canada and the French Antilles never came into the same relationship, though not for want of urging by Colbert or example by the intendant Talon. One of the unfortunate effects of the fur trade was to hold back New France's development as an agricultural colony. The French West Indies were thus compelled to rely for imported food on metropolitan France and on the English mainland colonies, neither satisfactory in the Atlantic wars of the eighteenth century.

For an explanation of the survival of the secondary cash crops, cotton, ginger, indigo, and of the relatively slow advance of sugar in Jamaica and Guadeloupe in the later seventeenth century, we must turn finally to marketing and prices. Sugar prices were falling gently before cane reached the English and French colonies. They continued to fall until about 1670, though not alarmingly. After 1670 they went down abruptly, reaching bottom in the mid-1680s. Just as tobacco prices had fallen between 1620 and 1645 by about 85 percent, so between 1645 and 1680 sugar fell by 70 percent.[138] Both ran into crises of overproduction, typical of colonial products that were easier to grow than to market. The whole Atlantic economy, Brazil included, was affected. In Amsterdam the

[135] Public Record Office, London, C.O. 138/2, pp. 110 et seq.
[136] Pares, *Merchants and Planters*, p. 22.
[137] Quoted in Bailyn, *New England Merchants*, p. 85.
[138] Pares, *Merchants and Planters*, p. 40.

price of raw sugar fell by one-third between 1677 and 1687.[139] In England *muscovado* in 1686 descended to a point not only lower than ever before but, there is reason to think, lower than at any time in the next two hundred years.[140] Production, the loudest complainants said, was being carried on at a loss. This may not have been literally true but it is certain that the boom conditions of the 1640s and 1650s had completely vanished. In 1700 when the worst was over Thomas Tryon, English agent of several Barbadian sugar planters, advocated crop restriction: his picture of the planter's "miserable consumptive life . . . filled with great Debts, perplexing Accompts, protested Bills of Exchange at Tenn per cent. loss" may be a little overdrawn, but there is no denying the reality of the depression through which sugar had passed.[141]

Recovery began with the outbreak of war between France and England in 1689. Military and naval operations in the West Indies and privateers in the English Channel sent London sugar prices from 16s.–18s. for 100 pounds to 35s. or even 50s. How much of the benefit went to planters and how much to shipowners and insurers it is difficult to say in this confused war period; if one may judge by Jamaica's enhanced capacity to absorb slaves in the first decade of the eighteenth century, the lot of the planters improved. After 1713 prices settled down at better than prewar levels, demand catching up with supply at least until the next slump in the 1730s. This necessarily rough summary of the course of European prices is an essential clue to understanding the spread of sugar in the Caribbean. Barbados, the tiny island of Nevis, and perhaps St. Kitts/St. Christophe apart, no English or French colony was fully committed to sugar before the depression of 1670–90. Other cash crops, requiring less investment, survived. With recovery after 1690 coinciding with improvements in the supply of slaves, the onward march of sugar across Guadeloupe, Jamaica, and St.-Domingue could be resumed.

Other Products

The North Atlantic economies of France and England in the seventeenth century rested upon these four products, tobacco, fish, furs, and sugar,

---

[139] Deerr, *History of Sugar*, II, 530; Mauro, *Portugal et l'Atlantique*, pp. 257, 526; Charles R. Boxer, *Portuguese Society in the Tropics* (Madison: University of Wisconsin Press, 1965), Appendix 20.

[140] For London prices in 1673–1713, see Davies, *Royal African Company*, Appendix IV; for London prices from 1728, see Deerr, *History of Sugar*, II, 530–531.

[141] Tryon, *Letters, Domestick and Foreign*, pp. 192–193.

and upon the trade to America in servants and slaves. No other commodity came near them in bulk, value, or influence. No other shaped the life of a colony as furs shaped New France or sugar Barbados, forcing them to be different from Europe. Three of these products — fish the exception — suffered the fate of being too successful, with prices tumbling to a point where colonists talked of ruin if they did not actually experience it. The beginning of the eighteenth century brought partial recovery in the staples, particularly sugar, but to thrive the Atlantic economies had to diversify. Purposeful experiments with new crops were started; by 1750 both French and English colonies had acquired a broader economic base.

The main contributors to diversification were rice, coffee, cocoa, and cotton, none of major importance in the seventeenth century. Rice was tried in early Virginia, and introduced to Carolina about 1685. Experiments were undertaken, strains imported from Madagascar, and by 1700 consignments were being sent to England and the West Indies.[142] In 1704 rice was important enough to be added to the list of enumerated commodities, which were required by law to be shipped only to English ports. Predictably it failed to make an impression on the Englishman's diet and in 1730 direct export to southern Europe was permitted. Twenty or thirty years later it was Georgia's as well as South Carolina's leading cash crop.

Coffee came later. In the seventeenth century Europe's supplies were drawn from Java, the East's monopoly not yet challenged by the Atlantic. An unsuccessful attempt was made to grow coffee in Martinique in 1716–17; in 1726 the plant reached Brazil, from Java by way of Amsterdam; and in 1730 it was introduced to Jamaica. In both places it did well, and in St.-Domingue it became one of the pillars on which that island's amazing prosperity was built.[143]

Cocoa like tobacco belonged to America. Chocolate began to be drunk in northern Europe about 1650, imported from Mexico and Venezuela, but for a long time it remained a luxury for the well-to-do. Jamaica was the leading English producer. As late as 1670 cocoa was described as the island's "chief produce," that is, outranking sugar, but disease and hurricanes stopped it from taking its place as a colonial staple.[144] Du Tertre

[142] David D. Wallace, *South Carolina: A Short History* (Chapel Hill: University of North Carolina Press, 1951), pp. 48–49, 83.
[143] May, *Histoire économique de la Martinique*, pp. 97 et seq; Rich and Wilson, *Cambridge Economic History of Europe*, IV, 296–297.
[144] Great Britain, Public Record Office, *Calendar of State Papers*, Colonial Series, America and West Indies, 1669–74 (London: H.M.S.O., 1889), nos. 144, 375.

recommended it as a crop from which money could be made, and in 1664 it was taken to Martinique from Venezuela. Here, as in Jamaica, there were difficulties, the hurricane of 1727 setting cocoa back several years.[145]

In the raising of cotton America's challenge to Asia was never more than halfhearted in the colonial period. Like ginger, it was a crop to which small planters turned in the early years, but according to du Tertre merchants disliked handling it on account of its bulk and susceptibility to fire.[146] Cotton was grown in many West Indian islands in the seventeenth and eighteenth centuries but nowhere as a major crop. In the southern mainland colonies it was raised for domestic use from early times but not as a cash crop until well into the eighteenth century.[147] As a major staple and important social influence it belongs rather to the nineteenth century.

These were Atlantic crops of the future, unknown in 1713 or only in infancy. Returning to the seventeenth century, dyestuffs stand out as the product or group of products which — next after the great staples — made a noticeable impact on Europe's economy. Here, demand existed before the Discoveries; madder and woad apart, Europe's range of native dyestuffs was not wide. Indigo reached Europe first from the East, but after 1650 several West Indian colonies began to cultivate it. Among the English, only Jamaica produced any quantity (130,000 out of 160,000 pounds of indigo reaching England from the colonies in 1688–89),[148] but the French seem to have taken it more seriously. In 1687 they had two *indigoteries* on Martinique, twelve on Guadeloupe, and no fewer than thirty-four on the little island of Marie-Galante, besides an unrecorded number in St.-Domingue.[149] Indigo, in the demands it made on capital and labor, stood midway between tobacco and sugar. Like tobacco, it grew fast, three months sufficing between planting and cutting, with a second harvest six weeks later from the same plants. On the other hand it can scarcely be ranked as a poor man's crop. Buildings and equipment were needed, though less elaborate than for sugar, for steeping the leaves in water, agitating the liquid and drying the solution until it could be cut

---

[145] Du Tertre, *Histoire générale des Antilles*, II, 184; May, *Histoire économique de la Martinique*, pp. 94–96.

[146] Du Tertre, *Histoire générale des Antilles*, II, 150.

[147] Gray, *Agriculture in Southern United States*, I, 182–184.

[148] Great Britain, Public Record Office, *Calendar of State Papers*, Colonial Series, America and West Indies, 1689–92 (London: H.M.S.O., 1901), no. 2757.

[149] Ly, *Compagnie du Sénégal*, p. 51.

into lumps and packed.[150] The *indigoterie* has rightly been called a "half-way house to plantership on the great scale."[151]

Indigo like rice helped to solve South Carolina's problem of what to do in a colony founded too late to thrive on tobacco and too far north to grow sugar. Barbadians who moved there took indigo, and seeds were fetched from Jamaica about 1700, but little progress was made until the 1740s. Thirty years later South Carolina produced ½ million pounds a year, indigo having become the colony's second cash crop after rice.[152] On the other side of the Atlantic, West Africa was the scene of several attempts to grow indigo in new ground. Between 1687 and 1697 the English experimented with it in Sierra Leone, while the Dutch tried to grow cotton, coffee, and sugar as well as indigo on the Gold Coast in 1697, and having failed with all of them tried again with indigo in 1712.[153] These experiments can be seen as attempts to take crops to labor instead of labor to crops. In the case of indigo, climate was blamed for failure, rain rotting the root and causing the leaf to fall before it was ripe.

Indigo gave blue dye and needed no mordant. Other Atlantic dyestuffs gave red (cochineal from Mexico, camwood, and braziletto), yellow (fustick from Central America and the Caribbean), orange (anotto from the West Indies), purple, black, and blue (logwood from the Bay of Campeche). If America did not supply, as early colonizers had hoped, a massive demand for European textiles, America at least made brighter and more variegated the clothes Europeans wore. Logwood did more than that: the quest for it led to a settlement, originally of retired buccaneers, on Spanish territory in Campeche Bay, which survived all efforts to dislodge it and became in time British Honduras. To judge by a report from Jamaica in 1679 that forty-seven ships had gone to Campeche to cut or collect, logwood was big business in post-buccaneer times, probably too big for Europe's needs. The price fell in the seventeenth century from £100 a ton to £30 by 1670, and to £16 by 1717, one more instance of the devastating effect of overproduction.[154]

---

[150] Du Tertre, *Histoire générale des Antilles*, II, 107–110.

[151] Pares, *Merchants and Planters*, p. 22.

[152] Wallace, *South Carolina*, p. 35; Gray, *Agriculture in Southern United States*, I, 290–296.

[153] Davies, *Royal African Company*, p. 221; Kwame Yeboa Daaku, *Trade and Politics on the Gold Coast, 1600–1720* (Oxford: Clarendon Press, 1970), pp. 44–45.

[154] Andrews, *Colonial Period*, IV, 91n4; Arthur M. Wilson, "The Logwood Trade in the Seventeenth and Eighteenth Centuries," in Donald C. McKay, ed., *Essays in the History of Modern Europe* (New York: Harper, 1936), pp. 13–14.

Wool, iron, water, and wood were the principal raw materials of European industries in the seventeenth century. Supplies of the first three were generally adequate; supplies of the last were not. With population growing in the later Middle Ages and some industrial expansion, chronic timber shortages were felt. These could be overcome, for certain purposes such as boiling and space heating, by the use of coal as a substitute; hence the rise of an English coal industry between 1540 and 1640.[155] From the same scarcity of timber proceeded the half-timbered house. But for other uses, above all for shipbuilding, there was no substitute. America seemed to have the answer, inexhaustible supplies of wood, some of excellent quality, at just the moment when more and bigger ships were needed. Yet American timber, while contributing much to the domestic economies of the colonies and to intercolonial trading, failed to become a major export to Europe in the seventeenth century or even in the eighteenth.

From the St. Lawrence to South Carolina the Atlantic coast was thickly forested with trees familiar to Europeans (oak, pine, cedar) and others they had not seen at home. The first settlers, chopping down trees to make fields, were probably more conscious of the forest as an enemy than as an economic asset. Nevertheless, cheap timber almost everywhere did something to balance high labor costs in colonial America, enabling New England's shipbuilding industry to get on terms with Old England's and helping the pioneers to be better housed than they would have been in Europe. In trade, too, lumber became important to all the seaboard colonies, the Caribbean not Europe being the chief market. Here, some of the smaller islands were soon short of wood. Barbados was almost entirely dependent on imports, trying to colonize nearby St. Lucia mainly for the sake of its wood.[156] Everywhere in the Caribbean, barrels were wanted for packing products destined for Europe. Barrel staves and hoops, oak and pine boards and shingles, with provisions, became mainstays of trade between the West Indies and the North American colonies.

A comparable trade was carried on between New France and the French West Indies but on a much smaller scale. In 1670 Intendant Talon sent three ships from Quebec with provisions for Cayenne and Tortuga, but no regular trade in Canadian-owned shipping appeared until the

---

[155] John U. Nef, *The Rise of the British Coal Industry*, 2 vols. (London: Routledge, 1932).
[156] Harlow, *History of Barbados*, pp. 151–152.

eighteenth century and then did not exceed ten ships a year.[157] Canadian grain and timber were carried to the Antilles by French-owned and French-freighted ships, sailing a triangular course from La Rochelle to Cape Breton, from Cape Breton to the Caribbean, and from the Caribbean home; but this trade was never great enough to get in the way of New Englanders and New Yorkers exchanging lumber for molasses in the French West Indies. From this illicit trade the English American colonies acquired, New France did not, the habit of defying government at home.

With freight costs three times those from the Baltic, American timber failed to make its way into European markets.[158] There were also doubts, probably exaggerated, about the fitness of American oak for ships' timbers, and doubts, probably not exaggerated, about the quality of American tar and turpentine. Masts were the exception: cargoes were shipped from Virginia as early as 1609 and from Massachusetts in 1634. The first Dutch war (1652–54) gave a fillip, and before the end of the seventeenth century the mast trade was "big business — bigger than any yet seen in New England."[159] Government at home was interested. Surveyors were appointed to select and reserve white pines. Bounties of £1 a ton on masts, £3 on turpentine, £4 on tar, and £6 on hemp were granted by Parliament in 1704, and naval stores put on the list of enumerated commodities in 1705. Between 1706 and 1714 about £4000 a year was paid by the British government in the form of bounties. Even so, and even in the mast trade, America did not effectively challenge the Baltic. The largest number of masts for the Royal Navy shipped in one year in the War of Spanish Succession was 261, enough to matter in New England, but few compared to 1981 of Baltic origin in the same year.[160]

Precious metals played a notable part in first promoting European interest in America, and it is appropriate to end this summary of the fruits of colonization with a reference to gold and silver. None was mined in the seventeenth century. Important quantities of bullion accrued to the Dutch from privateering, and all the northern countries earned silver by trading with Spaniards.[161] It was for this reason, among others, that the

[157] Allana G. Reid, "Intercolonial Trade during the French Regime," in *Canadian Historical Review*, 32:243–246 (1951).

[158] Robert G. Albion, *Forests and Sea Power* (Cambridge, Mass.: Harvard University Press, 1926), p. 240.

[159] Bailyn, *New England Merchants*, p. 133.

[160] Albion, *Forests and Sea Power*, pp. 251, 418.

[161] Curtis P. Nettels, *Money Supply of the American Colonies* (Madison: University of Wisconsin Press, 1934).

asiento was competed for with a persistence mocked by the fate of those unfortunate enough to win it. Most of the Spanish silver reaching Curaçao, Jamaica, and St.-Domingue in payment for slaves was immediately shipped to Europe. Little remained in the colonies, whose economies were chronically short of a circulating medium until relieved toward the end of the seventeenth century by inflationary issues of paper currency. The Canadians, to whom Colbert refused a currency of their own in 1676, alleviated the shortage in 1685 by an issue of playing cards, values stated on the face and signed by the intendant.[162] In the English colonies, war costs after 1689, coupled with an egregious reluctance to tax themselves even for defense, led to big issues of paper money, depreciating the colonial pound in the case of South Carolina to the level of 7:1 against sterling.[163] No special colonial coinage was supplied by either England or France, and no colony except Massachusetts dared to mint its own.[164] Colonies had to do the best they could with barter, credit, and Spanish-American or Portuguese coins, often much overvalued to stop them from being remitted to Europe. The rarity of coin encouraged a debtor mentality, reflected in colonial laws bearing hard on creditors and in the insouciance with which many planters regarded debts owed in Europe.

West Africa in part made good the disappointment of America. Here, the Europeans did not mine gold. Both Portuguese and Dutch tried to, at Egyira on the Gold Coast, but failed through local opposition. What they got, they bought from the Africans and not cheaply. An ounce of gold, nominally worth £ 4, was bought at Cape Coast Castle in 1687 with European goods costing 45s.–56s., giving a far from spectacular profit when overhead costs were taken into account. The total amount of gold annually taken from the Gold Coast (no other part of West Africa produced much) may have been as much as 7000 marks or £ 224,000 at the end of the seventeenth century.[165] This is Bosman's estimate for a good year about 1700, with the Dutch enjoying the major share. Such evidence as has survived, however, suggests that there were a good many years when the gold trade was interrupted by domestic African wars and purchases fell far

---

[162] Eccles, *Canada under Louis XIV*, p. 136.

[163] This was South Carolina's rate of exchange in the eighteenth century. In most other colonies the depreciation of paper money was less.

[164] A few coins were struck in England and shipped to Maryland in 1658; see Andrews, *Colonial Period*, II, 329–330.

[165] W. Bosman, *A New and Accurate Description of the Coast of Guinea* (2nd English ed.; London, 1721), p. 77.

below Bosman's figure. From 1668 to 1676, for example, the Dutch collected only 3150 marks, less than 400 marks a year. And in twelve years from 1705 to 1716 five of their forts on the Gold Coast (not including Elmina, their capital) took less than 2000 marks.[166] English figures are more complete: in forty-one years from 1673 to 1713 the Royal African Company received 548,327 guineas coined at the mint from African gold, with an annual average of 22,000 guineas for the years 1673 to 1689.[167] This suggests annual shipments from Cape Coast of about 700 marks in the period of more or less effective monopoly. These figures argue that seaborne imports of African gold at the end of the seventeenth century were not contributing much to easing Europe's shortage of that metal. Africa's output was lost in the product of the newly discovered mines of Brazil.

[166] Daaku, *Trade and Politics on the Gold Coast*, pp. 19, 27.
[167] Davies, *Royal African Company*, pp. 225, 360.

CHAPTER 5

GOVERNMENT

Freedom and Inequality

Most Europeans crossed the Atlantic to find work or make a fortune. Some, a minority, did so in order to escape from an oppressive religious establishment. Political freedom, in the secular sense, was not an important objective. Some French emigrants may have been influenced by heavy taxes at home; but few or none left Europe in order to vote at more elections, serve on more juries, attend more town meetings, or even to escape from an overgoverned community into one where the hand of government might be expected to be lighter. These were incidentals, relevant if a prospective settler could choose between one colony and another, but not material to the decision whether to stay in Europe or go. Probably most colonists who gave any thought to the matter assumed that they would find in America much the same political arrangements as they had known in Europe: monarchy or some reflection of it, supported by an elite of birth or wealth or both, in whose hands most of the power in the community would be vested.

New England furnishes the only examples in the seventeenth century of colonies founded with the conscious purpose of creating a society different from that left behind in Europe. The Puritan dynamic was in the first place theological and moral, not political in the secular sense, and it is perhaps a little difficult to see how the founding of Massachusetts has come to be regarded as a blow for freedom. The explanation is to be found in English domestic history where the battle for moral and ecclesiastical reform drew many Puritans, whether they liked it or not (and some obviously did), into political attitudes and action. It was feasible for a small group of nonentities like the Pilgrims to sneak quietly away from Europe and settle down in an empty and none too attractive corner of America. The Puritans who formed the Massachusetts Bay Company, conjured a charter out of the crown, and organized mass transports of settlers from East Anglia, were quite a different matter. They were known, vociferous critics of the Church of England; and in England, as in most of the rest of Europe, it was not possible to oppose the established church or even to decline to accept it without also being in conflict with the political system that supported and leaned upon the church. Church and state in Stuart England were so closely associated as to be one. To be free of episcopacy the Puritans had to be free of monarchy; to be free of William Laud, bishop of London, they had also to be free of King Charles I.

In this sense the founding of Massachusetts was a political act and may be claimed as an assertion of freedom; but it is better understood as a strategy for survival. In 1630 the Puritans who sailed for the New World were quitting a ship that was not merely in danger but actually appeared to be going down. This terrible decade — arguably the worst Protestants have ever known — began on November 8, 1620, with an hour's fighting at the White Mountain in Bohemia and ended on March 6, 1629, when Emperor Ferdinand, with his foot on the neck of German Protestantism, issued the Edict of Restitution. Between these two events Frederick, son-in-law of the king of England and the darling of European Calvinism, lost his newly acquired Bohemian crown and, soon afterwards, his hereditary lands in Germany. Nothing seemed able to stop the northward thrust of the Catholics. When Christian of Denmark took up the Protestant cause in 1626 he was promptly shattered at Lütter by Tilly. By 1629 the Hapsburg armies were on the shores of the Baltic. Nor was this all. The war between Spain and the Netherlands was renewed and for a while the Dutch got the worse of it: in May 1625, after a protracted siege watched by Protestants everywhere, Breda fell to Spinola. Two years later the French king, usually a reliable associate if not friend of European Protestants, turned on the Huguenots in his own country. For more than a year, La Rochelle, their greatest city, held out but starvation won in the

end. La Rochelle capitulated at the end of October 1628, and with its fall
vanished the security the Protestant cause had formerly enjoyed in
France. These blows were not isolated episodes in far-off countries. Puritans in England felt them. With Bohemia gone, Germany apparently
gone, France gone, the Netherlands in danger, Englishmen had no right
to expect immunity. Add the menacing moves at home by King Charles
and William Laud, and it must have seemed common prudence to run.

The new society which the Puritans hoped to make in America was not
dedicated to the pursuit of personal liberty. Early Massachusetts and early
Connecticut contributed enormously to American notions of independence and to the practice of self-government by the community. They
founded and styled American education. They planted the doctrine that
government should have a moral purpose. But the Puritans' best friends
cannot, or at any rate should not, claim that they brought with them or
nurtured in their settlements either the practice of personal freedom or a
generous conferment of political rights. Rhode Island (the repository of
New England's dropouts) apart, the Puritan colonies set no value on
personal freedom as a creative force or on the toleration of deviants without which assertions of freedom become mere tribal chanting.

The rulers of early Massachusetts, within the limits of their little community, were powerful men. There was no separation of authority. Governor and magistrates were the chief executives, either severally or together in council; they formed the upper house of the colony's legislature;
and, sitting as the court of assistants, they were also the supreme judicial
tribunal. Whether or not the charter made them legal sovereigns they
certainly acted as if that is what they were. The law they administered was
not pure English common law, but a compound of common-law precedents, Old Testament precepts, and improvised rules made up to cope
with situations which neither Sir Edward Coke nor Moses had foreseen.
In most civil matters including the law of property English precedents
were largely followed, though all feudal incumbrances on land were
specifically repudiated and English primogeniture was replaced by the
practice of a double portion for the eldest son. In criminal law, however,
the influence of the Old Testament is apparent in efforts to legislate
against sin as well as against crime. Death was the prescribed punishment
for idolatry, witchcraft, blasphemy, murder, bestiality, sodomy, adultery,
man stealing, perjury in capital cases, rebellion, and treason. It is the

presence of adultery in this list (subsection 9 of article 94 of the Body of Liberties of 1641) which most impresses the twentieth-century reader.[1] There were European states (Counter-Reformation Bavaria was one) where adultery was a capital crime but Caroline England was not among them. Fornication between unmarried persons was less severely (but probably more frequently) punished in early Massachusetts, generally by fine or whipping or both. It is of course true that both New and Old England feared the arrival of bastards chargeable on the community and so legislated against sexual irregularity in order to save money; but New England was also interested in fornication as a sin. Hence the punishment by fine in 1635 of a couple who had anticipated marriage; and hence the "comical incident" (narrated by Dutch traveler David Pietersz de Vries) at Hartford in 1639 when a young couple two months married were denounced by the bridegroom's brother for having engaged in premarital intercourse. Both parties were sentenced to be whipped and separated from one another for six weeks.[2]

It may be true that these laws were not rigidly enforced (very few laws were, anywhere, in the seventeenth century) and that "the colonial adulterer might well calculate his chances of evading punishment by the civil authorities" as good.[3] On the other hand, there is a case on record in 1643 of a man and a woman sentenced to death for adultery and, according to Cotton Mather, at least one example of execution.[4] It is also to be remembered that the civil magistrates were not the only agency for intruding into the lives of the citizens of early Massachusetts. The churches took upon themselves the regulation of the morals of their members, censuring those found guilty and in serious cases depriving them of church membership. In a community where church membership was a valuable privilege this was a heavy punishment.

The early laws of Massachusetts give the impression that the town officers who whipped convicted persons were the busiest men in the

[1] An easily accessible version of the "Body of Liberties" of 1641 is that printed in Louis B. Wright and Elaine W. Fowler, eds., *English Colonization of North America* (London: Arnold, 1968), pp. 61–71.

[2] J. Franklin Jameson, ed., *Narratives of New Netherland, 1609–1664* (New York: Scribner, 1909), p. 204.

[3] Emil Oberholzer, Jr., *Delinquent Saints* (New York: Columbia University Press, 1956), p. 142.

[4] Charles J. Hilkey, *Legal Development in Colonial Massachusetts, 1630–1686* (New York: Columbia University Press, 1910), p. 96.

colony. One should not, however, be too impressed by this, having regard to early colonial conditions. There were few jails in seventeenth-
century America and hardly any which could not be broken out of; nor
could a new community be expected cheerfully to shoulder the expense of
keeping prisoners for long periods. Punishments in Massachusetts and in
all colonies were mostly by fines for those who could pay them and the
whip for those who could not. One of the earliest forms of class distinction
in North America was that between those who were and those who were
not sentenced to corporal punishment. "Gentlemen" were not, or very
rarely; indentured servants were. The laws of Massachusetts for controlling the latter were as severe as those of any other colony.

The notorious instances of oppression and victimization in the history of
Massachusetts in the seventeenth century — the banishment of Mrs.
Hutchinson and others in 1638, the hanging of Quakers (including a
woman) in 1660, and the Salem witchcraft trials and executions in 1692 —
cannot be dismissed as aberrations: they are, rather, occasions when the
aims and principles of the founders and first rulers of Massachusetts were
carried to farther extremes than was generally the case. Together with
many less dramatic examples of intolerance and intrusion, they acquit the
colony of the charge of preoccupying itself with the furtherance of freedom in any but the most idiosyncratic sense.

The special case of Massachusetts apart, founders of colonies were more
concerned to plant unfreedom than freedom and made no special effort to
conceal it. This was natural, in the first place because a positive sense of
freedom was not part of the equipment which most colonists brought with
them from Europe. They came from societies where formal privileges out-
ranked common freedoms: where to vote was a privilege, to be exempt
from taxes a privilege, to work at certain trades a privilege, to govern or
judge a privilege. Most of these privileges were heritable, the birthrights of
a minority; some were conferred by favor, but sparingly so as not to dilute
them. To earn them was far beyond the capacity of ordinary people. It
does not follow from this that there were no common rights or common
freedoms at all in seventeenth-century Europe or that promises to colonists that by leaving their country they were not forfeiting the "rights
and liberties of Englishmen" were devoid of all meaning. No one in
England in 1600 could be deemed absolutely rightless; even the "poorest
he" had the right to be tried for his life or liberty by jury according to the

laws of the land and the right (purely notional in the case of the mass of the population) to consent to taxes imposed upon him. These rights are not to be despised, but they melt into insignificance beside the benefits of belonging to a privileged order: the peerage, the clergy, the freeholders, the freemen of a town, the masters of a craft.

The conditions immediately facing the founders of new colonies required the imposition of unfreedom. The first task was to ensure survival: food, defense, something to sell in Europe, were the priorities. To get them, work, disciplined and directed, was essential. Settlers had to be made to dig the land instead of living on fish and berries and hunting for treasure; then to stop digging fields and turn to building defenses against Spaniards or Indians or Caribs; then to stop growing too much tobacco and grow corn instead; and always to strive for a surplus above bare subsistence so that the communal facilities taken for granted in Europe — law courts, jails, churches, schools — could be provided. The interests of the community had to take precedence over the interests of the individual; and if no sense of community arose of itself, the individual had to be coerced. How was this to be done?

The simplest way to run a settlement of Europeans overseas was on military lines, with military rank and discipline, and no rights other than those conferred by rank. Thus were organized, throughout the seventeenth and eighteenth centuries, the Dutch, English, and French trading posts in West Africa and the English posts on Hudson Bay.[5] Here there were no voters and no elected assemblies, no civil magistrates, no trials by jury, not even the right to desert. Men came out with assigned ranks — governor, merchant, factor, lieutenant, tradesman, soldier — and kept them or were promoted according to how they pleased their masters. While in service they forwent the famous "rights and liberties" of Englishmen (or Frenchmen) as surely as if they had joined an army or a ship's company.

These were exceptional communities, settlements of temporary residents, with no land, no family life, and no accumulation of private fortunes. But traces of a military style of government can be found in early Virginia (the rule of Gates and Dale), in Dutch trading posts in New Netherland manned by West India Company officials and soldiers, and in

---

[5] On African establishments see A. W. Lawrence, *Trade Castles and Forts of West Africa* (London: Cape, 1963), pp. 46–65. On Hudson Bay, see E. E. Rich, *History of the Hudson's Bay Company*, 2 vols. (London: Hudson's Bay Record Society, 1958), I, 606–608.

the French colonies of New France and the Antilles. Every new settlement was to some extent a beleaguered garrison, the French most of all. In New France their misfortune in attracting the animus of the Iroquois meant that for half a century the Canadian *habitant* carried his life in his hands; all but the handful in Quebec were frontiersmen. And in the Antilles the Carib threat to the French was far more serious than to the English in Barbados: every colonist, *habitant* or *engagé*, had to be a soldier ready to leave the fields and fight. A mid-seventeenth-century French Caribbean colony was divided into *quartiers*, each *quartier* forming one or two *compagnies* of militia in which all served. This, not the *paroisses* or *baillis* of metropolitan France, was the basic territorial partition: the Conseil Souverain of the island, the supreme court in civil and criminal causes, was formed in early times of the captains of the *compagnies* and two principal inhabitants from each *quartier*.[6] In New France, militia officers did not participate ex officio in central government but the *capitaines de milice* had civil as well as military powers and functions, serving throughout the period of French rule as local agents of the intendant.[7]

Military rank was one way in which discipline could be imposed on a colonial community. Another way was by the introduction into America of the social and legal distinctions associated with European *féodalité*. It is a matter of definition, not evidence, whether western European society or any part of it should be termed "feudal" in the seventeenth century: if a "feudal society" is one in which land is held in return for military service rendered by tenant to lord and by lord to king, then western Europe was not such a society, for armies no longer consisted of feudal levies. On the other hand, many of the feudal forms, obligations, and privileges were still present, especially in France, and to these survivals collectively the term *féodalité* may be applied. Services and rents owed by many French tenants to their *seigneurs* were still regulated by custom, not by contract, and so continued until the end of the *ancien régime*. *Seigneurs*, in the age when colonization began, were still judges over their tenants, not because they had been commissioned by the king but in virtue of inheritance of the lands they held. Though well before 1600 royal justice had displaced seignorial courts for certain purposes, the *seigneurs* had not lost all their

---

[6] [J.-B.] du Tertre, *Histoire générale des Antilles* (Paris, 1667), II, 442–445.
[7] W. J. Eccles, *Frontenac, Courtier Governor* (Toronto: McClelland and Stewart, 1959), p. 214.

rights; it is still appropriate to describe the French countryside in the seventeenth century as under a *régime seigneurial*.[8]

In England *féodalité* lost ground sooner. Landlords and tenants from the fifteenth century onwards were turning away from custom and toward contract; and though the manorial court, attended by tenants and presided over by the lord or his bailiff, was still general in 1600 its usefulness was diminishing.[9] The English landowner ruled the country, not as a *seigneur* sitting in a manorial court, but as a justice of the peace, commissioned by the king, sitting alone in petty sessions or with his colleagues at quarter sessions. In France the alternative to a *régime seigneurial* was rule by professionals, by royal *officiers*, intendants and *subdélégués*; in England it was rule by J.P. Moreover, English landowners — through their preponderance in Parliament — were in a position to enact in statutory form the privileges for property owners, such as the game laws conferred, which in France depended on the inherited and carefully preserved rights of the nobility.

Turning to colonization and the urgent need to regiment colonial society, we should expect a less purposeful attempt to introduce *féodalité* to the English than to the French Atlantic possessions.[10] Vestiges of the English king's claim to suzerainty over the soil of the land he ruled can

---

[8] The most recent statement on this subject and on *féodalité* in Europe is in *L'abolition de la féodalité dans le monde occidental*, 2 vols. (Paris: Éditions du Centre National de la Recherche Scientifique, 1971), the proceedings of an international conference held at Toulouse in 1968.

[9] But not ended. See Carl Bridenbaugh, *Vexed and Troubled Englishmen* (New York: Oxford University Press, 1967), pp. 66–70, 240–243.

[10] Historians have looked for evidence of *féodalité* in the New World at two levels: in legal relations between king and proprietor or company as defined by charter; and in relations between the proprietor and his tenants within the colony. The following discussion proceeds at the second of these levels but it is perhaps necessary to refer briefly to the first. The language of some seventeenth-century charters is certainly evocative of grants of a much earlier time but it does not follow that they were feudal in spirit or substance. For example, Calvert was obliged to swear an oath of allegiance to the king as a condition of holding Maryland but the lands were given to him in free and common socage — as was Maine to Gorges in 1639 — with virtually no services to perform, i.e., in the form that the crown made grants in England *after* the abolition of feudal tenures in 1660. Many charters contained picturesque little sergeanties, e.g., the rendering of two Indian arrows a year to the king (Maryland), two beaver skins (Pennsylvania), two elk skins and two beaver skins when the king set foot in the territory (Hudson's Bay Company). As evidence of feudal relationships, these should not be taken too seriously. In Penn's charter (1681) the patentee was placed under numerous important obligations, e.g., to submit laws to the crown for approval and to enforce the Acts of Trade; but these were not in any sense "feudal" obligations. Charles Verlinden discusses *féodalité* at this level in *Abolition de la féodalité*, I, 341, and has done so at greater length in his other writings.

be seen in America in the attempt (not very successful) to exact quitrents from freeholders, but only in Maryland and Carolina was there a coherent intention to create a formally privileged nobility. Of the two Maryland is the better example of *féodalité* at work: it was founded nearly forty years earlier than Carolina and for a long time had a resident proprietor. According to charter, it was a palatinate (like the bishopric of Durham), divided into honors and manors, the lords of which were patented and granted powers of seignorial justice by the proprietor. About sixty manors were created, on paper at least, with courts baron and courts leet for petty cases as in England, and it is probable that some of these courts did business in the early years. Lords of manors were meant to be a hereditary nobility, a privileged order. There was a suggestion in 1639 — though it came to nothing — that a lord of Maryland should be tried only by his peers, that is, by other lords of manors; and for a time only lords were eligible for a seat in the colony's Council. Most of this apparatus had disappeared or ceased to work by 1700.[11]

The plans for Carolina, drawn up by John Locke, secretary of the proprietors, are breathtaking. Their avowed purpose was to "avoid erecting a numerous democracy" by introducing an outlandishly titled nobility and giving it a formidable share of land and power. "Each province shall be divided into countyes, each county shall consist of eight seignioryes, eight barronyes, & four precincts, each precinct shall consist of six collonyes. . . . To every county there shall be three as ye hereditary nobility of this pallatinate, who shall be called ye one a landgrave & ye other two cassiques, & shall have the place in the Parliament there, ye landgrave shall have four barronyes, and ye two cassiques each of them two a piece hereditaryly & unalterably annexed & settled upon the said dignity."[12] There was to be a high constable, treasurer, admiral, and chamberlain, each with his own court, a Palatine Court, and a Grand Council. This nobility was required to take up residence in the colony by 1700. Judical authority, both civil and criminal, was conferred on the landgraves and caciques and no leetman or leetwoman was to be free to leave the lord's estate without license. When all due allowance has been made for the natural conservatism of drafters of laws and constitutions and

[11] Charles M. Andrews, *The Colonial Period of American History* (New Haven, Conn.: Yale University Press, 1934–38; reprinted, 1964), II, 294–296.

[12] *Collections of the South Carolina Historical Society*, V (Charleston: South Carolina Historical Society, 1897), pp. 94–95.

for donnish ineptitude in practical affairs, Locke's vision of Carolina is still amazing for its unawareness of how a handful of ordinary Englishmen (let alone Barbadians) were likely to comport themselves when set down in swamp or forest.

Very little of what Locke planned came to pass. The proprietors tried for thirty years to impose some part of their constitution on the colony. Twenty-six landgraves and thirteen caciques were actually created and some seigniories were laid out, though there is no evidence of the exercise of hereditary judicial authority.[13] Carolina's "nobles" became just landowners, duplicates of untitled English gentlemen who ruled as J.P.'s and M.P.'s, not duplicates of a feudal baronage ruling through private courts.

New France was different. *Féodalité*, as already noted, was more pervasive and vital in France than in England. Feudal terminology came easily to French lawyers, however inappropriate it may now seem, as in the charter to the Marquis de la Roche who set out to colonize Acadia in 1598 with sixty convicts from the Rouen jails and powers to grant "fiefs, seigniories, chatellenies, countships, viscountships, baronies" to gentlemen and other persons of merit.[14] He did not succeed; but the Compagnie des Cent Associés (1627) created sixty seigniories in New France and more were erected in the later seventeenth century. By 1760, 250 Canadian seigniories had been granted comprehending nearly 8 million acres, three-quarters to laymen and one-quarter to the clergy, principally the Jesuit Order.[15]

This was the shadow, what of the substance? New France's *seigneurs* were obliged to render fealty and homage to the king's representative, and did so. They were also obliged to settle subtenants on the property, in default of which the grant might be revoked. Tenants were never plentiful in New France and some seigniories were vacated for nonsettlement; more were allowed to remain empty or half-empty of people. *Seigneurs* were further bound to pay to the crown a due or quint whenever the property was sold or inherited "other than in direct succession": since few

[13] David D. Wallace, *South Carolina: A Short History* (Chapel Hill: University of North Carolina Press, 1951), p. 25; Andrews, *Colonial Period*, III, 217, 219.

[14] William B. Munro, *The Seigniorial System in Canada* (New York: Longmans, 1907), p. 19.

[15] J.-P. Wallot, "Le régime seigneurial et son abolition au Canada," in *Abolition de la féodalité*, I, 363.

seigniories were sold in the seventeenth century this was not a heavy burden. Profits appear to have been as exiguous as outgoings. The *seigneur* could collect from his tenants, according to the Coutume de Paris introduced to New France in 1664, *cens, rentes,* and *lods et ventes,* payable either in money or kind annually or at the inheritance of a farm. All these dues were low, lower than in metropolitan France; the *corvée* was seldom exacted; and the obligation on a tenant to grind his corn at the lord's mill was not a grievance in the seventeenth century. *Seigneurs* also had the right to hold their own courts. Indeed they were granted *haute, moyenne et basse justice,* which meant that in law each could have his own prison and his own gallows. In practice seignorial justice was exercised only in petty matters arising on the estate; there is no record of a *seigneur* sentencing a tenant to death, let alone hanging him. All the important courts in New France were royal, and the plain fact is that, whereas in France seignorial justice could be made a thing of profit, in the colonies it could not.

The *régime seigneurial* of New France, whatever the law said, appears to have been short of substance; and this has led to its being dismissed as "simply irrelevant" to the most important aspects of Canadian life.[16] Economically this was true; and as a system of justice the *régime* was a failure. Yet as a device for introducing formal inequality into North America it is worthy of notice, particularly when coupled with the conferment of patents of nobility. *Seigneurs* were not necessarily noble. Titles in New France were bestowed separately and — in the later seventeenth century — sparingly, though freer use was made of the *lettres de noblesse* which gave the quality of nobility without a title.[17] These privileges were eagerly sought after, not because they carried exemption from direct taxation (there was no direct taxation), but simply out of snobbery. Gradually there emerged in New France something identifiable as a Canadian nobility, more formal than the upper class of the British colonies and expecting the deference of *roturiers* and tenants. It was very different from the provincial French aristocracy, let alone from Versailles; the Canadian nobility, for example, was allowed to engage in trade from 1685 without degrading itself.[18] But it was nonetheless a

[16] R. C. Harris, *The Seigneurial System in Early Canada* (Madison and Quebec: University of Wisconsin Press, 1966), p. 192.

[17] Munro, *Seigniorial System,* pp. 161–173.

[18] Wallot, "Le régime seigneurial," p. 371.

distinct class which the British recognized after 1763 as having a life and problems of its own.[19]

At first sight it seems extraordinary that nonnobles in New France should have accepted this emergence of hereditary social leaders. Certainly they were used to deferring to their betters at home, but with so much empty land why did immigrants accept the status of tenants (*censitaires*)? New France's ribbon development along the St. Lawrence and the Richelieu rivers is part of the answer. The seigniories occupied the best waterfronts, stretching back from the river a mile or more into the country. Every farmer wanted a frontage; the simplest way to get one was to farm within a seigniory. Moreover, with Iroquois constantly threatening, no one in his senses would settle far from a community capable of defending itself. *Seigneurs* did not render military service as a feudal obligation but in practice they led the fighting. In this way, and in the wars with England from 1689 to 1713, the social leaders of New France gave a good account of themselves. In command of Indian war parties they harried New England; they led Canadians to intrude on the English in Hudson Bay; and they took privateers to sea to attack the enemy's trade. In proportion to numbers, New France revealed far more military vitality than the English colonies; it is not farfetched to connect this vitality with the existence of a nobility. No English colony in the seventeenth century produced a fighter with the energy, resource, and panache of Pierre Le Moyne d'Iberville, grandson of a Dieppe innkeeper and son of Charles Le Moyne, *habitant*, created a baron of New France in 1668.[20]

Féodalité in New France more or less followed the rules of the mother country; its tenuousness proceeded not from the model but from its unsuitability in some respects to the population and conditions to which it was applied. The *féodalité* (if the term is permissible) brought by the Dutch to the Hudson Valley was a more corrupt version. It is not the case that *féodalité* had disappeared from the Netherlands by the time of colonization; much remained in the landward provinces, not to be abolished till

[19] For example, Lieutenant Governor H. T. Cramahé to the Earl of Hillsborough, July 25, 1772: "Far from complaining of slavery the Canadian noblesse often allege that from the freedom enjoyed under their present government the middling and lower sort of people daily lose of that deference and respect they used formerly upon all occasions to show their superiors." Public Record Office, London, C.O. 42/31, fo. 131.

[20] Nellis M. Crouse, *Lemoyne d'Iberville: Soldier of New France* (Ithaca, N.Y.: Cornell University Press, 1954).

French Revolutionary times, and some features — seignorial hunting rights for instance — lasted into the twentieth century.[21] At the same time, the urban and maritime growth of the Dutch seaward provinces in the fifteenth and sixteenth centuries had been accompanied by an obvious erosion of feudal institutions and practices, so that it is surprising to find a great commercial corporation like the West India Company engendering a quasi-feudal institution.

The patroonships advertised by the company in 1630 were not, as a matter of fact, genuinely feudal in character. To begin with, the term *patroon* was unknown to Dutch land law; it meant an entrepreneur in business, not a *seigneur*.[22] The grants themselves were allodial more than feudal; homage was required (though never performed) but enfeoffment was perpetual and the grantee empowered to dispose of his property by will. There were obligations besides homage but they related to planting settlers and respecting the company's trading rights and were not of a recognizably feudal nature. The patroon's tenants received leases, the terms of which were settled by contract, not — as in New France — by custom imported from Europe. Thus far patroonships did not much differ from the grants of "particular plantations" in Virginia.

Where they did differ was in the grant of rights of justice — *hooge en laage justitie* — a fusion of landholding and judicial authority that is certainly one of the hallmarks of a *régime seigneurial*. A *schout* (steward) presided in the patroon's court, assisted by four *schepens* (deputies); and these are recognizably feudal terms. Tenants were proceeded against in this court for criminal offenses as well as for nonpayment of dues, with right of appeal in major causes to the governor and Council of the colony. As in the seignorial courts of New France, there is no record in New Netherland of a patroon imposing the death penalty.[23]

Rensselaerswyck was the only patroonship to come into being, though several others were projected. By 1651 it had eighteen farms but, perhaps because the patroon was not in residence, was never prosperous. In 1664, following the English conquest, the right of jurisdiction was abolished — a small but important declaration of intent against *féodalité* — and in 1685

[21] I. J. Brugmans, "La fin de la féodalité aux Pays-Bas," in *Abolition de la féodalité*, I, 221.
[22] S. G. Nissenson, *The Patroon's Domain* (New York: Columbia University Press, 1937), p. 26, n. 7, p. 54.
[23] *Ibid.*, pp. 94–95, 126–132, 140.

the domain became the "Manor of Rennsselaerswyck," now apparently nothing but a large (one million acres) private estate. So, in law, it was. But the example of the great estate in New York seems to have been infectious: between 1686 and 1702 nineteen more manors were created in the province, some of great extent, making New York a colony in which inequality was more firmly entrenched in the distribution of land than anywhere else in North America.[24] And the term *patroon*, devoid now of legal meaning, continued to be used conversationally and was applied to other great landowners in the Hudson Valley, setting them apart from the mass like a title or honor.

These instances of the transfer of feudal or quasi-feudal practices from Europe to the colonies are of interest chiefly as tokens of the preoccupation of the founders of certain colonies with the avoidance of a "numerous democracy." Other and apter ways were found of achieving the same end. The rulers of Massachusetts did it by resolving (1631) that "noe man shalbe admitted to the freedom of this body polliticke, but such as are members of some of the churches within the limitts of the same."[25] This decision (a departure from the charter) was generally consistent with prevailing Puritan notions of election but was specially appropriate to a new community set down in the wilderness. New England had a moral purpose and its leaders meant it to be served. Their concern for education and their success in providing schools and colleges (far greater than anywhere else in America) prove the genuineness of this intention. But a price had to be paid. Only by confining power to persons who had passed a strict examination for church membership could purity of purpose be preserved. Massachusetts, the seaports especially, was full of indentured servants, tradesmen, fishermen, and sailors, bursting with unrighteousness, whose private and social lives needed investigation and who had to be excluded from decision making. The interest of the community — not of the majority — was paramount. It appears, though no one knows for certain, that among the first settlers of Massachusetts "at best a few hundreds in a total of twenty thousand inhabitants" were entitled to vote in elections for governor, magistrates, and deputies.[26] Perhaps one in five of the population was a church member, but not all church members had

[24] Wesley Frank Craven, *The Colonies in Transition, 1660–1713* (New York: Harper & Row, 1969), p. 280.

[25] Andrews, *Colonial Period*, I, 435.

[26] *Ibid.*, I, 443.

political rights.[27] Things were easier in the second and third generations. Following the Half-Way Covenant of 1662 and the softening effects of prosperity, votes in Massachusetts became easier to acquire.

New England, as in so many respects, went its own way. In the middle and southern English colonies and in the Caribbean (French as well as English) inequality — the sorting of colonists into those who owned, directed, and ruled, and those who worked and obeyed — came about less dramatically. Virginia's promoters envisaged a hierarchy of landlords, tenants, and laborers. Each purchaser of a share of £ 12 10s. in the company was to have a dividend of one hundred acres after seven years with the possibility of more. Tenant farming on three-acre lots was started in 1614, and large numbers of servants were brought to the colony. Few really big grants of land were made in the early years: between 1621 and 1625 only 4 out of 184 exceeded a thousand acres and most were for two hundred acres or less. Very different was the picture by the second half of the seventeenth century when the average size of a land grant in Virginia was 674 acres.[28] Quite early in the colony's history headright became the commonest way of acquiring land, not only peopling the colony but working steadily and smoothly to manufacture inequality. To bring indentured servants to the colony cost money. The richer a man was the more servants he could afford; the more servants he brought the more land he acquired; the more land he had the greater his standing in the colony.

Here, in the importation of servants and the unequal distribution of land, was the answer to the problem besetting the founders of colonies, how to get the many to obey the few. Calvert's and Locke's endeavors to create and sanctify inequality by importing antiquated European terminology and practice proved needless. Stability came, not from fealty and homage or *haute, moyenne et basse justice*, but from the employment of labor with minimal rights or no rights at all. In the West Indies the demands of tropical agriculture summoned into existence unfreedom to a degree and on a scale unknown in western Europe. As the blacks poured in, a version of capitalism was evolved, virtually outside public control and untrammeled by tradition or social restraint, which swamped all other influences and put political power firmly into the hands of a few great

---

[27] Samuel Eliot Morison, in *Builders of the Bay Colony* (revised Sentry ed.; Boston: Houghton Mifflin, 1962), has an interesting appendix discussing the "four out of five" non-Puritans in Massachusetts.

[28] Thomas J. Wertenbaker, *The Planters of Colonial Virginia* (Princeton, N.J.: Princeton University Press, 1922), p. 47.

slave owners. In such societies the vote was a privilege; probably no more than a quarter or a third of the white adult males in Barbados in 1680 served as jurors, sat as vestrymen, and elected the Assembly.[29] And even the vote, though a valuable possession, was by no means a decisive weapon. Leisure, education, money, family interest were the qualifications to hold the major offices and take the lead in West Indian politics: big planters (those with sixty slaves or more) held most of the positions of power in Barbados in 1680.[30] Other Caribbean colonies were slower to turn into slave-owning oligarchies but they all got there in the eighteenth century.[31]

No English colony on the mainland went anything like as far in this direction as Barbados in the seventeenth century. But the history of the franchise in North America furnishes little evidence of progress toward formal democracy. More of the population of Massachusetts had votes in 1700 than in 1635 (there could hardly have been fewer) but in the southern colonies the indications are of movement in the opposite direction. Though the evidence is unsatisfactory, it appears that in early Virginia all white adult males except servants (and perhaps some of them) voted in the election of burgesses; certainly Virginia was far more democratic at this time than either Old or New England.[32] In 1670, however, at the instance of the colony's Assembly, the freeman franchise was replaced by a suffrage restricted to freeholders (not including householders), that is, to owners of land. The old franchise was restored by the Assembly which sat at the time of Bacon's Rebellion (1676) but was lost again in 1684. Meanwhile, Maryland had also confined the vote to freeholders (1671), though here householders were counted as freeholders. Connecticut had the same qualification from 1657, New York from 1683, and New Jersey and Carolina from their beginnings.[33] Insofar as we can speak of a standard colonial qualification to vote at the beginning of the eighteenth century, it is the possession of freehold land, not by any means the restriction in empty America it was in crowded England but a restriction just the same.

[29] Richard S. Dunn, "The Barbados Census of 1680: Profile of the Richest Colony in English America," *William and Mary Quarterly*, 3rd series, 26 (no. 1):13 (1969).
[30] *Ibid.*, p. 19.
[31] Elsa V. Goveia's *Slave Society in the British Leeward Islands at the End of the Eighteenth Century* (New Haven, Conn.: Yale University Press, 1965) is the classic statement.
[32] Philip A. Bruce, *Institutional History of Virginia in the Seventeenth Century*, 2 vols. (New York: Putnam, 1910), II, 409–410.
[33] Andrews, *Colonial Period*, III, 115n.

Consultation and Resistance

Most governments of colonies were weak by European standards. What interior strength they had in the early years came from no-nonsense governors (Dale of Virginia, Frontenac of New France, Nicolls of New York), or as in New England from a community of principle between rulers and ruled. Institutions were new and fragile and governors a long way from home. They had to guess what to do in unforeseen situations and not infrequently learned six or twelve months later that they had guessed wrong. This engendered overcaution in some governors, a surrender of initiative to the colonists which is apparent down to the American Revolution.

No colonial government had much money at its disposal and none was in a position to win much support by the distribution of offices, sinecures, and privileges. This by itself was enough to modify European styles: from the sixteenth to the eighteenth centuries all governments in Europe depended to some extent on the skillful use of patronage. Many posts in the gift of an English or French king, in the army, navy, or civil service, had genuine functions attached to them and were by no means overrewarded; others were jobs at court about the person of the monarch, yielding pay in return for token or ceremonial or no duties; others were licenses to prey upon the public by the exaction of fees. Some offices were hallowed by antiquity; others were of recent creation, particularly in France where the sale of new offices in the sixteenth and early seventeenth centuries was the ordinary recourse of hard-up ministries.[34] The importance of office in securing obedience to the crown has perhaps been represented as more decisive in European history than it really was: not all officeholders fought for the king of England in 1642 and the French *officiers* massively turned against the crown in 1648.[35] But some effect is undeniable. Contrast the colonies, with no royal or princely courts, no standing armies, no traditional offices, and only limited means to create new ones. The task in English North America of building up the patron-

[34] Roland Mousnier, *La venalité des offices sous Henri IV et Louis XIII* (rev. ed.; Paris: Presses Universitaires de France, 1971), a much wider ranging book than its title might suggest.
[35] Gerald E. Aylmer, *The King's Servants* (London: Routledge, 1961); P. R. Doolin, *The Fronde* (Cambridge, Mass.: Harvard University Press, 1936). H. R. Trevor-Roper, *The Gentry, 1540-1640, Economic History Review* Supplement no. 1 (Cambridge: Economic History Society, 1953), greatly stimulated the study of the role of office in English politics in the seventeenth century.

age of governors and using it — as in the mother country — to give stability to political life proved a toilsome one, far from completed by 1775.

Without the customary resources to make their rule acceptable colonial governors must often have wished to resort to coercion. More or less disciplined European troops appeared in the colonies from time to time but nearly always for a specific task, fighting an extension of a European war or punishing the Indians, on completion of which they either turned into colonists or went home. Regular troops for peace keeping were not a feature of seventeenth-century colonial rule. The five infantry companies sent to Virginia to deal with Bacon's Rebellion were disbanded in 1681 and Andros's hundred grenadiers, landed at Boston in 1685 to impose the Dominion of New England, were a bodyguard not an army.[36] Governors facing aggrieved colonists had no ordinary recourse but to the militia, an institution transferred without much modification from the Old World to the New. Though usually reluctant and unexercised, colonial militias were of some use in defending frontiers from Indian raids and even, by 1689, from other Europeans; but for the suppression of riot and civil commotion they had their limitations. They had too much in common with the rioters. Where there were neither funds to buy obedience nor force to command it, prudence suggested frequent consultation between governors and governed. Thus, while some proprietors and some kings aspired to a colonial population at least as disciplined and regimented as that of Europe, this ideal was annihilated in the English colonies, compromised in the Dutch, and qualified even in the French.

The story of the planting of representative institutions in the English colonies has been told too often and too well to bear repetition in detail. Virginia led the way in 1619, Bermuda followed in 1620, enacting the first English colonial laws. The New England colonies acquired assemblies (albeit chosen by only a handful of voters) almost as soon as they had people. Maryland held her first assembly in 1638, Barbados in 1639, Jamaica in 1663, New Jersey in 1668, New Hampshire in 1680, Pennsylvania in 1682, and New York in 1683. In only two of these colonies was there opposition from home to the introduction of a popular element into government. King James I appears not to have liked the calling of Virginia's House of Burgesses and one reason for his dissolving the com-

---

[36] Craven, *Colonies in Transition*, pp. 149, 218.

pany was stated to be "the populousness of the government."[37] The king's
death soon afterwards removed the difficulty. In the other case James's
grandson, the Duke of York, failed to provide a representative assembly
in New York following its conquest in 1664. This was not unreasonable
considering the number of Dutchmen in the colony; it was less reasonable
in 1675 when the duke explicitly and on principle denied an assembly to
the colony. He refused again in 1676 though less uncompromisingly,
finally changing his mind and acceding in 1683.[38] New York had by then
been nineteen years without an elected assembly, the longest experience
of nonparliamentary government in any major English colony (Quebec
excepted which had to wait from the conquest till 1791) in the seventeenth and eighteenth centuries.

In these two instances the granting or withholding of an assembly was
viewed from England as an issue of principle. And so, to some extent, it
was: a confirmation or denial of the broad proposition that Englishmen
lived under a *dominium politicum et regale* and would continue to do so
despite removing to a colony. But to understand the proliferation of representative institutions in America and the West Indies we must also
summon up the argument of expediency. Assemblies were sanctioned and
even stimulated from home as a means of lending support to feeble civil
governments, of promoting stability in new societies, and perhaps above
all of pinning on the colonists financial liability for their own affairs. This is
aptly illustrated by the case of Bermuda where the first Assembly met in
1620. The population of the colony was then small, not much over 500,
and facing difficult times. So far as is known there was no irresistible
clamor for an assembly from the settlers themselves. The initiative came
from the company in London in an instruction to Governor Butler to
bring together "as many of the ablest and best understandinge men in the
Islands, both of the clergy and the laitie, as you and your counsell shall
thinck fitt, wherein we wish you rather to take too many than too fewe,
both because every man will more willingly obey laws to which he hath
yeilded his consent; as likewise because you shall the better discover such
things as have need of redrease by many than by fewe: and that in this
assembly you deliberately consult and advice of such lawes and constitutions as shalbe thought fit to be made for the good of the plantations, and

---

[37] Bruce, *Institutional History of Virginia*, II, 254.
[38] Andrews, *Colonial Period*, III, 112–113.

for the maintenance of religion, justice, order, peace and unitie among them."[39] This is very explicit and fully justifies Wesley Frank Craven's observation (which has application to Virginia too) that Bermuda's assembly "was used first as a forum for producing in the burgesses a consciousness of common interests. It was then relied upon in reaching a common agreement as to the projects that were essential to the protection of these interests. Finally, it offered the colonists a voice in the imposition of taxes necessary to the support of such projects."[40] It was this last consideration — the difficulty of raising money without consultation — that finally brought New York into line with other colonies. Thus, before 1700, the classic formation of governor, council, and assembly had been completed in England's empire. Variations abounded: whether the governor was appointed by king or proprietor and whether he was paid out of royal moneys or by vote of assembly; whether the council consisted of royal or proprietorial nominees or was elected by the assembly; what qualified a man to sit in and vote for an assembly. But the fundamental structure was common, and recognized by the government at home as the norm to which new colonies should be encouraged to conform.

The expediency of consultation between rulers and ruled is further demonstrated in colonies where there was less stimulus from home (even the contrary) and different or weaker European traditions of representative government. Though decentralization was the Dutch political hallmark in the seventeenth century, and though the United Netherlands possessed effective representative institutions in their provincial estates as well as a rather feeble States-General, there was no question of the West India Company's voluntarily introducing these features into their early establishments in North America or the West Indies. Company rule, as already pointed out, was more military than civil, styled for transient employees not for settlers. Nevertheless, when genuine colonists arrived in New Netherland and genuine colonial problems arose, some measure of consultation was forced on the company's representative. This began in 1641 when Governor Kieft called an assembly of heads of families which chose representatives known as the Twelve Men to advise on how to fight the Indians. In 1643 Eight Men were elected for the same purpose, and in 1647 when Governor Stuyvesant arrived in the

---

[39] *Ibid.*, I, 221–222.

[40] Wesley Frank Craven, "An Introduction to the History of Bermuda," *William and Mary Quarterly*, 2nd series, 18:37 (1937–38).

colony he summoned the Nine Men in the hope of raising money from the settlers.[41] All three bodies embarrassed the West India Company by calling for reforms. The Nine drew up the Representation of New Netherland (1650) which condemned the company for neglecting population, defense, and education and called for municipal self-government "somewhat resembling the laudable government of the Fatherland."[42] Concessions to the principle of decentralization were introduced but no formal representative institution emerged before the end of the Dutch regime, an omission that was surely more a source of weakness than of strength to a colony hemmed around by Englishmen. Elsewhere in the Dutch colonies the millstone of company rule hung equally or more heavily. Two seats out of ten in the Council of Polity at the Cape of Good Hope were given to burgher representatives in 1685, but it was not until the mid-eighteenth century that consultation with the planters began in Surinam (as the only way of raising money) and not until 1796 that that colony was granted an elective element in its constitution.[43] Seen in the light of the Dutch colonial record as a whole, the calling of the Twelve, the Eight, and the Nine in New Netherland shows how strong the pressure was on the government of an American colony of settlement to consult the governed.

French political institutions and practices in the seventeenth century were too complex and subtle to be adequately summarized. On the surface monarchy was carrying all before it. In 1614, before St. Christophe was founded and long before New France had enough inhabitants to think of a civil constitution, the Estates-General met for the last time before the French Revolution. Richelieu, Mazarin, and Louis XIV mowed down whatever opposition they met. A revitalized bureaucracy of intendants and *subdélégués* was formed to give effect to the royal will. These at least are the appearances and it would be wrong to deny them a large measure of substance. At the same time, a little below this surface, there was still some dialogue in seventeenth-century France between ruler and ruled. Two of the provinces most closely concerned with colonization, Normandy and Brittany, were *pays d'états*, i.e., possessed provincial assemblies which the king consulted on ways and means of raising money. The

[41] Jameson, *Narratives of New Netherland*, pp. 287, 333n1.
[42] *Ibid.*, p. 288.
[43] Charles R. Boxer, *The Dutch Seaborne Empire* (London: Hutchinson, 1965), p. 253; D. K. Fieldhouse, *The Colonial Empires* (London: Weidenfeld, 1967), pp. 53–54.

Estates of Normandy by the seventeenth century were acquiescent but those of Brittany (where no permanent royal intendant was fixed until 1689) were capable of driving a bargain. Additionally, there were assemblies of the French clergy meeting throughout the century principally to grant money to the king, and Assemblies of Notables called occasionally to advise on specific topics. These last were purely consultative and particularly apt for introducing to the colonies. Since the king chose the time and place of sitting, the persons summoned, and the business discussed, their existence did not theoretically diminish his authority; well managed, they could only strengthen his hand by engaging leading men to perform the undertakings they were brought to make. Such were the assemblies called by Louis XIII and Richelieu in 1624 and 1626–27. Further down the scale French towns enjoyed a large measure of self-government which the king might occasionally suspend or correct but which he had no intention of replacing by a system of royal *officiers*. This authority comprehended the maintenance of law and order, the regulation of markets, building and employment, the levying of rates, and services such as water and food supply. Even the countryside was required to take a share in its own government, with little assemblies of householders meeting to discuss and vote on ways and means of raising the money demanded by the king and on other matters of local concern.[44]

Frenchmen in the New World did not, therefore, go ashore with traditions of absolute and passive acceptance of an unexplained royal will; and even had they done so, colonial conditions would probably have enforced a measure of consultation between governors and governed. Elections were another matter: these were actively opposed by the king from the moment he took charge of New France in 1664. Thus the syndic, elected by the first Canadians to represent their causes at the Conseil Souverain, was suppressed by Colbert in 1673. And Frontenac's harmless vanity — the assembly called at Quebec on October 23, 1672, to welcome the new governor — was stamped on because it was ranged in orders too closely resembling an Estates-General.[45] At the same time consultation with bodies resembling petty Assemblies of Notables was not only tolerated by

[44] Roland Mousnier, *La plume, la faucille et le marteau* (Paris: Presses Universitaires de France, 1970), pp. 241–244, discusses local self-government in a paper entitled "La participation des gouvernés à l'activité des gouvernants dans la France des XVIIᵉ et XVIIIᵉ siècles."

[45] W. J. Eccles, *Canada under Louis XIV* (Toronto: McClelland and Stewart, 1964), pp. 17–18, 35; Eccles, *Frontenac*, pp. 66–67.

the king but actively encouraged. Such was the famous (and misnamed) Brandy Parliament at Quebec in 1678 to advise whether liquor should or should not be sold to Indians. No election of representatives occurred, merely the summoning of twenty leading men in the fur trade, their recommendations forming in due course the basis of a royal edict.[46] There were seventeen such meetings in New France between 1672 and 1700, enough for consultation to be regarded as part of the ordinary process of government.[47] No formal representative system grew out of these arrangements, nor did one emerge in any other French colony in the seventeenth century. Du Tertre mentions a meeting of "officiers & aucuns des bons habitants" at Martinique in 1668, but it was not until 1715 that a representative assembly met in that island, summoned for the usual reason, the raising of money.[48]

Enough has been said to suggest certain common political features and postures in the Atlantic colonies of the northern European colonies. Nearly every government was short of money and could be paralyzed by Indian troubles or European war. Taxation was not likely to work in a colony without some measure of prior consent. Even law enforcement was difficult unless at least the leaders of a community had approved the wisdom of the laws. These conditions did not automatically induce representative government but they gave a fillip to rule with consent, if not to rule by consent.

To discuss the American political inheritance merely in constitutional terms is not enough. There were ideals of political order and social restraint in Europe, and they were assiduously propagated by rulers, churchmen, and many political theorists. But the frequent reading of the *Homily against Sedition and Wilful Disobedience* in English parish churches and the hammering out of principles of submission in the *Mercure François* are not necessarily evidence of a society in which the common people accepted everything that was thrown at them; they may be just the reverse. European history of the sixteenth and seventeenth centuries is quite as remarkable for occasions of illegal political activity, conspiracy, assassination, riot, and revolution as it is for state building. Among the impressions which English and French colonists took across

[46] William B. Munro, "The Brandy Parliament of 1678," *Canadian Historical Review*, 2:172–189 (1921).
[47] Eccles, *Canada under Louis XIV*, p. 36.
[48] Du Tertre, *Histoire générale des Antilles*, IV, 138–140; Fieldhouse, *Colonial Empires*, p. 40.

the Atlantic was undoubtedly a familiarity with violent resistance to the demands of governments and the exactions of landlords.

Not all the unlawful activity in Europe contributed to the colonial inheritance. Some rebellions and conspiracies were straightforward aristocratic demonstrations by noblemen out of favor and trying to force their way back in. Such was the rising of the Earl of Essex in 1601 in which common people took no part; such were the frequent *prises d'armes* of the Duc de Condé in the first years of Louis XIII; and such was the Fronde Princière of 1649–52. With no courts, no aristocracies to speak of, and few sinecures worth fighting for, the colonies furnish no parallels to violence of this sort. More relevant to America were the occasions in Europe when political ends were pursued by arms after legitimate constitutional methods had been tried and exhausted: the Revolt of the Netherlands, the Great Rebellion in England, the first Fronde, and the Glorious Revolution. Between 1642 and 1647 Englishmen fought the lawful government, not in itself a novelty. They beat the king and took him prisoner; that was rarer. Then instead of patching up a settlement, they tried him and executed him, and for good measure abolished the monarchy and the House of Lords. These were the "unheard-of things" that caused men to fall into melancholy and women to miscarry.[49] In these great events the common people — the people who settled the colonies — were cast by their betters in the role of pike trailers and musketmen. But they could hardly fail to be aware of some of the issues in dispute, and once, just once, they were moved to speak for themselves and threaten rebellion within rebellion. This was in 1645, when the first Civil War was over and the New Model Army had leisure to articulate the aspirations of the men of little property more clearly than at any other time in the seventeenth century.[50] We can certainly assume that these aspirations crossed the Atlantic, probably accompanied from 1645 by the knowledge that they had once been pursued collectively by men with arms in their hands.

Behind these great rebellions occupying the foreground of European history are episodes of resistance, less well known but too numerous to ignore, when common people rose on their own initiative and with little hope of success. The exactions of landlords, with or without the enclosure

[49] Christopher Hill, *Intellectual Origins of the English Revolution* (Oxford: Clarendon Press, 1965), p. 5.

[50] For the Army debates, see A. S. Woodhouse, *Puritanism and Liberty* (Chicago: University of Chicago Press, 1951).

of common land, were the commonest cause in England, taxation in France. In both countries bad harvests, high food prices, and the billeting of troops created a groundswell of discontent. Poorly armed, usually badly led, with no money and no discipline, revolting peasants were easy game for royal troops, bowled over as Kett's men were by Northumberland in 1549 or Monmouth's followers by King James's regulars in 1685. Their best hope was to hit and run, disappearing to their homes or into the woods before the law arrived. Thus proceeded the agrarian riots in England in 1596, 1607, 1629–31, and sporadically through the Hungry Thirties when harvest after harvest failed. Anonymous, perhaps mythical, leaders arose, Captain Pouch in Midland England, Lady Skimmington in the West, to inspire resistance and — occasionally — to coordinate it.[51] Nothing was achieved in the short run; in the long run these demonstrations probably set limits to what it was prudent for government or landlords to attempt.

Violence in France was more pervasive. Every Frenchman in the later sixteenth century was familiar with civil war; many must have personally engaged in armed self-help. The Wars of Religion ended in 1598; there followed a few years of peace, then an outbreak of popular riot and rebellion coinciding with the beginning of French colonization.[52] In almost every instance taxation was the cause, imposed to pay for the aggressive deeds of Richelieu and Louis XIII. Towns as well as country were affected. There were troubles in Dijon in 1630, Aix in 1631, Lyons in 1632. At Bordeaux a new tax on wine was announced in 1635; the collector arrived in town on May 10; the riot began on May 14. Here, in the towns, there were forces of law and order, civic officers, guards, perhaps a representative of the king: urban riots did not generally last long. It was different in the country. The revolt of the Croquants in southwest France lasted from 1635 to 1637, with 60,000 reported up in Périgord and the cry raised: "Vive le roi sans la gabelle! Vive le roi sans la taille!"[53] In Normandy, the province which supplied more emigrants to the colonies than probably any other, the Nu-Pieds rose by the thousand between 1639 and 1641 in France's greatest popular rebellion before the Revolution. Simi-

[51] E. F. Gay, "The Midland Revolt of 1607," *Transactions of the Royal Historical Society*, new series, 18:195–244 (1904); D. G. C. Allan, "The Rising in the West 1638–1631," *Economic History Review*, 2nd series, 5:76–85 (1952).

[52] Boris Porshnev, *Les soulèvements populaires en France de 1623 à 1648* (Paris: S.E.V.P.E.N., 1963), has changed the appearance of this period of French history.

[53] *Ibid.*, pp. 76, 159, 303 et seq.

lar, if less widespread, demonstrations occurred throughout the 1640s and again in the middle years of the reign of Louis XIV. None appears to have been aimed against the king or the institution of monarchy; it is a matter of debate how far they were aimed against the *seigneurs* as a class.[54] Some were led by *seigneurs*, though in the later stages of a revolt radical tendencies were sometimes expressed by burning down chateaus. No political program was put forward that can compare with the manifestoes of the English Levellers or the Army Agitators. The French risings were massive bread-and-butter protests by men who found it hard enough to get a living in the best of times and, confronted by new taxes, chose to risk death by hanging or fighting rather than pay.

Such in barest outline was the violent political legacy of Europe to America. What did the colonists make of it? The French record in the seventeenth century is simpler than the English and will be discussed first. The rank and file of France's first colonists appear to have been much the same kind of men as those who made the great demonstrations of the 1630s and 1640s: a country people from Normandy and the Atlantic provinces. The immediate effect of putting them into a colonial environment was probably more to diminish than to enhance their propensity to resist. Most new settlers could see that with Iroquois or Caribs at the door and starvation round the corner discipline was needed. New France, because for so long threatened by Indians and because taxes were light and the taille nonexistent, furnishes no instance of popular rebellion in the period under examination. Laws, such as the prohibition of *coureurs de bois*, were flouted but there was no collective action by dissidents in arms. By contrast the Antilles, peopled by much the same kind of Frenchmen as New France, experienced two decades of violence which threatened to wreck their economies.

These colonies were founded by adventurers backed by the Compagnie des Îles d'Amérique which thus became the titular proprietor of the land with a monopoly of trade and the right to collect taxes. Governors were appointed for each principal island, some of whom also received commissions from the king, virtually his only involvement in the Antilles in the 1640s and 1650s. Finding that it was making no money and that the governors were "maistres absolus," the company decided to sell its in-

[54] Mousnier disputes Porshnev's inferences in "Recherches sur les soulèvements populaires en France avant la fronde," reprinted in Mousnier's *La plume, la faucille et le marteau*.

terests to the governors. This took place between 1649 and 1651, inaugurating a decade of proprietorial rule in the French Antilles not unlike the rule of the Calverts in Maryland. St. Christophe was sold to the Order of the Knights of St. John of Malta for 120,000 livres and left to Lonvilliers de Poincy, himself a knight, to govern much as he pleased. Martinique, with St. Lucia, Grenada, and the Grenadines, went to Jacques Dyel du Parquet, a nephew of d'Esnambuc, for 60,000 livres. Guadeloupe, with Marie-Galante, Desirade, and Les Saintes, was sold to Houel du Petit-Pré, a shareholder in the company, for the same price plus 11,500 livres for fixtures.[55] All three men were in control of their islands before these transactions took place and naturally continued to run them with an eye to their own profit.

The rule of the proprietors was probably no worse than the rule of the company had been. Both provoked violent reactions in the colonists. There was a rising in St. Christophe in 1640 led by Clement Bugaud; another in Martinique in 1646 under "General" Beaufort, a Parisian glovemaker; and another in St. Christophe in 1647 in which a thousand colonists are said to have taken part. The last two claimed to be, and probably were, risings against the company and for the king. Meanwhile faction fights were in progress involving du Parquet, de Poincy, Houel, and Noël de Patrocles de Thoisy, a courtier sent out hopefully by the Regent Anne of Austria as lieutenant general for the child Louis XIV; de Thoisy lost and fled. As an example of the excesses of these times, an *officier* in Guadeloupe was condemned to be a slave for twenty months merely for having acknowledged the authority of the king's lieutenant general. The effect of these disorders was to bring economic life to a standstill: "no one worked any more, many plantations were deserted, most of them nearly overrun by weeds."[56] This was what induced the company to sell in 1649–51.

The new proprietors, either for purposes of defense or for their own benefit, raised the taxes on each colonist from 50 to 100 livres of tobacco, not a vast sum but these were bad times for Caribbean tobacco growers. In Guadeloupe this tax produced a storm of opposition in 1658 before which Houel was obliged to yield; and in Martinique it produced an organized rebellion.[57] Du Parquet died in 1658, leaving his widow as

[55] Du Tertre, *Histoire générale des Antilles*, I, 442–447.
[56] *Ibid.*, I, 166–167, 328–329, 367, 386, 397.
[57] *Ibid.*, I, 521–529.

regent for two sons to whom the king confirmed the government of the colony. On July 22 a seditious assembly met. Madame du Parquet's house was searched; the finding of a copy of the works of Machiavelli was enough to confirm suspicions of her tyrannical ambitions. A Council of Regency was set up, with representatives of the colonists on it, reforms were proclaimed, and "a kind of republic was born."[58] The du Parquet interest was subsequently restored but enough had happened in the Antilles to convince the king and his ministers that the time had come to intervene. On October 19, 1663, the Marquis de Tracy was commissioned lieutenant general of all French possessions in America, with wide powers and a fleet of ships with which to introduce the king's authority. This he did. Sedition did not die out in Martinique immediately. There was trouble in 1665 with the *torqueurs*, the tobacco twisters whom du Tertre believed were at the root of all riots and rebellions in the Antilles, but it was firmly suppressed; two were hanged, the rest of the ringleaders sent to the galleys.[59] With this assertion of royal power the French islands became more peaceful, helped no doubt by their transformation into slave societies. As fears of revolts by slaves increased, fears of revolts by poor whites receded.

The history of rebellion in the early English colonies is a good deal less tidy, in some respects a puzzle to be explained only by reference to the diversity between colony and colony. In the first years of settlement there were few signs of sedition, let alone of anything deserving to be called armed opposition to lawfully constituted government. Spaniards and Indians threatened; the need to survive gave a temporary coherence to new colonies. There was plenty of bickering in New England but it was resolved by withdrawal or banishment, not by fighting. Here and elsewhere the people most likely to rock the boat were the indentured servants, generally without political rights and subject to strict codes of discipline. In New England they were closely watched. In Barbados a conspiracy of white servants was uncovered in 1649: like later slave conspirators they had planned to massacre their masters and take over the island. Eighteen were hanged, arguing either a widespread plot or unusually severe repression.[60]

[58] M. Delafosse and G. Debien, "Marchands et colons des îles," *Revue française d'histoire d'outre-mer*, 48:105 (1961).

[59] Du Tertre, *Histoire générale des Antilles*, III, 220.

[60] Vincent T. Harlow, *A History of Barbados, 1625–1685* (Oxford: Clarendon Press, 1926), p. 304.

The immediate effect of the Civil Wars in England was to face the colonies with a choice of loyalties that might have led to trouble. New England was naturally glad to see the end of Laud and Charles I but both Virginia and Barbados were inclined to neutrality. Both had governors more royalist than the people they governed. When parliamentary fleets appeared off these colonies in 1651, demanding submission to the de facto regime in England, there was a distinct possibility of civil war. Both governors mustered troops to oppose the Parliamentarians and some skirmishing took place in Barbados. Happily matters were accommodated. At the Restoration all the colonies renewed their allegiance to the monarchy, even Massachusetts though in so grudging a way that the king could scarcely accept it. Outwardly the enormous mid-century upheaval in the mother country had gone off remarkably smoothly in the colonies.

What of the longer term effects, if any? That there was some direct transmission of revolutionary ideas from England to the colonies is deducible from the presence in America of defeated Cromwellians and the conspiracy in Virginia in 1663 "to subvert the laws, liberties and religion of the people" set on foot by former Ironsides.[61] And it is tempting to see in the rebellious movements in the southern colonies in 1676–77 and the revolutions of 1689 in Massachusetts, New York, and elsewhere further examples of that ready resort to organized disobedience which Europe had experienced so often.

The troubles in the south fit well enough into the hypothesis of colonies following practices inherited from the mother country. They were not republican in tone and they were not jacqueries. Gentlemen, or what passed for gentlemen in seventeenth-century America, were prominent. Though such programs as the dissidents published were distinctly popular in purpose there was none of the radicalism of Anabaptists or Fifth Monarchy Men. The rebels declared themselves, and with some truth, to be opponents of innovations made by others, more like 1641–42 in England than like 1645 or 1649. Bacon's Rebellion in Virginia in 1676 was set off by Indian troubles. The rebels wanted a punitive expedition against the Susquehannahs; Governor Berkeley (whose friends if not himself

[61] Philip A. Bruce, *Economic History of Virginia*, 2 vols. (New York: Macmillan, 1896), I, 605. The spirit of 1649 was evidently still alive in the Leeward Islands in 1710 when Governor Parke reported that one of his political opponents "justified publickly King Charles' murder and bid me take warning" (Great Britain, Public Record Office, *Calendar of State Papers*, Colonial Series, America and West Indies, 1710–11, no. 230). Parke did not take warning and was murdered six months later by another of his opponents.

·were interested parties) wanted to trade with them.[62] It is dismaying indeed that a movement with some claims to be the first occasion in American history when a popular program was asserted by force should have had such origins. There was of course more to it than that. Beverley was surely right in putting at the top of his list of causes "the extream low Price of Tobacco, and the ill Usage of the Planters in the Exchange of Goods for it."[63] This affected everyone, rich and poor. Some of the gentlemen who joined Bacon may have resented Governor Berkeley's conferment of offices on his friends, but this is not certain. Once the rebellion was going a political program was devised. With the colony's government in their hands the rebels called a new Assembly and passed "Bacon's Laws" giving back to freemen the franchise they had lost to freeholders six years previously and increasing the popular element in officeholding and local government. At this point Bacon died. Governor Berkeley recovered control of the colony; five English companies arrived in 1677; "Bacon's Laws" were repealed; and twenty-three rebels were executed.[64] The rising failed to interrupt the formation in Virginia of something recognizable as a ruling class, that is, of a political system adjusted to the colony's growing economic inequalities. It failed, too, to persuade the king's government to do anything to relieve tobacco growers. There was further trouble in 1682 when the "rabble," working by night where expedient, destroyed large quantities of the crop in Gloucester and New Kent counties.[65] This disorder was not politicized: it began and ended as a protest by the poor.

Bacon's Rebellion was the signal for an unlawful assembly in Maryland in 1676, likewise prompted by a man of the "better sort." This declared no confidence in the proprietor's government, complained of taxes and of the plantation duty, and called for the restoration of the franchise to freemen. Though two leaders were hanged the meeting was more a demonstration than a rebellion. It inaugurated nevertheless a time of political instability in Maryland which added to Lord Baltimore's difficulties with the English government and contributed to the suspension of proprietary rule in 1691. In North Carolina, too, the proprietors were rocked by a Bacon-

---

[62] On Bacon's rebellion, see Wilcomb E. Washburn, *The Governor and the Rebel* (Chapel Hill: University of North Carolina Press, 1957).

[63] Robert Beverley, *The History and Present State of Virginia* (1705; reprinted, Chapel Hill: University of North Carolina Press, 1947, ed. Louis B. Wright), pp. 74–75.

[64] Craven, *Colonies in Transition*, p. 142n14.

[65] Great Britain, Public Record Office, *Calendar of State Papers*, Colonial Series, America and West Indies, 1681–85, nos. 524, 531.

type movement in 1677. This was in Albemarle County and a good deal more serious than the Maryland affair. Organized by George Durant, one of the colony's richest men, and with John Culpeper as leader, the rebels turned away the proprietors' governor and ran the colony "after their own fashion."[66] No proprietorial governor was seen in North Carolina again until 1683.

The colonial revolutions of 1689, at least the major movements in Massachusetts and New York, differ from the disturbances of the previous decade in the southern colonies. Far from displaying readiness to take up arms against an obnoxious political system, the history of the reign of James II reveals a distinct reluctance in the colonies to do so. William of Orange landed at Torbay on November 5, 1688, and was in London in early December; King James fled the country. A meeting of former M.P.'s advised the prince to call the Convention Parliament which met on January 22, 1689, and offered the crown to William and Mary. News of these events was received in Massachusetts not later than the beginning of April and then, and only then, was the yoke of James II cast off. The people of Boston rose on April 18 and arrested the royal governor and other officers. A Council of Safety was formed and William and Mary proclaimed. The other New England colonies followed suit with revolutions equally bloodless with that which had taken place in England, and a good deal safer for participants. Massachusetts's list of grievances against King James was a long one, beginning with his favoring of Roman Catholics and the colony's enforced inclusion in the Dominion of New England; but whether, without a signal from the mother country, it would then or at some later date have risen against the king is to say the least doubtful.[67]

The same doubt, indeed a greater one, exists with regard to New York. Here, too, the signal for revolution was the news from England. The militia mutinied in May 1689, the king's governor fled in June, and a revolutionary government came into being headed by Jacob Leisler, a Dutch-born New Yorker. There were plenty of people in the colony, including some rich men, who were glad to see the backs of James II and Governor Nicholson, and a mob of common folk could be spirited up as easily in New York as in Boston. But while there are signs of discontent in the colony in the years before 1689 there is nothing to show that it was

---

[66] Andrews, *Colonial Period*, III, 255, 343–344.
[67] On the revolutions of 1689 in Massachusetts and elsewhere, see Michael G. Hall et al., *The Glorious Revolution in America* (Chapel Hill: University of North Carolina Press, 1964).

about to erupt into armed opposition.[68] Bacon's rebels thought that the government in England ought to be told the true state of affairs in Virginia; in other words they hoped to appeal, as so many rebels have hoped, from local authority to remote authority. In Massachusetts and New York in James's reign that argument was not possible. Sir Edmund Andros and Governor Nicholson were doing the king's work and everyone knew it; to rise against them would be to rise against England, and this the colonies were apparently not ready to do. In Maryland likewise the revolution of 1689 was detonated by what had happened in England with the further parallel of being Protestant in character.[69] Here, however, and in the rebellions in the Carolinas the political purpose was not so much to reject King James as to cast off the yoke of the proprietors.

"Baconism" in 1676–77, the tobacco riots in 1682, and perhaps the events in the Carolinas in 1688–89 show us colonists at some risk to themselves turning to violent means in pursuit of economic or political ends. On the other hand, the reign of James II in Massachusetts and New York reveals a wariness of doing so until it was safe and more or less legitimate to do so: the risings of 1689 in these colonies were rebellions in leading strings, disobedience over a safety net.

To say this is not, however, to argue that European traditions of violent resistance to authority were dead by the end of the seventeenth century in the American colonies or any part of them. It may rather be that colonial governments, even those of James II's reign, recognized limits beyond which it was unsafe to pass. European experience suggests that radical traditions could lie dormant for a long time and not be altogether forgotten. In North America in the eighteenth century specific local influences were grafted onto whatever had been inherited from England, the frontier and the institution of slavery, for example, shaping societies in which violence could scarcely be contained. From these conditions sprang violence of a more public kind: the primitive populism of the North Carolina Regulators and the Green Mountain Boys. But while these opponents of authority were recognizably American, their manifestoes carry one back a hundred or two hundred years to the popular rebellions of France or England.[70]

[68] Craven, Colonies in Transition, pp. 227–228, discusses this point.
[69] Andrews, Colonial Period, II, 373–374.
[70] On the Regulators, see K. G. Davies, ed., Documents of the American Revolution, vol. II (Shannon: Irish University Press, 1973), pp. 185–189. On the people of Bennington, see ibid., vol. V (1974), pp. 108–112, 170–173.

Consolidation

The first French and English colonies were founded without much awareness of one another. The initiative and the means were mainly private, with varying amounts of government support, sometimes very little. Having struggled into existence and acquired a population and the means of subsistence, the colonies had to face the question whether the geographical limits prescribed by charter or defined by settlement corresponded with their own best interests, to say nothing of the policies and aspirations of the mother country. Was every colony to remain forever a self-contained community depending (more or less) on government at home but independent of any superior in the New World? or were economic needs, exigencies of defense, or administrative considerations to constrain colonies to cooperation and perhaps to redraw their boundaries in some more rational way? and, if not, how was the western expansion of the mainland colonies to be fitted into the patchwork laid out in the first years of settlement? Some of these problems belong to the eighteenth century; others were present from early times and must be taken into account in a discussion of the political aspects of empire building.

France's problems in North America were largely solved for it by the geographical fact of the St. Lawrence River. Quebec was queen, not merely because it suited the French king that she should be, but because Quebec controlled the approach to all New France save Acadia and Terre-Neuve, exemplifying the maxim "Whoever commands the country below will always rule the country above." Wherever New France extended in the seventeenth century, up the Ottawa and toward the Great Lakes, up the St. Lawrence and through Ontario and Erie to the Wabash and Illinois, it was still a single colony: a fine thread with one end held by Quebec. Separate governorships were, it is true, created for Acadia, Three Rivers, Montreal, and later Detroit but they were subordinate to the governor of New France at Quebec. Frontenac (governor 1672–82 and 1689–98) made the most of Quebec's primacy, partly because he had a private interest in western expansion and meant to keep an eye on it and partly because he was not the kind of man to brook rivals. In 1673, soon after beginning his first term, he defined his position by conscripting a large number of the inhabitants of Montreal to work on the building of Fort Frontenac at the entrance to Lake Ontario, a post of small military value but handy for Frontenac's fur-trading concerns. The inhabitants naturally protested and François-Marie Perrot, the governor of Montreal, put himself at the head of opposition. Frontenac summoned him to Quebec in 1674, arrested him, and threw him into prison. Perrot carried his case to Colbert but all he got was three weeks in the Bastille and permission to return to duty if he first apologized to Frontenac.[71] Colbert was not pleased with Frontenac's behavior on this occasion but had no choice but to uphold the supremacy of the governor of Quebec. Even Acadia's nominal dependence on Quebec was made to count: Frontenac himself appointed a governor there in 1678 who held office without royal commission and without salary for six years before being noticed and evicted by Versailles. This was an instance where Quebec's hegemony — on the whole beneficial — worked against French interests; Frontenac's man made his job pay by selling licenses to New Englanders to fish on the Acadian coast and dry their catch ashore.

A breach in Quebec's predominance came, however, with the establishment of Louisiana (1699). La Salle's expeditions into the Upper Mississippi Valley and the descent of the river itself (1681) had Frontenac's backing and were meant for his and Quebec's benefit. The initiative and first settlers at Mobile were supplied by Canadians under d'Iberville and the government set up there, like Acadia's, was nominally subordinate to New France. Thus when a Conseil Supérieur was instituted in Louisiana in 1714 the governor and intendant of New France were made titular members of it. But the conflict of interest between Louisiana's fur trade and Quebec's proved too acute and the distance too great for a colony on the Gulf of Mexico to be effectively controlled from the St. Lawrence. Louisiana became in practice an independent establishment.[72]

With New France divided into vast departments — Labrador and Hudson Bay, Canada including Terre-Neuve and Acadia, and Up Country (Lakes and Illinois)[73] — the king's representative at Quebec, albeit the ruler of a thinly populated, insecure, and impoverished land, was more a viceroy than a governor. So, in the later seventeenth century, was the French king's lieutenant general in the Antilles. Founded, as we have seen, by private enterprise, the French colonies in the Caribbean struggled on for several decades with hardly any royal help and correspond-

---

[71] Eccles, *Canada under Louis XIV*, pp. 82–83, 127–128.

[72] Marcel Giraud, *Histoire de la Louisiane française*, vol. I (Paris: Presses Universitaires de France, 1953), pp. 80–82, 279–280.

[73] J. Saintoyant, *La colonisation française sous l'ancien régime*, vol. I (Paris: Renaissance du Livre, 1929), pp. 139–140.

ingly little royal control. Governors like d'Esnambuc and l'Olive were in the first place governors de facto through having personally led pioneers to settle an island. Their position was regularized (though scarcely strengthened) by commissions from the Compagnie des Îles d'Amérique and in some instances by commissions from the king. Thus du Parquet, who succeeded d'Esnambuc by the latter's appointment in 1636, was "Gouverneur de l'Isle de St Christophe, pour les Seigneurs de la Compagnie des Isles de l'Amerique, & Lieutenant General pour Sa Majesté desdites Isles,"[74] an early but still theoretical statement of the principle of a single superior governor for the whole French Caribbean. De Poincy (1638) and de Thoisy (1644) received similar royal commissions, but de Thoisy was not a governor de facto and found it impossible to establish his authority over those who were; at St. Christophe, the main French settlement, he failed even to get ashore.[75] The king's power at this time was thus limited to recognizing established facts; and with the sale of the islands to their rulers in 1649–50 royal intervention and the promotion of any kind of union were virtually given up.

The rule of the proprietors (1650–63) was on the whole a demonstration of the need for royal control, and with the assertion of the king's authority over the Antilles in 1663 the principle of viceregal government was enacted. On October 19, 1663, the Marquis de Tracy was appointed lieutenant general not only throughout the Caribbean but for all North and South America.[76] This was an emergency measure. De Tracy was given a fleet and sent round France's Atlantic colonies to show the flag and proclaim the king's sovereignty, and he seems to have done his job well. There was no intention of putting New France and the Antilles permanently under the same government. What was envisaged was regional unification under de Tracy's successors. De la Barre (1665–67), de Baas (1668–77), and de Blénac (1677–90), were lieutenant generals over all French colonies in the Caribbean including the outposts of Cayenne and St.-Domingue, with a viceregal residence and a Conseil Souverain first at St. Christophe, later at Martinique.[77] Each major island continued to have its own governor and intendant; the effects of instituting a governor generalship must not be exaggerated. The main advantage

---

[74] Du Tertre, *Histoire générale des Antilles*, I, 115–116.
[75] *Ibid.*, I, 292.
[76] The commission is printed in *ibid.*, III, 15–19.
[77] Saintoyant, *Colonisation française*, I, 228–229.

of unification was in war when the French had to fight a more numerous but divided English enemy.

The English mainland colonies had no St. Lawrence; and even where there were strong geographical and economic arguments for federation — as in the Chesapeake colonies — diversity of origin and difference of religion proved stronger still. Broadly speaking the French colonists were united, the English divided, by religion. There were nevertheless several experiments in federation in England's empire in the seventeenth century which, though without lasting effect, testify to the presence of centripetal forces. The first was the Confederation of New England colonies mooted in 1637 but not formed until 1643.[78] An executive council was instituted but there was no union of legislatures and no surrender of "sovereignty." Religion was at once the unifying and the divisive force. Massachusetts, Connecticut, New Haven, and Plymouth were the associating colonies, all Calvinist-ruled, but Rhode Island was repeatedly refused admission on the ground of its anarchical (i.e., non-Calvinist) condition.[79] Defense, against Indians and Dutch, was the confederation's chief concern and some useful steps were taken toward military collaboration. The confederation also showed interest in regulating the Indian trade of its members. But in 1664 Connecticut absorbed New Haven, against the wishes of the other members, and the union was fatally weakened. Though still existing in a shadowy form, it was not effective in New England's great crisis — King Philip's War in 1675, when Massachusetts and Plymouth were threatened with annihilation by Indians.

The history of the New England Confederation reveals the obstacles in the way of intercolonial cooperation and the fragility of a supracolonial authority. Puritan suspicion of Rhode Island and Connecticut's imperialism were stronger than apprehensions of external danger. After very few years of existence, it seems, colonies acquired a kind of "nationalism" or at least a love of doing things their own way which remained a force to be reckoned with down to 1774. Any disturbance in the original pattern of self-contained colonies would have to be imposed from outside.

The Dominion of New England (1686–89) was an attempt to do just this and at the same time to tie up many loose political ends in the northern and middle colonies.[80] There was, to begin with, the problem of the

[78] Harry M. Ward, *The United Colonies of New England* (New York: Vantage Press, 1961).
[79] Andrews, *Colonial Period*, II, 24 n. 1.
[80] Viola F. Barnes's *The Dominion of New England* (New Haven, Conn.: Yale University

future government of Massachusetts whose charter was declared void on
October 23, 1684, and where the king wished to promote a greater liberty
of conscience than had prevailed under the superseded Puritan rulers.
Then there were fiscal problems clamoring for solution: the nonenforcement of the Acts of Trade and Navigation throughout New England to
which Edward Randolph, the king's overseer of Customs, had been drawing attention for the past ten years, and the noncollection of royal quitrents which had never been reserved in New England's land grants. New
York's status, now that the Duke of York was king of England, needed
redefining and perhaps her boundaries enlarging.[81] Timber for masts for
the Royal Navy needed protecting; and there were other lesser problems
of administration, the legacy of more than half a century of neglect. Above
all, there was the urgent requirement of defense. King James II was not
Louis XIV's yes-man: he was ready, for example, to back the Hudson's
Bay Company in its dispute with New France.[82] This business could have
led (and in formal diplomatic terms did actually lead in 1689) to war
between the two countries, hence to war between New France and New
England.

   The Dominion of New England came into being with the appointment
of Sir Edmund Andros as governor general in 1686 and the constitution of
a Council to advise him. Andros's commission at first comprehended only
Massachusetts, New Hampshire, Maine, and Plymouth but it was intended that Rhode Island and Connecticut should be added. In 1688 New
York and New Jersey were brought in, creating on paper at least a unified
government extending from the borders of New France to the Delaware.
The council was representative: seven members each from Massachusetts, Rhode Island, and New York, six from Plymouth, two each
from Connecticut and Maine, and one each from New Hampshire and the
Narragansett Country, with three commissioners from England, Randolph among them. There was talk of including Maryland but it came to
nothing.[83]

   However pragmatically the plan for the dominion was evolved, the idea

---

Press, 1923; reprinted, New York: Ungar, 1960) is a very careful investigation, strikingly
"Tory" in its conclusions.
   [81] Andrews, *Colonial Period*, III, 118–119, attaches much importance to this contributory explanation of the plan for the dominion.
   [82] Rich, *Hudson's Bay Company*, I, 223, quotes the king's reply to the company's request
for help: "Gentlemen, I understand your businesse, my honour and your money are concerned, I assure you I will take a particular care in it and see you righted."
   [83] Barnes, *Dominion of New England*, p. 73; Andrews, *Colonial Period*, II, 359.

in its final form was breathtaking, probably too ambitious for the time both in extent of territory and in program. It was not difficult to find arguments against the scheme. It was associated, unfortunately, with nonparliamentary government, though there was no essential reason why a dominion assembly should not have been instituted right away. It was associated, too, with a fiscal policy of making empire pay; and with Church of England preponderance, though not to the extent of withdrawing toleration from Dissenters. These associations could and should have been minimized by the English government: political union should have been striven for initially as an end in itself, with the rest of the program following only when the means were secure. Even so, there was no armed resistance to the dominion until news came of James's overthrow, and the verdict of the closest student of the subject — that the dominion was "satisfactory to England, and for the most part, to the colonists"[84] — cannot be lightly set aside. Collapse, when it came, was total. William III chose not to revive the dominion or indeed to do anything in America that might interfere with his dour and bloody struggle with Louis XIV in Flanders. This was a short view. Political union of the New England colonies and cooperation between them and New York were badly needed in the wars with New France from 1689 to 1713.

Practical schemes for federating the North American colonies perished with the Glorious Revolution and were not revived. In the eighteenth century the British government not only did nothing to bring about federation but opposed gestures in that direction by the colonists themselves. This was a mistake. A continental viceroy and court, presided over perhaps by a member of the British royal family supported by a North American peerage analogous to the peerage of Ireland; a continental bureaucracy with plum posts to distribute to the right people; a continental Parliament, the members of which would have gone back to their separate colonies to lead them to compliance with the purposes of an Anglo-American ruling class — such innovations might have Anglicized Atlantic America and brought to life dominion status and a federated commonwealth long before their eventual appearance in the nineteenth century. As it was, the failure of the Dominion of New England was final. No king after James and no leading minister till Pitt was interested in the colonies, and Pitt himself was interested in the broader aspects of colonial government chiefly when out of office.

[84] Barnes, *Dominion of New England*, p. 275.

The only other instance of federation of English colonies in the seventeenth century was in the Leeward Islands. Here were three small islands: St. Kitts (68 square miles), Nevis (50), and Montserrat (33), with a fourth, Antigua, considerably bigger (108 square miles), lying about forty miles to the east. Menaced to begin with by Caribs and ever afterwards by French (who occupied half of St. Kitts and had Guadeloupe within comfortable attacking distance), these colonies appear natural candidates for federation. In the time of proprietary government they were under Barbados, and when separated in 1671 they received from the crown a single governor or governor general. By this time, however, each island had acquired a deputy governor of its own (which they kept), a rudimentary executive, and an assembly: the latter was the stumbling block to federation, for once a community acquired a taste for making its own laws very strong persuasion or great force was needed to merge it into any larger unit. The push for federation in the Leewards resolved itself into a tussle between the governor general, backed by the government at home, and the separatist inclinations of the islanders.[85] Unlike the New England Confederation, the union of the Leewards was always an imposition from above. The objectives were a common legal system, common representation of the four islands by one agent in London, and common taxation particularly for defense. The means was a General Assembly, meeting for the first time to pass laws in 1684 and irregularly thereafter until 1711. Successive governors general, Sir William Stapleton, the two Codringtons, and Daniel Parke, cajoled and threatened the colonists, not without some success. Assemblies met, enacted some laws, and even voted taxes at the beginning of the War of Spanish Succession. If not wholly effective in opposing the French, the federation was better than nothing. The moment war was over, however, the islands reverted to separation: they declared enthusiastically for it in 1698 and achieved it in 1711 when the General Assembly met for the last time. Close to each other as they were, these colonies had differences which meant more to them than to Whitehall. Montserrat, for example, had a large Roman Catholic population of Irish origins, while Antigua — much bigger and richer than the rest — found itself in the classic position of the big boy in a small class, carrying the burdens of the others. Federation failed here as decisively as in New England, and the lesson seems to be that if the English govern-

[85] This paragraph is based on C. S. S. Higham, "The General Assembly of the Leeward Islands," *English Historical Review*, 41:190–209, 366–388 (1926).

ment could not bring enough persuasion or force to bear on the Leeward community it could do so nowhere else.

Centralization

On the day King Louis XIV assumed the government of France in person — March 10, 1661 — no French colony could properly be described as royal. All were in the hands of companies or private proprietors with minimal surveillance by king or ministers. On May 29, 1660, the day Charles II entered London to resume the kingdom from which he had been extruded for more than a decade, things were little better in the empire of England. Virginia was the only colony on the mainland of America, Jamaica the only Caribbean island, where the appointment of governor and Council was in the king's hands. No effective institutions existed at the center of either empire for governing the colonies, or even for collecting information about them. Few laws had been made by either country of application to the colonies; those made were largely ignored. In both countries there were plans on file for asserting central control: some grandiose schemes of Richelieu which might have been composed by a novelist so little did they conform to reality, and some more practical sketches by Martin Noell and Thomas Povey drawn up in the English Interregnum and tendered unavailingly to Cromwell.[86] All was to do.

It is a coincidence that new brooms went to work simultaneously in France and England but it is not a coincidence that centralizing policies were launched in the 1660s. Colonies by this time could be ignored no longer. With the appearance of sugar as the main Caribbean crop they had begun to emerge from the cloud of disappointment that had surrounded them ever since it became plain that France and England were not going to find treasure. Sugar interested the mother countries and necessarily created a further interest in the slave trade: both invited an assault on the Dutch carrying trade in the North Atlantic, a policy which accorded well with the European aims of Charles II from 1660 to 1674 and of Louis XIV from 1668 onwards.[87] These were the common impulses

---

[86] On Richelieu see Henri Hauser, *La pensée et l'action économiques du Cardinal de Richelieu* (Paris: Presses Universitaires de France, 1944), pp. 129 et seq. On Povey and Noell, see Charles M. Andrews, *British Committees, Commissions and Councils of Trade, 1623–1675* (Baltimore: Johns Hopkins University Press, 1908), pp. 49 et seq.

[87] Keith Feiling, *British Foreign Policy* (London: Macmillan, 1930); Louis André, *Louis XIV et l'Europe* (Paris: Michel, 1950).

toward taking the colonies in hand; and if they were not enough, the king of England had the further incentive of seeking to bring New England back into the family from which she had unilaterally declared a virtual independence.

Royal government of the French colonies may be dated from the mission entrusted to de Tracy in 1663 and carried out by him in 1664–65. Going first to Martinique, then to Guadeloupe, St. Christophe, and St.-Domingue, and finally to Quebec where he arrived on June 30, 1665, with troops for a punitive expedition against the Iroquois, de Tracy not only asserted the king's authority in each colony but also settled a number of urgent and outstanding problems. In Guadeloupe he abolished the excessive taxes levied by Houel; in Martinique he promulgated a code for the treatment of *engagés* and slaves; [88] and in New France he lifted — at least for a time — the shadow of the Iroquois and decreed the abolition of brandy in the Indian trade. [89] For the first time in French colonial history the king's representative, with full powers and troops at his back, made his presence felt. It is from this time that the French colonies, from being undergoverned by the mother country, began to be overgoverned, New France in particular. De Tracy returned to France in 1667; the rest was up to the king and his ministers, the royal governors and the royal intendants.

It was in the 1660s that the common and in some ways odd French style of colonial government was shaped, with power divided between governor and intendant in a way that left neither clearly superior to the other. The explanation of this arrangement lies in French history of the sixteenth and seventeenth centuries. Royal governors of provinces, cities, and strongholds proved unreliable instruments of the king's will during the troubled times of the Wars of Religion. Performing mainly military tasks, they had to be nobles or gentlemen; no bourgeois could be given command of troops. But because of their nobility and noble connections governors were difficult to dismiss and, when the crown was weak, impervious to control. Hence the institution of intendants, generally men of the law, civilians, not soldiers, and with training in administration. At first, and for a long time, their functions and commissions were temporary: to descend on some town or district where the king's orders were not being

[88] Du Tertre, *Histoire générale des Antilles*, III, 71–76. The code is printed in *ibid.*, III, 71–76.
[89] Eccles, *Canada under Louis XIV*, pp. 41–44, 72.

obeyed or where some problem existed beyond the competence of the regular local administration; to enforce the king's will or solve the problem; and to withdraw. In the course of the seventeenth century these temporary commissions turned into permanent ones, each intendant acquiring a staff of deputies (*subdélégués*) in his department. The ancient forms of local government in France were not thereby revoked; the intendant worked alongside governors and *officiers*, supervising, animating, and checking.[90]

This, approximately, is how the duality of governor and intendant worked in the colonies, though because the colonial intendants were on station as early as the first royal governors and before much existed in the way of a subordinate administration, they had more construction work to do than in France. The first royal intendants appeared in New France and the Antilles in 1664–65 and were permanent from the start.[91] No precise definition of their relations with the governors was laid down, leaving ample room for disagreements. Broadly, the governor was the colony's first citizen, responsible for military affairs and for diplomatic relations with colonies of other countries and with Indians. He also had judicial functions, presiding at New France's Conseil Souverain until 1675 when he lost the place to the intendant. The latter, as in France, was a civilian. Talon (1665–72), Duchesnau (1675–82), and de Meulles (1682–86) — though not de Champigny (1686–1702) — were career administrators, typical of the public servants Colbert recruited at home and a cut above the men who ruled and judged in English royal colonies. Their commissions empowered them to act in matters of *justice, finances,* and *police,* leaving very little in the life of a colony which they could not touch. *Justice* involved supervising the entire judicial machinery, sitting if not presiding in the Conseil Souverain, and holding (in New France) a court of first instance for major criminal causes. *Finances* included the collection of taxes and responsibility for the colony's budget. *Police* was nearly everything else: control of immigration, *engagés,* slaves, trade, and markets. From 1666 to 1676 land grants in New France were made by the intendant alone, from 1676 by him and the governor together. Talon —

[90] On the development of the intendant in France, see particularly Edmond Esmonin, *Études sur la France des XVII*e *et XVIII*e *siècles* (Paris: Presses Universitaires de France, 1964).
[91] The average length of service of an intendant in New France was between eight and nine years. See W. B. Munro, "The Office of Intendant in New France," *American Historical Review,* 12:15–38 (1906–7), on which this paragraph is based.

"the Colbert of New France" — also promoted industry and started trade between Quebec and the Antilles, seeking to blend his own and the colony's profit.

Both governor and intendant corresponded in detail with the responsible minister in France, and it remained a weakness of French colonial government throughout the seventeenth century that too much depended on the accident of the minister's interest in colonies or lack of it. No adequate bureaucracy was formed at the center. Richelieu, by making himself "Grand maître, chef et surintendant de la navigation et du commerce" in 1626 and buying out the ancient admiralties, had taken a step toward modernizing the administration.[92] But this office, after Richelieu's death, itself fell into the hands of sinecure seekers and had to be suppressed in 1666. Colonies were then attached to the Ministry of Marine and run by Colbert: well run, too, by him and his son, Seignelay, not so well by their successors, Pontchartrain (1690–99) and his son (1699–1715). What was lacking was a staff of specialist undersecretaries to keep business in motion when the minister was occupied elsewhere, a defect not remedied until 1710 when a Bureau des Colonies was formed within the Ministry of Marine. Until then French colonial administration was "morcellée."[93]

Colbert's monuments, apart from mountains of year-by-year correspondence with the colonies, are the great *ordonnances* regulating commerce (1673), marine (1671), and slaves (the Code Noir of 1685). All bore upon the colonies but the latter is of special interest as an instance of France's central administration tackling a problem to which England's never gave thought. In colonies like Barbados, Jamaica, and Virginia the planters were left alone or with very little guidance or control to shape slave laws as they saw fit.[94] In the French empire the Code Noir regulated every aspect of a slave's life:.his religion, marriage, food and clothes, relations with whites, legal status, and manumission.[95] It is true that these prescriptions were largely a codification of rules already existing in Martinique but it remains a striking indication of vitality at the center that

[92] Hauser, *Richelieu*, pp. 24–33.

[93] Saintoyant, *Colonisation française*, I, 108–110.

[94] Elsa Goveia, "The West Indian Slave Laws of the Eighteenth Century," in Laura Foner and Eugene D. Genovese, eds., *Slavery in the New World* (Englewood Cliffs, N.J.: Prentice-Hall, 1969).

[95] Printed among other places in Lucien Peytraud, *L'esclavage aux Antilles françaises avant 1789* (Paris: Hachette, 1897), pp. 158–166.

local practices were thus codified, universalized, and given additional weight by enactment as a royal edict. Nor is it a decisive objection to Colbert's work that neither the Code Noir nor his measures to turn New France into a compact agricultural colony fully achieved their purposes. Few plans of seventeenth-century governments did; and none for the colonies. What impresses about Colbert's work is that he made the colonists several degrees more aware of being Frenchmen.

The centralizing of authority in the English empire, such as it was, offers a number of points of contrast with the French. On the whole it was less dramatic. The English colonies were not quite so neglected by the mother country before 1660 as were the French, nor quite so closely regarded after. The transformation of Virginia into a royal colony in 1624, the dispatch by Parliament of Sir George Ayscue's fleet in 1651 to reduce the colonies that had not acknowledged kingless government in England, and Cromwell's Western Design eventuating in the capture of Jamaica, reveal considerable if patchy concern before 1660, though there are also instances of conspicuous neglect, notably New England. Possibly there lingered some vestiges of Elizabethan imperialism; certainly there was a continuing interest in the Atlantic trade on the part of English merchants in the first half of the seventeenth century and the opportunity (denied to the French) of voicing this interest in Parliament. The House of Commons debated Virginia as early as 1621 though the king denied that the subject was their business. With the king out of the way from 1649 to 1660 an opportunity offered for merchants to influence imperial policies from below.

It was in the Interregnum that the foundations of the Old Colonial System were laid, not so much by the Navigation Act of 1651, which was more concerned with European than Atlantic trade, as in an act of 1650 affecting the four contumacious colonies, Antigua, Barbados, Bermuda, and Virginia. The former act — requiring that goods should be brought to England directly from the country of origin and in ships of England or of that country — was a blow at the Dutch carrying trade but essentially a law about what goods and ships should *not* enter England. The latter — the act of 1650 — forbade the four colonies to trade at all with foreigners or in foreign ships, including of course the Dutch, i.e., it obliged the colonists to sell their products to Englishmen and no one else. It was a happy coincidence for English merchants and shipowners that the four colonies affected by this act produced nearly all the Atlantic staples in which the mother country was interested.

From 1660 successive Acts of Trade and Navigation laid down the lines of intended development of a consolidated imperial economy organized to England's profit. A new Navigation Act in 1660 revealed growing awareness of colonial products by enumerating sugar, tobacco, cotton, and dyewood as commodities which could be shipped by the colonies only to England or to other English colonies and only in English ships. The Staple Act (1663) dealt with trade in the reverse direction, obliging the colonies to obtain European goods only from England, i.e., forbidding direct purchase and shipment from France, Spain, Holland, etc. The Plantation Duty Act of 1673 imposed a duty on the shipment of enumerated commodities from one colony to another and introduced a system of bonds to ensure that cargoes leaving the colonies arrived at their stated and legitimate destinations. Later acts, particularly one in 1696, strengthened control and stopped loopholes, though none of these laws worked as well as their authors hoped and none (except in the time of the dominion) was effective in New England. In the colonies that mattered most to the mother country — Virginia, Maryland, and the Caribbean islands — the acts were reasonably well enforced. They also served to establish the principle (by no means clear before 1650) that Parliament could legislate for the trade of the colonies and even raise a revenue on goods passing from colony to colony and not intended for England.[96]

This economic centralization, outlined by Parliament and with details filled in by the Privy Council or Lords of Trade, was paralleled from 1660 by administrative centralization of a rather less purposeful kind. There was, first, the matter of the proprietary colonies and when and how far proprietary governors and councils should be replaced by royal. As already stated, there were only two colonies, Virginia and Jamaica, where no charter or proprietary rights or claims existed in 1660. A matter for immediate settlement by the Restoration government was whether these rights — dormant in the Interregnum — should be revived in Barbados and the Leeward Islands, the most valuable English colonies. The Earl of Carlisle, the prewar proprietor, had leased his rights to Francis, Lord Willoughby, in 1647. As lessee, but also with a commission from the

[96] The standard work is L. A. Harper, *The English Navigation Laws* (New York: Columbia University Press, 1939).

exiled Charles II, Willoughby had assumed the government of Barbados in 1650. He was smartly evicted in 1651 by Sir George Ayscue's parliamentary fleet and the next three governors were appointed by the government at home. With the king back in 1660, Carlisle's death in the same year leaving his rights to the Earl of Kinnoull, and Willoughby claiming with reason that he had suffered in the king's cause and anyway still held an unexpired lease of the Carlisle interest, the legal position of Barbados was as tangled as could be. The solution adopted in 1663 was sensible and momentous: Carlisle's patent was canceled, Willoughby was sent out as governor for the remainder of his lease but with a commission from the king.[97] Henceforth Barbados was a royal colony.

The Restoration government did not turn its back on proprietary rule everywhere. On the contrary it created new proprietaries in New York (the special case of the king's brother), New Jersey, the Bahamas, Carolina, Hudson's Bay, and finally Pennsylvania. By the time Penn got his charter, however, this method of colonization by delegation had substantially changed from earlier models. Pennsylvania was bound under the charter of 1681 to observe the Acts of Trade and Navigation and to admit royal customs officers to see that this was done; to submit its laws to the crown for approval; and to allow appeals from the colony to the Privy Council. Mainly because they obstructed trade policies, the tide in Whitehall was already running against charters. New Hampshire received a royal governor in 1680, New York on King James's accession in 1685. Following quo warranto proceedings Massachusetts lost her charter and was brought under royal government for the first time in the Dominion of New England (1686); though the dominion fell and Massachusetts got a new charter in 1691 the office of governor remained a crown appointment until the end of the colonial period. Maryland got its first royal governor in 1691, New Jersey in 1702, Nova Scotia in 1711, the Bahamas in 1717, South Carolina in 1719, North Carolina in 1729, and Georgia in 1752. By the time of the American Revolution only four proprietary or charter governments survived: Rhode Island, Connecticut, Pennsylvania, and Maryland (recovered by the Calverts in 1715), and the appointment of their governors had long been subject to royal approval.[98]

With the royal governors there moved into the colonies from 1673 a

[97] A. P. Thornton, *West-India Policy under the Restoration* (Oxford: Clarendon Press, 1956), chapter 2.

[98] Evarts B. Greene, *The Provincial Governor in the English Colonies of North America* (New York: Longmans, 1898), p. 22.

civil service of crown appointees, not very numerous and too widely scattered to be politically serviceable in the style to be developed in England in the eighteenth century. Most colonies acquired a secretary, receiver of revenues, auditor, and surveyor of lands, all appointed by the crown; these posts were freely treated as sinecures and given to absentees in England (i.e., contributing to the stability of British not American politics) with deputies to do the work. Above all there were the customs men: collectors, comptrollers, surveyors, searchers, naval officers, tide and land waiters. Appointments were made in ten colonies, not including New England, in 1673; extensions followed until a customs service existed in forty-nine North American and West Indian ports.[99] A surveyor general was appointed to preside over all in 1683, but the office did not become one of great influence. Just as in the course of the eighteenth century the British government fell into the posture of opposing union of the colonies, so it continued shy of continental administration in America. Thus no regular royal officer for Indian affairs was appointed until the Seven Years War and no American commissioners of customs were instituted until 1767. Whitehall's imagination seemed not to reach beyond dividing and ruling.

The years between 1685 and 1692 were the watershed in English colonial government. Edward Randolph's attempt in 1679–83 to bring New England within the newly defined system of political and fiscal control had failed.[100] To achieve this and other purposes, the charter of Massachusetts was revoked and the dominion erected, the boldest centralizing stroke attempted by any British government in North America during the *ancien régime*. Wider horizons called. Then came the Revolution in England and retreat. The dominion was abandoned; New York's government became like that of other colonies; Massachusetts got a new charter, losing her elected governor but keeping her elected Council. Replacement of proprietary by royal governors continued and the customs service was further extended but no determined effort made to enforce the Acts of Trade in New England. Retreat it was, solving some problems, shelving others, making the eventual secession of the mainland colonies not inevitable, but more likely.

England's institutions for colonial government at the center were dif-

---

[99] Andrews, *Colonial Period*, IV, 196.

[100] On which, and on all matters regarding Randolph's career and much besides, see Michael G. Hall, *Edward Randolph and the American Colonies* (Chapel Hill: University of North Carolina Press, 1960).

ferently styled from the French. There was no Colbert: rule was by committee, not by a single minister. The priority given to colonial business nevertheless fluctuated almost as much as in France, mirroring to some extent the interest or lack of it shown by the king and the court, high for example between 1660 and 1688, then falling. In principle the colonies were governed in the seventeenth century by the King in Council, that is, by the Privy Council, the highest tribunal in the country. In the Interregnum, it was of course the Council of State; then and at other times attempts were made to set up specialized bodies with executive power to deal with colonial matters. Frequently the Privy Council established subcommittees, ad hoc or standing, but more often with advisory than with executive functions. The different names given to these bodies are bewildering but it is important to see that nearly all the time the Privy Council was in charge.[101] The shortcomings of colonial administration did not come from matters being considered at too low a level but at too high. Colonial business often got pushed off the Privy Council's agenda and the practice of appointing fact-finding advisory committees was never very satisfactory. Thomas Povey wrote the epitaph on these toothless expedients: "Whatsoever Council is not enabled as well to execute as advise, must needs produce very imperfect and weak effects. It being, by its subordination and impotency obliged to have a continual recourse to superior Ministers, and Councels filled with other business, which ofttimes gives great and prejudicial delays and usually begets new or slower deliberations and results, than the matter in hand may have need of." [102] This stricture does not apply to the period of the Restoration when men with a genuine interest in the colonies, the Earls of Clarendon and Shaftesbury and the Duke of York, were in the Privy Council; but it does to the eighteenth century.

England's central colonial administration for the duration of the *ancien régime* took on something like its final shape in 1696. The Privy Council continued to be the supreme authority with a standing Committee for Plantation Affairs. One of the two secretaries of state gave to the colonies what time he could spare from diplomacy and other duties, sometimes very little; he was the nearest approach to a minister for the colonies. And the Lords Commissioners for Trade and Plantations (Board of Trade), created in 1696, found the facts and reported to the Privy Council. As in

[101] Andrews, *British Committees*, sorts out the confusion.
[102] Quoted in *ibid.*, p. 112.

the French administration there was fragmentation, getting worse not better in the eighteenth century. No unitary Colonial Office was created. Alongside the secretary of state and the Board of Trade, other departments of state (Treasury, Admiralty, War Office, Post Office, Ordnance, Customs) corresponded with their own representatives in the colonies. The result by the mid-eighteenth century was a mess, somewhat tidied up in the twenty years before the American Revolution but incomparably less efficient than the nineteenth-century British Colonial Office.

CHAPTER 6

IMPACT

Confrontation

The Discoveries confronted Europeans with situations for which they were by no means fully prepared. These situations arose from contact not merely with people of different races and colors but with people whose behavior and beliefs were unrecognizable and sometimes almost indescribable in European terms. For centuries before Henry the Navigator Christians had fought and traded with infidels — more of the first than the second, which may help to explain the caution with which Christians first approached the inhabitants of West Africa and India. But the Arabs and Turks of North Africa and the Levant, though unbelievers and enemies, were recognizable as fellow human beings. They were civilized (in European terms), more so in many respects than the Europeans themselves. They set store by books and learning, from which Europe borrowed extensively. Their political arrangements were at least as sophisticated as those of the Europeans: their rulers could be negotiated with and were strong enough to enforce the agreements they made. They had a religion, not Christianity but one equally coherent and binding. They had a commercial sense to match or outmatch that of the European traders. Above all, they had rules of behavior which, though different, could be learned; this made them predictable, something which Europeans have always been apt to demand of other people before admitting that they might be civilized.

Little was known in medieval Europe of the world beyond the Mediter-

246

· ranean. What could be gleaned from Marco Polo and Ibn Battuta nurtured an expectation of powerful rulers and rich cities. The early discoverers addressed themselves to kings. Some carried royal letters, forerunners of diplomatic missions and Christian attachés. Hence the importance of finding the legendary Prester John, not only a great king but thought to be a Christian already. Africa, in this light, was a disappointment; but elsewhere hopes were fed enough to engender confidence. In the East the Europeans found political organization, culture, Islam, and a commercial sense: no Christians, but otherwise much as expected. And in America, by the luck and the daring of Cortes and Pizarro, they quickly happened on the strongest and richest "empires" — Mexico and Peru — in the length and breadth of the two continents. These discoveries naturally prompted a search for more "empires" and "kingdoms" (Saguenay and Guiana are instances) and for the cities which Europeans took to be the most reliable evidence of affluence, culture, and social discipline. Needless to say they were disappointed. It is an important fact about the discovery of America that the best came early on; after the Aztecs and the Incas everything else was anticlimax.

French, Dutch, and English failed to find the kingdoms and cities to put them on level terms with Spain. They failed, equally, to discover religions in Africa or North America strong enough or coherent enough (in European terms) to be identified like Islam as an inveterate enemy, or weak enough to be uprooted and replaced by Christianity. It should go without saying that few Europeans were perceptive enough to see vital or respectable connections between the devil worship of Africans or American Indians and their natural environment and styles of living; it is, after all, necessary to have given up most of the traditional Christian doctrines in order to make that kind of appraisal of someone else's superstitions. Only a few rare spirits like Montaigne (and he never saw savages in their savagery) were capable of turning the Discoveries inwards and using them to make a fresh valuation of Christendom. Many Europeans despised the beliefs and practices they encountered, denying that they amounted to religion. Others went to convert and were confounded by pagan logic. What answer could the Jesuits make to the Hurons who, seeing missionaries baptize the dying, concluded that baptism was the cause of death? [1] By what arguments were Christians to refute the disarming

---

[1] Francis Parkman, *The Jesuits in North America in the Seventeenth Century* (Boston: Little, Brown, 1897), pp. 185–187.

proposition that their God was all very well for whites but no use for blacks or reds? This was frequently suggested, perhaps never more teasingly than by the Edo to Father Celestino, a missionary in Benin in the early eighteenth century: while ready to admit "that there is a God who is the creator of all, they say that the true God is the god of the white Christians and that theirs is the Devil, whom they worship because he is evil and wicked but tells them what they want to know, and also because by so doing he harms them less." [2] How could Christianity supplant gods who lifted the sun into the sky each morning, caused rain to fall in due season, found lost objects, sanctioned and aided desire and revenge, and were capable of frightful vindictiveness unless handsomely placated? How could a religion insisting on monogamy be presented to polygamists? The first missionaries were not armed with satisfactory answers to these questions. Christianity's poor record in Africa and North America in the seventeenth century owes much to lack of interest and bad example on the part of its carriers, but perhaps still more to the predictable failure of the Christians to perceive that heathen beliefs were often well adapted to heathen environment.

Northwestern Europe's ambassadors in Africa and most of North America were the traders. The people they met and with whom they did business were bound to have a different scale of values from that prevailing in Europe; this was appreciated by the whites and indeed relied on to enhance profits. What the traders were not ready for was an encounter with people who had no commercial sense at all or at least none they could recognize. This is Father du Tertre's description of the buying of hammocks, the only Carib product coveted by the Europeans: "Our Frenchmen are so much sharper and shrewder than the Caribs that they easily deceive them. They never trade a hammock in the evening, for these good folk [the Caribs] know well that they have an immediate use for them and won't sell at any price; but in the morning they will sell cheaply, without a thought for the next night when they will need them just as much. When night falls they invariably come back, bringing whatever they have traded, and say that they can't sleep on the ground: and when they realize that they can't have their hammocks back, they are ready to shed bitter tears." [3] No doubt this was an extreme case of incom-

---

[2] Alan F. C. Ryder, *Benin and the Europeans, 1485–1897* (London: Longmans, 1969), p. 123.

[3] [J.-B.] du Tertre, *Histoire générale des Antilles*, 4 vols. in 3 (Paris, 1667), II, 385.

prehension of the purpose of trade. African kings and merchants were more sophisticated and the Indians of North America picked up some of the rules as they went along; but nowhere, outside Asia, did the Europeans find a commercial sense to match their own. Time in European trading was money, bargaining a business to be concluded as quickly as possible, not in order to take one's ease but in order to make more bargains. To many non-Europeans, trade was more than a satisfaction of economic needs. On the Upper Guinea coast it was overlaid with rituals of hospitality and present giving.[4] At the English posts on Hudson Bay it was a social occasion, an annual fixture for the Indians with lengthy and well-established routines.[5] With the Abenakis, a Jesuit missionary reported, "gifts must be presented and speeches made to them, before they condescend to trade; this done, they must have the Tabagie, i.e. the banquet."[6] All this was a far cry from the swift application of the law of supply and demand to which Europeans were accustomed.

At certain points of contact in the New World a brief honeymoon ensued: non-Europeans pleased with the new goods, Europeans overwhelmed with the novelty of America and imagining it to be peopled with creatures of refreshing innocence. Explorers from Columbus to Cook were given to enthusing over the friendliness of the "natives" they encountered (and it was the explorers who wrote the books that were read in Europe). There is no reason to doubt the accuracy of the reports. The trouble began when exploiters followed explorers and the imaginary savage melted into the reality. Whatever the pronouncements of philosophers and literary men sitting safely at home, the prevailing attitude of traders and settlers to the "natives" had more in it of contempt and fear than of admiration. On all counts — their inadequate political and legal systems, their feeble superstitions, and their defective commercial sense — most of the inhabitants of West Africa, the Antilles, and North America failed to qualify, in the eyes of most Europeans who saw them at close quarters, as fully fledged members of the human race. There were exceptions but they were few. In one word, the Europeans found it hard to *respect* the "natives" or credit them with individuality.

[4] Walter Rodney, *A History of the Upper Guinea Coast, 1545–1800* (Oxford: Clarendon Press, 1970), pp. 195–196, 227.
[5] E. E. Rich, "Trade Habits and Economic Motivation among the Indians of North America," *Canadian Journal of Economic and Political Science*, 26:35–53 (1960).
[6] Quoted by Abraham Rotstein, "Trade and Politics: An Institutional Approach," *Western Canadian Journal of Anthropology*, 3:14 (1972).

Wholesale denunciations were common. Two examples will convey the style. First, Rev. Jonas Michaëlius, the first Dutch Reformed pastor in North America, on the Indians of New Netherland: "I find them entirely savage and wild, strangers to all decency, yea, uncivil and stupid as garden poles, proficient in all wickedness and godlessness; devilish men, who serve nobody but the Devil. . . . They are as thievish and treacherous as they are tall; and in cruelty they are altogether inhuman, more than barbarous, far exceeding the Africans."[7] Secondly, Willem Bosman, factor of the Dutch West India Company, on the Africans of the Gold Coast at the end of the seventeenth century: "The Negroes are all, without Exception, crafty, villainous and fraudulent, and very seldom to be trusted; being sure to slip no Opportunity of cheating an European nor indeed one another. A Man of Integrity is as rare among them as a white Falcon."[8] From verdicts like these it was not difficult to advance to a view of non-Europeans as the destined victims of a superior morality, a superior culture, and a superior technology.

Yet one must beware of explaining too much. It would have been amazing if Europeans had in general taken any other view or behaved other than they did toward non-Europeans. Europe in the seventeenth century, if one recalls the sack of Magdeburg, the massacre of Drogheda, the *dragonnades*, the persecution of Grotius and Galileo, the barbarous criminal codes, and the poverty of most of the people, was not a conspicuously civilized or sensitive place. The gulf in privilege and education between the top and the bottom was tremendous. There were not many Montaignes among the French, Dutch, or English colonists. At home Europeans perpetrated appalling things upon one another; much of what they proceeded to do to non-Europeans was an extension of that. For anything they did beyond the customary tariff of frightfulness they could find all the justification they needed in the "inhumanity" of the savages.

Europeans in West Africa

Europe's impact on West Africa in the seventeenth century was shaped in the first place by what is sometimes known as "the climate" but should more properly be called the disease environment. Malaria and yellow

[7] J. Franklin Jameson, ed., *Narratives of New Netherland, 1609–1664* (New York: Scribner, 1909), pp. 126–127.

[8] W. Bosman, *A New and Accurate Description of the Coast of Guinea* (London, 1721), p. 100.

fever — to which the Africans were largely immune — destroyed a majority of the Europeans exposed to them. There were no cures, scarcely any palliatives until the eighteenth century, not even accurate diagnosis.[9] Because of this there was no effective penetration of the African interior and no serious possibility of forming white colonies on the mainland. Instead, English, French, and Dutch built trading stations, sited by the sea or only a little way up-river, and fortified them against hostile Africans and white competitors.

Within these forts the death rate was very high. Precision is difficult to attain but a recent study of the staff records of the English Royal African Company, based on some 2000 recorded deaths on the West Coast including 460 new arrivals, shows that Africa was indeed the white man's grave at the end of the seventeenth century.[10] The incidence of mortality varied a great deal: from season to season, from place to place, and from year to year. In the Gambia more than four times as many white men died in the month of July as in the month of April and on the Gold Coast deaths in July were three times what they were in September. Broadly speaking, the Gold Coast was healthier than other stations, probably because there were more men there, continuous occupation of forts, and better facilities. There were "good" years at Cape Coast Castle when fewer than one white man in five died in twelve months; and "bad" years when that number was doubled. Clearly anyone who lasted a year improved his chances of living another year. To see the full effects of disease it is necessary to separate newcomers to the environment from old hands. The indications supplied by this sample of 460 new arrivals in Africa between 1695 and 1721 are that one in three died within four months of landing and three in five before completing their first year.

It is obvious that few whites would settle in Africa on these terms. Some Portuguese nevertheless did so; they and the transient traders in Upper Guinea fathered mulattoes who acquired immunity to the destroying diseases and in time formed a considerable element in the population of Senegal, Gambia, and what is now Portuguese Guinea. These were the *lançados*, particularly important in trade where they functioned as mid-

[9] Philip D. Curtin in *The Image of Africa* (Madison: University of Wisconsin Press, 1964), has a lucid discussion of the amassing of medical knowledge in and about Africa in the eighteenth century in his chapter "The Promise and Terror of a Tropical Environment."

[10] K. G. Davies, "The Living and the Dead," in Eugene D. Genovese and Stanley Engerman, eds., *Race and Slavery in the Western Hemisphere: Quantitative Studies* (provisional title), to be published by Princeton University Press in 1974.

dlemen between the Africans and other Europeans visiting the coast.[11] In time Dutch, French, and English fathered mulattoes of their own (though many fewer than the Portuguese) on the Gold Coast and elsewhere. In the eighteenth century men of Anglo-African descent worked as interpreters and brokers and at least one family of mixed Irish and African blood — the Brews of Anomabu — rose to be leading merchants of the coast.[12] A tiny number of English-born whites resided on or near the coast independent of the African Company; Nicholas Owen, who lived at Sherbro from 1746 to 1757, is the best known.[13]

This disease environment was a disappointment to Europeans who had once hoped to find a mighty empire in Africa and divert it to their own purposes and tastes. Great empires had as a matter of fact existed in western Africa in earlier times, of which the Europeans had heard quite a lot before the Discoveries began. Such were the empires of Ghana and Mali in the central and western Sudan; and later, about the time of the Discoveries, the empires of Songhai on the Middle Niger and Bornu on Lake Chad.[14] Themselves far inland, they had impressed the coastal lands culturally and economically but had given them nothing the Europeans could recognize as political unity. Nowhere on the Atlantic coast did the Europeans find satraps or mudirs representing distant powers; and nowhere except Benin was there a great city within reach of the sea. Benin naturally became the target of much interest. Portugal sent a mission there in 1486 and may have come close in 1516 to seeing a Christian on the throne.[15] The missionaries eventually failed but tried again in 1651–52, from which period comes this description of Benin: "The city has huge squares in which things are bought and sold. In one of them stands the great palace of the King which has three large courtyards; almost every day ceremonies, sacrifices and worship of the devil take place there. The streets of the city are so broad and straight that they appear to have been drawn perfectly with a level; the walls of the houses

[11] Rodney, *History of the Upper Guinea Coast*, pp. 76 et seq.

[12] Kwame Yeboa Daaku, *Trade and Politics on the Gold Coast, 1600–1720* (Oxford: Clarendon Press, 1970), pp. 96–98; Margaret Priestley, *West African Trade and Coast Society* (London: Oxford University Press, 1969); Rodney, *History of the Upper Guinea Coast*, pp. 216–220, discusses mulatto families of Anglo-African origin in Gambia.

[13] Nicholas Owen, *Journal of a Slave-Dealer*, ed. Eveline Martin (London: Routledge, 1930).

[14] J. D. Fage, *A History of West Africa* (Cambridge: At the University Press, 1969), chapter 2.

[15] Ryder, *Benin and the Europeans*, pp. 49–52.

are made of a red clay which is so smooth that they seem to be painted or polished; the roofs are covered with palm fronds." [16] Not Mexico City or Cuzco; but an improvement on the villages the Europeans had found on the coast.

Trade between Benin and the Europeans — Portuguese first, then Dutch — resulted from this contact. Pepper, ivory, and Benin cloth (which the Europeans sold elsewhere in Africa) were the kingdom's exports; textiles and metalware its imports. But Benin disappointed by refusing to sell male slaves to the Portuguese, who for their part banned the sale of firearms.[17] Toward the end of the seventeenth century the Dutch supplanted the Portuguese and, while continuing officially to forbid the trade in guns, in practice began to circumvent their own prohibition. Benin, hitherto somewhat indifferent to European goods, now permitted the export of male slaves, an indication perhaps of the difficulty of keeping aloof in a world increasingly permeated by imported manufactures.

Elsewhere no great cities came to light. The Europeans divided the coast into Upper and Lower Guinea, the former including Senegal, Gambia, and Sierra Leone, the latter the Gold and Slave coasts. They also traded further east in the Oil Rivers (Niger Delta) and further south in Angola. The points of contact extended, therefore, along more than two thousand miles of coastland, within which there was much diversity, economic, political, and cultural. This diversity was not fully appreciated in the seventeenth century, partly because some regions were little known, partly because the Europeans had not yet learned to look for anything but similarities to or dissimilarities from their own institutions and culture. Politically speaking, they found little evidence of compact organization in Upper Guinea but a host of petty "kings," some ruling no more than a village. "These people," wrote Nicholas Owen, "that goes by the names of kings and princes are only so in title. Thier substance consists of nothing more than a lace hat, a gown and a silver-headed cane and a mat to sit down upon, which serves to distinguish them from the rest of the negros. . . . In this light they apear to me, they are people of no magnificence or grandour." [18] Very likely this was an exaggeration of the

---

[16] *Ibid.*, p. 313.

[17] *Ibid.*, pp. 45–47. The king of Portugal wrote in 1514 to the Oba of Benin that he could have guns if he would accept baptism.

[18] Owen, *Journal of a Slave-Dealer*, p. 47.

political fragmentation of Upper Guinea; [19] a European naturally looked for courts, judges, and prisons, tax collectors, recruiting officers, and a ruling class distinguished by style of living, the only symbols of organized power he knew. If there was coherence here, of a moral or cultural rather than political kind, the Europeans would not have seen it.

South of Cape Mount — on the Grain and Ivory or Windward Coast — was a long stretch where the Europeans traded from their ships, built no residences, and knew next to nothing of the people. Gold and ivory were traded here, but few slaves. A little to the west of Cape Three Points the Gold Coast began, scene of Europe's most sustained efforts to trade and reside in Africa from the fifteenth to the eighteenth centuries. Here, by 1700, the English had six forts as well as a number of smaller unfortified factories, the Dutch had nine forts, the Danes one, and the Brandenburghers three. [20] On and near this coast the African states were more compact and coherent than in Upper Guinea, or at least seemed so to the Europeans who identified about a dozen distinct authorities between the Ankobra and Volta rivers. [21] From these states four leading powers emerged in the later seventeenth century, Akwamu, Akim, Denkyira, and the Fante Confederacy, all coastal or near the coast, and all by this time with a stake in maritime trade. Behind them, a hundred miles or so inland, was Ashanti, a tributary of Denkyira. Formerly a loose confederacy, Ashanti transformed itself from the 1680s into a relatively integrated state with a strong army. Between 1698 and 1701 the fruits of this reconstruction were gathered. Ashanti fought a decisive war of liberation with Denkyira, opened the way to the sea and became the strongest African power on the Gold Coast, a position it held until the nineteenth century. [22]

The existence of a number of states of roughly equal force, whether in Renaissance Italy or seventeenth-century West Africa, is an incitement to interference by foreigners. Although the Europeans came to the coast to trade and soon discovered that there were no empires to conquer or build, trade by itself was enough to draw them into African politics in the hope of winning concessions. How influential were they? Certainly the presence of

[19] Rodney, *History of the Upper Guinea Coast*, p. 31.

[20] A. W. Lawrence, *Trade Castles and Forts of West Africa* (London: Cape, 1963), pp. 14–15. English forts: Cape Coast Castle, Dixcove, Commenda, Anomabu, Winneba, Accra. Dutch: Elmina, Mouri, Cormantin, Apam, Accra, Commenda, Sekondi, Takoradi, Axim. Danish: Christiansborg. Brandenburgher: Akwida, Princestown, Takrama.

[21] Fage, *History of West Africa*, p. 105.

[22] *Ibid.*, pp. 107–110; W. W. Claridge, *A History of the Gold Coast and Ashanti* (London: Murray, 1915).

Europeans opened new possibilities for Africans and African states to acquire wealth and created new strategic situations in the control of trade routes leading to the forts; but it is by no means clear that European meddling was decisive in its effects. The rise of Ashanti, for example, was a struggle for freedom from Denkyira and a bid to break through to the coastal markets: it owed something to the European presence but nothing to European diplomacy. English and Dutch seem indeed scarcely to have heard of Ashanti before 1700 though they quickly remedied their omission, the Dutch sending an embassy there in 1701 and the English cultivating the king with presents, once the power of Ashanti had become clear.[23] It would be quite wrong to see these Gold Coast states about 1700 as puppets of the Europeans. Earlier, about 1650, the reverse would be truer, the Europeans being guests tolerated for the trade they brought. Later they began to meddle, spending much money and time on what an English factor in 1705 called "concerning our selves in the succession of their kings on suspicion that they may be more inclined to the Dutch interest than ours" and which he thought was wasted. "It is impossible to say," he concluded, "what this article hath cost both you and the Dutch, & I am very well sattisfyed that nothing has been done to less purpose on either side."[24]

Further east, on the Slave Coast, there was a European presence comparable to the Gold Coast but in less strength. At Whydah (Ouidah, Juda) there were English and Dutch residences in the later seventeenth century, joined in 1704 by the French. Hereabouts were a number of small African powers owing nominal allegiance to the inland Yoruba kingdom of Oyo, in decline by 1700. Very likely the Europeans meddled in local politics here, too, though less is known about the Slave Coast than the Gold Coast. But in the great happening in this region in the early eighteenth century, the rise of the kingdom of Dahomey, the Europeans seem to have played no more effective part than they had done in the rise of Ashanti. If anything they discouraged Dahomey, which responded about 1730 by stopping the export of slaves. Whydah and its environs normally furnished the Europeans with more slaves than any other part of Africa; a prolonged stoppage here would have crippled the Atlantic trade. By this time, however, each side needed the other and terms were quickly arranged acceptable to the Europeans and profitable to Dahomey which soon established itself as the

[23] Daaku, *Trade and Politics*, pp. 68–70, 144–145, 160 et seq.
[24] Report by John Snow, July 31, 1705, printed in K. G. Davies, *The Royal African Company* (New York: Atheneum, 1970), pp. 367–371.

outstanding, if not the first, example of an African coastal power reared on the profits of the slave trade. Further east still, in the Oil Rivers and New and Old Calabar, African rulers seem to have done well out of visiting ships by collecting a duty on slaves exported.[25]

Insofar as a complex situation, with much local diversity, can be reduced to a formula it would seem that the direct consequences of European meddling were slight. The Europeans did not become kingmakers, much as they may have wished to be so. To this extent Africa resisted Europe. In other respects, however, resistance was less effective. Against the flood of European manufactures the Africans, like the Indians of North America, had little defense: guns and gunpowder, metal goods, textiles (though Africans were well able to make their own), beads, and cowrie shells poured into the country in the late seventeenth century, losing the status of luxuries and turning into articles of common consumption. Benin, perhaps Dahomey, held out for a time against the tide but both capitulated in the end; nowhere can be found the icy and sustained indifference with which China regarded European technology. This consumer demand was Africa's weakness, "the fatal flaw" which made the Atlantic slave trade possible.[26]

Of these European goods, guns and gunpowder have naturally attracted the most attention for the influence they may have had on the style of African warfare and on the balance of power in different regions. It is certainly true that Africa had an *envie* for firearms. Benin wanted them as early as 1514 and Portugal's refusal to sell them was a principal reason for the slow development of trade between the two countries.[27] Ashanti had guns before 1700, obtained indirectly from Africans on the coast; the desire to buy them directly from the Europeans has often been represented, and probably was, a major objective of its aggressive policies. At first the Europeans refused African demands. Portugal forbade the trade everywhere and the Dutch, after selling a few guns in the early seventeenth century, stopped doing so from about 1610 to about 1650. The motive was concern for their own safety. At the same time both Portuguese and Dutch put firearms into the hands of their African auxiliaries, recruited for the defense of the towns which sprang up round the forts.[28]

[25] Fage, *History of West Africa*, pp. 76–77, 102, 103; Davies, *Royal African Company*, p. 230.

[26] The term "fatal flaw" is Rodney's in *History of the Upper Guinea Coast*, p. 253.

[27] Ryder, *Benin and the Europeans*, pp. 59, 63; R. A. Kea, "Firearms and Warfare on the Gold and Slave Coasts from the Sixteenth to the Nineteenth Centuries," *Journal of African History*, 12:185 (1971).

[28] Kea, "Firearms and Warfare," pp. 186–187.

The breakthrough in the arms trade came about 1650 and there seems to be no doubt that it was the English who swept aside the embargo. From the 1660s guns were sold on the Gold Coast in hundreds every year and by 1700 in thousands. In four years (1701–4) the English African Company alone sent out 32,954 muskets, pistols, and firearms of other types.[29] Other Europeans followed the English lead. By the beginning of the eighteenth century all inhibitions had gone. Thus when the Dutch West India Company tried to stop the sale of guns to Benin in 1717, their own director general suppressed the prohibition.[30]

The consequences of this trade are not easy to evaluate. Initially the impact of firearms in Africa must have been considerable; even a few weapons would have made a profound impact on those facing them for the first time. On the other hand, when most armies had guns the effect on morale was bound to diminish. It is also important not to exaggerate the practical value of the crude weapons of the seventeenth century. The smooth-bore musket was not very accurate. A musketeer hitting his mark at a range of a hundred yards was doing well; a skilled archer could do better. Loading was intricate and had to be done precisely, not easy when under attack. Rate of fire was absurdly slow compared to bows and arrows. Match-locks — which formed the greater part of the guns sold in Africa until the last quarter of the seventeenth century — were fired by applying a burning match to the touch hole and were apt to fail in bad weather. Firelocks, in which the powder was ignited by a spark from flint, were better but still vulnerable to damp. Most trade guns were of low quality and broke easily; though Africans eventually acquired the skill to repair them, this took time. It is not surprising, therefore, that some historians have moved from one extreme to the other, from claiming that firearms brought about a military and political revolution in Africa to denying that they had any profound effect.[31] Regional differences in this respect have begun to emerge: guns do not seem to have made much impact on Upper Guinea before 1700 but had a greater effect on the Gold Coast. Here, in the later seventeenth and early eighteenth centuries, armies were being reformed and tactics changed to accommodate the new weapon, despite its numerous deficiencies.[32] A possible longer term effect may have been to stabilize both external and inter-

[29] Davies, *Royal African Company*, p. 356.
[30] Ryder, *Benin and the Europeans*, pp. 148–149.
[31] Rodney, *History of the Upper Guinea Coast*, p. 177: "European firearms did not automatically influence the African balance of power."
[32] Kea, "Firearms and Warfare," pp. 207–212.

nal politics, to keep power in the hands of those who already had it and could use it to buy more and better arms. The most important consequence, however, was to increase Africa's dependence on Europe.

No other imported product acquired an equal status. Liquor was brought to Africa and used extensively by the traders for purposes of entertainment. But, presumably because Africans were able to mix strong drinks of their own, neither French brandy nor Dutch gin nor West Indian rum (which began to be shipped across the Atlantic about 1680) had the devastating consequences they produced in North America. It is difficult to gauge the impact of other goods: cloth, ranging from expensive scarlets down to cheap East Indian cottons brought first to Europe and reshipped to Africa, mirrors, bells, pewter, iron, glass beads, etc. Few or none of them were necessities; one is free to believe that they became symbols of status and contributed to sharpening the sense of inequality between Africa's rich and poor.

Europe's impact on Africa in the seventeenth and eighteenth centuries was not, however, wrought principally by imported goods, even firearms; it was wrought by Africa's exports, slaves. Some figures of the volume of the slave trade have already been presented:[33] low in the first half of the seventeenth century, it rose in the third quarter and rose again sharply in the last quarter, suggestively parallel to what is known of the sale of guns in Africa. It remains to indicate the consequences of the slave trade for Africans, always remembering that in 1700 it was still far from its zenith.

Much here is speculation; and speculation bedeviled by two centuries of breast-beating on the part of humanitarians as well as, more recently, the assertions of nationalists. To start with the obvious, the slave trade could not have existed without the full and willing cooperation of Africans. Entire communities of Indians in South America and the Caribbean were enslaved by *force majeure* but in Africa the acquisition of slaves by Europeans was business. If whites are to be found guilty of buying blacks, blacks must be found guilty of selling each other; there is no sliding round this. If it is urged that the principal African beneficiaries were a few kings and great merchants who conspired to exploit the mass of their own people (and this has so far been asserted more explicitly than it has been proved), it can also be argued that the profits drawn by Europeans from the trade fell mainly into few hands. Whites, too, were exploited by whites: the rank-and-file sol-

[33] See above, pp. 112–114.

diers who staffed the forts in Africa and the sailors who manned the slave ships got little out of the trade beyond a bare living and a much-enhanced expectation of death. In the West Indies the consequence of slavery was to enable a small number of sugar planters to dispossess a large number of pioneers, again an advantage to the few rather than to the many. Only in Europe itself can there be found diffused benefits arising from the institution of slavery: employment for makers of guns and cloth and builders of ships and cheaper sugar and tobacco for the people in general. Even here, it does not seem sufficient to explain the cruelties of the Middle Passage and the inhumanity of chattel slavery merely in terms of profit and loss. A key — perhaps the key — to understanding these things is the freedom with which Europeans had long been accustomed to maltreat other Europeans. Only when this freedom began to be questioned did there arise a considerable body of criticism of the slave trade.

Africans could be born in slavery or could enter slavery voluntarily in order to obtain some advantage for their families; they could be taken prisoners of war; or they could be enslaved for crime or debt. War and judicial process probably accounted for a majority of slaves shipped by the Europeans; and it is here that the effects of the trade on African society must be sought. For many years it was believed, more as an article of faith than from evidence, that African states at the height of the slave trade fought wars against each other solely, or primarily, in order to take prisoners. Such a view satisfied European guilt feelings and also accorded with an African view of the past in which white outsmarted black. Lately, however, it has been challenged, mainly on the strength of statements by rulers of Ashanti and Dahomey that they did no such thing. "One thing is clear," an African historian of the Gold Coast has written; "the motives of their wars were more political than economic, with the slaves as the incidental products of the wars."[34] Whether any ruler's explanation of why he began a war should be treated with this much respect is open to question; more evidence is needed. Meanwhile a recent study of Upper Guinea leaves no doubt that raids if not wars were organized there solely in order to get slaves.[35]

With demand rising as rapidly as it was after 1675 major responses on the supply side were bound to appear. Wars, whether undertaken for the sake of prisoners or not, were probably not able to furnish a regular enough flow

[34] Daaku, *Trade and Politics*, p. 32.
[35] Rodney, *History of the Upper Guinea Coast*, pp. 105, 109.

of slaves to fill the English, Dutch, French, Portuguese, German, Danish, and Swedish ships waiting to receive them. One response to this demand appears to have been an extension of enslavement by judicial process and a worsening of the status of slaves. It is claimed that in Upper Guinea, under the influence of the Atlantic trade, "sale into slavery was becoming the punishment meted out for an ever-increasing number of crimes, descending to the most trivial."[36] Enslavement for adultery is one example. Customary laws could be twisted for profit much as the laws and judicial processes of England were twisted in order to furnish convicts for the plantations. Life in Africa came to be lived under a growing threat of capture and sale.[37] Kidnapping of Africans by Africans became common. Worst of all, the status of serf appears to have been transformed into something close to chattel slavery, an inevitable change if owners were to have the right to sell their slaves overseas. In time, though probably not in the seventeenth century, a slave class emerged in parts of West Africa with no rights at all or at least with fewer than serfs had formerly enjoyed.[38] This, rather than depopulation, was the most baneful effect of the Atlantic slave trade on Africans who stayed behind.

There is not much to enter on the other side of the balance sheet. The European presence in Africa and the trade it engendered undoubtedly quickened the economic life not only of the coast but far inland. Before the Europeans came the whole region looked inwards toward the Middle Niger and beyond to the Sahara trade routes. By 1700, probably long before, the pull of the coast had become far stronger, impoverishing the center but enriching the periphery. Trade made possible the accumulation of wealth; some of the benefits must have percolated down from kings and merchants to less privileged people. New crops were introduced by the Europeans: maize, cassava, sweet potatoes, tobacco. Towns grew up round the forts with populations largely occupied in supplying food and services to the Europeans and provisions for the slave ships. A small beginning was made in the acquisition by Africans of new skills. But no new manufactures were introduced; some already in existence may have been weakened by competition. There were few cultural benefits in either direction, none at all in the seventeenth century, to relieve the monotonous record of goods exchanged for human beings. No heroic tales of explorers or missionaries, no

[36] *Ibid.*, p. 108.
[37] Fage, *History of West Africa*, p. 94.
[38] *Ibid.*, pp. 92–93; Rodney, *History of the Upper Guinea Coast*, pp. 259 et seq.

stories of dedicated administrators or devoted doctors dispel the melancholy induced by contemplating the meeting of Europe and Africa in these years. Both parties to the business showed themselves to worst advantage; the only moral issue worth discussing is whether either should have known better.

Arawaks and Caribs

The pre-Columbian inhabitants of the islands of the Caribbean — Columbus's original Indians — were Arawaks and Caribs.[39] Both, probably, came from South America; in the seventeenth century there were branches of both on the mainland, survivors of earlier migratory thrusts. The Arawaks were the first to start northwards along the great bow that stretches from Trinidad to the Leewards and curves west to the Greater Antilles. It is a reasonable guess that they arrived at Barbados about A.D. 800 and were evicted about A.D. 1200 by Caribs.[40] This pattern of successive occupation was probably repeated in other islands, Arawaks displacing inhabitants Europeans have called "Ciboneys" and in their turn being ousted by Caribs. By Columbus's time Caribs possessed the whole of the Lesser Antillean chain, the Arawaks having wheeled round to Hispaniola, Cuba, and Jamaica. Puerto Rico was the approximate dividing line, occupied by Arawaks but raided by Caribs.

These two peoples struck the Europeans as utterly unlike one another: the Arawaks gentle and welcoming, given to agricultural pursuits and amusement, living mainly on a diet of tapioca relieved by the occasional lucky capture of a manatee; the Caribs fierce and bloodthirsty hunters who ate their enemies and spent their leisure motionless in dark daydreams.[41] Doubtless inexpert observers exaggerated the divergencies. Aside from the common origins these people may have had, intermixing between them must have followed from the Carib practice of killing male captives and adopting the women. Du Tertre, who studied them in the mid-seventeenth century, reports that Carib men and women spoke languages somewhat different from one another and that they themselves attributed this to the custom of incorporating women prison-

---

[39] Carl O. Sauer, *The Early Spanish Main* (Berkeley and Los Angeles: University of California Press, 1969), provides an excellent picture of the immediate impact of the Spaniards on pre-Columbian people.

[40] Ripley P. Bullen, "Barbados and the Archaeology of the Caribbean," *Journal of the Barbados Museum and Historical Society*, 32:18 (1966).

[41] Du Tertre, *Histoire générale des Antilles*, II, 358, for dreams.

ers in the tribe.[42] Since most or all of these prisoners were Arawaks, and since women were responsible for so many of the objects made and used by the Caribs, cultural similarities must have resulted. Divergencies in behavior and style of life between Arawaks and Caribs, however, survived this mingling and are too well documented by the Europeans to be doubted; they had important consequences in the first two centuries of the European presence in the Caribbean.

The Spaniards did not trouble themselves much with the eastern islands of the Caribbean; but before passing on to the mainland of Central America they occupied the larger islands to the west. The Arawaks were, therefore, the first non-European people with whom Spaniards had extensive dealings and received the full weight of the latter's greed and ignorance. The precedent was a terrible one, more shameful than the slave trade. The Indians of the Greater Antilles were set to work by the colonists on terms that amounted to enslavement; in two decades they were virtually wiped out. Long before the French, Dutch, and English were on the scene these islands had been emptied. In 1518 a Spanish official in Hispaniola reported that the island's Indian population had been reduced from 1,130,000 to 11,000; the same happened in Jamaica and Puerto Rico and much the same in Cuba.[43] If genocide had been the Spaniards' avowed purpose the obliteration of the Arawaks could not have been carried out more efficiently. Hitherto unknown diseases and hitherto unknown compulsion to hard labor were the principal agents; a complete dislocation of what seems to have been an unusually well-balanced way of life was probably equally effective, perhaps more so. The Arawaks lost the will to live. "A well-structured and adjusted native society had become [by 1520] a formless proletariat in alien servitude, its customary habits and enjoyments lost. The will to live and to reproduce was thus weakened." [44] This is not rhetoric. The Arawaks' answer to marauding Caribs had been flight to the next island; their answer to the Spaniards was a declining rate of reproduction that can be documented from the records of their destroyers.

Hence, when the English conquered Jamaica and the French occupied St.-Domingue there were no Arawaks left. As settlers in the Lesser Antilles they knew them only in small numbers and as slaves. Needless to say

---

[42] *Ibid.*, p. 361.
[43] Sauer, *Early Spanish Main*, pp. 202–203.
[44] *Ibid.*, p. 204.

the English and French would have put them to work on tobacco farms and sugar estates had the opportunity arisen. To prove it, there is the well-known story of thirty Arawaks from Guiana who were talked into coming to Barbados in 1627 to help the first settlers. They were promised rewards and freedom to go home after two years; instead they were enslaved.[45] Probably the English acquired a few more Arawaks from Carib raiders but the number was never large: in 1684 there were only seventy-two Indian slaves in Barbados, a total which may have included Carib prisoners as well as Arawaks.[46] Enslaving either, and setting them to perform the tasks of tropical agriculture in the European style, was perfectly useless. According to du Tertre Arawaks in the French colonies grew melancholy and died, as their fellows had done under Spanish management. All that could be done was to make them "demy-esclaves," treat them kindly, and use them for hunting and fishing.[47] The French Caribbean census of 1683 gives a total of 105 "sauvages et sauvagesses," compared to 18,759 blacks, and this figure, too, probably includes Caribs.[48] Thanks to the Spaniards, the annihilation of the Arawaks is one crime that cannot be fastened on northwestern Europe.

It was the Caribs, a very different proposition, that the latecomers had to face, and perhaps one reason why the Spaniards had ignored the Lesser Antilles was the presence of these fierce people. About 1600 there were Caribs on all the major islands except Barbados, an exception that goes some way to explaining why that colony took a long early lead over all other English and French settlements. The hazards and backbreaking hardships of pioneering in thickly wooded and mountainous islands were great enough without the added peril of small parties of Caribs armed with poison-tipped arrows lying in the bush and cutting off even smaller parties of colonists. For at least the first thirty years of French and English colonization, longer in some islands, relations between whites and Caribs were more often than not on a war footing. Between English and Caribs hostility lasted throughout the seventeenth century; as late as 1772 the British had to mount a major punitive expedition, with two regiments

[45] Vincent T. Harlow, A History of Barbados, 1625–1685 (Oxford: Clarendon Press, 1926), pp. 5–6.
[46] Jerome S. Handler, "The Amerindian Slave Population of Barbados in the Seventeenth and Early Eighteenth Centuries," Journal of the Barbados Museum and Historical Society, 33:128 (1970).
[47] Du Tertre, Histoire générale des Antilles, II, 486.
[48] Abdoulaye Ly, La compagnie du Sénégal ([Paris]: Présence Africaine, 1958), p. 51.

brought from North America, against the Caribs of St. Vincent. It is extremely difficult — quite impossible here — to marshal the possible explanations for this mutual antipathy, let alone to apportion blame. Pursuing and killing Arawaks for several centuries had doubtless predisposed the Caribs to be hostile to strangers and it is unlikely that this feeling was moderated by their early contacts with Spaniards and privateersmen who went ashore for wood and water, careless of the impression they left behind. The Caribs were not, it appears, conspicuous forgivers. Revenge was a principal motive for their going to war: Father Labat, the French missionary, describes what looks like a ritualized procedure in which the old women of a tribe worked up a latent thirst for vengeance into warlike action.[49] By the time the English and French began the occupation of St. Kitts/St. Christophe the Caribs had probably discovered a good deal about white men and did not like what they had learned. There was no honeymoon such as Virginia had with the Indians. The St. Christophe Caribs soon called up their friends from neighboring islands and devised a plan to massacre the French. The French got wind of it and struck the first blow, killing a hundred Caribs or more and making slaves of the most beautiful women. Thenceforth and for a long time there was no trust between the two races. The Caribs opposed the French colonization of Martinique and Guadeloupe and a long war (1636–39) ensued, for which du Tertre held the French responsible. The Caribs were eventually evicted from both islands but elsewhere they held out longer. About 1640 they attacked the English in Antigua, killed forty and took four women prisoners including the governor's wife. They drove the French from St. Bartholomew in 1656, and in some islands it was their activities that determined which European power became the eventual proprietor. Thus the English badly wanted to colonize St. Lucia, partly in order to relieve overcrowding in Barbados and partly for its ample supplies of wood, a commodity of which Barbados soon ran short. An attempt at settlement was made but repulsed by the Caribs (1638–41); the French got a foothold there in 1650 which grew in time into a reasonably flourishing colony.[50] Grenada, another island of mountains and forests, had a similar early history. The English tried to settle here in 1609 but failed, withdrawing and leaving the island to the Caribs for a long time.

[49] Jean-Baptiste Labat, *Nouveau voyage aux isles de l'Amerique*, 6 vols. (Paris, 1722), IV, 320–321.

[50] Du Tertre, *Histoire générale des Antilles*, I, 82 et seq., 150, 416–418, 434–435.

Du Parquet planted a small group of colonists in 1650 whom the Caribs proceeded to pick off. Reinforcements were sent from Martinique including a hundred Walloon troops who had fled from Brazil. A large-scale Carib hunt was organized; some were killed; others to the number of about forty were surrounded on a cliff top above where the town of Sauteurs now stands.[51] Here took place the best known event in Carib history, the leap of the forty to death on the beach below rather than surrender to the French. Famous as it has become, this mass suicide should *not* be taken as a paradigm of white-Carib confrontation in the seventeenth century; usually the Caribs fought, always under cover and often with effect.

The Carib menace led in the early years of settlement to schemes for mutual defense between French and English in St. Kitts/St. Christophe and elsewhere. In 1660 a treaty was concluded between the Leewards, St. Christophe, and Guadeloupe to protect each other and to leave two islands unsettled, Dominica and St. Vincent, as Carib reserves.[52] The first part of the bargain was not kept. Somehow the French succeeded in winning the confidence of the Caribs after 1660, at least to the point of being able to use them as auxiliaries against the English.[53] This was an effective move to judge by English complaints of such an unnatural alliance between Europeans and savages, complaints which correspond with New England's lamentations over the deeds of the French Canadians' bloodthirsty allies. In the Caribbean the English never found the touch: they made treaties with the Caribs and enlisted their help in recovering runaway blacks but they failed to get through the barrier of suspicion that had existed from the beginning.

The Caribs are interesting and important for their relatively long resistance to Europeans and European influences. This resistance was not total even in the seventeenth century. They traded with the colonists in the intervals of fighting, selling turtles, pigs, fish, and other food and (rather more reluctantly) hammocks. They had, it appears from Labat, the common *envie* for guns, though probably even the most near-sighted

[51] *Ibid.*, pp. 426–432.

[52] Nellis M. Crouse, *French Pioneers in the West Indies, 1624–1664* (New York: Columbia University Press, 1940), p. 258. The treaty is printed in Vere L. Oliver, *The History of the Island of Antigua*, 3 vols. (London: Mitchell, 1894), I, xxvii–xxviii.

[53] C. S. S. Higham, *The Development of the Leeward Islands under the Restoration, 1660–1688* (Cambridge: At the University Press, 1921), chapter 6, is one of the few coherent treatments of Caribs by a historian.

trader could see that it was dangerous to sell them many. Perhaps because of this they kept up their skill with bow and arrow. Because they had so little to sell — no skins, few slaves — their headmen were not treated to expensive presents such as were often distributed in North America and which set standards to which others aspired. The Caribs were thus protected by their poverty as well as by their ferocity from some of the dislocating effects of European manufactures. Once an island had been "cleared" the French allowed Christianized or partly Christianized Indians to live there. Such was the group of Caribs Labat saw in Martinique in 1694. But these were very few; most retired to another island and went on living more or less as they had done before the Europeans arrived.[54]

Why were the Caribs able to resist? First, because the Europeans were afraid of them. English settlers, Governor Stapleton thought, "dread them heathenish villains more than a Christian enemy."[55] Useless as slaves, worthless as customers, hopeless as converts, the Caribs inspired little but fear in the whites. Even du Tertre, who saw many virtues in them, calls them "these barbarians in whose word no trust can be put and who, even in time of peace, never lose a chance to affront the Europeans."[56] Their style of fighting in the bush instead of in the open enhanced their reputation for treachery and the belief that they were man-eaters added to the fear they engendered. There is no reason to infer from du Tertre's chauvinistic claim that Frenchmen were considered best to eat and Spaniards so tough as to be almost uneatable that the Caribs regarded Europeans as food.[57] Nor does there seem to be any evidence that they ate brave enemies in order to acquire the estimable qualities of their victims. The Caribs ate, as they made war, for revenge.

This fierceness protected them; but they had another and rarer asset, a thorough knowledge of the sea and how to travel on it. It was this that enabled them to strike swiftly and unexpectedly at European coastal settlements or small islands, kill, and retire before their presence was known to any but their victims. Their tactics at sea were the counterpart of their tactics on land, concealment and surprise. Seapower also enabled them to aid each other and to concentrate relatively large numbers of warriors for particular operations. Thus in 1635, to defend Martinique against the

[54] Du Tertre, *Histoire générale des Antilles*, II, 384; Labat, *Nouveau voyage*, II, 8, 15, 20.

[55] Quoted in Higham, *Development of the Leeward Islands*, p. 131.

[56] Du Tertre, *Histoire générale des Antilles*, I, 542.

[57] *Ibid.*, II, 405–407.

French, help was summoned from Dominica, St. Vincent, and Guadeloupe; 1500 Caribs, du Tertre says, were assembled. In 1650 Caribs from Dominica and St. Vincent came to the aid of Grenada. In 1681 a small English colony on Barbuda was wiped out by Caribs, some of whom were said to have come from as far off as the mainland of South America. There are numerous other instances in the seventeenth century of Carib cooperation and use of sea power. Order and discipline seem not to have been wanting. Du Tertre described a fleet of war canoes "which came toward him in such good order that you would not see better in any navy in Europe" and tells how the ship in which he was sailing was attacked. At least once, in 1654, the French lost command of the sea to the Caribs between Martinique and Guadeloupe.[58]

The characteristic Carib vessel was the pirogue, about 40 feet long and up to 7 or 8 feet in the beam. This was built from a single block of wood by burning and shaping with stone hatchets (until the Europeans brought iron) and took a year to complete.[59] A pirogue measured by Labat at the end of the seventeenth century was only 29 feet by 4½ feet but he was also shown a *bacassa* 42 feet long and nearly 7 feet in the beam, big enough to be formidable to some of the small European craft which sailed in these waters. Propulsion was by oars and sails with two or three masts. Labat thought the vessels handy, able to turn as easily as a horse round a stake.[60] Caribbean waters are not the easiest in the world to navigate in but the Caribs appear to have been perfectly at home there; this competence in shipbuilding and navigation entitles them to a respect they have not always been accorded.

Carib resistance to Christianity was nearly total in the seventeenth century. George Fox, the Quaker, showed some interest in the "Taunies" at Barbados in 1671–72 but the English did not in general offer their religion to other races in the Caribbean.[61] The French did. Article XI of the charter to the Compagnie des Îles d'Amérique in 1635 stated that colonists, descendants of colonists, and all *sauvages* converted to and professing Christianity should be "deemed and reputed Frenchmen born, legally qualified for all offices." [62] Article XXXV of de Tracy's commission

[58] *Ibid.*, I, 102–103, 150, 429–430, 508–512; Higham, *Development of the Leeward Islands*, p. 136; Crouse, *French Pioneers*, p. 216.

[59] Du Tertre, *Histoire générale des Antilles*, II, 398.

[60] Labat, *Nouveau voyage*, II, 29–39.

[61] Handler, "Amerindian Slave Population of Barbados," pp. 126–127.

[62] Printed in du Tertre, *Histoire générale des Antilles*, I, 49.

in 1663 said the same,[63] so that conversion of the aboriginals and their incorporation in French society must be regarded as official objectives of French policy. Missionaries were early on the scene: four Dominicans with special responsibility for Caribs were sent out at the time of the colonizing of Martinique and Guadeloupe (1635).[64] Other orders followed. Two missionaries were martyred in 1654 but few converts were made in du Tertre's time. This he attributed, first, to the problem of language which he believed could be overcome, and secondly to the bad impression of Christianity which the Caribs had formed from the cruelty and greed of the whites.[65] Half a century later, in Labat's time, things were no better. The language difficulty had been overcome by the Caribs' picking up French but baptisms were few and dependable conversions nonexistent. Not that the Caribs at this time were reluctant to accept baptism; on the contrary the presents they were given by godparents to mark the occasion made them willing to undergo the ceremony as often as possible. But the missionaries had grown wary. Apart from men under sentence of death and dying children, baptism was given only to those on whose future conduct the priest could keep a close watch. Labat was convinced that a baptized Carib would continue as a Christian only for as long as he was separated from his own people; as soon as he resumed his former life apostasy was certain.[66] Here is further evidence of deep resistance to European influences.

Du Tertre, notwithstanding his occasional loss of temper with the Caribs, regarded the *sauvages* as possessing virtues which the French, like oversophisticated gardeners with wild plants, were corrupting by their "artifices." Despite all that had happened between French and Caribs he could still write: "The natives of these islands are the most contented, the happiest, the least vicious, the friendliest, the least malformed and the least plagued by diseases of any in the world. They are what nature has made them, that is, simple and innocent by nature. All are equal, rank and inferiority being almost unknown; it is scarcely possible to discover deference, even among kinsmen or by son to father. None is richer, none poorer, than his fellow: they desire only what is useful and strictly necessary and they scorn superfluity as not worth having." [67] This

[63] Printed in *ibid.*, III, 56–57.
[64] Crouse, *French Pioneers*, p. 45.
[65] Du Tertre, *Histoire générale des Antilles*, II, 414–419.
[66] Labat, *Nouveau voyage*, II, 26–27; Du Tertre, *Histoire générale des Antilles*, I, 467.
[67] Du Tertre, *Histoire générale des Antilles*, II, 357.

is worthy of Rousseau and seems too good to be true. Labat was cannier. He found in the Caribs "a natural indifference" toward religion and toward almost everything else. Three things only stirred them: their women, killed on the smallest suspicion of infidelity; revenge; and liquor. "Nothing, apart from these three things, can arouse them." [68] If Labat was right contact with the Europeans, however stoutly resisted to begin with, was taking its toll by 1700. Ennui leading to extinction was overtaking the Caribs as it had the Arawaks. In the later eighteenth century the British applied a virtual coup de grace so that, despite the survival of a small community in Dominica, there are few traces of the Caribs in the modern West Indies. Until archaeologists give them the attention they deserve there will be little to see apart from their leap — a tourist attraction — and a few rock graffiti. Neither they who resisted the Europeans, nor the Arawaks who capitulated, have descendants to protest at the past.

The Indians of North America

Heavy as it was, Europe's impact on West Africa in the seventeenth century was indirect, conveyed to Africans mainly by Africans. In the Caribbean the impact was direct and catastrophic. North America comes in mid-scale. The Europeans wanted fish, which could be taken with no disturbance of Indian life. They wanted furs, which the Indians on the whole were glad to provide in exchange for trade goods: metalware, knives, axes, cooking kettles; textiles; firearms; liquor. These goods were bound to bring about a certain amount of dislocation of Indian life, rendering traditional skills obsolete and inducing the trapping out of large areas of North America. There was no resistance: an *envie* for European goods gripped the Indians. "O, the infinite wisdom of the most holy, wise God," Roger Williams wrote in 1643, "who hath so advanced Europe above America that there is not a sorry hoe, hatchet, knife, nor a rag of cloth in all America but what comes over the dreadful Atlantic Ocean from Europe!" [69] Williams advised America not to be "discouraged" by this situation, but the Indians could hardly help losing confidence in their own technology when every day reminded them of its inferiority; at the least they were thrust into a position of perpetual dependence on the whites for

[68] Labat, *Nouveau voyage*, II, 25–26.
[69] Perry Miller, *Roger Williams: Prophet in a Wilderness* (New York: Bobbs-Merrill, 1953), p. 70.

powder and ball and repairs to easily broken trade guns. This shock might nevertheless have been assimilated had not the Europeans, and above all the English, wanted something else: land. This was the white *envie*, at least as cogent as the Indian longing for manufactures, which turned colonization into conquest. People not goods — or rather people with goods — overthrew the Indians.

Estimates of the pre-Columbian population of the North American continent (including Mexico) range between 60 million and 4.2 million; perhaps 30 million might be near the mark, with one-quarter to one-fifth of the total in Central America and a greater density of population on the west coast than the east.[70] Over most of what is now the United States there were fewer than sixty Indians to one hundred square kilometers (or between twenty-three and twenty-four to one hundred square miles) and over nearly all of what is now Canada much less than that. When farming was practiced, for example in the lands of the Powhatan confederacy where Virginia was planted, population was relatively thick (one or two to the square kilometer) but this was balanced by hunting territories which contained very few people. By the standards they were used to, there-fore, the Europeans entered a thinly populated land, and one moreover whose occupants attached no special importance to living close to the ocean. These facts aided first settlement.

In culture, styles of life, and forms of government the Indians of North America were more various than the Europeans.[71] Leaving aside the advanced culture of Mexico, of which French, Dutch and English had little experience, the differences observable between farming Indians and hunting Indians in North America were greater than those between dis-similar cultural groups in Europe. After centuries of movement, tribes of different stocks and languages had settled in proximity to one another but retained their separate identities, so that Virginia had Iroquoian and Siouan inhabitants in 1607 as well as Algonquian. This diversity was only partly perceived by the Europeans if one may judge by a description of the Indians of New Netherland given by Johan de Laet, a director of the Dutch West India Company, in *Nieuwe Wereldt*, first published in 1625:

[70] Harold E. Driver, *Indians of North America* (2nd ed.; Chicago: University of Chicago Press, 1969), pp. 63–64.

[71] Ben C. McCary, *Indians in Seventeenth Century Virginia* (Williamsburg: Virginia 350th Anniversary Celebration Corporation, 1957), pp. 8–10. For a documentary introduc-tion to the variety of Indian life and culture, see Harold E. Driver, *The Americas on the Eve of Discovery* (Englewood Cliffs, N.J.: Prentice-Hall, 1964).

The barbarians being divided into many nations and people, differ much from one another in language though very little in manners; they possess the same constitution of body as those that inhabit a great part of New France. Their clothing is composed of the skins of wild animals, especially beavers, foxes, and the like, sewed together in the manner of savages, with which they cover themselves entirely in winter, and slightly in summer. Their food principally consists of maize or Indian corn, from which they bake cakes resembling loaves of bread; fish, birds, and wild game. Their weapons are bows and arrows, the latter pointed with sharp flint stones or the bones of fishes. Their boats are one piece of wood, hollowed out by fire from the solid trunks of trees. Some of them lead a wandering life in the open air with no settled habitations; lying stretched upon the ground or on mats made of bulrushes, they take both their sleep and food, especially in summer, when they go nearer to the sea for the sake of fishing. Others have fixed places of abode, and dwellings built with beams in the form of an oven, covered above with the bark of trees, so large that they are sufficient for several families. Their household furniture is slight and scanty, consisting of mats and wooden dishes, hatchets made of hard flint stone by dint of savage labor, and tubes for smoking tobacco formed likewise of flint stone ingeniously perforated, so that it is surprising how, in so great a want of iron implements, they are able to carve the stone. They neither desire nor know riches. [72]

This is not a bad piece of observation of one region but the diversity was far greater, so much so that no summary statement is possible of Indian responses and attitudes to Europeans in the seventeenth century or vice versa. All that will be attempted here is an inventory of some of the commoner red-white situations which arose in the first hundred years of settlement.

The Honeymoon. "Welcome, Englishmen." [73] These were the words, spoken in English, with which Samoset greeted the Pilgrims in 1620 — encouraging words in one sense, promising the cooperation the colonists badly needed; deflating in another sense, obliging the newcomers to recognize that they had so far accomplished nothing very special. Nearly everywhere the colonists found that the Indians knew more about them than they knew about the Indians. The French had been fishing and gathering furs in the St. Lawrence long before Champlain; French and English sailors had coasted New England, landing for wood and water, for at least a century before the Pilgrims came; while in the south there had been not only the unhappy precedent of Roanoke but spasmodic Spanish

[72] Jameson, Narratives of New Netherland, p. 57.
[73] John Bakeless, The Eyes of Discovery (Philadelphia: Lippincott, 1950), p. 218.

and French visitations at earlier dates. The Pilgrims' experience of finding a local Indian who had spent a vacation in England must be deemed unusual, but it is broadly true to say that the seaside Indians of North America had been aware of the whites long enough to form at least provisional attitudes toward them.

What these attitudes were it is impossible to say for certain but, to judge by the reception given to settlers, they were more favorable than unfavorable. In Virginia there was an initial reserve, probably owing to fear that the whites wanted revenge for the destruction of Roanoke, but this was not the prevailing Indian attitude of the first years. The Indians here were farmers, well able to keep the colonists from starving by supplying them with maize, and later teaching them how to grow it themselves, where to catch fish, and what wild plants to eat. There was no doubt some apprehension that the English might prove difficult to manage and even more difficult to shift, and this would explain a certain ambivalence on Powhatan's part; on the other hand, the newcomers had something to offer as well as trade goods. The suggestion that Powhatan hoped to use the English to strengthen his hold over the confederacy and as auxiliaries against his enemies, though naturally difficult to prove, is highly plausible.[74] Here, as elsewhere, the Europeans were a new element in an existing complex of Indian relationships. It was perfectly natural to see them as allies, powerful allies too, considering the devastating effect of firearms at first encounter. Thus the Hurons, Algonquins, and Montagnais drew Champlain into their war with the Iroquois, so that one burst (four bullets) fired from his harquebus on July 30, 1609, inaugurated nearly a century of conflict. Most attention has naturally been given to Champlain's "blunder" in antagonizing the most formidable Indians east of the Mississippi; but it is equally correct to see this episode as part of a honeymoon between the French and the Indians they had met on the St. Lawrence.

In New England it would perhaps be inappropriate to designate as a "honeymoon" the early relations between the Indians and either the Pilgrims or the Puritans. But Thomas Morton's colony at Merrymount near Quincy, Mass. (1622–28), apparently deserved that description.[75]

[74] Nancy O. Lurie, "Indian Cultural Adjustment to European Civilization," in James M. Smith, ed., *Seventeenth-Century America* (Chapel Hill: University of North Carolina Press, 1959), pp. 43–44.
[75] Samuel E. Morison, *Builders of the Bay Colony* (revised Sentry ed.; Boston: Houghton Mifflin, 1962), pp. 14–18.

Here, according to Governor Bradford, the Indians were given more liquor than was good for them, shown how to use firearms, and invited, the women at least, to dance and frisk round the maypole and engage in "worse practises." [76] It would be quite wrong to make a hero of Morton: liquor and guns were not the finest flowers of Europe's culture and the maypole no answer to the long-term problems of race relations. The Pilgrims put a stop to these goings-on, probably as much because they feared the firearms as because they disapproved of the frisking about. What they wanted from the Indians was trade with as few complications as possible; it was only thus that they could survive and pay their way. One cannot see the first New Englanders having much skill in collecting furs themselves, so that they like the Virginians began in a state of dependence on Indian goodwill. That this was forthcoming probably owed something to the epidemic which had reduced the Indian population of New England just before the Pilgrims arrived and must have weakened any disposition to resist.

Symbolizing the honeymoon time between white and red is of course the marriage of John Rolfe to Powhatan's daughter in April 1614, undertaken, as the bridegroom put it, not only for love but "for the good of this plantation, for the honour of our countrie, for the glory of God, for my owne salvation, and for the convertinge to the true knowledge of God and Jesus Christ, an unbeleeving creature, namely Pokahuntas." [77]

Alliances and Trade. For the greater part of the seventeenth century relations between Indians and Europeans were ruled by three considerations: the pioneers' need for help; the colonists' quest for security; and trade. New colonies needed Indian friends to aid them in mastering the environment; but this phase was short, a few years at most. From 1622 in Virginia and from 1637 in New England (the Pequot War) Indians were viewed more as a threat to security than as auxiliaries in the work of colonization — a specially dangerous threat because of their unpredictability ("treachery"). At the same time trade with the Indians was, for most colonies, far too valuable an asset to cast aside. A balance had to be struck between the advantages of trade and the requirements of security, by no means easy to find in view of the Indian passion for guns and ammunition. Selling guns to Indians was plainly bad security; but it was equally obvi-

[76] Wilcomb E. Washburn, ed., *The Indian and the White Man* (New York: New York University Press, 1964), pp. 28–34.

[77] *Ibid.*, p. 22.

ously good business, and often essential business when French, Dutch, and English were in competition with one another. Hence the ambivalence of New France, New Netherland, Virginia, and Massachusetts toward the arms trade, changing their rules (or rather their attitudes toward those rules) according to how vulnerable they felt to Indian attack.[78] Usually commercial considerations prevailed; in the second half of the seventeenth century it seems to have been possible for any Indian who could afford a gun to have one.

As the coastal lands were cleared of fur-bearing animals the stayers in the fur trade naturally emerged as the colonies with easiest access to the west: New France, New York, and Pennsylvania in the north, South Carolina and Louisiana in the south, increasingly in collision with one another as the geography of the west was learned. Until this time there had been little in the relations between Indians and Europeans that could be called *haute diplomatie*, on the European side anyway. From about 1680 the first indications can be glimpsed — in exchanges between Sir Edmund Andros and Governor Dongan in New York and Governors Frontenac and La Barre in New France — of an attempt to use Indians in European strategic rivalry: to view them, in other words, as allies or perhaps as tools, instead of as customers if they had any furs or nuisances if they had none.[79]

This change in relations between Europeans and Indians from the bread-and-butter business of the early years to the affair of high strategy they became in the eighteenth century was first manifest in encounters with the Iroquois, the Five Nations of Indians (Seneca, Cayuga, Onondaga, Oneida, and Mohawk) living in the angle formed by the St. Lawrence and Lake Ontario on one side and the Hudson and Lake Champlain on the other. These were Indians the Europeans learned to fear, sometimes to the point of exaggerating both their strength and their cunning. Whatever else may explain the reputation of the Iroquois it was not numbers: at the height of their power there were not more than 15,000 of them,[80] i.e., about the same as the Indian population of Virginia in 1607

---

[78] On arms trade, see Allen W. Trelease, *Indian Affairs in Colonial New York: The Seventeenth Century* (Ithaca, N.Y.: Cornell University Press, 1960), pp. 94–100; Douglas E. Leach, *Flintlock and Tomahawk* (New York: Macmillan, 1958), pp. 20 et seq.; Charles M. Andrews, *The Colonial Period of American History*, 4 vols. (New Haven, Conn.: Yale University Press, 1934–38; reprinted, 1964), I, 363n1, III, 87–88; Paul C. Phillips, *The Fur Trade*, 2 vols. (Norman: University of Oklahoma Press, 1961), I, 164–165, 175, 210.

[79] Trelease, *Indian Affairs*, pp. 260 et seq.

[80] *Ibid.*, p. 16.

or as the Hurons in 1649 and rather fewer than the number of Indians living in southern New England at the time of King Philip's War. Probably the Five Nations had about 2500 warriors, though no such number ever took the warpath at one time. Nor should too much be made of the unity of purpose of the Five Nations. Each nation had the right to pursue policies of its own, including war, and frequently did so. Despite the famous confederate organization there is reason to think that a lot of Iroquois fighting was done by private parties looking for plunder or glory.

Why, then, did the Iroquois become renowned — probably the only Indians known by name to well-informed people in Europe in 1700? They were warriors, but so were most Indians. They were cruel to their enemies, but so were the Abenakis. More than anything else the Five Nations owed their achievements and the reputation built on those achievements to the geographical position they occupied in relation to the fur trade which the Europeans created. *They* alone could trade with equal facility with the Dutch at Albany, the English in New England, or the French on the St. Lawrence; *they* alone could threaten impartially the forward bases of the three European powers; *they* alone could interrupt the flow of furs from the Great Lakes to New France and bend it toward New Netherland. From this happy position, created for them by the European presence, they could extract the prices they wanted for their furs and insist on the guns they coveted; they could be sure of sympathetic Dutch or English at their backs when they raided Canada; and they could threaten neutrality or even a French alliance to carry a point with the English. These were the cards they held. The cards had still to be played, and one should not expect to find that the Five Nations invariably made the best use of the hand they had been dealt. They were not, after all, "economic men" with a European passion for the infinite acquisition of wealth. War was their way of life, often undertaken when it would have been more in their material interests to stay at peace. In winning the respect, or at least the fear, of the Europeans the Iroquois overextended and weakened themselves. Their greatest days as warriors and conquerors were in the middle of the seventeenth century: the neutral posture they took up fifty years later may have owed as much to exhaustion as to shrewdness.

The French met the Iroquois when Champlain fired at them in 1609.[81]

[81] Robert A. Goldstein, *French-Iroquois Diplomatic and Military Relations, 1609–1701* (The Hague: Mouton, 1969), p. 50.

Champlain led another expedition against them in 1615 and was worsted. In 1621–22 the Iroquois raided the French settlements for the first time. Peace, more or less, prevailed until 1636 when there began thirty years of running warfare that would be tedious to describe in detail but which was of great importance in constricting the growth of New France as a colony. Not only the fur trade and mission work were interrupted but also agriculture: French farmers working in the fields took their arms with them as a precaution against surprise attack. From 1664, when royal troops and more settlers arrived, the colony grew stronger. A large-scale punitive expedition was undertaken against the Mohawks in 1666 and a period of relative peace ensued. From about mid-century, however, the territory of the Five Nations appears to have been showing signs of exhaustion as a source of furs; [82] to stay in business the Iroquois were forced to hunt further west or to plunder canoes going down the river to French markets. Both occupations diverted furs from Montreal to Albany and brought them into renewed conflict with the French.

This long-lived hostility between French and Iroquois owed a good deal, no doubt, to the desire for revenge on both sides for grievances accumulated since 1609. But matters would probably have come to a satisfactory settlement had it not been for the presence of the Dutch at Albany to 1664 and of the English thereafter. Though they sent emissaries into the Mohawk and Oneida countries as early as 1634 — the first Europeans to describe the Iroquois at home [83] — the Dutch had no ambition to regard the Indians as anything but customers; nor do the Iroquois at this time appear to have viewed the Dutch in any but the same light. It was only with the coming of the English to Albany and the gradual unfolding of the geography of the west that the key position held by the Five Nations became perfectly clear. It was a position from which neither English nor French could draw much satisfaction. True, the Iroquois were generally friends to the English and in 1684 the Onondaga and Cayuga — though not yet the other three nations — acknowledged themselves subjects of the English. True, too, the Iroquois generally brought their furs to Albany. But it was also the case that they constituted a formidable barrier to English penetration of the west. Both Andros and Dongan were aware of this; the latter employed a time of bad French-Iroquois relations to promote English trading expeditions to Michilimack-

[82] Trelease, *Indian Affairs*, pp. 118–119.
[83] Jameson, *Narratives of New Netherland*, pp. 138 et seq.

inac and the Ottawa country between 1685 and 1687.[84] For a moment it looked as if the entire French western design was about to be frustrated. But Dongan's reach exceeded New York's grasp; as well as being too dependent on Iroquois friendship, his plans were too expensive for one colony to bear. No other colony could find a reason to help to win the west for New York and no aid could be expected from home for what was, economically speaking, a narrow interest. New France by contrast, though poorer, was able to concentrate its resources on defending what was for the Canadians a matter of vital concern.

King William's War (1689–97) was a decisive time in the evolution of the triangular relationship between Iroquois, French, and English. The Five Nations, resenting French aggressions in 1687–88, began the war ready to fight on England's side and delivered a terrible blow by the massacre at Lachine on August 4, 1689.[85] But Massachusetts, where the money was, chose a maritime style of war against New France and fought on land only in defense of her frontier. The southern colonies were naturally indifferent and King William did not give much to the war except his name. New York could do little alone and Frontenac skillfully avoided provoking the Iroquois. The policy of the French from 1689 to 1713 was to win the Five Nations to neutrality and in this they were largely successful.[86] The Iroquois were ready, when it suited them, to be the "children" of the governor of New France or the "subjects" of the king of England. The statesmen of Europe, assembled at Ryswik in 1697, set up a commission to decide which; [87] presumably it was beyond them to grasp that by luck and shrewdness — it is impossible to say how much of each — the Iroquois had won a position where, at least for a time, they could continue to be their own masters.

No other Indians acquired the standing of the Iroquois in the seventeenth century. There were bloody little wars — in New Netherland with the Algonquins of Long Island, in Virginia with the Susquehannah, in South Carolina with the Westo — and plenty of diplomacy of a bread-and-butter sort to fix boundaries (pro tempore), obtain land, and safeguard trade, but little on either side that deserves to be called a strategy. Toward the end of the period with which this book is concerned two

[84] Trelease, Indian Affairs, pp. 268–274.

[85] Goldstein, French-Iroquois Diplomatic and Military Relations, pp. 164–165.

[86] W. J. Eccles, The Canadian Frontier, 1534–1760 (New York: Holt, Rinehart & Winston, 1969), pp. 133–134.

[87] Trelease, Indian Affairs, pp. 342–343.

developments were working to lift white-Indian relations in the southwest into a class perhaps below but certainly comparable to relations with the Iroquois. Traders, cattle drivers, and hunters from Virginia and especially from South Carolina were beginning to encounter the formidable nations of Creeks, Cherokees, and Choctaws; and the French were arriving in Louisiana to dispute the trade in skins and check English expansion to the Mississippi.[88] Here, as in the north, the scene was being set for European competition for worthwhile Indian alliances. And here, as elsewhere, the whites were to pay tribute to the Indians by adopting their styles and idioms in diplomacy and treaty making. Hence the congresses of the eighteenth century attended by hundreds, sometimes thousands, of Indians expecting and receiving presents and subsisted for the duration of the meeting by the whites; hence the designation of an accredited representative as "beloved man," the discourses on "brightening the chain of friendship" and "making the path white again," and the appearance in treaties of images like "as long as the sun shines and the rivers run." The Indian seldom came best out of these exchanges; but he went down in his own style.

Conversion. There is no reason to doubt the genuineness of the European *intention* to convert the Indians to Christianity. What must be questioned is the high priority claimed for it in contemporary statements about the purposes of exploration and settlement; for nearly all Europeans it came a long way second to making money. For a start, conversion was expensive; Morison puts the cost of Massachusetts's "praying Indians" at £10 a head, not much less than an indentured servant.[89] Then, while missionary work did not necessarily conflict with other purposes of colonization such as fur trading and farming, in practice it often did. Finally, conversion was difficult, much more difficult than the Europeans can have imagined before work began. To make Indians into Christians, it was necessary first to learn their speech and to turn spoken languages into written ones. This done — and it was done with commendable speed in both New France and New England — the Indians had to be persuaded of the truth of the message tendered to them. This was not impossible, but to have any lasting effect on the wandering style of life followed by many Indians in the northern parts of North America the missionaries had either to live with the tribes or induce them to take up new forms of

---

[88] On which see generally Verner W. Crane, *The Southern Frontier, 1670–1732* (Ann Arbor: University of Michigan Press, 1956).

[89] Morison, *Builders of the Bay Colony,* p. 306.

existence in special settlements where backsliding could be checked. The first course was both dangerous and slow. The second was to cut off the Indians from the springs of their material as well as their cultural lives and reduce them to a state of baptized dependence on European charity. No way out of these difficulties was found. It is a temptation to wish that the missionaries had left North America alone, but one that can be resisted by turning toward regions such as the Carolinas where scarcely any attempt was made to offer Christianity to the Indians and where relations between the races were if anything worse than elsewhere.

The principal English effort to convert Indians was undertaken by Massachusetts. Nothing was attempted for the first fifteen years; the colony had too much else on its hands and the ministers who came out from England, though first class at their work with congregations, were unsuited to the task of explaining Christianity to the heathen. In 1644, however, following the Pequot War, the government of Massachusetts began to consider instructing the Indians within the colony in "the good knowledge of God." [90] It is important to see that this and most of what followed was not an attempt to carry Christianity into the forests of Maine or across the Connecticut River into the lands of the Iroquois but an operation to mop up heathen survivors in the settled or soon-to-be-settled parts of the colony. Security considerations were at work as well as the evangelical spirit.

Most of the history of the Massachusetts mission is contained in the life of John Eliot, minister at Roxbury from 1632, who began to take Christianity to the Indians in 1646 and who translated the entire Bible into the Algonquin language. [91] This huge task was completed in 1663, by which time Eliot had brought into existence a number of villages of "praying Indians" supported by funds raised in England by the Society for Promoting and Propagating the Gospel of Jesus Christ in New England (chartered in 1649). An Indian college at Harvard must be reckoned a failure but Eliot's main work prospered. By 1674 there were a dozen "praying villages" in the colony with about 1400 Indian residents ruled by laws and a tariff of fines which included 20s. for fornication, 5s. for long hair (men), idleness for a fortnight, or breaking lice between the teeth, and 2s. 6d. for naked breasts (women). [92] Whether this was or was not the right way to

[90] Washburn, *The Indian and the White Man*, p. 183.
[91] Morison, *Builders of the Bay Colony*, pp. 312–315.
[92] Washburn, *The Indian and the White Man*, p. 186.

promote good race relations is a question which later generations have good reason to be diffident in answering.

King Philip's War (1675) did not quite put an end to missionary work in Massachusetts but its effect was to reduce the number of Indians within the province. The "praying Indians" for the most part stayed loyal to the colony; it is the opinion of one of New England's greatest historians that, but for the work of Eliot and his few conpanions, Massachusetts would have been exterminated.[93] It is from this time, however, that most New Englanders took up battle stations against the Indian, a posture in which they were confirmed by the border raids of 1689–1713. The notion that the only good Indian was a "praying Indian" yielded to another, better known piece of folk wisdom.

In New France the style of tendering Christianity to the Indians was more outgoing, as befits a church in which the priest precedes the congregation. Though Indian communities were set up within the colony — for example, the remnants of the Hurons at Quebec in 1650 — the missionary's place was on the frontier or beyond it. This meant living with the Indians in conditions of great discomfort; it might mean dying horribly at their hands. But the French missionaries, Récollets and Jesuits, were specialists, spiritually prepared for the work if not trained for it, a *corps d'élite* supported by the French king and court and by the morale of the European Counter-Reformation, not eccentrics like Eliot.

No one can read the *Relations* and fail to be impressed by the courage and selflessness of the Jesuits. If there were any heroes at all in the history of Europe's impact on North America in the seventeenth century, Jean de Brébeuf, Isaac Jogues, Paul Le Jeune, and the others of this company would come first. But, this said, the missions of New France cannot be reckoned a convincing success in human terms, though it became part of Protestant legend that they were. The insuperable difficulty, already mentioned, was the same that Labat met in the Antilles: to convert an Indian you had first to change his life or at the very least anchor him to one spot. Baptizing Montagnais or Neskaupis and leaving them free to roam over southern Labrador was merely to chalk up technical victories: "we shall work a great deal and advance very little, if we do not make these Barbarians stationary," Le Jeune wrote in 1634.[94]

[93] Morison, *Builders of the Bay Colony*, p. 317.

[94] The standard edition of the *Relations* is that edited by Reuben G. Thwaites, *The Jesuit Relations and Allied Documents*, 73 vols. (Cleveland, Ohio: Burrows, 1896–1901). For a

Not all Indians were nomads. In the Hurons, a people numbering perhaps 16,000 living between Lake Huron and Lake Ontario, the missionaries found promising material to work on: a nation of farmers, growing maize, beans, and squash, moving every ten or twelve years when the land ceased to bear but sedentary between times.[95] The Huron mission was opened in 1615 and lasted for thirty-five years: twenty-nine missionaries were engaged in it, of whom seven lost their lives.[96] Here the Jesuits labored strenuously to combat the Devil and baptisms could be counted in hundreds, if one included the dying and children baptized when their parents were not looking. It was Christianity's showpiece in North America, and it was utterly destroyed in 1649–50 by the Iroquois. Hundreds of Hurons were killed, thousands fled, the nation ceased to exist. A few fragments were collected in the comparative safety of Quebec but the work of the mission in the field was ended.

The Jesuit response was to send a mission to the Iroquois (1655), but it is important to remember not only the heroism of this decision but also that the Iroquois mission achieved little except at the Caughnawaga settlement and was withdrawn in 1687.[97] Elsewhere the Jesuits had better luck. The Tadoussac mission did not come to much in the seventeenth century because of the wandering ways of the Indians but considerable success was obtained with the Abenakis and Micmacs of the Bay of Chaleur. One may doubt the claim that the Micmacs were "entirely converted to the Catholic faith"[98] but it is certainly true that the French interest prevailed over the English in this region for many years to come. The same is true in the field of operations of the Ottawa mission which extended as far as the Illinois country. This ultimately was the most material consequence of the French missions: to Frenchify more Indians than ever were Anglicized. If the Jesuits made few conversions of the quality to satisfy a purist like Pascal, they certainly impressed the Indians by their patience and their model lives. In this way they helped to weave a net of Frenchness over the Indians on the northern and western bound-

---

useful evaluation, see an article by Charles W. Colby in *American Historical Review*, 7:36–55 (1901–2). For the effect of the *Relations* on opinion in Europe, see G. Chinard, *L'Amérique et le rêve exotique* (Paris: Hachette, 1913). A selection of the *Relations* has been edited by Edna Kenton, *Black Gown and Redskins* (New York: Longmans, 1956); see p. 51 for this quotation.

[95] Kenton, *Black Gown and Redskins*, p. 139.

[96] *Ibid.*, p. xxxix.

[97] *Ibid.*, p. xliii.

[98] *Ibid.*, p. xxix.

aries of the English colonies, a net that not even the Peace of Paris could altogether break.

Enslavement. The Indians of North America enslaved one another before the Europeans arrived. In some tribes the ownership of a slave comprehended the right to kill him, but this was not common. Usually slaves were survivors of the captives taken in war, mainly women and children, the men having been put to death.[99] They do not appear to have performed specially degrading tasks and they had good prospects of being freed by adoption into the tribe. There may have been some trading in slaves but it is difficult to see what economic purpose it could have served until the Europeans appeared. On the whole, enslavement was incidental to Indian war, a token of victory like scalping.

Neither French nor Dutch nor English seriously aspired to subdue the Indians of North America in order to live on their labor in the Spanish style. Coming to fish, collect furs, and farm, they had no call to enslave Indians in the early years of colonization; and when, later, slavery became the foundation of southern agriculture, it was widely believed that Africans were better at that kind of work. The Indian slaves who were employed on southern plantations in the eighteenth century did the same tasks as the Africans and were subject to the same discipline; but they seem generally to have commanded lower prices. Numbers were small in all colonies, but sufficient to show that, whatever the objections on grounds of principle or expediency, the owning of Indian slaves was neither illegal nor shocking. South Carolina in 1708 is said to have had as many as 1400 men, women, and children, but this may have been an exceptional time when Indian wars were inflating the total. In New France there was no explicit recognition of Indian slavery in the seventeenth century but its legality was implied in the eighteenth. Louisiana in 1726 had 229 Indian slaves compared to 1540 blacks.[100]

"Man-stealing" was a capital crime in Massachusetts and this presumably included the kidnapping of Indians. But kidnapping was not the way slaves were ordinarily acquired. A few were gifts to explorers or traders, some were bought from the Indians, and others were prisoners taken in war. There is evidence that some of the slaves exported from Charleston to the northern colonies and to the West Indies were prisoners taken in

[99] Driver, *Indians of North America*, p. 270.

[100] Almon W. Lauber, *Indian Slavery in Colonial Times within the Present Limits of the United States* (New York: Columbia University and Longmans, 1913), pp. 91, 106, 298–299.

wars fought by one Indian tribe against another solely for that purpose, but no systematic trade arose. Nor was there any genuine parallel to Spanish slave raiding up from Mexico or the periodic Portuguese expeditions into the interior of Brazil to bring back captives for the sugar plantations on the coast. South Carolina's Indian wars in the early eighteenth century, undertaken partly for plunder and partly for strategic purposes, are probably the nearest approaches to these Iberian practices.[101]

In New England the economic incentive to enslaving Indians, though probably never absent, was second to considerations of order. King Philip's War was considered less as an invasion of the colonies by an independent people and more as a domestic rebellion.[102] Captives were held to be at the mercy of their captors: some of the Indians taken in the fighting were executed, many were sold as slaves in the West Indies, some men and most of the women prisoners were sentenced to terms of servitude to be spent in New England. In punishing the Indians in these ways the colonies were following the example of the mother country which rid itself of rebels by transporting them to America.

Warfare. Although the Indians took to the use of firearms and became expert in handling them, they kept to their own style of making war by small fast-traveling parties which ambushed the enemy, cut off stragglers, plundered traders, or descended on lonely farmsteads or isolated villages and slaughtered the inhabitants. In nearly everything they did, surprise was the effect the Indians strove for, thus enhancing their reputation for "treachery" in the eyes of the whites. That surprise was so often achieved argues, besides the whites' failure to read the enemy's intentions, a considerable Indian talent for secrecy or, more likely, an absence of elaboration both in making the decision to attack and in preparing to do so. The pattern was made plain on March 22, 1622, when 347 Virginians were slain in a few hours, and was repeated in the same colony on April 17, 1644, when a like number or perhaps more perished.

The adoption of an Indian style of fighting by the Europeans is one of the two outstanding instances of borrowing from the pre-Columbian inhabitants of North America (the other was the birchbark canoe). In the early colonial period the newcomers naturally tried to fight in their own way. Thus New France in the winter of 1666 dispatched a punitive expe-

---

[101] *Ibid.*, p. 170. The subject is also discussed in Crane, *Southern Frontier*, pp. 112 et seq.

[102] Leach, *Flintlock and Tomahawk*, p. 225.

dition against the Mohawks, consisting of 600 men, half regulars of the Carignan-Salières regiment and half Canadians. Although useful as a show of force the venture cannot be deemed a military success. The regulars were overloaded and did not know how to use snowshoes properly.[103] They found, too, that there was little to attack in Indian country except Indians, and no chance of encountering them with a column that announced its coming well in advance of its arrival. New England made similar mistakes in King Philip's War, sticking too closely to the maneuvers and formations which had won the English Civil War for the Puritans but which were unsuited to swamp or forest fighting.[104] From experiences like these the colonists evolved an American style of fighting that confounded General Gage at Lexington and Concord in 1775.

Even in the seventeenth century there were indications of a disposition to learn. Laying hands on the enemy's leaders before war began was something the Europeans needed no instruction in, but it is interesting to find Governor Kieft of New Netherland organizing a surprise massacre as early as February 25, 1643. On that night, at Pavonia and Corlaer's Hook, between 80 and 120 Indians were slaughtered without warning by enthusiastic Dutch colonists.[105] Both French and New Englanders, at first appalled by what Indians did to prisoners, grew more tolerant and connived at tortures performed by their Indian allies.[106] Scalping was not merely tolerated but officially encouraged by the payment of rewards in cash during King William's and Queen Anne's wars.[107] Above all, Indian tactics of surprise attacks and swift retreats came into use in the border warfare that began in 1689. In this kind of fighting there was no room for European drill manuals and no place for regular troops. The side that had the keener Indian allies and learned more from them, not the side with the bigger population or even the greater wealth, was likely to win. How else could New France have held out for so long and struck back so boldly against the English colonies?

Dispossession. The French wanted furs, souls, and a little land; the English wanted furs, very few souls, and all the land they could get. This, more than reputed French and English national characteristics of a pro-

---

[103] Goldstein, *French-Iroquois Diplomatic and Military Relations*, pp. 94–95.
[104] Leach, *Flintlock and Tomahawk*, pp. 71, 93.
[105] Trelease, *Indian Affairs*, pp. 72–73.
[106] For example, Leach, *Flintlock and Tomahawk*, p. 172.
[107] Francis Parkman, *Count Frontenac and New France under Louis XIV* (Boston: Little, Brown, 1897), pp. 312, 407n.

founder kind, explains the broadly different attitudes toward the Indian taken up in New France and the English colonies. For all the main purposes of the French in the seventeenth century, above all for exploration, the Indian was an essential ally; for all the main purposes of the English he was the victim. Firearms changed the hunting methods of the Indians; metal pots made their lives more comfortable; liquor debauched them — all three put them in a state of dependence on Europeans. But none was as final in effect as the loss of land ceded to or simply taken by the colonists.

The early English were a little troubled by the question of their right to be in America and their title to the land they occupied, at least to the point of considering theories to justify what they were doing. There were, according to Rev. John Cotton's valedictory sermon to the emigrants for Massachusetts in 1630, three ways in which "God made room for a people": conquest, an invitation to settle by the inhabitants in possession, and emptiness of the land in question.[108] Most later thinking on the subject is contained in this formula, reinforced by Locke's derivation of a right of property from the mixing of labor with land. A right of conquest was not proclaimed in the early years for the obvious reason that no conquest had taken place. It became important after the Virginia massacre of 1622 and subsequent operations against the Indians, which from this point of view were welcome resolutions of a moral difficulty. As an apologist put it in 1622: we "may now by right of Warre and law of Nations invade the Country and destroy them who sought to destroy us. . . . Now their cleared grounds in all their villages (which are situate in the fruitfullest places of the land) shall be inhabited by us, whereas heretofore the grubbing of woods was the greatest labour." [109]

Explicit invitations to settle were unusual but the sale of land by Indians to colonists could be construed as an act of consent. Acquisition of "Indian title" was recommended in the seventeenth century by Roger Williams, Penn, and others, and was practiced in some colonies partly as an act of justice, partly because it was sometimes the only way in which any kind of right could be obtained previous to the conferment by royal charter of the power to grant land. Thus Rhode Island and New Haven in 1638 had no other warranty for erecting civil government or for being

[108] Washburn, *The Indian and the White Man*, pp. 102–105.
[109] Quoted by Wilcomb E. Washburn, "The Moral and Legal Justification for Dispossessing the Indians," in Smith, *Seventeenth-Century America*, p. 21.

where they were than that implied by Indian land cessions. In the Dutch West India Company's charter no title was conferred to land; settlers in New Netherland, able to establish ownership only by purchase, appear to have bought all the land they occupied in the early colonial period, some of it like Staten Island three times over.[110] In chartered colonies "Indian title" was less necessary but seems often to have been acquired. Thus the Virginia Company did not recognize it as a necessary part of land granting but in practice, both before and after 1622, some purchases were made in the colony. In the eighteenth century a fairly systematic attempt was made to combine "Indian title" and colonial grant by having the Indians sell to the crown which, through its governor, granted the lands to those who had put up the purchase money; in this way some abuses were controlled. But neither this nor any other device could curtail the land hunger of the colonists. Reservations were fashioned for the Indians in Virginia before the middle of the seventeenth century but most Indians vanished from the Atlantic coast like sand castles before a tide. Many died of smallpox or the effect of liquor; a few were killed in war or enslaved; the rest retreated. By 1770 it was possible for the colonists to wonder where the Indians had gone. Thus William Bull, third-generation American and lieutenant governor of South Carolina: "I cannot quit the Indians without mentioning an observation that has often raised my wonder: that in this province, settled in 1670 (since the birth of many a man now alive) then swarming with tribes of Indians, there remains now except the few Catawbas nothing but their names within three hundred miles of our sea coast, no traces of their emigrating or incorporating into other nations, or any accounting for their extinction by war or pestilence equal to the effect." [111] The third of the justifications for colonizing America urged by Rev. Mr. Cotton — absence of other inhabitants — had come to pass at last.

---

[110] Andrews, *Colonial Period*, II, 156; Trelease, *Indian Affairs*, pp. 36, 40–45, 63.

[111] K. G. Davies, ed., *Documents of the American Revolution*, vol. II (Shannon: Irish University Press, 1973), p. 275.

CHAPTER 7

REPERCUSSIONS

The Atlantic in International Relations

The Discoveries brought about a revision of European international relations by giving kings and ministers new targets to aim at and, in the long
run, by changing the balance of power. At the end of the fifteenth century
some such revision was overdue. Renaissance diplomacy had become
stylized. Its restricted agenda resembled the menu of a dull restaurant
with Italy year after year as the specialty of the house and a crusade
against the Turks an often-advertised but seldom-tasted dish. Royal marriages were the bread and butter of international relations, disputed suc-
cessions the occasional treats. With so much to talk about and so little to
do, professionals were taking over and devising diplomatic games of small
relevance to the situation of most European people.

Early in the sixteenth century European diplomacy was given new
purposes, new dimensions, and (incidentally) a new relevance to people's
lives by the Reformation and the Discoveries — by the first to a far
greater extent than the second. Whatever the long-term consequences
may have been, the course of international relations in the next hundred
years owed much more to Luther and Calvin than to da Gama and Columbus. In nearly all the great events — the civil wars in Germany and
France, the revolt of the Netherlands, the Great Rebellion in England,
the Thirty Years War — religious alignments were paramount and
thoughts of the Atlantic and America, if present at all, a long way behind.

287

This is not to argue that all rulers in sixteenth-century Europe were *dévots*, only that religion was the metaphor in which they generally reasoned and expressed themselves. Every ruler was concerned, as in the past, to stay in power, enhance his revenues, beat down opposition at home, and hand on an unblemished inheritance to his successor. What was novel was that a Catholic ruler now saw the main threat to this program coming from Protestants while a Protestant ruler saw it coming from Catholics, and each feared that the enemy within his realm was certain to be sustained by coreligionaries elsewhere.

Though the Discoveries came second to the Reformation, their effect on the relations of the European powers was from the beginning not negligible. They did not upset the prevailing distribution of power; rather they confirmed it and even exaggerated it by making the strong stronger. The Mediterranean in 1500 was still the motor of Europe's diplomacy and to a large extent of her economy too. There Aragon, a component of Spain, had built a maritime empire and was rendering it formidable; there the Italian question, with France intervening, was still unsolved; there the Turks were rampaging; there the pope wheeled and dealt. Economically, Italy was in advance of all Europe in industrial techniques and banking methods. Venice still dominated the trade in spices coming overland from the Orient and still controlled the distribution of those commodities to northern Europe. Culturally Italy's preeminence was everywhere acknowledged. Insofar as Europe in 1500 had common models, styles, and a focus, Italy supplied them.

None of this came suddenly to an end with the Discoveries. A portion of the spice trade was shifted to Lisbon, and Antwerp became the distributor of Portuguese spices in northern Europe. But the overland route was not put out of business by the Cape for many decades to come; about 1570 it was still active and still bringing profits to Venice.[1] As for the Atlantic, it was some while before the profit and prestige of navigating the foggy coasts of Newfoundland or calling on stone-age Indians in the tropics were seen to repay the risks involved. China, the advertised objective, was no nearer. Only after the conquest of Mexico (1519) and Peru (1535) and the beginning of silver mining in America (1545) were exploration and discovery seen to pay noble royalties. By then Castile, an Atlantic king-

---

[1] Fernand Braudel, *La Mediterranée et le monde mediterranéen à l'époque de Philippe II* (Paris: Colin, 1949), pp. 423 et seq. A large part of this book is devoted to proving the continuing vitality of the Mediterranean world in the sixteenth century.

dom but merged with a Mediterranean power, had taken the New World in her grip. There was no dramatic shift in Europe's "center of gravity" to the north. It was the power and prestige of a southern European country, Spain, that was furthered by American treasure. It was this treasure flowing into Seville that serviced the Spanish hegemony and helped to pay for the reduction of Italy to obedience, the defeat of the Turks in the western Mediterranean, the conquest of Portugal, Spain's interference in the French Wars of Religion, the long defensive action in the Netherlands, and the enterprise against England.[2] At no time in the sixteenth century can the profits won from the Atlantic by France, England, and the Netherlands, added together, have amounted to a fraction of what Spain drew from America.[3] Viewed from Madrid, northwestern Europe can seldom have looked smaller than it did in the first year of Philip II. Nor was Spain the only country in southern Europe to be advantaged by the Discoveries. Portugal profited from Africa, Asia, and Brazil while keeping largely aloof — until 1580 — from the rest of Europe. Within the Mediterranean Italy, though turned into a political backwater by the Spanish conquest, was a beneficiary of American silver, some of which was conveyed to Genoa and helped to postpone economic decline until the next century.[4]

Spain's achievement in the New World was a shot in the arm for southern Europe; it was also an incitement to competitors, first French, then English, lastly Dutch. Broadly speaking, the positions taken up by European countries in regard to this new battleground did not conflict with their alignments in religion. France, it is true, had Catholic kings who nevertheless authorized their subjects to attack Spaniards in America; but much of this attacking was done by French Protestants and in any case was virtually over by 1570. For the English and Dutch who took up the burden of plundering the Spanish empire, considerations of national advantage, private gain, and God's service were in pleasing correspondence. Fighting Spain in the later sixteenth century for reasons that at first had little to do with the Atlantic, these countries were drawn into closer contemplation of America because that was where the enemy ac-

---

[2] J. H. Elliott, *Imperial Spain, 1469–1716* (London: Arnold, 1963), p. 263.

[3] Figures for Spanish silver imports are in Earl J. Hamilton, *American Treasure and the Price Revolution in Spain, 1501–1650* (Cambridge, Mass.: Harvard University Press, 1934), p. 34, summarized in Elliott, *Imperial Spain*, p. 175.

[4] Braudel, *La Mediterranée*, pp. 385 et seq.

quired the means to support his pretensions in Europe. Spain, it was found, could be hurt and humiliated more effectively by sea than by land, more cheaply in America than in Europe.[5]

The leading problem contributed by the Discoveries to international relations in the sixteenth century was, therefore, whether the New World was to stay the property of one crown. By 1600, with Spain and nearly everyone else fought to a standstill in Europe, it was clear (except to the Spaniards) that America must be partitioned. Spain did not formally concede the principle to France in 1598 or to England in 1604, but it was accepted de facto north of the Florida Channel when (through impotence) Spain failed to evict the English from Virginia and Bermuda. Within the Caribbean Spain's resistance was tougher. French and English colonization of the West Indies did not begin until the mid-1620s by which time Spain was committed to war in Germany, to the reconquest of the Netherlands, and to the defense of Brazil from Dutch attack. Overextended, she could deliver no more than occasional counterstrokes in the Caribbean (St. Kitts in 1629, Providence Island in 1641, Tortuga in 1654). Empty islands were effectively occupied by other Europeans, and in 1655 Spain underwent the further humiliation of losing one of her own colonies, Jamaica, to the English. At last, in 1670, she was brought to recognize explicitly England's right to have possessions in America.[6]

The Dutch won a similar recognition, by inference and temporarily in the Truce of 1609, and formally by the Treaty of Münster in 1648. But their concern was more with New World trade than with the planting of colonies. What they wanted from Spain was, first, an acknowledgment of their right to sail to American waters in search of trade and not ipso facto be treated as pirates; and, secondly, to be allowed to trade with the Spanish colonists. The first was given them in 1609 and confirmed in 1648 but only at the price of renouncing the second; they had to promise not to visit Spanish settlements without permission.[7] This left them with four options in America: to trade with the Indians not under Spain's rule, an affair of little profit; to found or conquer colonies of their own in order to grow tropical produce, an affair of too much investment of money and people and to be avoided if possible; to trade with the colonies of other

[5] See above, pp. 25–28.
[6] Max Savelle, with M. A. Fisher, *The Origins of American Diplomacy: The International History of Angloamerica, 1492–1763* (New York: Macmillan, 1967), p. 67.
[7] *Ibid.*, pp. 32–34.

European countries more complaisant than Spain; and finally to trade with the Spanish colonies either illicitly or by special license.[8] The Dutch in the seventeenth century did all these things, the last two more than the first two. No difficulty was at first encountered in trading with the English and French colonists; on the contrary, the Dutch were welcomed for their reliability and low costs and for the terms they extended to credit-hungry pioneers. More than one settlement owed its survival to them.[9] Left to themselves, Virginia, Barbados, St. Christophe, and Martinique would have gone on trading with the Dutch for many years. But the time of complaisance was short. The more the Dutch did, the more notice was taken by rival governments in Europe. By an act of 1650 and by the Navigation Act of 1660 the English forbade Dutch participation in all their most profitable colonial business; and by Colbert's tariffs of 1664 and 1667 the French did the same. Neither country was able totally to enforce its will in America, but the Dutch were severely hampered by these measures: they fought and negotiated in Europe and smuggled in the Caribbean but they never recovered the freedom they had enjoyed between 1620 and 1650.

There remained the Spanish colonies, by now an easier nut to crack. The Dutch probably never meant to keep their promise of 1609; all it signified was that a Dutchman caught trading in a Spanish colony could be punished and his goods confiscated without occasioning diplomatic resentment in Europe. Illicit trade continued after 1609 and after 1648, aided by an unsatisfied demand in the Spanish empire for slaves. This was the key the Dutch hoped to use to unlock the door to a trade in manufactures. Particularly after 1640, when Portugal's revolt from Spain ended all expectations of slaves from that quarter and the *asiento* was suspended, the Spanish colonial authorities were forced to connive at a certain amount of smuggling.[10] From 1667, when the *asiento* was revived, the Dutch by one means or other contrived to get a foot in legitimate business. But here, too, action in Europe took from them the fruits of acumen and low costs. They did not win from Spain an acknowledgment of their

[8] Another option was to trade indirectly with the Spanish colonies through the agency of Spanish merchants in Seville: an important alternative to fighting and smuggling. See Jean O. MacLachlan, *Trade and Peace with Old Spain, 1667–1750* (Cambridge: At the University Press, 1940).

[9] For example, St. Christophe. See [J.-B.] du Tertre, *Histoire générale des Antilles* (Paris, 1667), I, 23, 36–37.

[10] See above, pp. 125–126.

right to trade in anything but slaves; no country won that right until 1713 when it was given in restricted form to the English, to whom the supply of slaves was also passed over. The Dutch at the beginning of the eighteenth century still had the commercial capacity; they still had the slaves to sell; what they lacked was enough weight at the peace conference to insist on the concession.[11]

These were problems arising from the claim to an Iberian monopoly of the New World, its land, people, and trade, which Spain asserted in the sixteenth century, and which it took most of the seventeenth century to solve. But the statesmen at European peace conferences from Breda to Utrecht had also to find solutions to problems which had come into view for the first time in the seventeenth century, problems of Anglo-French and Anglo-Dutch rivalry beyond the confines of Europe.

Anglo-French relations. Anglo-French rivalry first became serious in the Antilles. In St. Kitts/St. Christophe the two sides skirmished as early as 1629 but were obliged by the approach of a Spanish fleet to put their antipathy aside. Fear of Spain and of the Caribs and frequent internal distractions in the French colonies kept them at peace until after 1660. The first major collision came in the Second Dutch War (1664–67) when France joined the United Provinces against England. In European waters there was hot naval warfare between the two maritime powers but no extensive involvement on the part of France: Louis XIV's presence in the war was a not too enthusiastic gesture toward allies he never loved and was soon to hate. In the Caribbean, however, French and English fought with gusto and bitterness, which suggests that the declaration of war in Europe served less to elicit a patriotic response in the West Indies, more to release pent-up antagonisms. With sugar just then supplanting tobacco and slaves replacing white labor, there were plenty of broken smallholders and unemployed ex-servants ready to turn to plunder for compensation. Lord Willoughby raised a substantial force in Barbados on this expectation.[12] Enthusiasm for fighting seems to have been less marked in later Caribbean wars; in other respects, a pattern was established to be repeated down to 1783. Fleets came out from Europe: two French, under La Barre and de Baas; one English, under

[11] The decline of the Netherlands as a force in European international relations (evident before 1713) preceded economic decline. For a summary of continuing Dutch material prosperity in the eighteenth century, see Charles Wilson, "The Economic Decline of the Netherlands," *Economic History Review*, 9:111–127 (1939).

[12] Vincent T. Harlow, *A History of Barbados, 1625–1685* (Oxford: Clarendon Press, 1926), pp. 164–166.

Sir John Harman who beat La Barre off Martinique in 1667. The French, with a smaller population, made up by recruiting blacks and Caribs and proved themselves better at island raiding. They conquered St. Kitts in 1666, expelling 8000 English; they took Antigua; and they plundered Montserrat.[13] In reply Willoughby took his fleet to attack the French islands, failed, and was lost in a storm. At the Treaty of Breda conquests by each country upon the other were restored.

The Anglo-French war of 1689–97 ran on similar lines. The French again took St. Kitts but lost it in 1690. Royal warships came out from Europe, tilting the balance of naval power now this way, now that. The English raided Martinique and Guadeloupe but could conquer neither; the French raided Jamaica and did not try to conquer it, contenting themselves with carrying off slaves. Governor Codrington of the Leeward Islands did what Willoughby had done in 1666, raising local troops and leading them against the French, but the decisive force was that which was applied from outside. Already the Caribbean was becoming for Europe's navies what Belgium was for Europe's armies, a good place for a fight. After an intermission of less than five years, the English began the War of Spanish Succession with the advantage of having a fleet (Benbow's) on the spot before the fighting began and by taking St. Christophe before the French could take St. Kitts. But they failed to beat the French at sea. Extended by naval war in the Mediterranean and by Marlborough's costly campaigns on the Rhine and Danube, they could not send enough force to defend the islands. The planters suffered. Most of the smaller English islands experienced devastating raids in France's *guerre de course*: the Bahamas, St. Kitts, Nevis, Antigua, Montserrat.[14] Yet it was Britain that won the peace in 1713, keeping St. Christophe and winning the entrée to Spanish colonial trade.

Fighting between English and French in North America can be dated from 1613 when Argall went up from Virginia to destroy Port Royal in Acadia. This, like Kirke's capture of Quebec in 1629, was a piece of private enterprise, undertaken for profit and perhaps because Englishmen regarded a state of hostility between themselves and the French as so natural that not even an empty continent could keep them apart. Although some friction was inevitable it was not until the decade 1680–

---

[13] On this and later Caribbean wars, see Nellis M. Crouse, *The French Struggle for the West Indies, 1665–1713* (New York: Columbia University Press, 1943).

[14] J. H. Parry and P. M. Sherlock, *A Short History of the West Indies* (London: Macmillan, 1956), p. 100.

90 that strategic situations developed to which war might be thought the appropriate remedy. By then New France's fur trade was feeling English competition in Hudson Bay; New York feared recent French aggression against the Iroquois; and the English colonies in general were stirring to what in the eighteenth century was to be a mighty dread, encirclement by French posts on the Mississippi. In Europe these dangers did not go unnoticed: an Anglo-French treaty was signed on November 8, 1686, which was meant to neutralize America and stop disagreements there from fouling up European diplomatic arrangements.[15] It was just too late: when they signed the treaty, the French knew, but the English did not, that the Chevalier de Troyes had led a tiny expedition overland from Canada and had taken Moose Factory, one of the Hudson's Bay Company's lodges, on June 21, 1686. Fort Rupert, Albany, and the *Craven* trading ship of forty tons also fell into French hands; the company assessed its damages at £50,000.[16] No restitution was made. Along with other colonial incidents, this aggression was cited as a *casus belli* in William III's declaration of war in 1689. That did not mean that William went to war on behalf of the Hudson's Bay Company or indeed for any reason other than his long-standing dispute with Louis XIV. At the same time it is important to see that at least in one quarter of North America a warlike situation existed. This was the true beginning of the Anglo-French struggle which terminated in 1763.

Following the declaration of war there was fighting in Hudson Bay almost every year until 1697 with posts changing hands as warships arrived from Europe, a Caribbean war in miniature. The English narrowly survived, ending with Albany in their hands and a promise at the Treaty of Ryswik that the dispute would be referred to commissioners. This was done in 1699 but no agreement reached. When war restarted in 1702 the Hudson's Bay Company passed through the grimmest years in its three centuries of life. No royal warship could be spared for the Bay; the company, in debt, could do little for itself; beaver lay unsold for want of demand; no dividend was paid for twenty-eight years.[17] Fortunately the French were in little better shape. In 1709 they tried another overland expedition against Albany but were spotted and beaten off. By the skin of

[15] Savelle, *Origins of American Diplomacy*, p. 106.
[16] E. E. Rich, *The History of the Hudson's Bay Company*, vol. I (London: Hudson's Bay Record Society, 1958), pp. 212–218.
[17] K. G. Davies, "The Years of No Dividend," in Malvina Bolus, ed., *People and Pelts* (Winnipeg: Peguis, 1972).

their teeth the English held on to enjoy the fruits of Marlborough's victories and St. John's diplomacy at Utrecht. As in the Caribbean, so in Hudson Bay, the English had the worse of the fighting and the better of the peace: in 1713 the company's whole claim to the Bay was acknowledged by the French.

Elsewhere in North America "King William's War" was less an affair of spontaneous combustion, more a gift by that monarch to his new subjects. There were tensions, as already stated, over the Iroquois and over the French garrison in Port Royal, but left to themselves neither side would have chosen to start fighting in America at that moment. To some extent the war gathered point, if not momentum, as it went along. French border raids, accompanied by Indians, were of a savagery not to be forgotten or forgiven. The Anglo-American dogma of the eighteenth century — that there was no room in North America for two empires — probably owed more to memories of burning New England villages and battered babies than it did to a collision of material interests.

These raids were the principal operations on land.[18] From Schenectady and Salmon Falls in 1690 to Haverhill in 1697 the French launched ten or a dozen. Parties of one hundred to three hundred Canadians and Indians approached by night, burst into the chosen village, killing indiscriminately in the assault, and carrying off prisoners, some of whom were likely to be murdered on the way home. New York tried to hit back in 1690 and 1691 but achieved somewhat less. Very little help came from England but this was not the sole reason for Anglo-American lack of success. Equally important was the failure of the northern and middle colonies to pool their resources or even to agree upon a common strategy. This affected the Indian allies. At the start of the war the Iroquois were ready to take revenge on the French but the inability of the English colonies to put respectable forces in the field and Frontenac's sweep into Mohawk country in 1693 convinced them that the English were not good allies. They withdrew, first into inactivity, later into neutrality.[19] Without Indians, border raiding by the English lost some of its feasibility and most of its terrors. By contrast the Abenakis, New France's allies, were nearly always ready to move with or without Canadian leaders.

At sea England's failure to provide naval aid was more serious and

[18] On military affairs, see Howard M. Peckham, *The Colonial Wars, 1689–1762* (Chicago: University of Chicago Press, 1964), and W. J. Eccles, *The Canadian Frontier, 1534–1760* (New York: Holt, Rinehart & Winston, 1969).

[19] Peckham, *Colonial Wars*, p. 55.

shorter sighted. Of ships of force the Americans had none; of big guns, siege trains, and competent engineers, virtually none. Judicious help from King William might have won him at least some useful cards to play at the next peace congress. As it was, Massachusetts was left to fight the war at sea almost singlehanded. Sir William Phips was sent by Boston with 700 men to take Port Royal in May 1690. This was easily accomplished and in August of the same year 2000 men and thirty-four ships were found for the same commander to try for the greater prize of Quebec. All things considered — the inexperienced troops, the late season, the numerically superior garrison — Phips's men did not do badly; but they did not take Quebec. Exhausted by these efforts, Massachusetts did little more than stand on the defensive. It is scarcely necessary to add that the Treaty of Ryswik restored the status quo.

Queen Anne's War in North America was "a spasmodic, halfhearted sort of war,"[20] as if the colonists had been caught once and were not to be caught again. There were border raids including the notorious attack by Abenakis, Caughnawagas, and Canadians on Deerfield (1704), but fewer than in King William's War. New York was not raided (Iroquois neutrality was too useful to New France to be put in jeopardy) and played almost no part in what war effort there was. In 1707 Massachusetts launched one more attack on Port Royal but even this consolation eluded it. With the war in danger of fizzling out, England at last stirred, promising a major expedition against Quebec in 1709. American troops gathered at Albany, N.Y., to attack by land as soon as news came of the fleet's approach. It did not come in 1709 and it did not come in 1710. At last in 1711 the great armada sailed: a well-found force of 60 ships and 5000 troops under Admiral Walker and General Hill, more than enough to cut off New France's head. A thousand men were lost by shipwreck in the Gulf of St. Lawrence; incredibly the commanders decided that they had suffered enough. Quebec was never reached, ships and survivors turned for home.[21] This humiliation, however, did not stop England from collecting Acadia (Nova Scotia) at the Treaty of Utrecht.

Broadly the role of the Atlantic and America in the strategy and operations of Anglo-French wars can be summarized as the assumption by both countries of responsibility for the main offensive and defensive operations

[20] *Ibid.*, p. 74.
[21] An account of the expedition and its British setting is in Gerald S. Graham, ed., *The Walker Expedition to Quebec, 1711*, Champlain Society Publications, vol. 32 (Toronto: Champlain Society, 1953).

in the Caribbean and the abdication by both countries of a like responsibility in North America. Of course there are some exceptions. The dispatch of fleets to the West Indies was fitful not systematic. North America was never entirely ignored. France always kept some regular troops in Canada, though not many and not of the best quality. Both countries sent royal ships to fight in Hudson Bay in King William's War though neither did in Queen Anne's. There were lightweight English station ships at principal colonial ports to frighten away privateers. None of this can be called grand strategy. Walker's expedition against Quebec in 1711 was quite a new idea, exceptional in every respect.

The allocation of so much more of the available resources to the Caribbean than to North America faithfully reflects the European preference for tropical colonies; if Virginia and Maryland had been seriously threatened English attitudes to the mainland might have been different. But it is important to see that, even in the Caribbean theater, only a fraction of European naval strength was put forth. French naval strategy after 1690 evolved toward keeping royal fleets in Toulon and Brest but waging the main war on England's trade with cruising squadrons of brilliant privateersmen working out of the ports of Picardy, Normandy, and Brittany; the Antilles got what could be spared. England's response was to fill the Channel with ships of all rates, to promote the Mediterranean to be the second theater of operations in 1702–13, and to give the West Indies what could be- spared.[22] The accompanying tabulation shows the distribution of the Royal Navy at two dates in the War of Spanish Succession. "Abroad" for this purpose includes the East Indies and West Africa as well as North America and the West Indies; in 1708 it accounted for one ship and one sailor in five.[23]

	1704		1708	
	Ships	Men	Ships	Men
Home waters ...	85	15,600	111	24,200
Mediterranean ...	64	21,600	44	13,300
Abroad	26	6,600	38	9,500

This synopsis of Anglo-French conflict in America has been necessary in order to consider the question when and how deeply colonial interests penetrated into the policies of these countries toward one another in the

[22] J. H. Owen, *War at Sea under Queen Anne, 1702–1708* (Cambridge: At the University Press, 1938), pp. 36, 64.
[23] *Ibid.*, pp. 274, 276.

century ending with Utrecht. This penetration was not a steady process nor did it proceed at the same pace in both countries. Styles of government made a difference. An absolute monarch might decide, for well-considered reasons, to adopt policies of colonial or commercial aggrandizement; but he might as easily jettison those policies when they jarred with something closer to his heart. A constitutional monarch might reason in the same way but would find it harder to revise a policy that had advantages for his subjects. The contribution of the House of Commons to England's foreign policy was to write into it a somewhat more *consistent* awareness of trade and empire than can be found in French. Even so, there were other pressures from below acting on an English king besides the commercial. We must not, therefore, expect to find a steady permeation of Atlantic awareness throughout the seventeenth century. There were lurches forward by England about 1650, about 1660, and about 1710; and there were lurches in the opposite direction, as in 1688 when William III took control of English resources and tied them to a European land war against Louis XIV. There was progression in France in 1661 when the monarch made himself king in fact of New France and the Antilles; and there was regression in 1672 and 1688 when the same monarch gave all his attention to fighting in Europe.

Until 1660 at the earliest there is no reason to think that Anglo-French relations in Europe were seriously informed or affected by Atlantic or American considerations. Rivalry between the two sets of colonists, as we have just seen, was stifled by fear of Spain in the West Indies and by poverty and distance in North America. Stimuli from both crowns were weak or absent. When Charles I's subjects captured Quebec in 1629 he was willing to return it to France on condition of receiving the unpaid balance of his wife's dowry.[24] Parliament, both in opposition and in power, displayed greater awareness of the Atlantic but favored either old-style maritime war against Spain or new-style maritime war against the Dutch. France, commercially, was not yet an important competitor; relations with her could proceed on lines dictated by ideology or the convenience of the moment. Hence such episodes as the English expeditions against the Île de Ré and to relieve La Rochelle (1627–28) which were intended to succor French Protestants and had nothing to do with Atlantic trade or empire. The French, for their part, gave America equal

---

[24] A decision which, though inevitably attracting derision later, was probably correct at the time.

or even lower priority. For all his rhetoric on the subject of colonies, Richelieu's vision of international relations did not extend far beyond his mission to abase Spain in Italy and Germany.[25] The spur to his building a French Navy was supplied more by the spectacle of Huguenot and English ships going in and out of La Rochelle when he was besieging it than by the contemplation of wider horizons. If he was aware that Spain could be hurt in the Atlantic he allocated little of France's resources to that theater. England, an unsatisfactory ally and ineffectual enemy, he regarded as peripheral to his purpose. Mazarin, his successor, was even less interested in the Atlantic.

Between 1660 and 1713 America crept into Anglo-French relations in Europe. The process cannot be described in detail here but some trends can be noted and some landmarks identified. The importance of America as a contributory cause of war in Europe and the importance of America in negotiations for peace will be examined in turn.

Concern for America was not the major cause of any war between France and England between 1660 and 1713. Louis XIV entered the Second Dutch War on January 6, 1666, without enthusiasm and after prolonged and sincere attempts to make peace between the two belligerents. He did so because the United Provinces had been his ally since 1662 and had a part to play in his longer term plans against Spain.[26] America was not the issue. The war he entered was undoubtedly a colonial and commercial one, brought on by worldwide Anglo-Dutch rivalry, but his concern was different; if trade had been in his mind, he would have fought against the Dutch, not for them. On England's side trade was a consideration only inasmuch as France might or might not use its influence to force the Dutch to make concessions in Africa, Asia, and America.

The War of the League of Augsburg (begun by Louis's rupture of the Truce of Ratisbon on September 24, 1688; England's declaration of war was on May 7, 1689) marks a new development in Anglo-French relations but as yet only a minor one. Thanks to Colbert France was more of a

[25] The contrary view is sometimes put. Mine is arrived at by comparing the papers on colonial questions in Georges d'Avenel, *Lettres, instructions et papiers d'état du Cardinal de Richelieu* (Paris, 1856–61), and the pronouncements on the same subject in Louis André, ed., *Testament politique* (Paris: Noël, 1948), with the way Richelieu actually conducted war and diplomacy against Spain. If he saw the possibilities of the Atlantic he did not follow them up.

[26] Keith Feiling, *British Foreign Policy, 1660–1672* (London: Macmillan, 1930), pp. 139–150.

commercial competitor in Europe than twenty-five years earlier;[27] in the same time Anglo-French rivalry in the West Indies and North America had become keener. These clashes were important to James II — still king when Louis invaded Germany — though it is unlikely that he would have gone to war for the sake of them.[28] Within a few months, however, James had been expelled and William III had taken his place. America was of little importance to William; but it was certain that he would lead England into war with France as soon as he was safely on the throne. When the English made him king instead of James, they got a Protestant instead of a Catholic; they also got a man who had spent much of his life fighting and scheming against Louis. Colonial questions were, as a matter of fact, given prominence in his declaration of war but this means little more than that there was a public opinion to be courted. We cannot dismiss American issues entirely from the antecedents of the war of 1689 but we must confine them to a secondary status.

Upon the causes of the War of Spanish Succession (fighting began in Italy in 1701; England's declaration of war was on May 15, 1702), there has been much debate.[29] First and foremost this was a war to decide who should be king of Spain following the death of Carlos II. Austria, the party disappointed in hopes of a share of the Spanish inheritance, was certain to fight from the moment Louis publicly accepted Carlos's bequest of the Spanish crown to his grandson (November 16, 1700), but why did England go to war to keep a Bourbon off the throne of Spain when she had already agreed to it twice and was to do so again in 1713? Has Anglo-French rivalry in the extra-European world any explanation to offer? The answer to both questions lies in the actions of the king of France between his acceptance of the will and England's entry into war. In 1700 William III had little ground for thinking that he could once more pull England behind him into an expensive land war with France; by the date of his death (March 8, 1702) he could be confident that his life's work was to go on. Louis made this possible by what he did in 1701, principally four things: he poured French troops into the Low Countries, frightening both Dutch and English; he used his new influence at Madrid to obtain the *asiento* for the French Compagnie de Guinée (February) and let it be

[27] Margaret Priestley, "Anglo-French Trade and the 'Unfavourable Balance' Controversy," *Economic History Review*, 2nd series, 4:37–52 (1951).

[28] David Ogg, *England in the Reigns of James II and William III* (Oxford: Clarendon Press, 1955), pp. 190–194, discusses James's relations with Louis.

[29] Summarized in M. A. Thomson, "Louis XIV and the Origins of the War of Spanish Succession," *Transactions of the Royal Historical Society*, 5th series, 4:111–134 (1954).

known that French traders were to expect more privileges in Spain and the Spanish empire; he recognized James III (the Old Pretender) as king of England; and he prohibited almost all trade between France and England (October).[30] Whether these acts should be ranked as causes of war is immaterial; they were what reconciled English parliamentary and public opinion to the prospect of renewed fighting. Thus an American issue crept into Anglo-French relations as one explanation among several why hostilities began. Queen Anne's War was still a war given by Europe to America, to a greater extent probably than King William's had been; but it is possible to say that at last an English interest in America had played an influential part in the antecedents of an Anglo-French war in Europe.

To conclude this view of Anglo-French relations and the part played in them by the Atlantic and America, we must look briefly at the peace treaties of 1667, 1697, and 1713 which ended the wars between the two countries.[31] Few European treaties have seemed equivalents of the fighting which has preceded them, certainly not Breda or Ryswik. Despite the warlike activities in the Caribbean, Breda recorded no important change in Anglo-French colonial relations: each side returned its conquests to the other. This meant that in 1667 England had to surrender Acadia and France St. Kitts. There is nothing to suggest that the English hesitated over the bargain while the French put up only a token resistance by insisting that the slaves they had taken in St. Kitts should be given the choice whether to return to their English masters or not.[32] At Ryswik in 1697 conquests were again restored. The treaty was no more than a truce. Everyone wanted a break from fighting in Europe; a discussion of American issues would have been a perfect nuisance. When the Hudson's Bay Company sent private representatives to the conference they were fobbed off with the promise of a commission to consider their claims. So much for America in King William's peace.

Had the War of Spanish Succession ended in 1708–9, as it probably would have done but for the allies' insistence that Louis XIV should help them to run his grandson out of Spain, the terms respecting America might have been once again little more than a restoration of the status quo, with England perhaps picking up some concessions in the Spanish

---

[30] Louis André, *Louis XIV et l'Europe* (Paris: Michel, 1950), pp. 297–306.

[31] Printed in Frances G. Davenport, *European Treaties Bearing on the History of the United States and Its Dependencies* (Washington, D.C.: Carnegie Institute), vol. II (1929) for Breda and Ryswik, vol. III (1934) for Utrecht.

[32] Feiling, *British Foreign Policy*, p. 225.

empire. But the English Whigs were looking to humiliate the Bourbons in Europe. That was where they had fought the war, starving the West Indies of ships and neglecting North America to do it, and that was where they expected to gather the fruits of their victories. Sadly for the Whigs, Louis refused to eat dirt. England, tired of an expensive war, chose a Tory House of Commons in 1710. A new ministry, headed by Robert Harley and Henry St. John, initiated fresh policies both at home and abroad, policies with important consequences for America. There was as a matter of fact nothing original about rejecting England's involvement in continental warfare and pressing for a maritime and colonial alternative; it had been stock-in-trade for the parliamentary op- position in the early seventeenth century. A section of the Tories took it up in 1702, arguing the case without much success as long as Marlborough rolled out victories in Europe.[33] In 1710 all changed. The opposition became the government and, more surprisingly, began to carry out much of what it had promised or threatened to do. America's priority, low under the Whigs, rose suddenly both in respect to the allocation of resources for war and, more important, in the objectives of negotiations for peace. The Walker-Hill expedition to Quebec, a plan the Whigs had considered but postponed, was the first result. Difficult as it may be to take this enterprise seriously, in the light of the craven conduct of the commanders, the effort must be made. Compared to what had gone forth before from England to North America (Ayscue in 1651, Nicolls in 1664), it was magnificent. More was to come. In May 1711 Harley unfolded the breathtaking South Sea scheme and the Tories settled to the task of making peace and getting what they could for England in the New World. They did well. Ditching their European allies, they acknowledged a Bourbon king in Spain and accepted the *asiento* and the right to send one ship a year to Porto Bello with trade goods. They let France off the hook in Europe and accepted Hudson Bay, Acadia, and St. Christophe, solid gains not just for English merchants but for colonists too. Massachusetts was relieved from the threat of Port Royal (renamed Annapolis, Nova Scotia); the Leeward Islands planters were safer with the French out of St. Kitts. France was far from finished either in the Caribbean or in North

[33] Geoffrey Holmes, *British Politics in the Reign of Anne* (London: Macmillan, 1967), pp. 71–81. Swift's *Conduct of the Allies* puts the arguments as clearly as one would expect. W. J. Ashley in his *Surveys, Historic and Economic* (London: Longmans, 1900) has an interesting paper entitled "The Tory Origin of Free Trade Policy."

America but England made a start at Utrecht in the direction of exchanging victory in Europe for benefits in the wider world.

Franco-Dutch relations. Where French diplomacy was dictated mainly by dynastic considerations, Dutch policies were formed more by economic interests. The Dutch survived as an independent country in the first half of the seventeenth century by means of their trade and fishery. With the lowest manufacturing and handling costs, the biggest and most efficient mercantile marine, and the lowest rate of interest in Europe, they appeared increasingly from mid-century as conservators of the good things they had won. Others envied and tried to imitate them. "Coûte que coûte," England's supreme commander in the Second Dutch War said, "England must be allowed its share in world trade";[34] Colbert wanted at least the same for France. Unfortunately for the Dutch they were never able to found their European policies solely on commercial interests. Geography was against them. Hardly was the Eighty Years War with Spain over (1648) than their landward frontier was threatened by France and had to be defended in three long and expensive wars from which they emerged in 1713 as a second-class European power, still prosperous but unable to support worldwide pretensions by diplomatic action.

Thus, while commercial and even specifically Atlantic interests were sometimes present in Dutch relations with France, they were always secondary to considerations of defense and often of no weight at all. From 1624 to 1667 Richelieu, Mazarin, and Louis XIV sought to manipulate the Dutch to serve French purposes against the Hapsburgs, to which the Dutch for the most part cordially responded because a French alliance was their best defense in diplomatic terms against Spain.[35] Trade came into it little, America not at all. In 1667 a *renversement des alliances* took place, initiated by the Triple Alliance of Holland, England, and Sweden. Louis from trying to use the Dutch turned to trying to destroy them. In a brisk diplomatic offensive he easily demolished their house of cards and in 1672 he invaded the Republic. It has sometimes been argued that economic (including colonial) considerations were at the bottom of this assault, that Colbert had identified the Dutch as stubborn opponents of his plans for France, and that the war of 1672 was the pursuit by military

[34] Quoted in Feiling, *British Foreign Policy*, p. 95.
[35] Discussed at length in A. Waddington, *La République des Provinces-Unies, la France, et les Pays-Bas espagnols de 1630 à 1650*, 2 vols. (Paris: Masson, 1895–97).

means of purposes laid down in the tariffs of 1664 and 1667. It is certainly
true that Colbert was ready to fight the Dutch. "As we have destroyed
Spain on land," he wrote, "so we must destroy Holland on the sea. The
Dutch have no right to arrogate all trade to themselves, on which they
have founded their state."[36] Doubtless Louis was pleased to find his
minister, more a man of peace than a man of war, of this mind. But it
would be at variance with nearly all that is known of *le roi soleil* to think
that Colbert's arguments were the decisive ones in 1672. Louis hated the
republic of maggots and meant to punish the Dutch for having concluded
the Triple Alliance; he wanted war, not exactly for its own sake, but for
the glory he was sure it would bring him. When he thought about
France's trade and colonies (and sometimes he did) it was largely as
expressions of his own grandeur, easily forgotten when the opportunity
arose nearer home to pit his army against that of another European
power. As a field in which to study the rise of American issues in European international relations, Franco-Dutch diplomacy in Louis's time
is a disappointment.

Anglo-Dutch relations. Relations between England and the Netherlands are less of a disappointment. It is here that economic considerations
were weightiest and here that we find the strongest pull exerted by the
wider world. There was, to begin with, a tradition to build on that was
older than the Dutch Republic, older even than the Discoveries. Thus in
1660, when Dutch envoys opened negotiations with English on the subject of the Navigation Act, they began by unfurling the *Intercursus
Magnus*, a commercial treaty made between the two countries in 1496.[37]
As the major international market for broadcloth the Netherlands was
vital to English prosperity well before the end of the fifteenth century.
Until the breach with Spain under Elizabeth I it was a constant objective
of English diplomacy to keep at peace with the ruler of the Netherlands
whoever it might be. When the seven northern provinces revolted from
Spain in 1568 Elizabeth, fearing to offend King Philip, did not rush to
their aid; when, reluctantly and belatedly, she gave support, trade played
a smaller part in the decision than concern for her own security,
threatened by the massing of Spanish armies just across the English
Channel. Trade, however, resumed its former importance when the new
republic established its independence, and Amsterdam fell heir to part of

[36] Quoted in André, *Louis XIV et l'Europe*, p. 121.
[37] Feiling, *British Foreign Policy*, p. 98.

the economic sway over northern Europe once wielded by Antwerp. All through the seventeenth century and for much of the eighteenth Holland was the destination of a large part of England's exports and reexports, of London's especially.[38] This formed an argument for peace not war between the two countries, one that had to be balanced against an opposition of interest in the East Indies or America or in the North Sea fisheries.

While it was never the case that commercial interests pointed clearly and consistently either to war or to peace between England and the Netherlands, it is equally true that relations between the two countries were seldom decided by trade alone. Sometimes bitter hostility arising from commercial conflict inside or outside Europe had to be laid aside for other reasons. One instance is the Treaty of Southampton, a defensive alliance made in 1625, just two years after the darkest event in the whole of Anglo-Dutch history, the execution of ten English factors at Amboina in the East Indies.[39] Twenty-six years later, when England and Holland were at war, Oliver Cromwell thought it wrong that two Calvinist countries should fight when there were so many papist enemies available in Europe and outside, an instance of the common religion pulling one way, commercial rivalry another.[40] Another example is the treaty obtained by the Earl of Danby in 1677 for the marriage of William of Orange and Mary, daughter of the Duke of York. English and Dutch were still trade rivals all over the world but fear of France drew them closer together. In 1689 they came closer still, learned to live with economic jealousies and fought the common enemy.[41] Insofar as Holland's commercial greatness was sapped by war, it was when fighting at England's side not against England that most of the damage was done.

Thus, while trade never stopped being important to both countries, their alliances and alignments had to take account of other considerations. G. N. Clark believed that "throughout the later seventeenth century and ever since, economic and colonizing quarrels took a leading place, and often the first place, in the antecedents of European wars."[42] This was

[38] Using the inspector general's records, which are imperfect but not absurdly so, Elizabeth B. Schumpeter in *English Overseas Trade Statistics, 1697–1808* (Oxford: Clarendon Press, 1960), p. 17, gives destinations of exports and reexports from England and Wales in five-year periods. The value of what was going to Holland was double that to any other country until 1725. Holland did not lose first place until 1756.

[39] Savelle, *American Diplomacy*, pp. 41–42.

[40] Robert S. Paul, *The Lord Protector* (London: Lutterworth, 1955), pp. 257–258.

[41] G. N. Clark, *The Dutch Alliance and the War against French Trade, 1688–1697* (Manchester: Manchester University Press, 1923).

[42] G. N. Clark, *The Seventeenth Century* (Oxford: Clarendon Press, 1929), pp. 25–26.

written at a time when historians were hopeful of finding rational explanations for almost every human idiosyncrasy; it probably needs revision. While economic and colonial rivalry furnished major causes of the First and Second Dutch wars, it was less important in the antecedents of the Third, and less still in the War of the League of Augsburg when Dutch and English fought on the same side. And of course it does not follow that because the First Dutch War was commercial in origin, American trade was the thing contended for. On the contrary, this war (1652–54) was mainly about European economic questions (North Sea fisheries, salutes to the English flag, the operation of the Navigation Act of 1651 in regard to the German hinterland of Holland) plus endemic conflict in the Far East.[43] The Atlantic and America scarcely came into it: in the colonies a kind of "No war beyond the Line" prevailed.[44]

By a process of elimination we arrive at the Second Dutch War (1664–67) as the prime (sole?) example of a war in Europe with predominantly colonial, including American, antecedents. Circumstances in England were favorable to this. With Charles II there came into power and prominence in 1660 a number of men exceptionally interested in the wider world, post-Cromwellian imperialists who rejected the Puritan vendetta with Spain and identified Holland as the more dangerous enemy.[45] At the top were James, Duke of York, governor of the Company of Royal Adventurers trading to Africa and patentee of New York, and Prince Rupert, later to be an active governor of the Hudson's Bay Company. In the ministry were Edward Hyde, Earl of Clarendon, architect of much of Restoration colonial policy, and Ashley Cooper (later Shaftesbury) in whom concern for America and hatred of the Dutch were perfectly blended. At court were the Earl of Craven, protector of the Winter Queen of Bohemia, who now put money in trading companies, John, Lord Berkeley, brother of Virginia's governor and collector of directorships, Sir Philip Carteret, and others. As ambassador at The Hague there was Sir George Downing, Harvard's first graduate and Barbados's first schoolmaster to win a European reputation, albeit an unenviable one.[46]

[43] M. P. Ashley, *Financial and Commercial Policy under the Cromwellian Protectorate* (London: Oxford University Press, 1934).

[44] Savelle, *Origins of American Diplomacy*, p. 53.

[45] Wesley Frank Craven, *The Colonies in Transition* (New York: Harper & Row, 1968), pp. 56–57, discusses the association of some of these men in the Carolina project. See also E. E. Rich, "The First Earl of Shaftesbury's Colonial Policy," *Transactions of the Royal Historical Society*, 5th series, 7:47–70 (1957).

[46] There is a life of Downing by John B. Beresford, *The Godfather of Downing Street* (London: Cobden-Sanderson, [1925]).

With London's merchants more interested in distant trades, through the chartered companies, than at any time since the reign of James I, City and court were in fair harmony, something that has not always been the case in English history.

Not everyone wanted war with the Dutch even in 1664. The king thought himself "almost the only man in my kingdom who doth not desire war" but he exaggerated; neither Clarendon nor Southampton nor Arlington was enthusiastic.[47] There was disagreement about how much the wider world mattered. To Downing's "Go on in Guinea, if you bang them there they will be very tame" must be opposed the king's "And, pray, what is Cape Verde? a stinking place, is this of such importance to make so much ado about?"[48] Asia, where the Dutch were refusing to give up Pulo Run despite their agreement of 1654, and Africa probably counted for more in English calculations than America, but the time was certainly ripe to take New Netherland. One may go further and say that New Netherland *had* to be taken in order to stop smuggling and make sense of Restoration colonial and commercial policy.

Sir Robert Holmes's expedition to West Africa sailed in November 1663 with orders to enforce the Royal Adventurers' right to trade.[49] Holmes interpreted his orders widely and attacked the Dutch trading stations in Guinea, taking every one except Elmina. On his return to England at the end of 1664 it was open to the king to repudiate these doings but he did not: Holmes's brief stay in the Tower was a "matter of jest" only.[50] Long before Holmes got back from Africa, even before news of the full extent of what he was doing to the Dutch had reached Europe, Richard Nicolls had sailed (May 1664) with his little force to effect the conquest of New Netherland. The Dutch could not overlook these blows. Their response was to send de Ruyter to Africa to recover the lost posts (which he did) and to sail on to attack the English West Indies (he bombarded Bridgetown, Barbados, but ineffectively). War was formally declared on March 4, 1665. When it ended, at the Treaty of Breda in 1667, England kept New Netherland, adding to the security of all her North American colonies and making the implementation of imperial economic policies at least feasible. On the Gold Coast she kept Cape Coast Castle, to be the headquarters of the Royal African Company. The Dutch kept Surinam

[47] Feiling, *British Foreign Policy*, pp. 84, 131.
[48] Both quotations in *ibid.*, pp. 125, 130–131.
[49] There is a life of Holmes by Richard Ollard, *Man of War* (London: Hodder, 1969).
[50] Pepys's phrase, in his *Diary* for January 9, 1665.

which they had conquered from the English in February 1667, thereby acquiring what proved to be their principal colony of settlement in the New World. Suitably the war which colonial issues had helped to start closed with a peace which is an important landmark in Anglo-Dutch (though not in Anglo-French) colonial relations.

Once the great matter of the sixteenth century had been decided — whether Spain could keep America for itself — the problems in international relations set by America, Africa, and Asia became fragmentary and disjointed. Too often a country's interests in those regions were at variance with its interests in Europe: nearly always the latter were held to be the more urgent. America had to call attention to itself, by agriculture, trade, and population, as an object deserving the concentrated notice of European statesmen. From about 1660 the West Indies began to earn this notice but even there progress was unsteady. North America took longer. England's gains at the Treaty of Utrecht are sometimes advanced to prove the emergence of America as a major concern of European diplomacy by 1713; they could just as well, perhaps better, be used to prove the opposite.

The Atlantic and the European Economy

We have seen that the New World's earliest major impact on political relations between European states came when gold was looted from the Aztecs and Incas and when American silver began to be mined. This is what incited other European countries to turn explorers and, disappointed, to become raiders preying on Spain's colonies and Spain's treasure ships. The same bullion also made America's first and greatest impact on Europe's economy: until the eighteenth century, perhaps until the nineteenth, nothing that America grew or made or thought or did matched the depth and pervasiveness of bullion's influence. This book is concerned with North America and the West Indies and with England, France, and the Netherlands, not with South and Central America or Spain. Silver mining, therefore, falls outside the present zone of discussion except insofar as it aroused the envy of northwestern Europe. No survey of the economic effects of the Discoveries, however, could omit at least a mention of bullion, dwarfing as it does the impact on Europe of other Atlantic products.

Four centuries ago, in the time of Jean Bodin and the anonymous author or reviser of the *Discourse of the Common Weal of This Realm of*

England, there was debate on exactly how and how far American silver was contributing to the unprecedented rise of European price levels that had begun about 1500.[51] Before the end of the sixteenth century it was a widely held view that inflation was monetary, caused by the enlargement of the quantity of precious metal in Europe. Adam Smith discussed the subject in the eighteenth century, though not at great length.[52] In the last forty years this debate has been revived and developed as part of the systematic writing of Europe's price history. The chronology of bullion shipments has been carefully studied and reliable figures obtained. Much work has been done on prices in different parts of Europe.[53] Other agents of inflation besides American silver have been positively identified, among them the growth of Europe's population in the sixteenth and early seventeenth centuries affecting food prices more than manufactures, and the manipulation of currencies by European governments which certainly explains some of the most hectic bouts of inflation. Weaknesses in the quantity theory of money, unperceived by John Maynard Keynes, have been exposed.[54] Yet it is safe to say that the bullion hypothesis, if modified, has not been dismissed and present indications are that it will not be. If the silver of Zacatecas and Potosí did nothing more, it *allowed* Europe's prices to rise (or at least stopped them from falling) by easing a shortage of circulating medium, a shortage that would otherwise have constricted economic activity. It is at present near to an orthodox belief that shipments of American silver had a buoyant effect on European economic life, particularly on the most sophisticated parts of it. Spain's craft industries may have been priced out of existence by Spain's receiving the earliest and fullest impact of the treasure; peasants with insecure tenures may have been rack-rented or evicted by landlords striving to keep pace with the cost of living; but regular shots of bullion were

[51] Henri Hauser, ed., *La response de Jean Bodin à M. de Malestroit* (Paris: Colin, 1932); Bodin wrote in 1568. Elizabeth Lamond, ed., *A Discourse of the Common Weal of This Realm of England* (Cambridge: At the University Press, 1929). The author did not mention American treasure as a cause of inflation in the first manuscript, composed about 1549, but it appears in the revision of 1581; see p. 187 of the Lamond edition. For other appreciations in Europe of the effects of American bullion, see Marjorie Grice-Hutchinson, *The School of Salamanca* (Oxford: Clarendon Press, 1952).

[52] *Wealth of Nations* (1776; Everyman ed., London: Dent, 1910), I, 175 et seq.

[53] Fernand Braudel's chapter "Prices in Europe from 1450 to 1750" in E. E. Rich and C. H. Wilson, eds., *The Cambridge Economic History of Europe*, vol. IV (Cambridge: At the University Press, 1967), makes an impressive introduction to the subject. There is a bibliography containing 315 items attached thereto.

[54] John Maynard Keynes, *A Treatise on Money* (New York: Harcourt, 1930), II, 148–163.

stimulants to the business of bankers and international traders. Of the years after 1580, when Spanish imports of silver were at their height, Braudel has written that "every arrival of bullion from the New World had a profound effect on the financial and commercial life of all Europe."[55] Ready money surged through the fairs and money markets, paying debts and discharging bills, supporting credit and generating optimism. More concretely, American silver enabled an extensive trade to be developed with Asia by the Dutch and English East India companies. This trade was necessarily fed by silver exports from Europe; without America it could not have flourished.

This mention of bullion and its effects is intended only to establish a mark against which other American influences on the European economy can be measured. Bullion apart, those influences in the first century after the Discoveries must be accounted slight, equally in the northern European trading zone — the English Channel, the North Sea, and the Baltic — and in the southern trading zone — the Mediterranean. No major shift of economic power between the two zones was induced before the last years of the sixteenth century. Braudel's case for the survival, and in some directions growth, of the Mediterranean economy has been mentioned. Venice lived. Italian industry did not collapse until after 1600. The Dutch and Hanse "conquest" of the Mediterranean did not come until the closing years of the sixteenth century.[56] Advocates of the view that Europe's "economic center of gravity" was swiftly changed by the Discoveries might point to Antwerp, the sun round which the northern trading zone revolved, at the height of its wealth and influence about 1550. But it is Antwerp itself that furnishes proof, if proof be needed, that the economy of northern Europe functioned for most of the sixteenth century more efficiently but on much the same lines as it had before the Discoveries.

Guicciardini's famous description of Antwerp was written about 1560, sixty-eight years after Columbus's landfall in the Bahamas and sixty-two years after da Gama went ashore at Calicut. Discussing Antwerp as a commodity market, Guicciardini gave estimates of the value of its different components which are interesting, not for their precision or authenticity, but as rough indications of the weight attached to each part by an intelligent observer.[57] He put the aggregate annual value of Antwerp's

---

[55] Braudel in Rich and Wilson, *Cambridge Economic History of Europe*, IV, 447.
[56] Braudel, *La Mediterranée*, part III, chapter 3.
[57] A convenient way to read Guicciardini's description of Antwerp is in his own French translation printed in R. H. Tawney and Eileen Power, eds., *Tudor Economic Documents* (New York: Longmans, 1924), III, 149–173.

trade at about 15 million golden crowns, the constituents of which are shown in the tabulation. Antwerp appears from these figures as a last flowering of the late medieval economy in northern Europe rather than a harbinger of an Atlantic or world economy. The freedom for foreigners to enter the city and do business was untouched by the modern xenophobia

	Value in Million Crowns
From Italy	
Silk and other textiles	3.00
From Germany	
Fustians	.60
Wine	1.50
From the Baltic	
Grain	1.68
From France	
Wine	1.00
Woad	.30
Salt	.18
From Spain	
Wool	.625
Wine	more than wool
From Portugal	
Spices	1.00
From England	
Wool	.25
Cloth	5.00

which countries like England were already beginning to display; and the major commodities, textiles, wine, spices, were the staples of a medieval trade. Guicciardini's picture is brushed by the Discoveries only at one point: the spices Antwerp handled were Lisbon's, brought via the Cape, not Venetian. They were important, Guicciardini insisted, but they formed only one-fifteenth part of Antwerp's trade. The Atlantic (except subtly, through American silver influencing Antwerp's bankers) was nowhere.

Antwerp went down soon after this time, not through a collapse of the economic system over which it presided, but as a result of the Revolt of the Netherlands (1568), the sack of the city by Spanish troops (1576), and the closing of the Scheldt. Some of Antwerp's functions remained to be performed and were taken over by Amsterdam in the seventeenth century, though not all and not in the same way. Here, about 1660, the effects of the Discoveries on the economy of northern Europe can be assessed; as in 1560, Asia led America. The Dutch East India Company was the biggest and probably the most sophisticated business corporation in the world. All over Europe merchants watched for news of the arrival of its fleets.[58] To a large extent, by regulating supplies, it controlled European prices of pepper, spices, East India textiles, and later of tea and coffee. Beside it, the Atlantic seems a secondary business, almost a sideshow. The history of the Dutch West India Company has yet to be written; it will be less spectacular and less revealing than that of its contemporary, because of the failure to retain a monopoly of Atlantic trade save in respect of slaves. Most of the American products reaching Amsterdam in the seventeenth century belonged not to the company but to private merchants. Quantities are not known but appearances suggest that they could have formed no very large fraction of the city's aggregate business. Records of Amsterdam's imports and exports have survived for only one year in the seventeenth century (1667–68), and then in a somewhat unsatisfactory form.[59] In weight sugar imports of all kinds amounted in this year to about 7 million pounds, reexports to just over 2 million. Tobacco, the other major American product, was imported to the value of just over a quarter of a million florins (i.e., about £ 25,000 sterling) though exported to the value of more than half a million. These figures may be compared (but only in a general way) with accounts of London's trade for the year 1668–69.[60] London's import of sugar was then 166,776 hundredweight of brown and 23,720 hundredweight of white, valued together at nearly £ 300,000 sterling; and of tobacco 9,026,046 pounds valued at £ 225,000. On this evidence London was already ahead in both commodities.

No great weight can be put on such fragmentary data but they may prepare us to appreciate that, despite Amsterdam's prominence in sugar refining, these American products were just two constituents among many in that city's commercial greatness. Even the Dutch East India trade, spectacular as it was, needs to be thought of with restraint. The

[58] Kristof Glamann, *Dutch-Asiatic Trade, 1620–1740* (The Hague: Nijhoff, 1958), p. 29.

[59] Printed by H. Brugmans, "Statistiek Van Den In-En Uitvoer Van Amsterdam, 1 October 1667–30 September 1668," in *Bijdragen en Mededeelingen Van Het Historisch Genootschap*, vol. XIX (The Hague: Nijhoff, 1898), pp. 125–183. This list sometimes gives quantities and sometimes values without saying how these values were computed.

[60] There is a well-known (though never printed) statistical account of London's trade in 1662–63 and 1668–69 in the British Museum, Additional Manuscripts, no. 36,785. Davenant thought that exports were fairly valued in this record, but imports overvalued. I do not think that his caution is necessary in respect to sugar.

foundations of Amsterdam's, and indeed of Dutch, prosperity were and were recognized to be the fisheries of the North Sea, the timber trade of the Baltic, the grain trade from north Germany and Poland to southern Europe, and the building of ships. It was estimated in 1666 that three-quarters of the capital active on the Amsterdam Bourse was at work in Baltic business.[61] Dutch fishermen throughout the seventeenth century beat off hopeful English intrusions into European herrings and whales. As for shipbuilding and operating, some thought this the rock on which all else was built. As Sir George Downing put it in his rough colonial way: "If England were once brought to a Navigation as cheape as this Country, good night, Amsterdam."[62] One cannot say that America is nowhere in Dutch trade in the 1660s nor can one overlook mighty Dutch efforts in the first half of the seventeenth century to conquer Brazil and to make the Atlantic unsafe for Spanish bullion ships. What must, however, be acknowledged is that the Dutch failed in both directions and failed, too, to keep Virginia and Barbados within their trading empire. In one way or another sugar and tobacco continued to arrive at Amsterdam and other Dutch ports (some of the tobacco was of European growth), but they were not the things by which the prosperity of the United Provinces stood or fell. Hence the ease with which the Dutch economy survived a curtailment of their Atlantic interests.

The Atlantic trades meant more to England and France between 1660 and 1713 because neither had anything like so large a share of the European trades as the Dutch. The rise of tobacco and sugar in England's imports and reexports and of north Atlantic cod in her invisible exports has already been remarked.[63] Much of it happened after 1660. As a consequence, England — whose trade had formerly been restricted by dependence on virtually one export, broadcloth, and that not vendible throughout Europe — became by 1700 an exporting country with more to offer. Serviced by the East India and Atlantic trades, London became a reexporting center, an entrepôt, rivaling and in the eighteenth century eclipsing Amsterdam. By 1700, it is probably true to say that England was

[61] Violet Barbour, *Capitalism in Amsterdam in the Seventeenth Century* (Baltimore: Johns Hopkins University Press, 1950), p. 27. This book helps toward understanding Amsterdam's trade in many ways. For the importance of the Baltic, see also Axel E. Christensen, *Dutch Trade to the Baltic about 1600* (The Hague: Nijhoff, 1941).

[62] Quoted by Charles Wilson, *England's Apprenticeship, 1603–1763* (London: Longmans, 1965), p. 168.

[63] See above, pp. 145–146, 160–161.

the country, anyway in northern Europe, with the greatest stake in the Atlantic. In this long run, her early investment in colonization and the planting of people was now paying off. France had made a bigger investment in
European war and a lesser one in Atlantic empire and, partly for this
reason, was drawing smaller dividends. With no London and no Amsterdam, France looks a poor third about 1700, but this is to some extent an
optical illusion. America's impact on the French economy was unspectacular because dispersed: many smaller cities did the job of one or two
great ones. By 1700 the ports of western and northwestern France can
certainly be said to have learned to handle Atlantic products and to be
ready for the great strides to be taken in the eighteenth century by the
French Caribbean colonies in general and by St.-Domingue in particular.

An assessment of the influence of the Atlantic on Europe's economy
should not stop at trade patterns. American products created new industries and extended old ones, beaver-hat making, sugar refining, and
(through vegetable dyes) textiles. Together with the East India trade, the
Atlantic called into being bigger and stouter ships than those which usually carried the European trade, with a consequential demand for timber,
cordage, tar, and sails. In such ways, and by the longer voyages which
crews had to make in the Atlantic, work was created for Europeans and
their standard of living was lifted a little. Their diet, too, was improved, as
we have already seen,[64] though slowly because, however cheap American
products became, there were still plenty of people in Europe unable to
afford them. Newfoundland fish and American tobacco had probably
penetrated deepest into the consumption patterns of the masses by the
end of the seventeenth century: one healthful, one baneful offering by the
New World to the Old. Emigration, on the other hand, cannot be reckoned a serious contribution to the raising of European standards of living,
as it was to be in the eighteenth and nineteenth centuries. Except
perhaps in England between 1620 and 1640, there was too little of it to
make more than a localized impression on Europe's poverty and unemployment.

Merchants were the people most directly affected by the Discoveries.
Ways of doing business had to be devised or at least adapted to cope with
voyages lasting a year or more. More capital certainly, more credit probably, were needed to send a venture across the Atlantic than across the

[64] See above, pp. 157–158.

Channel.[65] Greater risks were involved and these had to be shared either by marine insurance or by a pooling of resources. As a consequence of the Discoveries, the large business corporation made its appearance in the commercial life of Europe: a premature appearance to judge by the small number of successes and the large number of failures. One reason for failure was that these corporations were encouraged, or rather compelled, to assume functions that were not immediately profitable and for which they were unprepared, political or quasi-political responsibilities that were shoved onto them by governments wishing to save money and avoid commitment. The seventeenth-century experiment was thus less than fair to the large-scale business. If trading profits were exceptionally good (as they were in the Far East), and if the political responsibilities were not, to begin with, overwhelming, the big company might prosper. But the use of companies in the Atlantic, particularly the use of companies to promote *colonization*, appears to have been doomed to failure; one cannot imagine the Virginia Company, had King James let it live, turning into anything like an East India Company. In the course of the seventeenth century the large corporation retreated or was driven not only from colonizing but from nearly every corner of the Atlantic trade. It reappeared briefly in the form of the South Sea Company (chartered in 1711) but this was first and foremost a scheme for managing the British national debt, with Spain's commercial concessions tacked onto it to attract investors. By the beginning of the eighteenth century sole traders and partnerships of traders, assisted by agents (correspondents, factors) at major ports in America and the West Indies, were running most of Europe's trade in the Atlantic much as they had managed Europe's trade in Europe for centuries past. Far from engendering confidence in companies as the appropriate way of conducting long-distance trades, the seventeenth-century experiment failed so conclusively that it probably retarded the growth, anyway in England, of large-scale organization. America extended Europe's business experience more than it changed Europe's business methods.

It is hard to say with any assurance how far the Discoveries affected economic thinking as opposed to practice. The tenor of recent writing has been to present "mercantilism," if it was anything at all, as a collection of

[65] For bills of exchange in the Atlantic trade, see J. Sperling, "The International Payments Mechanism in the Seventeenth and Eighteenth Centuries," *Economic History Review*, 2nd series, 14:446–468 (1962).

fairly simple responses of governments to such recurring crises as unemployment and the outflow of gold and silver, not as a body of coherent ideas.[66] If an ethos attached itself to a particular measure, this was more likely to have come after than before the passing of that measure, to be an effect rather than a cause. The English Navigation Acts could be cited as an instance, perhaps the best instance, of this process of accretion; in the eighteenth century they acquired almost the status of sacred writings until blown upon in 1776 by *The Wealth of Nations* and the Declaration of Independence. It is difficult, it has to be admitted, to deduce anything theoretical from these acts. If they had an organizing idea it was a negative one: that the interest of individuals and the interest of the community (*commonwealth* was the usual term) were distinct and often at variance with one another and that if men were left to their own devices they would always trade advantageously to themselves but sometimes disadvantageously to the community. This is set forth clearly in chapter 7 of Thomas Mun's *England's Treasure by Forraign Trade* entitled "The Diversity of gain by forraign Trade" but Mun was not saying anything new or anything profound.[67] The assumption of such a "diversity" was a commonplace both before and after England entered the Atlantic trade, just as it has returned to be a commonplace of the twentieth century. Except as the antithesis of a genuine economic idea, Smith's "invisible hand," it scarcely qualifies as economic theory.

Most of the economic writing of the seventeenth century was done by men with axes to grind and causes to plead, by merchants in particular. Mun wrote *England's Treasure* about 1625 to defend the opinion that the

[66] There is now a formidable volume of modern criticism, a good deal of it hostile to the nineteenth-century attempt to build up "mercantilism" as a system of ideas. There is something strange about the fervor and urgency with which the paper tiger is repeatedly attacked. A second line of criticism has been to show how right the "mercantilists" were. A few landmarks in the study of the subject are the following: A. V. Judges, "The Idea of a Mercantile State," *Transactions of the Royal Historical Society*, 4th series, 21:41–70 (1939); Eli F. Heckscher's *Mercantilism* already cited and his article "Mercantilism," *Economic History Review*, 7:44–54 (1936–37); Jacob Viner, *Studies in the Theory of International Trade* (New York: Harper, 1937); D. C. Coleman, "Eli Heckscher and the Idea of Mercantilism," *Scandinavian Economic History Review*, 5:3–25 (1957); Charles Wilson, "Mercantilism: Some Vicissitudes of an Idea," *Economic History Review*, 2nd series, 10:181–188 (1957); B. E. Supple, *Commercial Crisis and Change in England, 1600–1642* (Cambridge: At the University Press, 1959).

[67] *England's Treasure by Forraigne Trade* was reprinted, with other tracts of the seventeenth century, by J. R. McCulloch in the nineteenth century. This reprint has itself been reprinted (Cambridge: Economic History Society, 1952). The chapter cited begins on p. 146 of both editions.

East India Company (of which he was a director) should be allowed to export bullion to Asia despite an apparent shortage at home. His argument, that goods were obtained from Asia that could be reexported to other countries and that the balance of trade would thereby be improved, is not a particularly sophisticated one; but it represents an advance on some earlier discussions of balance-of-trade problems. In the sixteenth century the common responses to an outflow of bullion had been a reduction of imports, exchange control, and tougher measures to stop the smuggling of specie. Such nostrums seem to reflect an inelastic economy with few possibilities of widening the range of exports and no possibility of increasing their volume by lowering real costs: not, on the whole, inaccurate assumptions about the English economy in the late sixteenth century and much what the Hakluyts argued when campaigning for an empire.[68] Mun was at least propagandizing in broader terms; it is the logic of his argument that there was a wider world of trade where England could win assets with which to solve her problems nearer home. It must certainly have been difficult, after the emergence of sugar and tobacco, for anyone to argue or even to assume that the volume of trade in the world was limited or a country's share of it more or less predetermined by natural resources. The rise of Holland to commercial greatness (a country of poor natural resources), the flow of East India goods, and the Atlantic trade — perhaps in that order — blew that notion away. Not every European merchant in the year 1700 would have endorsed Adam Smith's later, and still startling, assertion that "the discovery of America, and that of a passage to the East Indies by the Cape of Good Hope, are the two greatest and most important events recorded in the history of mankind."[69] But the Discoveries, if not parents of a revolution in either mercantile thinking or practice, can hardly have failed to stir up the traditions and modify the assumptions of an older and smaller world.

America as an Idea

Viewed from Europe, there was not one America but two: the America of the savages, revealed by explorers, and the America of the colonists to which ships put out from European ports with manufactures and emigrants, reappearing six months later with cargoes of tobacco and sugar;

[68] See above, pp. 141–142.
[69] *Wealth of Nations*, Everyman ed., II, 121.

a romantic, beautiful America, inhabited by innocents and stuffed with curiosities, and a prosaic, workaday America peopled by expatriates making a living and Puritans who by 1700 had begun to look like relics of a bygone age.[70] Not surprisingly it was the first which captured and held the imagination of Europeans more than the second, and on which they chiefly exercised their intellects.

The correct spirit in which to approach Europe's intellectualization of America seems to be one of restraint. Enormous claims have been filed for the effects of the Discoveries on Europe, both materially and mentally, not only by Europeans like Adam Smith but by modern writers viewing America's impact from outside Europe. To one, America has been Europe's "Great Frontier" dominating politics, economics, and ideas as completely as Frederick Jackson Turner's frontier is presumed to have dominated the history of the United States;[71] to another, the finding of America and its treasure was crucial in the evolution of European capitalism;[72] to a third, it was plantation slavery on which England reared her Industrial Revolution.[73] Perhaps there is more in these claims than the common desire of a historian to make the best possible case for a subject on which he may have spent many years; perhaps it is a characteristic of colonial and ex-colonial societies not only to snatch at anything that lays stress on their own distinctiveness but also to seek to erase (retrospectively) the supposed indignity of colonial status by proving that it was really the tail that wagged the dog. Not one of these sweeping theories is without interest; not one is without its element of truth. Their weakness is their parochialism: the unconcern of their proponents with so much that was happening in Europe independently of the wider world.

Restraint, then, is the suggested spirit and humility the recommended posture on entering the phantasmagorial world of intellectual history. Figures like Luther, Descartes, and Newton cannot be weighted and sunk in the Atlantic Ocean. The Discoveries were but one influence

[70] Alan Simpson, *Puritanism in Old and New England* (Chicago: University of Chicago Press, 1955), p. 34, writes of the reduction of the New England way to a "provincial anachronism." The Massachusetts witch trials in 1692 and 1693 must have reinforced any disposition in Old England to regard New England as half a century behind the times. A recent book, Chadwick Hansen, *Witchcraft at Salem* (London: Hutchinson, 1970), provides a useful introduction to all that has been written on this subject.

[71] Walter P. Webb, *The Great Frontier* (Boston: Houghton Mifflin, 1952).

[72] Earl J. Hamilton, "American Treasure and the Rise of Capitalism," *Economica*, 9:338–357 (1929).

[73] Eric Williams, *Capitalism and Slavery* (Chapel Hill: University of North Carolina Press, 1944).

forming "the European mind"; and America was no more than half the Discoveries. It is true that Africa made only a slight impact on European thinking until the nineteenth century, but Asia's was immediate and probably greater than America's. The useful statistic established by Geoffroy Atkinson is relevant here: between 1480 and 1609 eighty books were published in France on the subject of Turkey and the Turks, fifty on the East Indies, fifty more on other parts of Asia, and only forty on America.[74] With the Reformation in full motion at home, the Turks threatening southern Europe, and the Portuguese uncovering the mysteries of the East, America could not always be front-page news in the sixteenth century. Arguing for a kind of delayed effect of the Discoveries, J. H. Elliott has written: "It is as if, at a certain point, the mental shutters come down; as if, with so much to see and absorb and understand, the effort suddenly becomes too much for them, and Europeans retreat to the half-light of their traditional mental world."[75] Possibly the explanation should be simpler: that they had other and more pressing things to think about.

The mere fact of finding a large land mass where none had been looked for could not fail to impress at a very simple level. Add the discovery of bullion mines and the constituents are to hand for an obvious literary conceit. Thus John Donne to his mistress:

> Licence my roaving hands, and let them go,
> Before, behind, between, above, below.
> O my America! my new-found-land,
> My kingdome, safeliest when with one man man'd,
> My Myne of precious stones, My Emperie,
> How blest am I in this discovering thee!

This was written at the height of Elizabethan privateering when licensed (and some unlicensed) English ships were roving the Atlantic and thrusting rudely into the Caribbean in search of plunder. It is nearly, if not exactly, contemporary with Raleigh's first expedition to Guiana and the publication of the *Discoverie* in which he described that unexplored country as one that "hath yet her Maydenhead."[76]

The image of America as a woman to be rifled by virile Europeans was

---

[74] Geoffroy Atkinson, *Les nouveaux horizons de la Renaissance française* (Paris: Droz, 1935), pp. 10–12.

[75] J. H. Elliott, *The Old World and the New, 1492–1650* (Cambridge: At the University Press, 1972), p. 14.

[76] Vincent T. Harlow, ed., *The Discoverie of the large and bewtifull Empire of Guiana* (London: Argonaut Press, 1928), p. 73.

heightened by the beauty that impressed itself upon some who voyaged there and on none more than Raleigh: "I neuer saw a more beawtifull countrey, nor more liuely prospectes, hils so raised heere and there ouer the vallies, the riuer winding into diuers braunches, the plaines adioyning without bush or stubble, all faire greene grasse, the ground of hard sand easy to march on, eyther for horse or foote, the deare crossing in euery path, the birds towardes the euening singing on euery tree with a thousand seueral tunes, cranes and herons of white, crimson, and carnation pearching on the riuers side, the ayre fresh with a gentle easterlie wind, and euery stone that we stooped to take vp, promised eyther golde or siluer by his complexion."[77] This, from one of the most popular travel books ever written, seems to have been what Europeans wanted to read, not Puritan descriptions of a "howling wilderness."

America the beautiful awaiting the ravisher: already we are into a dream world remote from the harsh facts of seventeenth-century colonization, the exploitation of white servants, plantation slavery, the fur trade, fishing and farming, the world of men making a living and not caring much how they did it. And when we turn from virgin America to the savage inhabitants of the New World the gulf separating the view of the European intellectual from that of the colonist becomes wider still. For, until Cook and Bougainville furnished much-needed alternatives in the South Seas, it was in America that Europeans elected to locate "le bon sauvage," the "natural man," the "noble savage" — in America or else in Utopia.

To understand the fashioning of this powerful myth and the vigor with which it was propounded in the eighteenth century, it is important to see that its lineage is more ancient than the Discoveries themselves.[78] That there had been a golden age of heroism and innocence preceding the iron age of ordinary men was central to the view held by the Greeks of their own past; that their ancestors had lived in a virtuous simplicity shaming to their decadent descendants was widely believed in late Republican Rome. These classical traditions, well studied in the fifteenth and sixteenth centuries, allowed that innocence might have survived here and there in pastoral settings where rustics were not only happy but virtuous, and even admitted that somewhere out in the ocean there might be

[77] *Ibid.*, pp. 54–55.
[78] Hoxey N. Fairchild, *The Noble Savage* (New York: Columbia University Press, 1928), pp. 2–7.

Fortunate Islands where whole communities of innocents would one day be found. Christian myths were not entirely hostile to these traditions. The Garden of Eden and the Fall expressed the same rueful sense of departed virtue, though leaving less room to hope that it might ever be recaptured.

The discovery of America and encounters with free, naked, "natural" men did not therefore break into European cultural traditions wholly unprepared to receive and assimilate the news. On the contrary, high-ranking intellectuals like Peter Martyr and Montaigne seem to have needed only the slenderest evidence on which to attribute to the savages of America the virtues wanting in their own societies.[79] Their excitement, such as it was, is understandable if seen as the reaction of men who were accustomed to look backwards in time for evidence of simple virtue and who suddenly perceived the possibility of finding that evidence in the present, much as twentieth-century men, who have invented a future in order to evaluate their own present, might react to the discovery of some more advanced technology.

It is, perhaps, easier to explain the making of the myth of the "noble savage" than it is to account for its survival and extension in the seventeenth and eighteenth centuries in the face of a good deal of experience which appeared to run in a contrary direction. Part of the explanation for this tenacity, probably the greater part, is to be found in Europe's need of the myth, heightened toward 1700 by the formalization of so much of French, and by imitation European, upper-class life: manners, styles of dress, language, architecture, gardens, town planning. Versailles was the consummation of a will to subject as much as possible of life to timetables and rules, to expel or at least to tame nature. As formality became tainted with artificiality, the reassertion of the merits of "natural" behavior became a more pressing need. At the same time, once the myth had been planted in the contemporary world instead of in the past, even if in faraway America, it had to be clothed in some kind of verisimilitude, at least as much as is demanded, say, of Disneyland's reconstruction of the American Wild West. This was feasible. The American Indians *were* free in a sense that Europeans were not; they *were* sometimes naked and never ashamed of it; they *were* hospitable; and they *were* careless of the

[79] Elliott, *Old World and the New*, p. 26. Montaigne's "On Cannibals" is in all editions of his essays, for example, that selected and edited by J. M. Cohen, *Montaigne: Essays* (Harmondsworth, England: Penguin, 1958).

infinite accumulation of riches. But just as Disneyland leaves out the stings, so the European view of "le bon sauvage" discounted the part that nature can take as man's jailer, playing down the savage's dirt, ignorance, and cruelty, not to mention his obsessive preoccupation with dreams. Not all who made use of the myth had seen savages in their savagery. Montaigne's visit to the "Brazilians" at Rouen was like an afternoon spent at a zoo: each can serve to point a moral attitude but neither is a qualification to write about men or animals encountered in their wild state. Other savages followed the "Brazilians" to Europe in the seventeenth and eighteenth centuries, enabling all to see what they wanted to see: moral sensibility joined to innocence. What they were really seeing was the behavior of visitors so overwhelmed by new experiences and so completely alone in an alien world that every natural trait was suppressed and subordinated to a desire to please the hosts.

The intellectualization of America relied, however, more on the written word than on personal impressions or experiences. Between the philosopher — from Montaigne to Rousseau — and his American savage stood the reporter. How, if the damning comments on Africans and Indians (quoted in a previous chapter) by Europeans in daily contact with them were at all representative of the information fed back from the frontiers, was it possible for intellectuals at home to take so different a view? How, when one set of Europeans — the colonists in North America — were in bloody conflict with the savages, could another set of Europeans — the intellectuals (though not of course all of them) — have attributed moral excellence to the Indians? Was this a *trahison des clercs*, a mere belaboring of European civilization with no evidence at all that the natural savages existed in the shapes assigned to them? Part of the answer to these questions may lie in the identity of the reporters. Explorers, missionaries, and travelers published more books than colonists and inclined in their judgment of the savages to be more temperate, perhaps more humane, certainly more detached.

Explorers nearly everywhere were well received by the Indians and in most instances responded by writing well of the people they encountered. Colonists followed, and in most instances were soon at the Indians' throats. We do not have to assume that most explorers were egregiously virtuous or even that most colonists were egregiously vicious. Nor does it seem likely that the Indians at first meeting were innocent — in the intended sense — and were immediately and irredeemably corrupted by the Europeans and their goods. It is far more plausible to think of the exploring and colonizing situations as quite different, the one temporary, the other permanent. Explorers, needing help, are apt to be on their best behavior; colonists, making a living, tend to be impatient. The literature of voyages is naturally, if not universally, optimistic on the subject of race relations; that of colonization tends in the opposite direction. Furthermore, explorers and travelers, safely home again, commonly have the leisure to tell their stories as well as an audience to tell them to; colonists, hacking a living from a strange environment, seldom have either.

Much of the information about North American savages available in seventeenth-century France was furnished by missionaries. Annually from 1632 to 1673 the volumes of Jesuit *Relations* were published in the mother country for the benefit of supporters seeking to be assured that the work going forward in New France was worth the money they raised for it. These forty volumes were easily the biggest storehouse of current information about any European colony available to the general public; yet they do not in general lend support to the attribution of nobility to savages. Their chief import is that the free (disorderly) life of the Indians needed to be totally destroyed, the savages corraled and brought under surveillance, and their culture obliterated in order to fit them to retain the Christian message. Such purposes had no place in eighteenth-century secular criticism of European civilization and the glorification of natural man. The volumes of *Relations* were keenly read by *dévots* as they came out but do not appear to have influenced secular writing to any great extent,[80] perhaps because they were "works of propaganda, not scientific reports,"[81] perhaps because the Jesuits and all their works entered a period of intense and almost universal unpopularity toward the end of the seventeenth century, perhaps simply because European intellectuals found it easy to ignore what they did not want to hear provided some alternative was available.

In seventeenth-century France there were alternatives: the Dominican missionary Jean-Baptiste du Tertre who worked in the Caribbean and published his *Histoire générale des Antilles* in 1657, and the Baron de Lahontan who went to New France as a soldier in 1683, deserted,

---

[80] This is stated by Thwaites in the Introduction to his edition of the *Relations*, reprinted in Edna Kenton, ed., *Black Gown and Redskins* (New York: Longmans, 1956), p. li.
[81] Gilbert Chinard, *L'Amérique et le rêve exotique* (Paris: Hachette, 1913), p. 124.

traveled widely in America, and returned to France in 1692 to write his memoirs. Du Tertre, in Gilbert Chinard's estimation, did more than anyone else to establish the characteristics of "natural man" depicted by Rousseau.[82] Certainly, the *Histoire générale* is the only book about French colonization fit to stand alongside the great Spanish histories of the conquest and settlement of America. Du Tertre was capable of writing with great force and feeling on the virtues of the savages and on the harm done to them by contact with Europeans (see above, page 268); and in the frequent fighting between Caribs and colonists, he did not always blame the Caribs. If it seems strange that a Catholic missionary should express such views, we must recall Chinard's suggestion that inside every missionary were two men: the priest, who saw the savages as monsters, if not demons; and the classical scholar who saw them as innocents posted to the Caribbean from a golden age of antiquity.[83] Du Tertre's work, then, was a notable quarry for Europeans in search of "le bon sauvage." At the same time, it must be admitted that he was so closely involved with the struggles of the colonists for survival that *au fond* he wanted them to win. This makes for inconsistency and leaves him at times contemplating cruelty to the savages with more indifference than befitted an admirer of their virtues. Du Tertre compromises: more, probably, out of a genuine confusion than out of a sense of impartiality. The "colonial view" and the "European view" are both presented; the reader can take which he likes.

With de Lahontan there is no confusion. Disgruntled at the loss of his family's property, which is what drove him abroad in the first place, he found little to admire in the Canadians. Contemptuous of their priest-ridden society, in which a visitor could find no diversion but reading, eating, and drinking, de Lahontan is Molière's Dom Juan in a New World setting. He takes easily to the natural life and anarchical ways of the savages, though it is perhaps worth noticing that there are few expressions of enthusiasm in the letters he wrote while actually in New France and which he published as the *Voyages* (1703). All his admiration was saved for the *Dialogues avec une sauvage* (1703) composed after he was safely home, in which natural man disputes with civilized man and gets the better of him.[84] This is the work Chinard has called "the clarion call of a

[82] *Ibid.*, p. 39.
[83] *Ibid.*, p. 138.
[84] The English translation of 1703, edited by Reuben G. Thwaites, *New Voyages to North*

revolutionary journalist,"[85] the first considerable formulation of a new secular treatment of the "noble savage" theme that culminated in Rousseau.

England had no *Relations*, no du Tertre, and no de Lahontan in the seventeenth century. Instead, she had Puritan reports of New England's triumphs and disasters, less well informed on the subject of North American Indians than the *Relations* but even more hostile to the attribution of virtue to them; journalism like Richard Ligon's *True and Exact History of the Island of Barbadoes* (1657) and Dalby Thomas's *Historical Account of the Rise and Growth of the West-India Collonies* (1690); topography like John Ogilby's *America* (1671); and John Oldmixon's prosaic, much criticized, but often consulted *British Empire in America* (1708). It is not, on the whole, a list to impress, inferior to the French and far inferior to the Spanish. Indeed, after Hakluyt (who chronicled voyages not colonization) and some might say *The Tempest*, no major English literary work of the seventeenth century comes to mind that breathes an Atlantic air or takes the American empire for its theme.

Putting aside mere propaganda, two broad categories of historical writing can be distinguished in the seventeenth and early eighteenth centuries.[86] The Puritans occupy first place, as befits the only colonists who continuously saw themselves *sub specie aeternitatis*. Although Bradford's *Of Plymouth Plantation* and Winthrop's *Journal*, the two principal sources for the modern view of New England's beginnings, remained unpublished in full until the nineteenth century,[87] the loss was made good in volume and weight by Edward Johnson's *Wonder-Working Providence* (1653), Nathaniel Morton's *New Englands Memoriall* (1669), the writings of Increase Mather and William Hubbard on King Philip's War (1676–77), and Cotton Mather's *Magnalia Christi Americana* (1702). As historian, however, the Puritan had the defect of his quality: he saw

---

America, 2 vols. (Chicago: McClurg, 1905), contains the letters, the memoirs, the discourses, and the dialogue. See also Gilbert Chinard, ed., *Dialogues curieux* (Baltimore: Johns Hopkins University Press, 1931), which has an important introduction.

[85] Chinard, *L'Amérique et le rêve exotique*, p. 185.

[86] There are good introductions to this subject by Michael Kraus, *The Writing of American History* (Norman: University of Oklahoma Press, 1953), and Richard S. Dunn, "Seventeenth-Century English Historians of America," in James M. Smith, ed., *Seventeenth-Century America* (Chapel Hill: University of North Carolina Press, 1959).

[87] Bradford's book was published in full in 1856. An annotated edition was published by the Massachusetts Historical Society in 1912. Winthrop's *Journal* was first published in 1790 with additions in 1825: it, too, has been published with notes by the Massachusetts Historical Society.

himself and his friends in a perspective that stretched backwards and forwards to eternity but did not extend anything like so far in a lateral direction. This concern, sometimes obsession, with themselves no doubt guaranteed the early New England historians a readership within the ranks, but the disposition to ignore everyone else must have limited their lay audience. One need not be a Catholic in order to read du Tertre; but any attempt to get through the Mathers is greatly helped by being a Puritan.

The second category, secular history, was smaller. Virginia, unless one counts Captain John Smith or Rev. Alexander Whitaker, produced no historian in the seventeenth century, though Robert Beverley made up for the omission in his *History and Present State of Virginia* (1705), the most elegant and (to a modern reader) congenial English colonial history written to that date, and one incidentally in which the happy savage, if not the noble savage, makes a brief appearance.[88] Beverley's book has rather too much "Present State" and not enough "History" in it, sliding over the harder parts of the subject and plunging into current political controversy, but it is redeemed by a skeptical view of the past and a robust commitment to Virginia's future, two qualities that Europeans learned to expect from colonials. Thus, while some of the Puritan historians of the later seventeenth century seem not to be rooted in America, Beverley unmistakably was.[89]

Ligon's history of Barbados, like Beverley's, is more descriptive than historical and takes too little trouble to overcome difficulties. But Ligon has the further disqualification of writing to please the people who had helped him during his stay in the island from 1647 to 1650. This made him quick to praise the planters, enthusiastic about the opportunities for men with money to make more money, and slow to criticize. Only on one subject, slaves, did he express a mildly independent line: not that he condemned slavery as such, only its indiscriminate nature. "Though there be a mark set upon these people, which will hardly ever be wiped off, as of their cruelties when they have advantages, and of their fearfulness and falseness; yet no rule so general but hath his acception: for I believe, and I have strong motives to cause me to be of that perswasion, that there are as honest, faithful, and conscionable people amongst them, as amongst

---

[88] The modern edition is by Louis B. Wright (Chapel Hill: University of North Carolina Press, 1947).

[89] Dunn, "Seventeenth-Century English Historians," p. 221.

those of Europe, or any other part of the world."[90] When he met a slave who wanted to improve himself and was wishful of being baptized, Ligon was told flatly that this was not the Barbadian way of doing things; he does not seem to have insisted.

In Oldmixon's *British Empire in America* we arrive at something like a historical equivalent of the Navigation Acts: a schematic history of all the colonies in North America (including Hudson Bay) and the West Indies, written by a man who had never visited any of them but was firmly convinced of the benefit they brought to the mother country. The grounds of proof, inevitably, are material: so much sugar, tobacco, lumber, fish, furs enriching Britain. More than a century before, Richard Hakluyt in the *Discourse of Western Planting* had put forward a number of different arguments on behalf of colonization. Not surprisingly, profit was the one that had survived to Oldmixon's time. There was nothing necessarily harmful to the imperial connection in Britons and Americans getting rich together. The poison began to work with Britain's failure to give her colonies, in their third and fourth generations, a sufficient sense of belonging to a community with other purposes besides making money. "Damn your souls, make tobacco": words which perhaps were and perhaps never were spoken by a metropolitan minister of the crown to a colonial minister of religion, but which in any case come too close to the prosaic truth for comfort. The colonists had found out for themselves how to make tobacco; at a pinch they could learn to look after their own souls.

[90] *True and Exact History of the Island of Barbadoes* (2nd ed.; London, 1673), p. 53.

EPILOGUE

So much was started in the North Atlantic in the seventeenth century that
it is easy to trap oneself into filing inflated claims for the relevance of those
pioneering times to all that came afterwards, forgetting the failures, the
blind alleys, and the things that did not happen. With an effort it is
possible to imagine Europe's interest in America taking a form quite
different from that in which it was finally cast; and the effort is worth
making because it helps to identify the forces and counterforces that
blended to produce the results with which we are familiar. The alternatives to colonization were, first, the conquest of the pre-Columbian inhabitants of America, their conversion to Christianity, and their absorption into empires run by Europeans mainly for the benefit of Europeans;
and, second, the planting of *comptoirs* or trading posts at suitable sites to
tap the commerce of the New World. Why did these alternative styles fail
in North America and the Caribbean?

There was never any likelihood of the first of these alternatives being
adopted in the regions colonized by England and France. Adventurers —
inspired by Cortes — might dream of conquest and subjugation but the
Indian inhabitants were unfit to play the parts written for them. Some were
too weak (physically) to survive contact with European diseases and
European ruthlessness; others were too fierce to be tamed; others were
too fleet and had too much space to retire into. Raleigh's quest for the
Golden Man was the beginning and virtually the end of England's attempt
to imitate Spain.

Exploiting the New World by means of *comptoirs* was a more feasible alternative and might have become the prevailing Dutch, French, and English style in America, anyway for a century or two. It was by a *comptoir* that the Dutch expected to run the fur trade at Albany and actually did so for a number of years; it was of *comptoirs* that New France largely consisted until touched by the hand of Colbert; it was *comptoirs* not colonies that the English planted on the shores of Hudson Bay. Wherever the Indians had furs to trade, the *comptoir* became the natural and appropriate way to get them. And it was by settlements no stronger and no more permanent than *comptoirs* that the Europeans sought in Newfoundland, Acadia, and the Gulf of St. Lawrence to conduct their fishing interests well into the eighteenth century. Neither of these New World staples summoned colonies into being.

What needs to be kept always in view is that commercial exploitation without colonization or dominion was the style of a great deal of Europe's expansion into the wider world in the seventeenth century. It is what the Europeans sought for and got in West Africa and it is what the Portuguese, Dutch, and English settled for in India, the East Indies, and Japan. Trading places were occupied, small enclaves directly governed, the seas controlled by European navies, local rulers advised and domineered over; but the Europeans did not colonize those regions in the seventeenth century to a point where they either evicted the inhabitants or assumed responsibility for them. The North American empires of England and France, put in world context, appear as the exceptions, not the rule.

It was the English who invented the new colonial genre in America and numerous explanations have been urged why this should have been so: the precedent of Ireland, the failure to find gold in their part of the New World, the insufficiency of the fur trade on the western shores of what became the United States, a climate that could be endured, a soil suitable for European farming. All are important, none is enough. At the back of nearly all the permanent achievements in England's Atlantic empire in the seventeenth century was the remarkable readiness of Englishmen to leave their homes and make for North America or the West Indies, either because they were "vexed and troubled" or simply to try their luck. Somewhere in English history there must lie the secret formula of colonization, the particular social chemistry that turned Englishmen, above all others, into willing or at least resigned colonists. It was the working of this formula that put an end to the regime of *comptoirs* in America and peopled the Atlantic seaboard with Englishmen. This book may not have solved the mystery; but it has been written on the assumption that the formula existed and that there were other formulas in the history of other European countries which produced different results.

The *comptoir* is perhaps the outstanding instance of a seventeenth-century blind alley. Others, *féodalité*, federation, the introduction of Mediterranean staples such as silk and wine, have been mentioned in the preceding pages, but all were conditional upon the decision to plant people. The people needed to set and keep going colonies of settlement were forthcoming from England and, to a lesser extent, from France. People from Europe were reinforced and in places far outnumbered by people from Africa. New communities arose and prospered which we customarily say were linked to the other side of the Atlantic by ties of language, culture, and material interest. How strong were these links? and were they by the close of the seventeenth century becoming stronger or weaker? Even to employ a term such as the *North Atlantic World* is to take a selective view of the past, to lay stress on those things which worked for the togetherness of Europe and America (or West Africa and the West Indies) at the expense of those which worked for their separateness. Was there in any sense a North Atlantic community about the year 1700; or, if this begs too many questions, was there an identity of purpose between those who had settled in the colonies and those who stopped at home?

These questions have been glanced at more than once in the preceding pages. Here one can only draw lines of the crudest kind. Viewed first from America, the mother country can never have been more important to the colonist than at the moment of first settlement. It was from the mother country that all life had to come; were the umbilical string to be broken, the child would die. Much that happens in colonial history from this point onwards is a growing away from the parent; a grappling with unfamiliar problems leading to the acquisition of new and different skills, ultimately to different values; an enforced self-sufficiency generating a sense of separateness, ultimately a sense of independence. This awareness of being different was visible in nearly every colony by the eighteenth century; but in some it was restrained by the development of ties of a material kind which bound the colonial economy very closely to the metropolitan. Such, because of the prevailing monoculture, was the position of the sugar colonies. Jamaicans, for example, behaved in their legislature in the 1760s and 1770s much as the leaders of South Carolina and Massachusetts behaved in theirs, used the same arguments, struck the same attitudes. The logical end of much of what they said was independence from Britain.[1] The difference was that the Jamaicans were playing games; they knew that they could not afford to act as the Americans did and tell Britain where to get off. Jamaica, if an extreme case, was not a unique one — a colony that resented colonial status but had to bear it. The point to be grasped is that it was not only in the New England colonies, with their distinctive history and much less dependent economies, that the aspiration to run their own affairs was expressed by colonists. This was so general that we might as well think of it as "natural."

Merely by being born and bred in a colony, an American or West Indian was differentiated from a European or an African. Until recently it would have been considered inappropriate to illustrate this point other than by white experience; it is now permissible to offer a black example, though necessarily one that reaches us through white reporters. In 1736 three justices of the peace in Antigua compiled a report on the subject of a slave conspiracy which had been detected in that island.[2] The plan of the slaves was, as usual, to kill the whites when they were off their guard, this time by blowing up the governor's ball. "The slaves chiefly concerned," wrote the justices, "were those born on the Gold Coast whom we style coromantees . . . and those born in the colonies whom we call creoles." The "coromantee" leader was flattered with being made king when the revolt succeeded "but the creoles had privately resolved to settle a commonwealth and make slaves of the coromantees." Thus far the white reporters might have been deceiving themselves, inventing the divisions among the slaves they wished to find there. But the report goes on, more tellingly, to describe a ritual war dance performed at the instance of the "coromantees" which signified the willingness of both dancers and spectators to engage in the plot. "The bystanding slaves huzzaed three times, the coromantees knowing but the creoles not understanding the engagement entered into." In other words, the slaves born in slavery had already forgotten or had never known the purport of this piece of African ritual. Telling this story and giving weight to it is far from denying the

[1] George Metcalf, *Royal Government and Political Conflict in Jamaica 1729–1783* (London: Longmans, 1965).
[2] Great Britain, Public Record Office, *Calendar of State Papers*, Colonial Series, America and West Indies, 1737 (London: H.M.S.O., 1963), no. 20iii.

transmission of cultural traits from one side of the Atlantic to the other; rather it is meant to suggest that important elements could get lost in the new environment so that what survived, with new accretions, might in time constitute a new culture with only superficial resemblances to the old.

If it is true that people from Africa and Europe put down new roots in a new world and *tended* to grow away from their origins, the "North Atlantic World" cannot be thought of as something toward which the separate communities were steadily advancing. On the contrary, the colonist's sense of belonging to an ancient society must have diminished even where his material interests kept him tied closely to it. Economically the North Atlantic world was much closer knit in 1700 than it had been fifty years earlier, but culturally it had probably begun to disintegrate.

Viewed from Europe, the mother country's awareness of a colony follows a different plan. It is nearly correct to say that colonies were never less important in the seventeenth century than at the moment when they were first planted: not quite correct, because a country's prestige might be at stake, as it was in the founding of Virginia. But who in France or England cared if Guadeloupe, Antigua, Maryland, Connecticut, or for that matter New France, lived or died? The answer is that not many in Europe were even aware that these communities were struggling to life. Colonies, to be of public interest, had to succeed; the more successful they became, the more thought Europeans gave to them, the more the colonists were regarded as members — albeit humble — of a community headed by the mother country. This seems to be the paradox of seventeenth- and eighteenth-century colonization. The same triumphs — in overcoming and adapting to a strange environment, making a living and producing a surplus for sale — that bred a sense of independence in the colony bred a sense of proprietorship in the mother country. The same things that made the American colonists resolute in seeking independence made the British resolute in denying it. The idea of a North Atlantic community, with common moral and political ground rules as well as an interlocking economy, began with the Hakluyts as an argument to induce pioneers to go to America, an assurance that they were not thereby cutting themselves off from Europe. It ended as an appeal to Americans to go on accepting an alien set of ground rules when they not only were fully competent to devise their own but had, to a large extent, already done so.

BIBLIOGRAPHICAL
NOTE

Many of the volumes mentioned in the following pages contain book lists on special aspects of the North Atlantic world in the seventeenth century though it is to be remembered that the best books do not always have the best bibliographies. Frédéric Mauro, in *L'expansion européenne (1600–1870)* (2nd ed.; Paris: Presses Universitaires de France, 1967), pp. 5–86, has made a brave attempt to cover the whole field, arranging works by European countries and by extra-European regions. On the European side, the chapter bibliographies in E. E. Rich and C. H. (Charles) Wilson, eds., *Cambridge Economic History of Europe*, vol. IV: *The Economy of Expanding Europe in the Sixteenth and Seventeenth Centuries* (Cambridge: At the University Press, 1967), are useful; some are very full indeed. For the western shores of the North Atlantic, Oscar Handlin et al., *Harvard Guide to American History* (Cambridge, Mass.: Harvard University Press, 1954) is an obvious point of departure. It can be extended and updated by the elegant bibliographical essay at the close of Wesley Frank Craven's *The Colonies in Transition, 1660–1713* (New York: Harper & Row, 1969); by the appropriate section (pp. 563–573) of Norah Story's *Oxford Companion to Canadian History and Literature* (Toronto: Oxford University Press, 1967); and by the recommended reading in J. H. Parry and P. M. Sherlock, *A Short History of the West Indies* (3rd ed.; London: Macmillan, 1971). West Africa, historically speaking the region with the fastest growth rate in the world, is a special problem: new areas of the subject are prospected, if not developed, every year.

Probably the reader cannot do better than begin with the note on further reading in J. D. Fage, *A History of West Africa* (4th ed.; Cambridge: At the University Press, 1969), pp. 221–229.

Some of the most original work is first announced in periodicals, and some of it gets no farther. It is not easy to know how to keep up with a subject to which scores, if not hundreds, of periodicals are in some degree relevant. Only a few articles have been mentioned in the suggestions below; rather more have been cited in the footnotes to the text above, but it may be useful to give a general indication of the periodicals of greatest value. First in point of relevance, and outstanding in quality, is the *William and Mary Quarterly* (Williamsburg, Va.: Institute of Early American History). This takes in, as well as the early history of North America, the English colonies in the Caribbean. In the latter field there is now to be added the *Caribbean Historical Review* (Barbados: Caribbean Universities Press) which publishes articles of all periods and is concerned with the Spanish, French, and Dutch past of the region as well as the English. Local history is served by the periodicals supported in each of the seaboard states of the United States (some are excellent); by the *Jamaican Historical Review* (Kingston: Jamaican Historical Society) and by the *Journal of the Barbados Museum and Historical Society* (Barbados Museum and Historical Society). For French colonization in North America the *Canadian Historical Review* (Toronto: University of Toronto Press) has more to say on the early period than either its American or its English counterpart. For New France, Acadia, the Antilles, and French colonial history generally, the *Revue française d'histoire d'outre mer* (Paris: Societé Française d'Histoire d'Outre-Mer) is essential reading. It has twice changed its name. From 1913 to 1931 it appeared as *Revue de l'histoire des colonies françaises* and from 1933 to 1958 as *Revue d'histoire des colonies*. West African history is well served by the *Journal of African History* (Cambridge: At the University Press) which comprehends all periods.

The European Context

The study of New France or New England, Virginia or Jamaica, Guadeloupe or Curaçao, must begin in Europe. Events in Europe shaped colonial history, sometimes directly, more often in the seventeenth century indirectly, raising or lowering the attention and resources Europeans were able or willing to allocate to their colonial interests. For these events the series edited by William L. Langer under the general title "The Rise of Modern Europe" is as handy as any. Three volumes in this series cover the period from 1618 to 1715: Carl J. Friedrich, *The Age of the Baroque, 1610–1660* (New York: Harper, 1952); Frederick L. Nussbaum, *The Triumph of Science and Reason, 1660–1685* (New York: Harper, 1953); and John B. Wolf, *The Emergence of the Great Powers, 1685–1715* (New York: Harper, 1951).

More influential than events were the institutions, political, economic, and legal, of the mother countries; the social frameworks from which the emigrants emerged (or failed to emerge); the economies which generated the funds to carry them to a new world; and the life-styles and cultures they took with them. A book written nearly half a century ago, G. N. Clark's *The Seventeenth Century* (Oxford: Clarendon Press, 1929), provides the best brief introduction to all these aspects of European history, though in some respects it is out of date. Edward P. Cheyney's *European Background of American History* (New York: Harper, 1904) is even older but well worth reading. Among more recent books, volume IV of the *Cambridge Economic History of Europe* (already cited) is a useful *point de départ* for matters of population, trade, and prices, and B. H. Slicher van Bath's *Agrarian History of Western Europe, 500–1850* (London: Arnold, 1963) for agriculture. Fernand Braudel's *Capitalism and Material Life* (London: Weidenfeld, 1973) is the work of a master of professional history who reveals a talent for enlightening the unlearned as well. On economic institutions and the role of the state in economic life, the ideas of Eli F. Heckscher have not won general acceptance though his book, *Mercantilism*, 2 vols. (London: Allen & Unwin, 1935), because it contains so much information, continues to be read. Charles Wilson's *Profit and Power* (London: Longmans, 1957) is a short book in the same general field which has not, perhaps, received the notice it deserves.

For European religion and cultural life, also viewed internationally, there are convenient starting places in E. Préclin and A. Javy, *Les luttes politiques et doctrinaires aux XVIIe et XVIIIe siècles* (Paris: Bloud & Gay, 1955); Paul Hazard, *The European Mind, 1680–1715* (London: Hollis, 1953); and H. R. Trevor-Roper's essay "The European Witch-Craze of the Sixteenth and Seventeenth Centuries" in his *Religion, the Reformation and Social Change* (London:Macmillan, 1967). The reader who wishes to study the European, as opposed to the mere English, beginnings of the radical Protestantism later planted in America should find all he needs in a remarkable book by George H. Williams, *The Radical Reformation* (London: Weidenfeld, 1962). J. H. Elliott, *The Old World and the New* (Cambridge: At the University Press, 1972), briefly examines the effects of discovery and empire on early modern Europe, an aspect of the subject hitherto studied only in patches. Max Savelle, with M. A. Fisher, in *The Origins of American Diplomacy: The International History of Angloamerica, 1492–1763* (New York: Macmillan, 1967), has written the history of America's entry into European international relations.

To turn from Europe at large to separate countries, there are obvious reasons why English social, religious, political, and legal institutions and life should have been more thoroughly studied than those of any other country for the light cast upon early American history. Two books by leading scholars point the way: Wallace Notestein, *The English People on the Eve of Colonization* (London: Hamilton, 1954), and Carl Bridenbaugh, *Vexed and Troubled Englishmen, 1590 to 1642* (New York: Clarendon Press, 1967). Among a very large number of books not written expressly to elucidate the social and economic context of colonization, but which nevertheless do so, my personal selection includes Mildred Campbell, *The English Yeoman under Elizabeth and the Early Stuarts* (New Haven, Conn.: Yale University Press, 1942); Christopher Hill, *Society and Puritanism in Pre-Revolutionary England* (London: Secker, 1964); Louis B. Wright, *Middle-Class Culture in Elizabethan England* (Chapel Hill: University of North Carolina Press, 1935); Charles Wilson, *England's Apprenticeship, 1603–1763* (London: Longmans, 1965); B. E. Supple, *Commercial Crisis and Change in England, 1600–1642* (Cambridge: At the University Press, 1959); and Peter Laslett, *The World We Have Lost* (London: Methuen, 1965). Two books by William Haller, *The Rise of Puritanism, 1570–1643* (New York: Columbia University Press, 1938) and *Liberty and Reformation in the Puritan Revolution* (New York: Columbia University Press, 1955), are giants in a field cultivated by several historians of rare distinction. All matters of law can be referred to Sir William Holdsworth, *A History of English Law*, 17 vols. (London: Methuen, 1903–72). J. G. A. Pocock's *The Ancient Constitution and the Feudal Law* (Cambridge: At the University Press, 1957) should not be overlooked.

Readers who, after a time, become suspicious of "national history" should begin their study of English counties with Thomas G. Barnes, *Somerset, 1625–1640* (London: Oxford University Press, 1961); and of English towns with Wallace T. MacCaffrey, *Exeter, 1540–1640* (Cambridge, Mass.: Harvard University Press, 1958).

Seventeenth-century studies in France have changed nature and direction in the past thirty years more completely than in perhaps any other European country. The change, overdue considering the repetitiousness of pre-1939 court history, has been chiefly wrought by Roland Mousnier, who has studied French institutions in their social context; and by historians connected with the Centre de Recherches Historiques. Any selection of general works must include Pierre Goubert, *The Ancien Regime: French Society 1600–1750* (London: Weidenfeld, 1973); R. Mandrou, *La France aux XVIIe et XVIIIe siècles* (Paris: Presses Universitaires de France, 1967); and a collection of essays by some of the leading historians of France published under the title *La France au temps de Louis XIV* (Paris: Hachette, 1966). The student who wishes to penetrate more deeply into the subject must be prepared to read big books, e.g., Roland Mousnier, *La venalité des offices sous Henri IV et Louis XIII*, first published in 1945 and recently reprinted (Paris: Presses Universitaires de France, 1971), much wider in purpose than its title may suggest; Pierre Goubert, *Beauvais et le Beauvaisis de 1600 à 1730* (Paris: S.E.V.P.E.N., 1960), the best entrée to the structure of French provincial society; Boris Porshnev, *Les soulèvements populaires en France de 1623 à 1648* (Paris: S.E.V.P.E.N., 1963); E. Esmonin, *Études sur la France des XVIIe et XVIIIe siècles* (Paris: Presses Universitaires de France, 1964); and Louis Pérouas, *Le diocèse de La Rochelle de 1648 à 1724* (Paris: S.E.V.P.E.N., 1964).

A beginning in Dutch social and institutional history in the seventeenth century can be made with the English translation of Pieter Geyl's study, *The Netherlands in the Seventeenth Century*, 2 vols. (London: Benn, 1964). This book narrates events but also contains scholarly and penetrating comment on society and culture. Briefer expositions will be found in G. J. Renier, *The Dutch Nation* (London: Allen & Unwin, 1944), and Charles Wilson, *The Dutch Republic* (London: Weidenfeld, 1968). Oceanic interests enter naturally into all books on Dutch life in the seventeenth century. One which knits together with rare skill the Dutch at home and the Dutch abroad is Charles R. Boxer, *The Dutch Seaborne Empire, 1600–1800* (London: Hutchinson, 1965). Violet Barbour's *Capitalism in Amsterdam in the Seventeenth Century* (Baltimore: Johns Hopkins University Press, 1950) is essential reading for the Dutch economy and there are two fine books which say little about the Atlantic but a great deal about Dutch business methods and organization: Axel E. Christensen, *Dutch Trade to the Baltic about 1600* (The Hague: Nijhoff, 1941), and Kristof Glamann, *Dutch-Asiatic Trade, 1620–1740* (The Hague: Nijhoff, 1958).

Precolonization

J. H. Parry's *The Age of Reconnaissance* (Cleveland: World, 1963) is the proper place to begin the study of European exploration and discovery; it is particularly strong on the important technical aspects of the subject, cartography, shipbuilding, marine instruments, etc. Early voyages to and contacts with the different Atlantic regions can be followed in J. W. Blake, *European Beginnings in West Africa, 1454–1578* (London: Longmans, 1937), A. P. Newton, *The European Nations in the West Indies* (London: Black, 1933), and J. B. Brebner, *The Explorers of North America* (London: Black, 1933). Each of these books considers the subject internationally. What the explorers found in North America is recounted by John Bakeless, *The Eyes of Discovery* (Philadelphia: Lippincott, 1950).

French precolonial history is introduced by C.-A. Julien, *Les voyages de découverte et les premiers établissements* (Paris: Presses Universitaires de France, 1948). Charles de la Roncière's *Histoire de la marine française*, vol. III (Paris: Plon, 1923), is valuable for reference. Samuel Eliot Morison's *Samuel de Champlain, Father of New France* (Boston: Little, Brown, 1972) is the latest biography of France's greatest colonizer, and also the latest example of Admiral Morison's unique historical method combining mastery of the archives with mastery of the winds, currents, and navigational hazards which explorers encountered. There is a large literature on early English maritime activity, much of it celebrating the exploits of the seadogs: Julian Corbett's *Drake and the Tudor Navy*, 2 vols. (London: Longmans, 1899), and J. A. Williamson's *Hawkins of Plymouth* (London: Black, 1949) are examples of the genre. R. B. Wernham's *Before the Armada* (London: Cape, 1966) coolly puts these exploits into perspective. The master of early English oceanic history is David B. Quinn: any book, article, or document edited by him is certain to enlighten. See particularly his *The Voyages and Colonising Enterprises of Sir Humphrey Gilbert*, Hakluyt Society Publications, 2nd series, vol. 73 (London: Hakluyt Society, 1938); *The Roanoke Voyages, 1584–1590*, Hakluyt Society Publications, 2nd series, vols. 104–105

(London: Hakluyt Society, 1955); and *The Elizabethans and the Irish* (Ithaca, N.Y.: Cornell University Press, 1966). Readers who are daunted by the Hakluyt Society's *The Principal Navigations, Voyages, Traffiques and Discoveries of the English Nation* (Glasgow: MacLehose, 1903–5) in twelve volumes should make trial of an abridgement entitled *Voyages and Discoveries* (Harmondsworth, England: Penguin Books, 1972). Of major importance, finally, for the years in which England's interest in the Atlantic was first aroused is Kenneth R. Andrews, *Elizabethan Privateering* (Cambridge: At the University Press, 1964), which shows who the privateers were, how funds were raised, and what profits were made, and explores connections between privateering and the founding of Virginia.

West Africa and the Slave Trade

Twenty years ago this region's history rested mainly on the work of British civil servants: J. M. Gray, *History of the Gambia* (Cambridge: At the University Press, 1940); W. E. F. Ward, *History of the Gold Coast* (London: Allen & Unwin, 1948); and Sir Alan Burns, *History of Nigeria*, first published in 1929 (7th ed.; London: Allen & Unwin, 1969). It is right that these pioneers should be honored but any issue of the *Journal of African History* will show how different things are today. Beginners in the seventeenth century should start with Fage's *A History of West Africa* (already cited) and go on to the following regional studies: Walter Rodney, *A History of the Upper Guinea Coast, 1545–1800* (Cambridge: At the University Press, 1969); Christopher Fyfe, *A Short History of Sierra Leone* (London: Longmans, 1962); K. Y. Daaku, *Trade and Politics on the Gold Coast* (Oxford: Clarendon Press, 1970); Alan F. C. Ryder, *Benin and the Europeans* (London: Longmans, 1969); A. J. H. Latham, *Old Calabar, 1600–1891* (Oxford: Clarendon Press, 1973); and Phyllis M. Martin, *The External Trade of the Loango Coast* (Oxford: Clarendon Press, 1972). Philip D. Curtin's *The Image of Africa* (Madison: University of Wisconsin Press, 1964) deals with a somewhat later period of European activity in and attitudes toward West Africa, but much of what he says can be applied in some degree to the seventeenth century.

The history of the European slave trade owes much to Elizabeth Donnan, ed., *Documents Illustrative of the History of the Slave Trade to America*, 4 vols. (Washington, D.C.: Carnegie Institution, 1930); but it has lately been transformed by Philip D. Curtin, *The Atlantic Slave Trade*

(Madison: University of Wisconsin Press, 1969), a book which, it is to be hoped, has ended extravagant guesswork on the subject. For one reason or another the reader may still find it worth his while to consult H. A. Wyndham, *The Atlantic and Slavery* (London: Oxford University Press, 1935); Gaston-Martin, *Histoire de l'esclavage dans les colonies françaises* (Paris: Presses Universitaires de France, 1948); George Scelle, *Histoire politique de la traite négrière aux Indes de Castille*, 2 vols. (Paris: Librairie de la Societé du Receuil, 1906); Abdoulaye Ly, *La compagnie du Sénégal* ([Paris]: Présence Africaine, 1958); and K. G. Davies, *The Royal African Company* (London: Longmans, 1957; reprinted, New York: Atheneum, 1970). The last two books have something to say on company organization in the African trade and on the development of slave economies in the Caribbean. What work has hitherto been done in the archives of the Dutch West India Company has not resulted in a major exposition of that country's slave trade. Johannes Postma's "The Dimension of the Dutch Slave Trade from Western Africa," *Journal of African History*, 13:237–248 (1972), is an important step in this direction.

The Caribbean and Sugar

Two eminent historians, Richard Pares and Gabriel Debien, have had special interests in the Caribbean. Pares worked more in the eighteenth century than the seventeenth, but his *Merchants and Planters* (Cambridge: Economic History Society, 1959) is a brilliant epitome of the problems of English and French colonization and settlement in this region. The early chapters of his *A West-India Fortune* (London: Longmans, 1950) and parts of his *Yankees and Creoles* (London: Longmans, 1956) are also relevant to this period. It is difficult to imagine what French Caribbean studies would be like without Debien; he is as much at home in the seaports of western France as he is in the Antilles and West Africa, an authentic historian of the Atlantic. His numerous papers have unfortunately not been collected into easily accessible volumes and have to be tracked down in periodicals. My indebtedness to his "Les engagés pour les Antilles (1634–1715)," *Revue d'histoire des colonies*, 38:7–261 (1951), is, I hope, apparent.

J. H. Parry and P. M. Sherlock's *A Short History of the West Indies* (already cited) is easily the best introduction to this region: it is one of the few books to treat the subject internationally. There are several older books, pioneer works in their time but by no means dispensable today. They include Stewart L. Mims, *Colbert's West India Policy* (New Haven, Conn.: Yale University Press, 1912); C. S. S. Higham, *The Development of the Leeward Islands under the Restoration, 1660–1688* (Cambridge: At the University Press, 1921); Vincent T. Harlow, *A History of Barbados, 1625–1685* (Oxford: Clarendon Press, 1926); Louis-Philippe May, *Histoire économique de la Martinique* (Paris: Rivière, 1930); A. P. Newton, *The Colonising Activities of the English Puritans* (New Haven, Conn.: Yale University Press, 1914); J. A. Williamson, *The Caribee Islands under the Proprietary Patents* (London: Oxford University Press, 1926); and Clarence H. Haring, *The Buccaneers in the West Indies in the XVII Century* (London: Methuen, 1910). Noel Deerr's *The History of Sugar*, 2 vols. (London: Chapman & Hall, 1949), assembles a great deal of information, statistical and otherwise; it is indispensable.

Among more recent works, A. P. Thornton's *West-India Policy under the Restoration* (Oxford: Clarendon Press, 1956) is a study of the centralizing efforts of Charles II's government. Michael Craton and James Walvin, in *A Jamaican Plantation: The History of Worthy Park, 1670–1970* (London: W. H. Allen, 1970), have broken new ground with a continuous history of a West Indian estate from the beginning to the present. Richard S. Dunn's *Sugar and Slaves* (Chapel Hill: University of North Carolina Press, 1972) examines the rise of the planters in the English West Indies in a way foreshadowed in his article "The Barbados Census of 1680: Profile of the Richest Colony in English America," *William and Mary Quarterly*, 3rd series, 26:3–30 (1969). Carl and Roberta Bridenbaugh, in *No Peace beyond the Line* (New York: Oxford University Press, 1972), have produced a worthy Caribbean companion to the former's *Vexed and Troubled Englishmen* (already cited); both books, with more to come, are parts of a work entitled *The Beginnings of the American People* which seems certain to be a major landmark.

Outstanding among books written about the Caribbean in the seventeenth century are Richard Ligon, *A True and Exact History of the Island of Barbadoes* (London, 1657; 2nd ed., 1673); and Jean-Baptiste du Tertre, *Histoire générale des Antilles*, 4 vols. in 3 (Paris, 1667). The latter is one of the few classics of early European colonization (as opposed to exploration and discovery).

English North America

General

Charles M. Andrews, *The Colonial Period of American History*, 4 vols. (New Haven, Conn.: Yale University Press, 1934–38; reprinted, 1964), is not quite flawless: it gives a relatively poor deal to the inhabitants of North America before the Europeans arrived. This apart, nothing but respectful gratitude can be accorded to a book, albeit forty years old, in which evidence and argument are blended with such skill. Wesley Frank Craven's *The Colonies in Transition, 1660–1713* (already cited) comes near to matching Andrews; and it is especially valuable for introducing readers to some of the new themes that were occupying American historians at the time of writing. The same service was performed by James M. Smith, ed., *Seventeenth-Century America* (Chapel Hill: University of North Carolina Press, 1959). A volume of this kind once a decade would be a becoming task for historians in such a well-worked field.

Smith's volume includes two papers on Indians: Nancy O. Lurie's "Indian Cultural Adjustment to European Civilization" and Wilcomb E. Washburn's "The Moral and Legal Justification for Dispossessing the Indians." Readers coming to this subject without much knowledge should begin with Harold E. Driver, *Indians of North America* (2nd ed.; Chicago: University of Chicago Press, 1969). This is the work of an anthropologist, concerned with Indians as such rather than with Indians as victims of the white man. Two books by historians amply redress the balance: Douglas E. Leach, *Flintlock and Tomahawk* (New York: Macmillan, 1958), a study of King Philip's War; and Allen W. Trelease, *Indian Affairs in Colonial New York* (Ithaca, N.Y.: Cornell University Press, 1960). Alfred G. Bailey's *The Conflict of European and Eastern Algonkian Cultures, 1504–1700* (St. John, N.B.: New Brunswick Museum, 1937) is wide ranging and acute. Almon W. Lauber's *Indian Slavery in Colonial Times within the Present Limits of the United States* (New York: Columbia University and Longmans, 1913) remains the only comprehensive treatment of this important subject. There is an invaluable collection of documents edited by Wilcomb E. Washburn, *The Indian and the White Man* (New York: New York University Press, 1964).

Smith's volume contained no essay on African slavery in the North American colonies. The great surge of interest in this subject since 1959 has been mainly in the eighteenth and nineteenth centuries. Curtin's use of perspective has shown how unimportant North America was in the Atlantic slave trade to 1713. Even a brief bibliography of the seventeenth century must, however, find room for Winthrop D. Jordan, *White over Black* (Chapel Hill: University of North Carolina Press, 1968); David B. Davis, *The Problem of Slavery in Western Culture* (Ithaca, N.Y.: Cornell University Press, 1966); and Laura Foner and Eugene D. Genovese, eds., *Slavery in the New World* (Englewood Cliffs, N.J.: Prentice-Hall, 1969).

Current preoccupations with slavery will not, it is to be hoped, swamp the subject (statistically more important in the seventeenth century) of white indentured service. The two major books, Abbot E. Smith's *Colonists in Bondage* (Chapel Hill: University of North Carolina Press, 1947) and Richard B. Morris's *Government and Labor in Early America* (New York: Columbia University Press, 1946), were published more than a quarter of a century ago; perhaps the subject is ripe for further exploration. Mildred Campbell's "Social Origin of Some Early Americans" in J. M. Smith's *Seventeenth-Century America* examines indentured servants from the English end, as does Bridenbaugh's *Vexed and Troubled Englishmen* (already cited).

On imperial policy toward North America, volume IV of Andrews's *Colonial Period* is a very full account, as are L. A. Harper's *The Navigation Laws* (New York: Columbia University Press, 1939) and Leonard W. Labaree's *Royal Government in America* (New Haven, Conn.: Yale University Press, 1930). The curious reader may wish to consult two minor classics of imperial history by George L. Beer, *The Origins of the British Colonial System, 1578–1660* (New York: Macmillan, 1907) and *The Old Colonial System* (New York: Macmillan, 1912). Centralizing policies in post-Restoration times are considered by Viola F. Barnes, *The Dominion of New England* (New Haven, Conn.: Yale University Press, 1923; reprinted, New York: Ungar, 1960), and by Michael G. Hall, *Edward Randolph and the American Colonies* (Chapel Hill: University of North Carolina Press, 1960). Resistance to those policies is one (but not the only) theme of Michael G. Hall et al., *The Glorious Revolution in America* (Chapel Hill: University of North Carolina Press, 1964).

Louis B. Wright's *The Cultural Life of the American Colonies* (New York: Harper, 1957) is an important reminder that there is more to the subject than New England; and Carl Bridenbaugh's *Cities in the Wilderness* (New York: Alfred A. Knopf, 1964) that urban life was one of Europe's most important exports to America.

Tobacco and the Southern Colonies

Two major books map the history and economy of this region: Wesley Frank Craven, *The Southern Colonies in the Seventeenth Century* (Baton Rouge: Louisiana State University Press, 1949), and Lewis C. Gray, *History of Agriculture in the Southern United States to 1860*, vol. I (Washington, D.C.: Carnegie Institution, 1933). There is much to be said for two old books by Philip A. Bruce, *Economic History of Virginia in the Seventeenth Century*, 2 vols. (New York: Macmillan, 1896), and *Institutional History of Virginia in the Seventeenth Century*, 2 vols. (New York: Putnam, 1910). The second is not as interesting as the first and is best used as a work of reference. A notable practitioner in this field was Thomas J. Wertenbaker; of his numerous books perhaps the most useful is *Planters of Colonial Virginia* (Princeton, N.J.: Princeton University Press, 1922). The social history of Virginia is best studied at first hand in Richard B. Davis, ed., *William Fitzhugh and His Chesapeake World* (Chapel Hill: University of North Carolina Press, 1963), a work which leads naturally to Louis B. Wright's edition of Robert Beverley's *History and Present State of Virginia*, originally published in 1705 (Chapel Hill: University of North Carolina Press, 1947). Verner W. Crane's *The Southern Frontier, 1670–1732* (Ann Arbor: University of Michigan Press, 1956) is important for Indian as well as Spanish relations.

No general history of tobacco is as good as Deerr's work on sugar but there is an excellent regional study in Arthur P. Middleton's *Tobacco Coast: A Maritime History of Chesapeake Bay in the Colonial Era* (Newport News, Va.: Mariners Museum, 1953). Jacob M. Price's *The Tobacco Adventure to Russia*, in *Transactions of the American Philosophical Society*, new series, vol. 51, part 1 (Philadelphia: American Philosophical Society, 1961), is an impressive reconstruction of an episode on the marketing side. For the growth of mixed farming in the later seventeenth century there is work of high scholarship in Susie M. Ames's *Studies of the Virginia Eastern Shore in the Seventeenth Century* (Richmond, Va.: Dietz Press, 1940).

New Netherland and the Middle Colonies

Henry M. Kessler and Eugene Rachlis, *Peter Stuyvesant and His New York* (New York: Random House, 1959), and S. G. Nissenson, *The Patroon's Domain* (New York: Columbia University Press, 1937), are informative on the Dutch period. The latter is especially important for the history of European attempts to plant a species of unfreedom in the New World. J. Franklin Jameson, ed., *Narratives of New Netherland, 1609–1664* (New York: Scribner, 1909), prints many important documents in translation. For a general history of the period, one can do worse than to go back to E. B. O'Callaghan, *History of New Netherland; or New York under the Dutch*, 2 vols. (New York: Appleton, 1846–48), which is based on a respectable knowledge of primary sources. Among a number of books on particular episodes and persons in the later seventeenth century mention must be made of Jerome R. Reich, *Leisler's Rebellion: A Study of Democracy in New York, 1664–1720* (Chicago: University of Chicago Press, 1953).

New Jersey is better off than New York. There is an excellent history (where in the seventeenth century is there not?) by Wesley Frank Craven, *New Jersey and the English Colonization of North America* (Princeton, N.J.: Van Nostrand, 1964), as well as two books by John E. Pomfret, *The Province of West New Jersey, 1609–1702* (Princeton, N.J.: Princeton University Press, 1956) and *The Province of East New Jersey, 1609–1702* (Princeton, N.J.: Princeton University Press, 1962). Penn and the beginnings of Pennsylvania are comprehensively dealt with by Catherine O. Peare in her *William Penn* (Philadelphia: Lippincott, 1957). The nearest approach to a regional study of the middle colonies is by Thomas J. Wertenbaker and is called *The Founding of American Civilization: The Middle Colonies* (New York: Scribner, 1938).

New England and Puritanism

Samuel Eliot Morison's *Builders of the Bay Colony* was first published in 1930 and has been revised and enlarged in the Sentry edition (Boston: Houghton Mifflin, 1962); this, if anything, can win friends for the early Puritans. It was followed by the same author's *The Intellectual Life of New England*, published in 1936 under a somewhat different title and republished (New York: New York University Press) in 1956. For the subtleties, sometimes contortions, of Puritan theology and morality the reader will naturally turn to the writings of Perry Miller, notably *The New England Mind: The 17th Century* (New York: Macmillan, 1939) and *Errand into the Wilderness* (Cambridge, Mass.: Harvard University Press, 1956); and for a wider view of the Puritans to a collection of their writings edited by Perry Miller and Thomas H. Johnson, *The Puritans* (New York: American

Book Company, 1938). Other notable books in the field are Edmund S. Morgan, *Visible Saints* (Ithaca, N.Y.: Cornell University Press, 1965), and A. Simpson, *Puritanism in Old and New England* (Chicago: University of Chicago Press, 1955).

Without the Puritans American family life would have been very different; for a start, there would have been much less of it in the seventeenth century. The subject has been investigated by Levin L. Schucking (mainly from the European evidence) in *The Puritan Family* (London: Routledge, 1969); by Edmund S. Morgan in *The Puritan Family* (New York: Harper Torchbooks, 1966), which is specifically about New England; and most recently by John Demos, *A Little Commonwealth: Family Life in Plymouth Colony* (New York: Oxford University Press, 1970). This last book also serves as an introduction to a relatively new science, seventeenth-century American demography, in which a fair amount of work has already been published in periodicals.

Other aspects of New England life and history are illuminated by Bernard Bailyn, *The New England Merchants in the Seventeenth Century* (Cambridge, Mass.: Harvard University Press, 1955); Isabel M. Calder, *The New Haven Colony* (New Haven, Conn.: Yale University Press, 1934); George D. Langdon, *Pilgrim Colony: A History of New Plymouth, 1620–1691* (New Haven, Conn.: Yale University Press, 1966); Harry M. Ward, *The United Colonies of New England, 1643–1690* (New York: Vantage Press, 1961); John F. Sly, *Town Government in Massachusetts, 1620–1930* (Cambridge, Mass.: Harvard University Press, 1930); William Haller, Jr., *The Puritan Frontier: Town-Planting in New England Colonial Development, 1630–1660* (New York: Columbia University Press, 1951); and, a recent contribution to an ever-interesting topic, Chadwick Hansen, *Witchcraft at Salem* (London: Hutchinson, 1969).

Furs, Fish, and New France

As much for its connection with the exploration of North America as for its economic importance, the fur trade has attracted and continues to attract historians of distinction. Paul C. Phillips's *The Fur Trade*, vol. I (Norman: University of Oklahoma Press, 1961), has the great merit of drawing together the history of the trade of the whole continent. Harold A. Innis's *The Fur Trade in Canada* (New Haven, Conn.: Yale University Press, 1930) contains a full appreciation of the European market and its

vagaries, as does E. E. Rich's *History of the Hudson's Bay Company*, vol.
I (London: Hudson's Bay Record Society, 1958). Grace Lee Nute's
Caesars of the Wilderness (New York: American Historical Association,
1943), a study of Radisson and Groseilliers, and Arthur S. Morton's indispensable *History of the Canadian West to 1870-71* (London: Hutchinson,
[1939]) show the relationship of fur finding to discovery.

As fur encouraged exploration by land, so fish promoted exploration
by sea. The works cited above under Precolonization cover this aspect of
the subject. To them should be added the consideration of fish as a regular
business by Harold A. Innis, *The Cod Fisheries* (rev. ed.; Toronto: University of Toronto Press, 1954), which like his book on the fur trade is
strong on European connections; Ralph G. Lounsbury, *The British
Fishery at Newfoundland, 1634-1763* (New Haven, Conn.: Yale University Press, 1934); and Charles B. Judah, *The North American Fisheries to
1713* (Urbana: University of Illinois Press, 1933). Bailyn's *New England
Merchants* (already cited) has good things to say on this subject.

Fish and furs are the main part of New France's economic history. They
enter largely into Marcel Trudel's *Histoire de la Nouvelle-France*, vol. I: *Les
vaines tentatives, 1524-1603*; vol. II: *Le comptoir, 1604-1627* (Montreal:
Éditions Fides, 1963-66), a major work of scholarship. The same author
has furnished a briefer version in English: *The Beginnings of New France,
1524-1663* (Toronto: McClelland and Stewart, 1973) in the Canadian
Centenary Series, which also contains W. J. Eccles's *Canada under Louis
XIV* (Toronto: McClelland and Stewart, 1964). George M. Wrong's *The
Rise and Fall of New France*, 2 vols. (London: Macmillan, 1928) is solid.
Books of importance on particular aspects of New France include William
B. Munro's *The Seigniorial System in Canada* (New York: Longmans,
1907) and a modern book on the same subject, R. C. Harris's *The Seigneur-
ial System in Early Canada* (Madison and Quebec: University of Wiscon-
sin Press, 1966); W. J. Eccles's *Frontenac, Courtier Governor* (Toronto:
McClelland and Stewart, 1959); and Nellis M. Crouse's *Lemoyne
d'Iberville: Soldier of New France* (Ithaca, N.Y.: Cornell University Press,
1954). Anglo-French rivalry in North America is well served by Howard
M. Peckham, *The Colonial Wars, 1689-1762* (Chicago: University of
Chicago Press, 1964); W. J. Eccles, *The Canadian Frontier, 1534-1760*
(New York: Holt, Rinehart, 1969); and Gerald S. Graham, *Empire of the
North Atlantic: The Maritime Struggle for North America* (Toronto: Uni-
versity of Toronto Press, 1950). French colonial policy in its broader

aspects must be studied in J. Saintoyant, *La colonisation française sous l'ancien régime*, vol. I (Paris: Renaissance du Livre, 1929). This is a subject to which more attention might now be given, but (after many years of faith) French historians stay skeptical of the effects of the policies laid down in Versailles.

Finally, two works must be noted that have been more influential than any hitherto mentioned. The first is Reuben G. Thwaites's edition of *The Jesuit Relations and Allied Documents*, 73 vols. (Cleveland, Ohio: Burrows, 1896–1901). Abridgements exist; my own citations come from Edna Kenton's *Black Gown and Redskins* (New York: Longmans, 1956). The second is a true classic or rather several true classics — Francis Parkman's books on the French in North America. Written and published as separate works, they were revised and republished under the general title of *France and England in North America* (Boston: Little, Brown, 1897; reprinted 1963). Titles of the individual volumes are *Pioneers of France in the New World; The Jesuits in North America; La Salle and the Discovery of the Great West; Count Frontenac and New France under Louis XIV; The Old Regime in Canada*; and so on into the eighteenth century. It is a tribute to the author that they can be read as Victorian adventure stories.

Index

INDEX